Turbo Pascal Program Library

Tom Rugg
Phil Feldman

Que™ Corporation
Indianapolis

Library of Congress Catalog No.: LC 86-60590

ISBN 0-88022-244-1

90 89 88 87 86   8 7 6 5 4 3

Interpretation of the printing code: the rightmost double-digit number is the year of the book's printing; the rightmost single-digit number, the number of the book's printing. For example, a printing code of 87-4 shows that the fourth printing of the book occurred in 1987.

Dedication

To Gabby Johnson,
for clearly stating what needed to be said.

About the Authors

Tom Rugg

A native Californian, Mr. Rugg received his B.S. degree in Quantitative Methods from California State University in 1969. His 20 years of experience in computer programming and systems analysis include positions with GTE Data Services, Inc., the U. S. Army (Pentagon), and Jet Propulsion Laboratory. He has written or co-authored many articles in personal computer magazines and has coauthored with Phil Feldman a number of books, including *32 BASIC Programs for the Apple Computer* and *More Than 32 BASIC Programs for the IBM Personal Computer*. Mr. Rugg is president of 32 Plus, Inc., a software development and consulting firm.

Phil Feldman

Mr. Feldman received his B.A. degree in Physics from the University of California in 1968 and did graduate work in Computer Science at U.C.L.A. For 15 years he worked at TRW Systems, Inc., where he was a member of the Technical Staff and Project Manager of Software Development on Aerospace Engineering Projects. He has written or coauthored many articles in engineering technical journals and personal computer magazines, and has coauthored with Tom Rugg a number of books, including *TRS-80 Color Programs* and *Mind Moves*. Mr. Feldman is chairman of 32 Plus, Inc.

Table of Contents

Subprograms for Sorting and Searching

Subprograms That Manipulate Data (Text)

Subprograms of Useful Utilities

Full Programs

Preface

Our design philosophy for the *Turbo Pascal Program Library* is easily stated: "Make it a programming companion. Create a reference for repeated use." Contained in these pages is a comprehensive library of practical Turbo Pascal subprograms (procedures and functions).

At first glance, it may seem odd that our *program* library is composed of *subprograms*, not programs. The reason is that Pascal encourages a modular programming style in which most of a program's detailed tasks are delegated to subprograms. The subprograms are then assimilated into the full program to form one cohesive unit.

This book is a library of subprograms that are meant to be building blocks toward your finished programs. Think of these subprograms as the foundation stones on which your programming construction projects are built. Whether your undertaking is simple or complex, you should find in this book useful components that will save you time and trouble.

Is this book for you? If you program in Turbo Pascal, the answer is yes. By taking advantage of our ready-made routines, you can improve your productivity immediately. The first time you use one of these subprograms, you should be able to justify the cost of the book in the hours you save by not having to develop original code. And if you use any of our complete programs, your savings are even greater.

If you are an intermediate or advanced programmer, think of this book as an instant software reference library. For you, its primary benefits are simplified program development and expediency. If you are a beginner in Pascal, you receive the additional benefit of practical program components you might otherwise be unable to develop yourself.

We assume that you know how to program in Pascal, at least rudimentarily. This book is neither a tutorial on Pascal in general nor a tutorial on Turbo Pascal in particular. (Many excellent books that teach these subjects are available.) At a minimum, you should know how to get Pascal running on your computer, type a program, save it on disk, compile the program, and run it.

Even if you are just beginning to learn Pascal (especially if you are a "learn by doing" person), this book will be a useful companion. We explain many programming tips and techniques throughout the presentation of these subprograms. Additionally, the exposure to well-structured, useful subprograms and full programs will help you understand more than just the rules of Pascal. Pascal encourages a clean, structured, top-down programming style, and we have tried to exemplify it. We hope this book will help you become a more knowledgeable programmer.

Our target audience is the largest group of Turbo Pascal users—those with IBM PCs or compatibles. However, those who use Turbo Pascal on other computers (CP/M® computers, Apple®, etc.) should find the subprograms helpful, as will users of other versions of Pascal. You may have to make some changes, though, to enable certain programs to work.

Acknowledgments

The work of a few is always the result of many. We are especially grateful . . .

To Maria Katinos for the figures and research. She never floundered.

To the imponderable Dave Feldman. His contributions are simply not explainable.

To everyone at Que. Their faith and perseverance made this book a reality. Special thanks to Ginny Noble, Pegg Kennedy, and Chris DeVoney.

To Philippe Kahn, president of Borland International. His vision resulted in a watershed software product. Turbo is much more than just a Pascal compiler for microcomputers. It is a well designed programming environment. Its power, ease of use, and fair price have created a standard for future software products. The growing popularity of Turbo Pascal is a testament to this foresight.

And, finally, to Louisa Gillette for her understanding and support. We love her.

Product Development Director
Chris DeVoney

Editorial Director
David F. Noble, Ph.D.

Managing Editor
Gregory Croy

Editor
Virginia Noble, M.L.S.

Technical Editor
Art Sterling

Composed in Garamond and Que Digital
by Que Corporation

Cover designed by
Listenberger Design Associates

Trademark Acknowledgments

How To Use This Book

The Structure of a Pascal Program

We can view a Pascal program as consisting of three sections. Let's call section 1 the "global declarations section," section 2 the "subprograms section," and section 3 the "mainline logic section." The word *subprograms* is Pascal terminology for the program components that comprise procedures and functions. Here is a "pseudoprogram" with numbers at the right to indicate the sections:

```
program MainProgram;                                    {1}
   {global declarations for MainProgram and}            {1}
   {all subprograms.                       }            {1}

function FunctionA;                                      {2}
   {local declarations and logic of FunctionA}          {2}
function FunctionB;                                      {2}
   {local declarations and logic of FunctionB}          {2}
procedure ProcedureA;                                    {2}
   {local declarations and logic of ProcedureA}         {2}
procedure ProcedureB;                                    {2}
   {local declarations and logic of ProcedureB}         {2}

BEGIN                                                    {3}
   {logic of MainProgram}                                {3}
END.                                                    {3}
```

Most authorities recommend that the mainline logic section be short. Rather than perform all the detailed logic of the program in the mainline section, you should design individual chunks of logic called subprograms and put them in the subprograms section. Then your mainline logic section can simply invoke each subprogram to do its work as necessary. This method of organization simplifies the processes of designing and testing the program, thus improving productivity.

We strongly endorse this programming approach. That's why the *Turbo Pascal Program Library* contains subprograms, not programs. Think of this book as a library for *constructing* programs, not as a library *of* programs.

At one time or another, most programmers find themselves caught in the "reinvention of the wheel" syndrome. This typically happens during the writing of subprograms. At one of these frustrating moments, have you ever asked yourself, "I bet someone has written a subprogram to do this before. Why can't I just borrow theirs and save myself some time and trouble?" Well, that's our cue.

The Program Library Concept

The *Turbo Pascal Program Library* contains over 100 useful subprograms designed to give you the "wheels" so that you can concentrate on your mainline logic. You can choose subprograms to enter data from the keyboard, detect errors, produce graphics effects, manipulate disk files, sort data, calculate curve fits, do matrix algebra, and accomplish many other useful tasks.

Each subprogram has been used in "real world" full programs and has shown its practical value under firing-line conditions. Chapter 18 presents 10 full programs that demonstrate how easy it is to assimilate the subprograms. More than 40 of the subprograms in this book are used in those full programs.

The Assimilation Process

Once you have a subprogram saved on disk, you can easily incorporate the subprogram into your main program. You can do this in two ways. For each method, we assume that you're composing a main program with the Turbo editor.

The first method is to create a complete source copy of the subprogram in your main program. To do this while using the Turbo editor, you position the cursor where you want the subprogram to appear. Then you press Ctrl-K (press and hold down the Ctrl key while you press also the K key) followed by the R key. This sequence causes the Turbo editor to prompt you for the name of a disk file to be read into your main program. You simply give the name of the subprogram you want. A complete copy of the subprogram appears at the cursor location.

The second method is to use Turbo's {$I} compiler directive. You include just one line in the subprograms section of your program. The syntax for the compiler directive is

```
{$I filename}
```

in which the file name will be one of your subprogram names. The {$I} directive tells the compiler to include the subprogram within your main program at compile time. This approach saves considerable space in your program listings. The full programs in Chapter 18 are good examples of this method.

A Disk Offer for Lazy Typists

Typing annoys many programmers—especially typing "canned" code from a book like ours. Because we don't want any undue suffering, we've put all the source code from this book onto disk software for the IBM® PC and compatibles. Included are all the subprograms, Sample Usage programs, and full programs found in the book. When you use this software, typing hassles will fade into distant memory. See the disk offer at the back of the book.

Hardware and Software Configurations

All the programs and subprograms in this book were developed with Turbo Pascal® Version 3.01A on a standard IBM PC running under DOS V2.0. A dual floppy disk system is assumed with at least 128K of RAM (random-access memory). See Appendixes A and D.

Documenting the Subprograms

Each subprogram is accompanied by a detailed explanation, designed to help you decide whether the subprogram fits your particular needs and how to take full advantage of it when it does. We've standardized the form of these write-ups, creating a "template" for each subprogram explanation. This template consists of the following parts.

A Quicklook Box

This handy "quick reference" box, providing a thumbnail description of the subprogram, contains the following:

> Name (the full name of the subprogram)
> Type (procedure or function)
> Purpose (a brief explanation of what it does)
> Calling Sequence (the parameters passed)

The *Name* is the unique, descriptive name we have assigned to the subprogram. The name can contain up to eight characters. For example, the subprogram

```
GetReply
```

gets a reply from the keyboard. Capitalization is used in the subprogram name for clarity but is ignored by DOS and Turbo. When saving the subprogram to disk, we add the extension .PSL (for Pascal Subprogram Library; these subprograms, the Sample Usage programs, and the full programs make up the *Turbo Pascal Program Library*). PSL is always in uppercase. Thus, GetReply is saved on disk as

```
GetReply.PSL
```

The *Type* indicates whether the subprogram is a procedure or a function. If the subprogram is a function, the kind of function is also given, such as a real function, an integer function, a boolean function, and so on.

The *Calling Sequence* shows the exact syntax you use to invoke the subprogram from your main program. This information enables you to see at a glance the parameters required to use the subprogram. For example, the Calling Sequence for GetReply is

```
GetReply(First, Last, Reply)
```

Description

This section contains a one-paragraph explanation of what the subprogram does and when it might be used.

Input

The Input section describes everything required by the calling routine before the subprogram can be called. This section usually contains a list of the parameters (variable names) that must be passed to the subprogram so that it can perform its intended function. The three-column list contains the variable name, the variable type, and a short description of what the variable does and how to use it. Note that you do not need to use the same variable names as ours, but your type declaration for each variable must be the same as ours.

Sometimes a subprogram has other requirements, such as a global variable or a type declaration that needs to be defined, another subprogram that must be called first, or a specific state to which the computer must be set (high-resolution graphics mode, for example). When global variables or type declarations are required, you must use the same names we use, unless you modify the subprograms' names to match your global names.

Output

Similar to the Input section, Output describes the output expected from the subprogram. This section includes the variables set and the actions performed.

Limitations and Error Conditions

This section contains the limitations of the subprogram, any error conditions it detects, and the actions the subprogram takes when encountering an error.

Sample Usage

To illustrate the use of each subprogram, we've included a short sample program that contains the subprogram presented. This Sample Usage program assimilates the subprogram, using the {$I} compiler directive explained previously. You can type this sample program and run it to test the subprogram, but you first must have on disk a copy of the subprogram with the correct name.

Typically, the output of the Sample Usage program is shown also, illustrating how the program works and demonstrating the use of the included subprogram.

Subprogram Listing

This is a complete listing of the Turbo Pascal source code for the subprogram. The listing is printed on a shaded background for easy reference.

Variables

All the variables defined inside the subprogram are listed, along with explanations of their uses. These variables are local to the subprograms (and any embedded blocks) and are not defined at the level of the main program.

Discussion

This section contains information to help you make effective use of the subprogram. This section may include cross-references to other subprograms; applications that may not be obvious; theoretical foundations; details about the programming techniques used; and information about speed, memory use, or other resource requirements.

Modifications

Sometimes you want a subprogram to work slightly differently. In this section are specific changes you can make in the subprogram's source code so that you can tailor the subprogram to your exact needs.

Style Conventions

There are no rigid rules covering the "correct" way to write a Pascal program. Each programmer has a unique style for capitalization, indentation, identifier names, etc. Our approach and recommendations are covered in detail in Appendix C.

How To Get Started

If you are a grizzled Turbo Pascal veteran, you probably know exactly how you want to enter and run these subprograms, and how you'll add them to your existing subprogram library. For those who would like some advice on how to get started, refer to Appendix A. There you'll find recommendations about entering and testing the subprograms, fixing typing errors, building a subprogram library, and solving problems.

2

Getting Keyboard Input

Computer programs aren't very useful without data on which to operate, and nearly all data is input from the keyboard at one time or another. This chapter provides nine subprograms to aid you in constructing programs that require use of the keyboard.

GetReply, GetKey, and KeyHit are useful when your program requires detection of a single key pressed. GetReply is designed to get a reply within a specified consecutive range, such as after displaying a menu of options from 1 through 5. GetKey detects any keystroke that you indicate to be allowable, whether consecutive or not. KeyHit retrieves a key that has been pressed, if any, without causing your program to pause. All three subprograms require only a single keystroke; you don't need to press the Enter key afterward.

You should use GetNumR or GetNumI in programs that call for entry of a numeric value. Turbo Pascal aborts your program with a run-time error if you accidentally type an illegal character when a readln procedure requests a numeric variable. These two subprograms avoid this problem. Use GetNumR for real variables, and GetNumI for integer variables.

WaitKey displays a message and waits for a key to be pressed before the program continues. This simple procedure is often needed in programs.

Finally, this chapter has three subprograms for filling arrays with data entered from the keyboard. KeyArr is designed for entry of data into a one-dimensional real array. With a simple modification, you can use KeyArr for an integer array instead. Key2Arr is for entering data into a two-dimensional real array, and KeyTxt is for keying text data into a string array.

GetReply

Name:	*GetReply*
Type:	*Procedure*
Purpose:	*To detect a keystroke within a specified range*
Calling Sequence:	GetReply(First, Last, Reply)

Description

GetReply first prompts you to enter a reply (press a key) and then displays both the first and the last key of the acceptable range. You may specify the range to be whatever you want. Other replies are ignored. When you press a key, its value is returned in Reply.

Input

First char In ASCII sequence the lowest key that is an acceptable reply

Last   char In ASCII sequence the highest key that is an acceptable reply

Output

Reply char The key you press

The subprogram prompts you to Enter reply from [First] to [Last]. and waits for you to press an acceptable key.

Limitations and Error Conditions

First and Last are displayed in ascending ASCII sequence, even when you specify them in descending order. If the two are equal, then only that one key satisfies the condition. Note that alphabetic ranges are sensitive to upper- and lowercase. For instance, if you specify the range from ´A´ to ´G´, you are requiring uppercase entries, whereas ´a´ to ´g´ requires lowercase entries. You can specify the entire "normal" keyboard (that is, not counting special-function keys, such as F1 through F10, Home, Del, etc.) as acceptable entries by using the range of ´ ´ (a blank space) to ´z´. Special-function keys that cause a two-byte result ("Escape" plus a code) cause Reply to be set to zero. Thus, these keys are ignored unless you set First or Last to a value of chr(0). Note that the subprogram does not display the key pressed. Your main program must display the reply if that is what you want.

Sample Usage

```
program SampleUsageOfGetReply;

var
   First, Last, Reply: char;

{$I GetReply.PSL}

BEGIN
   First := '1';
   Last  := '5';
   GetReply(First, Last, Reply);
   writeln('Reply = ', Reply);
   GetReply('Z', 'A', Reply);
   writeln('Second reply = ', Reply)
END.
```

This sample program produces the following output on the screen if you press the 3 key after the first prompt, and the Z key after the second prompt:

```
Enter reply from 1 to 5.
Reply = 3
Enter reply from A to Z.
Second reply = Z
```

Subprogram Listing of GetReply.PSL

```
procedure GetReply(First, Last: char; var Reply: char);

var
   Temp: char;

begin
   if First > Last then
      begin
         Temp  := First;
         First := Last;
         Last  := Temp
      end;
   writeln('Enter reply from ', First, ' to ', Last, '.');
```

```
  repeat
    read(kbd, Reply);
    if (Reply = #27) and keypressed then
      begin
        read(kbd, Reply);
        Reply := #0
      end
  until (Reply >= First) and (Reply <= Last)
end;
```

Variables

Temp   Temporary char variable used in interchanging First and Last, if necessary

Discussion

GetReply has two common uses. First, you can retrieve a reply to a menu of choices. Such choices are generally labeled 1 through 5, or A through K, or some other consecutive range of values. (If your choices are not consecutive, see GetKey.) Your mainline program can then use Pascal's case statement to take appropriate action depending on which Reply you get. The second common use arises when your program displays a screenful of data and has more to come. You can ask for a key to be pressed to continue with the display or, if a special key is pressed, to take some other action. GetReply (unlike Turbo's built-in keypressed procedure) enables you to see which key was pressed. When using GetReply in this second way, you will want to replace its prompting message with one of your own to indicate the choices. In some cases, GetKey will be a more appropriate subprogram.

Modifications

None

GetKey

> **Name:** *GetKey*
>
> **Type:** *Procedure*
>
> **Purpose:** *To detect a keystroke from an eligible list*
>
> **Calling Sequence:** GetKey(KeyList, Reply, Reply2)

Description

GetKey detects which key is pressed from a list of eligible keys you specify in
KeyList. No prompting message is shown, and the key pressed is not echoed on
the screen. If you make KeyList the null string (two consecutive apostrophes with
no space between them), then any key is accepted. When the Esc (Escape) key
(#27, or ASCII decimal 27) is included in the list, the special-function keys (F1
through F10, Home, Del, etc.) are allowable replies. When you press a special-
function key, Reply returns #27 (Escape), and Reply2 returns the value of the key
as shown in Appendix K of the *Turbo Pascal Reference Manual*. If you don't include
the Esc key in the list (or imply the Esc key with a null KeyList), then Reply
contains the key value, and Reply2 is #0. If the Esc key itself is pressed, Reply is
#27, and Reply2 is #0.

Typical uses of this subprogram are to detect when a key is pressed without requiring the Enter key to be pressed afterward, and to require one key from a limited
list to be pressed, but no other keys. This second use is common if you want
someone to press Y or N (for yes or no) in response to your message but want
to ignore any other replies.

Input

KeyList   string   List of allowable keys to press. If null, any key is
                        allowable.

You must also specify the following global type declaration in your main program.
The string length of 10 is an example.

```
type
   KeyListType = string[10];
```

The string needs to be only as long as KeyList but must be at least 1.

Output

Reply   char   The value of the key pressed. For special-function
                       keys, Reply has the value #27.

Reply2   char   The second value for a special-function key (see
                       Appendix K of the Turbo manual), or #0 otherwise

Limitations and Error Conditions

Upper- and lowercase keys are differentiated. If, for example, you want both Y and
y to be allowable keys, you must include both in KeyList.

Sample Usage

```
program SampleUsageOfGetKey;

type
   KeyListType = string[10];

var
   KeyList       : KeyListType;
   Reply, Reply2 : char;

{$I GetKey.PSL}

BEGIN
   writeln('Press Y for yes or N for no');
   GetKey('YyNn', Reply, Reply2);
   writeln(Reply);
   writeln('Press any key');
   KeyList := '';    {null string - no spaces between apostrophes}
   GetKey(KeyList, Reply, Reply2);
   writeln(ord(Reply):4, ord(Reply2):4)
END.
```

This sample program produces the following output on the screen if you press the Y key after the first prompt (it ignores all other keys except y, N, and n), and the F1 special-function key after the second prompt:

```
Press Y for yes or N for no
Y
Press any key
  27  59
```

Subprogram Listing of GetKey.PSL

```
procedure GetKey(KeyList: KeyListType; var Reply, Reply2: char);

begin
   Reply2 := chr(Ø);
   repeat
      read(kbd, Reply);
      if (Reply = #27) and keypressed then
         read(kbd, Reply2);
      if length(KeyList) = Ø then exit;
   until pos(Reply, KeyList) > Ø
end;
```

Variables

None

Discussion

GetKey is useful when you have a limited number of nonconsecutive single keys you want to allow to be pressed in a program. Thus, GetKey is unlike GetReply, which is meant for replies from menus with consecutive keys from which to choose. Note that Reply is #27 for either the Esc key or any of the special-function keys, but Reply2 is either #0 for the Esc key or other values for the special-function keys. You can use code like this to determine the keystroke when Reply is #27:

```
GetKey('', Reply, Reply2);
if Reply = #27 then
   if Reply2 = #Ø then
      writeln('Esc key')
   else
      writeln('special-function key: ', ord(Reply2))
else
   writeln('not Esc or special-function key: ', Reply)
```

Modifications

None

KeyHit

> **Name:** *KeyHit*
>
> **Type:** boolean *function*
>
> **Purpose:** *To detect whether a key has been pressed and, if so, which one*
>
> **Calling Sequence:** KeyHit(Reply, Reply2)

Description

KeyHit detects whether a key has been pressed. If a key has not been hit, the function returns a boolean value of false. If a key has been pressed, a boolean value of true is returned, and the parameters Reply and Reply2 contain the value of the key pressed. These parameters return values of type char and indicate the key with a return code as shown in Appendix K of the Turbo manual. For "regular" keys, Reply has a value other than #27, and the value of Reply2 is irrelevant. For special-function keys (F1 through F10, Home, Del, etc.), Reply is #27 (Escape), and Reply2 contains the value of the key. If the Esc key itself is pressed, Reply is #27, and Reply2 is #0.

Input

None

Output

KeyHit	boolean	The function that indicates whether a key has been hit. A value of true means that a key has been pressed. A value of false means that no key has been pressed.
Reply	char	The value of the key pressed. For special-function keys, Reply has the value #27.
Reply2	char	The second value for a special-function key (see Appendix K of the Turbo manual), or #0 otherwise

Limitations and Error Conditions

KeyHit reads possible keystrokes by using Turbo's logical input device, designated kbd, which does not buffer input. As a result, if more than one key is pressed before the call to KeyHit, only the first keystroke is detected. The subsequent keystrokes are lost.

The values of Reply and Reply2 are meaningless if KeyHit returns the value of false.

Sample Usage

```
program SampleUsageOfKeyHit;

var
   Reply, Reply2 : char;
   Counter       : integer;

{$I KeyHit.PSL}

BEGIN
   clrscr;
   Counter := 0;
   while not KeyHit(Reply, Reply2) do
      begin
         gotoxy(1,3);
         Counter := Counter + 1;
         writeln('Time counter = ', Counter);
         delay(50)
      end;
   writeln;
   writeln('Key''s return code is', ord(Reply):5, ord(Reply2):5)
END.
```

This sample program continually updates an incremental counter in the upper left corner of the screen. When a key is pressed, the counter stops, and the value of the key is displayed. In the sample output that follows, the F1 key is pressed when the counter reaches 98:

```
Time counter = 98

Key's return code is   27   59
```

Subprogram Listing of KeyHit.PSL

```
function KeyHit(var Reply, Reply2: char): boolean;

begin
   Reply2 := #0;
   if keypressed then
      begin
         KeyHit := true;
         read(kbd, Reply);
         if (Reply = #27) and keypressed then
            read(kbd, Reply2)
      end
   else
      KeyHit := false
end;
```

Variables

None

Discussion

This function is useful in interactive programs when you want to detect whether a key has been pressed, yet want execution to continue if no key has been pressed. KeyHit does not wait for a key to be pressed; it merely detects whether one has been pressed. A typical use for KeyHit is in a "turtle" graphics sketching program, in which a line is continually drawn on the screen by the "turtle." If certain keys are pressed, the turtle changes its direction, speed, or color. If no key is pressed, the turtle simply continues straight ahead.

Remember that Reply is #27 if either the Esc key or a special-function key is hit, but Reply2 is either #0 for the Esc key or other values for the special-function keys. The Discussion section of GetKey contains sample code to determine the actual keystroke when Reply is #27.

This subprogram provides the solution to a problem that crops up during Turbo Pascal program development. When you want to have your program pause before it ends and returns control back to Turbo, an apparent solution is to use the code repeat until keypressed as your last program statement. The problem is that Turbo interprets the key you press as the first key pressed after Turbo regains control. The result, depending on which key you press, is that Turbo generally clears the screen and returns to its editor menu. A better solution is to use the

KeyHit subprogram by saying repeat until KeyHit(Reply, Reply2). KeyHit removes from the buffer area the key that was pressed, thus preventing the key from being interpreted by Turbo when it regains control.

Modifications

None

GetNumR

Name:	*GetNumR*
Type:	*Procedure*
Purpose:	*To get a real number (or a special character) typed from the keyboard*
Calling Sequence:	GetNumR(Number, CharFlag, Code)

Description

You are prompted to provide data entry from the keyboard. If you input a real number, GetNumR returns its value. If you input a single (nonnumeric) character, that character is returned. If you press only the Enter key, that is detected. Other replies are flagged as illegal. The subprogram avoids Turbo's usual run-time error that occurs when you make an illegal entry for a numeric value in response to a readln statement. All input strings are terminated with the Enter key.

Input

None

Output

Number	real	The real number entered from the keyboard
CharFlag	char	Nonnumeric character entered from the keyboard
Code	integer	Flag indicating the type of keyboard input provided, namely

-2: Only Enter key was input.

-1: Single nonnumeric key was input; its value is in CharFlag.

0: A real number was input; its value is in Number.

>1: Illegal entry; Code contains the position of the first character that cannot be interpreted as part of a real number.

Limitations and Error Conditions

Other than the standard alphanumeric keys, only the Shift key and the Enter key are intended for use with this subprogram. Data strings containing other specialized keys (such as Esc, tab, Ctrl, Alt, F1 through F10, cursor-movement keys, etc.) cause strange results. In most cases, Code is set to a nonzero value. These keys, however, do not cause a run-time error. Ctrl-C or Ctrl-Break interrupt the program.

Any input string longer than 30 characters is truncated to 30 characters before the subprogram processes the string.

GetNumR uses Turbo's built-in val procedure to interpret your input strings as real numbers. The rules defining legal strings are generally the same as the rules for defining real constants, but there are some surprises. The only allowable characters are the plus sign (+), the minus sign (-), the decimal point (.), the exponential indicator (e or E), and the 10 digits (0–9). Any other character causes the string to be illegal as a real number. Blanks are illegal, even if they lead or trail the rest of the input string. The plus sign is legal only after the exponential indicator (and the + is optional there). The plus sign cannot lead the number. (The minus sign can lead a number, of course.) A comma cannot appear in the string. The decimal point is optional if the number has an integral value. Numbers expressed in exponential form must be within Turbo's allowable range for real numbers (absolute value from 1.0E-38 to 1.0E+38). The exponential indicator must be followed by an (optional) plus or minus sign and at least one numeric digit.

Some examples of legal expressions are -23.481, 3E4, 3.e+4, 14., 14, ., -, E0, and -0. The last four expressions evaluate to zero. Some illegal expressions are +23.0 (leading + sign), 42E42 (too big), 13.1 45 (contains a blank), and 29.E (nothing following the exponential indicator). When Code is set to a nonzero value, the contents of Number are left unchanged.

Sample Usage

```
program SampleUsageOfGetNumR;

var
   Number   : real;
   CharFlag : char;
   Code     : integer;

{$I GetNumR.PSL}

BEGIN
   repeat
      GetNumR(Number, CharFlag, Code);
      case Code of
         -2: writeln('You hit only the [Enter] key');
         -1: writeln('You hit the nonnumeric character: ',
                   CharFlag);
          0: writeln('You entered the real number:', Number)
      else
         writeln('You made an illegal entry')
      end
   until
      (Code = -1) and (CharFlag = 'Q')
END.
```

The following is a possible session produced with this program. The sample program terminates after you press Shift-Q.

```
Entry? 23.14
You entered the real number:  2.3140000000E+01
Entry? -18e4
You entered the real number: -1.8000000000E+05
Entry? 46..21
You made an illegal entry
Entry?
You hit only the [Enter] key
Entry? +
You hit the nonnumeric character: +
Entry? Q
You hit the nonnumeric character: Q
```

Subprogram Listing of GetNumR.PSL

```pascal
procedure GetNumR(var Number: real; var CharFlag: char;
                  var Code: integer);

const
   PromptString = 'Entry? ';                              {Mod. #1}

var
   Entry: string[30];

begin
   write(PromptString);
   readln(Entry);
   val(Entry, Number, Code);
   case length(Entry) of
     0: Code := -2;
     1: if Code > 0 then
           begin
              Code     := -1;
              CharFlag := Entry
           end
   end
end;
```

Variables

PromptString	String constant displayed to prompt you for input
Entry	Data string entered from the keyboard

Discussion

This subprogram is designed to facilitate numeric input when you may need special replies but want to avoid run-time errors for nonnumeric entries. For a simple example, suppose that you are writing a checkbook-balancing program. You need the user to provide the amounts of the checks written during the last month, one check at a time. The program prompts the user for each amount (expressed as a real number in dollars and cents). But you also might allow some special replies to be made. One reply might be M, indicating that a mistake was made in the last value and the user wants to reenter it. Another reply might be F, indicating that the data entry is finished and all values have been entered. This type of keyboard input is perfect for GetNumR.

Modification

PromptString is the message displayed to prompt the user for input. You may want to change PromptString to a more suitable message for your particular application. If you make PromptString the null string, no message is displayed.

GetNumI

Name:	*GetNumI*
Type:	*Procedure*
Purpose:	*To get an integer number (or a special character) typed from the keyboard*
Calling Sequence:	GetNumI(WholeNumber, CharFlag, Code)

Description

You are prompted to provide data entry from the keyboard. If you input an integer number, GetNumI returns its value. If you input a single (nonnumeric) character, that character is returned. If you press only the Enter key, that is detected. Other replies are flagged as illegal. All input strings are terminated with the Enter key. The subprogram avoids Turbo's usual run-time error that occurs when you make an illegal entry for a numeric value in response to a readln statement.

Input

None

Output

WholeNumber	real	The integer number entered from the keyboard
CharFlag	char	Nonnumeric character entered from the keyboard
Code	integer	Flag indicating the type of keyboard input provided, namely

-2: Only Enter key was input.

-1: Single nonnumeric key was input; its value is in CharFlag.

0: An integer number was input; its value is in WholeNumber.

>1: Illegal entry; Code contains the position of
     the first character that cannot be interpreted
     as part of an integer number.

Limitations and Error Conditions

Other than the standard alphanumeric keys, only the Shift key and the Enter key
are intended for use with this subprogram. Data strings containing other specialized
keys (such as Esc, tab, Ctrl, Alt, F1 through F10, cursor-movement keys, etc.) cause
strange results. In most cases, Code is set to a nonzero value. These keys, however,
do not cause a run-time error. Ctrl-C and Ctrl-Break interrupt the program.

Any input string longer than 30 characters is truncated to 30 characters before the
subprogram processes the string.

GetNumI uses Turbo's built-in val procedure to interpret your input strings as integer numbers. The rules defining legal strings are generally the same as the rules
for creating integer constants, but there are some surprises. The only allowable
characters are the minus sign (-) and the 10 digits (0–9). Any other character
causes the string to be illegal as an integer number. Blanks are illegal, even if they
lead or trail the rest of the input string. The plus sign is illegal; it cannot precede
positive integers. (The minus sign can lead a number, of course.) A comma cannot
appear anywhere in the string. Also illegal are the decimal point and the exponential
indicator, which are both legal in real numbers. Numbers must be within the range
allowed in Turbo's integer precision (from -32768 to 32767).

Some examples of legal expressions are -23, 4, -, and 000. The last two expressions
evaluate to zero. Some illegal expressions are +23 (leading + sign), 33800 (too
big), 13 45 (contains a blank), 29.0 (contains a decimal point), and -45E2 (contains
the exponential indicator).

Sample Usage

```
program SampleUsageOfGetNumI;

var
   WholeNumber, Code : integer;
   CharFlag          : char;

{$I GetNumI.PSL}
```

```
BEGIN
  repeat
    GetNumI(WholeNumber, CharFlag, Code);
    case Code of
      -2: writeln('You hit only the [Enter] key');
      -1: writeln('You hit the nonnumeric character: ',
                   CharFlag);
       0: writeln('You entered the integer number: ',
                   WholeNumber)
    else
      writeln('You made an illegal entry')
    end
  until
    (Code = -1) and (CharFlag = 'Q')
END.
```

The following is a possible session produced with this program. Pressing Shift-Q ends the sample program.

```
Entry? 567
You entered the integer number: 567
Entry? -21
You entered the integer number: -21
Entry? 32,000
You made an illegal entry
Entry?
You hit only the [Enter] key
Entry? +
You hit the nonnumeric character: +
Entry? Q
You hit the nonnumeric character: Q
```

Subprogram Listing of GetNumI.PSL

```
procedure GetNumI(var WholeNumber: integer; var CharFlag: char;
                  var Code: integer);

const
  PromptString = 'Entry? ';                              {Mod. #1}

var
  Entry: string[30];
```

```
begin
   write(PromptString);
   readln(Entry);
   val(Entry, WholeNumber, Code);
   case length(Entry) of
      0: Code := -2;
      1: if Code > 0 then
            begin
               Code    := -1;
               CharFlag := Entry
            end
   end
end;
```

Variables

PromptString   String constant displayed to prompt you for input

Entry   Data string entered from the keyboard

Discussion

This subprogram is the companion to GetNumR. You use GetNumI when integer numbers are needed for input, and GetNumR when real numbers are required. See the Discussion section of GetNumR for additional details.

Modification

PromptString is the message displayed to prompt the user for input. You may want to change PromptString to a more suitable message for your particular application. If you make PromptString the null string, no message is displayed.

WaitKey

> **Name:** *WaitKey*
>
> **Type:** *Procedure*
>
> **Purpose:** *To make a program pause until a key is pressed*
>
> **Calling Sequence:** WaitKey

Description

WaitKey is a simple procedure that displays a message on the screen and waits for you to press a key to continue the program. Many programs require that this be done repeatedly, and using a procedure is preferable to using in-line code.

Input

None

Output

The message PRESS ANY KEY TO CONTINUE is displayed on the screen, the procedure waits until you press any key, and then the procedure ends, thus causing the mainline program to continue.

Limitations and Error Conditions

Nearly any key on the keyboard will satisfy this subprogram and cause the program to continue. Some keys, however, will not work, including the Alt, Ctrl, Shift, Caps Lock, and Num Lock keys.

Sample Usage

```
program SampleUsageOfWaitKey;

{$I WaitKey.PSL}

BEGIN
   writeln('This message displayed first.');
   WaitKey;
   writeln('This one after a key is pressed.')
END.
```

This test program produces the following output:

```
This message displayed first.

** PRESS ANY KEY TO CONTINUE **
This one after a key is pressed.
```

Subprogram Listing of WaitKey.PSL

```
procedure WaitKey;

begin
   writeln;                                    {Mod. #1}
   writeln('** PRESS ANY KEY TO CONTINUE **');
   repeat until keypressed
end;
```

Variables

None

Discussion

WaitKey displays its message and repeatedly calls Turbo Pascal's keypressed function until a key is pressed. For procedures that wait for a key to be pressed and enable you to examine which key it is, refer to the GetKey and GetReply subprograms.

Modification

You may want to delete the blank line displayed before the message by deleting the indicated statement. Our experience, however, is that the extra line is normally desirable for readability.

KeyArr

Name: *KeyArr*

Type: *Procedure*

Purpose: *To enter numeric data from the keyboard into an array*

Calling Sequence: KeyArr(NumArray, Count)

Description

This subprogram enables you to enter numeric data from the keyboard into a one-dimensional array. KeyArr uses real data, but modifications for integer data are provided. The subprogram prevents the run-time error that normally occurs when nonnumeric data is entered for a numeric variable.

Input

NumArray	real	Array in which data is to be stored
Count	integer	Number of elements currently in the array. (Normally this number should be zero before using KeyArr.)

In addition, you must specify the following global const and type declarations in your main program. The number 100 is an example; your array size may vary.

```
const
   ArraySize = 100;

type
   ArrayType = array[1..ArraySize] of real;
```

Output

NumArray	real	The same array, now containing data entered from the keyboard
Count	integer	Number of elements now in the array

Limitations and Error Conditions

Unlike most programs, this subprogram does *not* get a run-time error if you erroneously enter nonnumeric data. Instead, the subprogram displays the message ** Illegal. Please reenter. ** and asks for the same entry again. You enter the word END (all uppercase) to terminate data entry; otherwise, you fill the array full to ArraySize entries. A null entry is treated as nonnumeric data. If an entry is longer than 20 characters, only the first 20 are used. Count does not have to be zero before you use KeyArr. If, for example, you have 5 entries in you array and you want to enter more, set Count to 5. KeyArr willl put the next entry into element number 6.

Sample Usage

```
program SampleUsageOfKeyArr;

const
   ArraySize = 100;

type
   ArrayType = array[1..ArraySize] of real;          {Mod. #2}
```

```
var
   NumArray : ArrayType;
   Count, J : integer;

{$I KeyArr.PSL}

BEGIN
   Count := 0;
   KeyArr(NumArray, Count);
   writeln('Here is the data entered from the keyboard.');
   for J := 1 to Count do writeln(NumArray[J]:12:4)      {Mod. #2}
END.
```

When you enter and run this test program, it displays the following output:

```
** Enter real data.  Array size = 100 **
** Enter END to end data entry. **
Entry number 1: 37.2
Entry number 2: 15.61
Entry number 3: -4.03
Entry number 4: END
** Data entry complete **
Here is the data entered from the keyboard.
      37.2000
      15.6100
      -4.0300
```

Subprogram Listing of KeyArr.PSL

```
procedure KeyArr(var NumArray: ArrayType; var Count: integer);

const
   EndFlag = 'END';

var
   Entry   : string[20];
   Code    : integer;

begin
   Entry := '';
   writeln('** Enter real data.  Array size = ',          {Mod. #2}
           ArraySize, ' **');
```

```
   writeln('** Enter ', EndFlag, ' to end data entry. **');
   while (Entry <> EndFlag) and (Count < ArraySize) do
      begin
         Count := Count + 1;
         write('Entry number ', Count, ': ');
         readln(Entry);
         if length(Entry) = 0 then Entry := 'bad';        {Mod. #1}
         if (Entry <> EndFlag) and (Count <= ArraySize) then
            begin
               val(Entry, NumArray[Count], Code);
               if Code <> 0 then
                  begin
                     writeln('** Illegal.  Please reenter. **');
                     Count := Count - 1
                  end
            end
      end;
   if Entry = EndFlag then Count := Count - 1;
   writeln('** Data entry complete **')
end;
```

Variables

EndFlag	Text entered by user to indicate no more entries ('END')
Entry	User's string entry, converted to numeric value for placement into array
Code	Condition code set by Turbo's val function, indicating whether Entry was successfully converted to a numeric value

Discussion

This subprogram is a handy way to enter numeric data into an array and is compatible with several other array-handling subprograms (ShowArr, SortSIR, SortHR, LoadArr, and SaveArr). For two-dimensional arrays, see Key2Arr. KeyArr avoids the common problem encountered by Turbo programs in which keying illegal numeric data causes the program to blow up (that is, get a fatal run-time error). The solution is to use readln to enter the keyboard data into a string variable, which is then converted into a numeric value by Turbo's val procedure. If the entry can't be converted correctly, it must have been nonnumeric, and KeyArr asks the user to reenter the data. See GetNumR to determine exactly what constitutes a legal numeric entry for val.

Modifications

1. To allow a null entry (that is, pressing the Enter key with no data) to signal the end of data entry, change 'bad' to 'END' in the line indicated by {Mod. 1}.

2. To enter data into an integer array instead of a real one, change the global type definition to indicate an integer array. You will also want to change the subprogram's first writeln statement to Enter integer data instead of using Enter real data. To use the Sample Usage program, you also need to delete :4 from the last statement before the END. statement.

Key2Arr

> **Name:** *Key2Arr*
>
> **Type:** *Procedure*
>
> **Purpose:** *To enter keyboard data into a two-dimensional array*
>
> **Calling Sequence:** Key2Arr(Num2Array, RowCount)

Description

You use this procedure to enter numeric data from the keyboard into a two-dimensional real array. Our sample program uses an array that is 100 (rows) by 2 (columns), but you can specify any size you need. The subprogram prevents the run-time error that normally occurs when nonnumeric data is entered for a numeric variable.

Input

Num2Array	real	Array in which data is to be stored
RowCount	integer	Number of rows currently in the array. (Normally this number should be zero before you use Key2Arr.)

In addition, you must specify the following global const and type declarations in your main program in order to indicate the exact number of columns and the maximum number of rows in the array. The numbers 2 and 100 are examples; your array size may vary.

```
const
   ColSize = 2;
   RowSize = 100;

type
   Array2Type = array[1..RowSize, 1..ColSize] of real;
```

Output

Num2Array   real   The same array, now containing data entered from
                        the keyboard

RowCount   integer   Number of rows now in the array

Limitations and Error Conditions

Unlike most programs, this subprogram does *not* get a run-time error if you erroneously enter nonnumeric data. Instead, the subprogram beeps and displays the message ** Illegal. Please reenter. ** and asks for the same entry again. To terminate data entry, you enter the word END (all uppercase) when prompted for the first entry in a row; otherwise, you fill the array full to RowSize rows of entries. You must enter full rows of data. (In other words, you cannot enter END for the second column of a row, only for the first column.) A null entry is treated as nonnumeric data. If an entry is longer than 20 characters, only the first 20 are used. RowCount does not have to be zero before you use Key2Arr. If, for example, you have 5 rows of entries in your array and you want to enter more, set RowCount to 5. Key2Arr will prompt you for entries beginning with the sixth row.

Sample Usage

```
program SampleUsageOfKey2Arr;

const
   ColSize = 2;
   RowSize = 100;

type
   Array2Type = array[1..RowSize, 1..ColSize] of real;

var
   Num2Array      : Array2Type;
   RowCount, J, K : integer;
```

```
{$I Key2Arr.PSL}

BEGIN
   RowCount := 0;
   Key2Arr(Num2Array, RowCount);
   writeln('Here is the data entered from the keyboard.');
   for J := 1 to RowCount do
      begin
         for K := 1 to ColSize do
            write(Num2Array[J, K]:12:4);
         writeln
      end
END.
```

When you enter and run this test program, it displays the following output:

```
—Row number 1—
   Entry [1, 1]: 24.431
   Entry [1, 2]: 61.92
—Row number 2—
   Entry [2, 1]: 19.6195
   Entry [2, 2]: 142.857
—Row number 3—
   Entry [3, 1]: -13.003
   Entry [3, 2]: 1028.71
—Row number 4—
   Entry [4, 1]: END
** 3 rows entered. **
** Data entry complete **
Here is the data entered from the keyboard.
      24.4310      61.9200
      19.6195     142.8570
     -13.0030    1028.7100
```

Subprogram Listing of Key2Arr.PSL

```
procedure Key2Arr(var Num2Array: Array2Type;
                  var RowCount: integer);

const
   EndFlag = 'END';

var
   Entry            : string[20];
   Code, ColCount : integer;

begin
   {
   writeln('** Enter real data for 2-dimensional array. **');
   writeln('** Maximum array size = ', RowSize, ' rows. **');
   writeln('** There are ', ColSize, ' columns per row. **');
   writeln('** Enter ', EndFlag, ' to end data entry. **');
   }                                                  {Mod. #1}
   if RowCount >= RowSize then
      begin
         writeln(chr(7));
         writeln('** RowCount too large. **');
         exit
      end;
   repeat
      RowCount := RowCount + 1;
      writeln('—Row number ', RowCount, '—');
      if RowCount = RowSize then
         writeln('** Last row **');
      ColCount := 0;
      repeat
         ColCount := ColCount + 1;
         write('  Entry [', RowCount, ',', ColCount, ']: ');
         readln(Entry);
         if length(Entry) = 0 then Entry := 'bad';
```

```
            Code := 0;
        if (Entry <> EndFlag) or (ColCount <> 1) then
            begin
                val(Entry, Num2Array[RowCount,ColCount], Code);
                if Code <> 0 then
                    begin
                        writeln(chr(7));
                        writeln('** Illegal.  Please reenter. **');
                        ColCount := ColCount - 1
                    end
            end
    until ((Entry = EndFlag) and (ColCount = 1) and (Code = 0))
        or
            (ColCount = ColSize)
    until (Entry = EndFlag) or (RowCount = RowSize);
    if Entry = EndFlag then
        RowCount := RowCount - 1;
    writeln('** ', RowCount, ' rows entered. **');
    writeln('** Data entry complete **')
end;
```

Variables

EndFlag	Text entered by user to indicate no more entries ('END')
Entry	User's string entry, converted to numeric value for placement into the array
Code	Condition code set by Turbo's val function, indicating whether Entry was successfully converted to a numeric value

Discussion

Just as KeyArr is used for entering data into a simple one-dimensional array, Key2Arr works with two-dimensional arrays. It is compatible with the family of subprograms handling two-dimensional arrays presented in this book (Show2Arr, SortSI2R, SortH2R, Load2Arr, and Save2Arr) and can be used with the matrix-handling subprograms (MatAdd, MatMult, Determ, etc.).

Modification

To cause the subprogram to display introductory messages before data entry begins, delete the line indicated by {Mod. #1} and the line five lines above it. This removal of the open and closed braces activates the four writeln statements treated as comments in the standard version of Key2Arr.

KeyTxt

> **Name:** *KeyTxt*
>
> **Type:** *Procedure*
>
> **Purpose:** *To enter text data from the keyboard into an array*
>
> **Calling Sequence:** KeyTxt(TextArray, LineCount)

Description

KeyTxt is a procedure for entering text data from the keyboard into a string array. Once the data is in an array, you can save the data on disk with SaveTxt, reload the data into an array with LoadTxt, and manipulate the data with the text-manipulation subprograms.

Input

TextArray   string   Array in which data is to be stored

LineCount   integer   Number of lines of text currently in the array. (Normally this number should be zero before you use KeyTxt.)

In addition, you must specify the following global const and type declarations in your main program. TextSize is the maximum number of lines of text allowed, and LineSize is the maximum length of each line. The numbers 100 and 80 are examples.

```
const
   TextSize = 100;

type
   LineSize = string[80];
   TextArrayType = array[1..TextSize] of LineSize;
```

Output

TextArray   string   The same array, now with data entered from the
                           keyboard

LineCount   integer   Number of lines of text now in the array

Limitations and Error Conditions

If, during data entry, the number of lines you enter reaches TextSize, the subprogram automatically ends and returns control with the array full and LineCount
equal to TextSize. If you enter text lines longer than LineSize, they are truncated
(chopped off) after the first LineSize characters. No error message is issued.
LineCount does not have to be zero before you use KeyTxt. For example, if you
have 5 lines in your array and want to enter more, set LineCount to 5. KeyTxt will
put the next line into entry number 6 of the array and continue from that point.

Sample Usage

```
program SampleUsageOfKeyTxt;

const
   TextSize = 100;

type
   LineSize = string[80];
   TextArrayType = array[1..TextSize] of LineSize;

var
   TextArray    : TextArrayType;
   LineCount, J : integer;

{$I KeyTxt.PSL}

BEGIN
   LineCount := 0;
   KeyTxt(TextArray, LineCount);
   writeln('The text data entered is:');
   for J := 1 to LineCount do writeln(TextArray[J])
END.
```

Here is the output of this test program with data entered by the user:

```
** Enter text data.  Array size = 100 lines **
** Enter END to end data entry. **
    1: Now is the time for all good people
    2: to come to the aid of their
    3: sociopolitical entities.
    4: END
** Data entry complete **
The text data entered is:
Now is the time for all good people
to come to the aid of their
sociopolitical entities.
```

Subprogram Listing of KeyTxt.PSL

```
procedure KeyTxt(var TextArray: TextArrayType;
                 var LineCount: integer);

const
   EndFlag = 'END';

var
   ThisLine: LineSize;

begin
   ThisLine := '';
   writeln('** Enter text data.  Array size = ',
           TextSize, ' lines **');
   writeln('** Enter ', EndFlag, ' to end data entry. **');
   while (ThisLine <> EndFlag) and (LineCount < TextSize) do
      begin
         LineCount := LineCount + 1;
         write(LineCount:3, ': ');
         readln(ThisLine);
         if (ThisLine <> EndFlag) and
            (LineCount <= TextSize) then
            TextArray[LineCount] := ThisLine
      end;
   if ThisLine = EndFlag then LineCount := LineCount - 1;
   writeln('** Data entry complete **')
end;
```

Variables

EndFlag   The text entered by the user to indicate no more entries
                           (´END´)

ThisLine   The contents of each line as it is typed. ThisLine is moved
                           into TextArray after verification that ThisLine isn't equal
                           to EndFlag.

Discussion

There are many ways to enter text data into an array so that a program can process the data. A method obvious to a Turbo programmer is to use the "Turbo editor" built into Turbo Pascal. You can use the editor to enter any text data the same way you enter a Pascal program. After you save the text data on disk, you can load the data into an array with the LoadTxt subprogram in this library and then operate on the data by using the other text-processing subprograms.

You may require text data entry as part of a larger program, however. It is impractical to tell the person using the program to stop your program, create a file with the Turbo editor (or a word processor), and then go back to your program. Instead, you need to ask for the text input directly as part of your program. In such a case, KeyTxt can do the job.

Modification

Replace or delete the three writeln statements in the subprogram in order to alter the two prompting messages before and the one after the text data entry. You may want to replace these three statements so that you can customize the messages for your application, or you may want to delete the statements and provide similar messages in your main program instead.

3

Creating Graphics Effects

Effective graphics are a welcome enhancement to most programs, providing animation, lucid presentation, friendliness, and just plain fun. Fortunately, Turbo Pascal provides easy access to the PC's graphics modes and capabilities. (We use the term *graphics* a little loosely here. It refers not only to textual effects such as scrolling but also to higher-resolution pixel graphics.)

This chapter presents 10 subprograms in two categories: subprograms that require the Color/Graphics Adapter and those that work with either adapter (Monochrome or Color/Graphics). The subprograms are designed for maximum flexibility. All of them work with black-and-white monitors yet are easily modified to support color, windows, and Turbo's various text and graphics modes (as appropriate). None of the subprograms requires the use of anything other than standard Turbo Pascal. None uses the add-on machine-language routines for "extended graphics." (Nor do the subprograms duplicate any of the capabilities included in these routines.)

Three subprograms are strictly for use in one of Turbo's text modes. These subprograms work on PC systems with either of the display adapters (Monochrome or Color/Graphics). In addition, each of these subprograms is compatible with color and 40-column text modes for systems with the Color/Graphics Adapter. TextBox uses text characters to draw a rectangular box. This box can frame windows or highlight important text. Scroll performs scrolling of text in any direction: left, right, up, or down. CursorOn toggles the cursor either on or off.

The remaining seven subprograms require the Color/Graphics Adapter. Each of these subprograms is nominally configured for black-and-white graphics but can be easily modified for color graphics. In addition, each subprogram works in any of Turbo's graphics modes—medium or high resolution. GrCursor positions the cursor by using graphics coordinates on a graphics screen, thus facilitating the mixing of text and graphics on the same screen. GraphBox draws a rectangular box and can shade it in any of several styles.

Two-dimensional graphs (X versus Y) are an impressive presentation tool for appropriate data. Drawing and labeling the axes can be a headache, however. This chapter includes five coordinated subprograms designed to relieve the pain. They work together, sharing common parameters and thus simplifying the task of designing and labeling a graph. DoXAxis and DoYAxis draw a horizontal axis and a vertical axis, respectively, complete with two-tiered tick marks if desired. AnnXAxis and AnnYAxis annotate the axes, including the labeling of tick marks. Finally, AxisText stores a text array for use by the annotation subprograms. Chapter 18 contains two full programs that use these subprograms to create a complete graphing capability. BarChart draws bar charts and histograms. XYGraph plots curves of "X versus Y."

Many of the Sample Usage programs in this chapter are accompanied by figures. These figures were created on an EPSON® printer by using the PC's Shift-PrtSc key combination to produce on paper an image of the screen. The GRAPHICS.COM program (included with PC DOS V2.0 and higher) was used. This program permits Shift-PrtSc to work with graphics on an IBM 80 CPS Graphics Printer and other compatible graphics printers.

TextBox

Name:	*TextBox*
Type:	*Procedure*
Purpose:	*To draw a "graphics" box while the computer is in text mode*
Calling Sequence:	TextBox(UpLeftX, UpLeftY, LoRightX, LoRightY)

Description

While the computer is in one of Turbo's text modes, TextBox draws a rectangular box. The location of the box is defined by the text coordinates of its upper left and lower right corners. The subprogram is fully compatible with any of Turbo's text modes, color settings, and windows. After drawing the box, TextBox repositions the cursor to where it was before the procedure call.

Input

UpLeftX	integer	The X location of the upper left corner of the box in standard text coordinates
UpLeftY	integer	The Y location of the upper left corner of the box in standard text coordinates
LoRightX	integer	The X location of the lower right corner
LoRightY	integer	The Y location of the lower right corner

All these coordinate locations are relative to any active window. That is, the upper left coordinates of the active window are always UpLeftX = 1 and UpLeftY = 1.

The computer should be in one of Turbo's text modes when the procedure is called.

Output

TextBox draws a rectangular box at the coordinate position defined by the input variables.

Limitations and Error Conditions

TextBox makes sure that the requested location of the box is within allowable limits. UpLeftX must be at least 1 but less than LoRightX. UpLeftY must be at least 1 but less than LoRightY. LoRightY cannot be more than 25. The procedure determines whether the computer is in 40- or 80-column text mode by interrogating hex memory location 44A. LoRightX cannot be more than 40 or 80, depending on the current mode. If any of these restrictions is violated, the procedure is simply bypassed, and no box is drawn.

No special checks are made for an active user-defined window. Incorrectly defined box locations (outside the active window) may cause box fragments on the screen. See the Discussion section.

If the computer is in a graphics mode, no visible effect occurs. The memory-mapped area for text display is altered, however.

Sample Usage

```
program SampleUsageOfTextBox;

var
    UpLeftX, UpLeftY, LoRightX, LoRightY: integer;

{$I TextBox.PSL}

BEGIN
   clrscr;
   UpLeftX  := 15;
   UpLeftY  := 5;
   LoRightX := 31;
   LoRightY := 8;
   TextBox(UpLeftX, UpLeftY, LoRightX, LoRightY);
```

```
    window(UpLeftX + 1, UpLeftY + 1, LoRightX - 1, LoRightY - 1);
    gotoxy(1, 1);
    write('TextBox frames windows nicely');
    window(1, 1, 80, 25);
    gotoxy(1, 15)
END.
```

This sample program draws a box around a text window and then writes a message inside the window. Figure 3.1 shows the result. Note how the text wraps to a second line when the text reaches the edge of the text window.

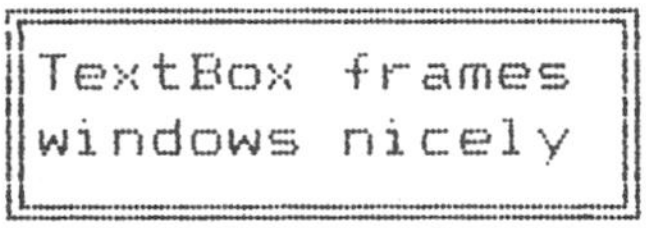

Fig. 3.1. *A demonstration of* TextBox.

Subprogram Listing of TextBox.PSL

```
procedure TextBox(UpLeftX, UpLeftY, LoRightX, LoRightY: integer);

const
    UpLeftChar   = #201;                                {Mod. #1}
    LoLeftChar   = #200;                                {Mod. #1}
    LoRightChar  = #188;                                {Mod. #1}
    UpRightChar  = #187;                                {Mod. #1}
    HorizChar    = #205;                                {Mod. #1}
    VertChar     = #186;                                {Mod. #1}

var
    X, Y, NumToDoX, CursorX, CursorY: integer;

begin
    if (UpLeftX >= LoRightX) or (UpLeftY >= LoRightY) or
                (UpLeftX < 1) or (LoRightX > mem[0:$44A]) or
                (UpLeftY < 1) or (LoRightY > 25) then
        exit;
    CursorX := wherex;
    CursorY := wherey;
    gotoxy(UpLeftX, UpLeftY);
    write(UpLeftChar);
```

```
   NumToDoX := LoRightX - UpLeftX - 1;
   for X := 1 to NumToDoX do
      write(HorizChar);
   write(UpRightChar);
   for Y := UpLeftY + 1 to LoRightY - 1 do
      begin
         gotoxy(LoRightX, Y);
         write(VertChar);
         gotoxy(UpLeftX, Y);
         write(VertChar)
      end;
   gotoxy(UpLeftX, LoRightY);
   write(LoLeftChar);
   for X := 1 to NumToDoX do
      write(HorizChar);
   write(LoRightChar);
   gotoxy(CursorX, CursorY)
end;
```

Variables

UpLeftChar	The ASCII character for the upper left corner
LoLeftChar	The ASCII character for the lower left corner
LoRightChar	The ASCII character for the lower right corner
UpRightChar	The ASCII character for the upper right corner
HorizChar	The ASCII character for horizontal sides
VertChar	The ASCII character for vertical sides
X	The current X location in text coordinates
Y	The current Y location in text coordinates
NumToDoX	Length of the box's horizontal sides
CursorX	The X location of the cursor when the procedure is called
CursorY	The Y location of the cursor when the procedure is called

Discussion

TextBox uses text characters from the standard IBM PC character set. These characters are in the ASCII range above 127. You may redefine the characters. See the Modification section.

The coordinate system that defines the location of the box is the standard system used by Turbo. A location is specified by an X value and a Y value. X runs from 1 at the left of the screen to 40 or 80 (depending on the text mode) at the right of the screen. Y runs from 1 at the top of the screen to 25 at the bottom of the screen.

If you have defined a window, text coordinates are relative to your window. Be careful not to request that any part of the box be drawn outside the active window. If you do, undesirable box fragments are the likely result.

A common use of `TextBox` is to draw a frame around a text window. The Sample Usage program illustrates this technique. If you have a window to be defined by `window(XL, YL, XR, YR)`, then the appropriate frame can be drawn with

```
TextBox(XL - 1, YL - 1, XR + 1, YR + 1)
```

Be sure that the call to `TextBox` precedes the call to `window`!

`TextBox` is fully compatible with all of Turbo's text modes and features. Both 40- and 80-column modes are acceptable, in color or black and white. For color mode, the current foreground and background colors are used. `TextBox` works with both the Monochrome Adapter and the Color/Graphics Adapter as long as the computer is in text mode.

Modification

To draw the box, we chose characters that produce a "double border." You can have a simpler one-line border by changing the ASCII character constants in the lines indicated by `{Mod. #1}` to the following:

```
UpLeftChar   = #218;
LoLeftChar   = #192;
LoRightChar  = #217;
UpRightChar  = #191;
HorizChar    = #196;
VertChar     = #179;
```

Many other character choices are possible, of course. You can get a solid border, for example, by setting each of these constants to #219. For other possibilities, consult a listing of the ASCII character codes. The IBM BASIC manual contains such a list in Appendix G.

Scroll

Name:	*Scroll*
Type:	*Procedure*
Purpose:	*To scroll text in any of four directions*
Calling Sequence:	`Scroll(UpLeftX, UpLeftY, LoRightX, LoRightY, Direction)`

Description

This procedure scrolls text left, right, up, or down. You define a scrolling window, and only the text within that window scrolls. The scrolling text moves one character position in the indicated direction. Blanks are written into the trailing row or column. `Scroll` is compatible with any of Turbo's text modes, including 40- or 80-column modes, color settings, and windows.

Input

`UpLeftX`	`integer`	The X location of the upper left corner of the scrolling window
`UpLeftY`	`integer`	The Y location of the upper left corner of the scrolling window
`LoRightX`	`integer`	The X location of the lower right corner of the scrolling window
`LoRightY`	`integer`	The Y location of the lower right corner of the scrolling window
`Direction`	`integer`	Scrolling direction, namely

0	Scroll left
1	Scroll right
2	Scroll up
3	Scroll down

`UpLeftX`, `UpLeftY`, `LoRightX`, and `LoRightY` define the scrolling window in standard text coordinates. These variables always reference the entire visible screen, even if you have an active text window created with Turbo's built-in `window` procedure. (Thus, regardless of any active text window, for the purposes of a scrolling window, the upper left corner of the screen is always `UpLeftX` = 1 and `UpLeftY` = 1. The lower right corner of the screen is always `LoRightY` = 25 and `LoRightX` = 40 or

80. The latter value depends on the active text mode.) If you set the scrolling window outside the active text window, you can scroll the entire active text window. To scroll only inside your text window, set the scrolling window with the same parameters used in the call to window.

Output

All text within the scrolling window scrolls one character position in the indicated direction. The trailing row or column fills with blanks.

Limitations and Error Conditions

The procedure is bypassed with no effect if Direction is negative or greater than 3. Be careful that you set the scrolling window correctly. No range checking occurs. If UpLeftX is greater than LoRightX or if UpLeftY is greater than LoRightY, the procedure is simply bypassed, and no great harm is done. If, however, one of the four coordinate positions is outside the screen boundaries (for example, LoRightY is greater than 25), you may possibly hang the system, lose the cursor, or generate spurious screen images.

Be especially careful with LoRightX. If the computer is in one of Turbo's 40-column text modes, LoRightX's maximum meaningful value is 40. In one of Turbo's 80-column text modes, LoRightX can have a value up to 80.

Be careful also that you call Scroll only while the computer is in a text mode. Unpredictable screen alterations will result from a call while the computer is in a graphics mode.

You'll have a minor annoyance with screen "flicker" if all of the following are true: (1) you call Scroll while the computer is in one of the 80-column modes, (2) you request a relatively large scrolling window, and (3) your system is using the IBM Color/Graphics Adapter. This problem originates with the hardware video circuitry and takes considerable software manipulation to overcome. The problem does not occur with the Monochrome Adapter or with the Color/Graphics Adapter using one of the 40-column text modes.

Animated effects are sometimes dulled on IBM's monochrome monitor because the phosphors on that monitor vanish relatively slowly. Images, therefore, fade rather than crisply disappear. Try changing the delay time as explained in the Discussion section.

Sample Usage

The following program demonstrates scrolling in each of the four directions. The screen is filled with characters while the computer is in Turbo's 40-column, black-and-white text mode. Four separate scrolling windows are defined one at a time, and text scrolls inside each window. A message at the bottom of the screen indicates the current scrolling direction just before scrolling occurs.

```
program SampleUsageOfScroll;

var
   J, K, M: integer;

{$I Scroll.PSL}

BEGIN
   textmode(bw40);
   for J := 1 to 15 do
      for K := 1 to 40 do
         write(chr(K + J + 63));
   writeln;
   for J := 0 to 3 do
      begin
         M := 10 * J;
         case J of
            0: writeln('Scrolling left');
            1: writeln('Scrolling right');
            2: writeln('Scrolling up');
            3: writeln('Scrolling down')
         end;
         delay(1000);
         for K := 1 to 8 do
            begin
               delay(250);
               scroll(M + 2, 3, M + 9, 12, J)
            end
      end
END.
```

Subprogram Listing of Scroll.PSL

```
procedure Scroll(UpLeftX, UpLeftY, LoRightX, LoRightY,
                          Direction: integer);

var
   Column, ColFactor, Row, RowFactor    : integer;
   Segm, Off, ScreenWidth, ScreenWidth2 : integer;

   procedure Horizontal(LastCol, Delta: integer);

   begin
      ColFactor := Column - 1;
      for Row := UpLeftY to LoRightY do
         begin
            RowFactor := (Row - 1) * ScreenWidth;
            Off       := (RowFactor + ColFactor) * 2;
            if Column = LastCol then
               mem[Segm:Off] := 32
            else
               begin
                  mem[Segm:Off]     := mem[Segm:Off + Delta];
                  mem[Segm:Off + 1] := mem[Segm:Off + Delta + 1]
               end
         end
   end;


   procedure Vertical(LastRow, Delta: integer);

   begin
      RowFactor := (Row - 1) * ScreenWidth;
      for Column := UpLeftX to LoRightX do
         begin
            ColFactor := Column - 1;
            Off       := (RowFactor + ColFactor) * 2;
            if Row = LastRow then
               mem[Segm:Off] := 32
            else
               begin
                  mem[Segm:Off]     := mem[Segm:Off + Delta];
                  mem[Segm:Off + 1] := mem[Segm:Off + Delta + 1]
               end
         end
   end;
```

```
begin
  if mem[0:$449] = 7 then
    Segm := $B000
  else
    Segm := $B800;
  ScreenWidth  := mem[0:$44A];
  ScreenWidth2 := 2 * ScreenWidth;
  case Direction of
    0: for Column := UpLeftX to LoRightX do
           Horizontal(LoRightX, 2);
    1: for Column := LoRightX downto UpLeftX do
           Horizontal(UpLeftX, -2);
    2: for Row := UpLeftY to LoRightY do
           Vertical(LoRightY, ScreenWidth2);
    3: for Row := LoRightY downto UpLeftY do
           Vertical(UpLeftY, -ScreenWidth2)
  end
end;
```

Variables

Column	Current text column
ColFactor	Component of Off due to the current column
Row	Current text row
RowFactor	Component of Off due to the current row
Segm	Segment address of the screen area in memory. This address depends on the type of video adapter present (Monochrome or Color/Graphics).
Off	Offset address of the screen area. This address is the number of bytes into the memory area where the current character is to be read or written.
ScreenWidth	Width of the screen in units of text coordinates. This width is 40 or 80, depending on the current text mode.
ScreenWidth2	Twice ScreenWidth
LastCol	Column to be filled with blanks. This variable is in the embedded procedure Horizontal.
LastRow	Row to be filled with blanks. This variable is in the embedded procedure Vertical.

Delta   Term added to Off to get the correct memory offset. This
                              variable occurs in the two embedded procedures.

Discussion

Scroll enables you to create many fancy effects in text mode. The means to scroll
left and right are not often found in other program sources. One good example
of this capability is the "moving ticker tape." Here, new text enters from the right,
and a general scrolling to the left creates easy reading. See the NewsWire program
in Chapter 18 for a demonstration of this technique.

Because Scroll only scrolls one row (or column), the procedure is usually used
inside a loop. Repeated calls create a general scrolling effect. Experiment with
placing a delay procedure between the calls to Scroll in order to find out what
the most pleasing scrolling speed is for your application. Adjusting the argument
in the delay call greatly changes the appearance of the scroll. Repeated calls to
Scroll with the same input arguments continually scroll the text inside the given
crolling window.

The IBM PC uses memory-mapped displays. This means that the image of what's
on the screen is kept in a section of memory. The video-refresh circuitry continually
"looks" at this memory area to display what you see on the screen. Scroll works
by directly changing this area of memory. As such, the procedure has autonomous
control over the screen image regardless of the text mode, color setting, or text
window set by other Turbo statements. Scroll looks at two special memory
addresses in low memory. Hex 449 indicates the adapter (Monochrome or
Color/Graphics) being used, which affects the segment address of the video
memory-mapped area. Hex 44A indicates the current screen width (in characters).
Scroll needs the screen width in order to determine correct address offsets for
proper scrolling.

Scroll contains two embedded procedures: Horizontal and Vertical. They do
the bulk of the needed work for horizontal scrolling and vertical scrolling,
respectively.

Modifications

None

CursorOn

Name:	*CursorOn*
Type:	*Procedure*
Purpose:	*To turn the cursor on or off while the computer is in text mode*
Calling Sequence:	CursorOn(TurnOn)

Description

This handy procedure lets you control whether the cursor is visible. An invisible cursor is nice if you are doing special effects in text mode (such as scrolling or drawing character "graphics"). The reason is that a blinking cursor can be distracting when a considerable amount of information on the screen needs to be absorbed. In this case, CursorOn enables you to remove the cursor. Of course, the procedure can restore the cursor as well.

Input

TurnOn   boolean   Indicator for the effect you want, namely

> true   Turn on the cursor
> false Turn off the cursor

The computer should be operating in (any) text mode when you invoke this procedure.

Output

The cursor becomes invisible if TurnOn is set to false. The cursor becomes visible if TurnOn is set to true.

Limitations and Error Conditions

Results are unpredictable if the computer is in one of Turbo's graphics modes. Such modes support intermixed text and sometimes display the cursor. It is possible to lose the cursor completely if you use this subprogram while the computer is in a graphics mode.

Turning the cursor on restores it to the default shape for your adapter card (Monochrome or Color/Graphics). If another routine changes the cursor's shape or size, CursorOn restores the cursor to the default shape.

Sample Usage

This sample program displays explanatory messages while it turns the cursor off and then back on again.

```
program SampleUsageOfCursorOn;

{$I CursorOn.PSL}

BEGIN
  clrscr;
  writeln('Cursor will disappear in 5 seconds, but...');
  delay(5000);
  CursorOn(false);
  writeln;
  delay(3000);
  writeln('It will reappear in 5 seconds.');
  delay(5000);
  CursorOn(true)
END.
```

Subprogram Listing of CursorOn.PSL

```
procedure CursorOn(TurnOn: boolean);

type
  RegList = record
    AX, BX, CX, DX, BP, SI, DI, DS, ES, Flags: integer
  end;

var
  Reg: RegList;

begin
  if TurnOn then
    if mem[0:$449] = 7 then
      Reg.CX := $0C0D
    else
```

```
      Reg.CX := $0607                              {Mod. #1}
   else
      Reg.CX := $2000;
   Reg.AX := $0100;
   intr($10, Reg)
end;
```

Variables

Reg   A record of integer variables representing the
                        microprocessor's registers and flags. Reg is used to pass
                        values to Turbo's intr procedure.

Discussion

This procedure is compatible with any of Turbo's text modes using color or black
and white.

When the cursor is invisible, you can still display text as usual. The cursor is logically
there, moving to the next character position as text is displayed. The cursor is
exactly where you would expect it to be; it's just not visible. When you use CursorOn
to restore the cursor, it appears at the correct updated position.

Access to cursor control is possible through the PC's ROM-resident BIOS (Basic
Input/Output System). You use Turbo's intr procedure to invoke the ROM BIOS
video service interrupt (hex 10). Service 1 sets the cursor to the size specified in
the CX register. Because the default cursor size depends on the adapter card present,
memory address hex 449 is read to indicate which adapter card (Monochrome or
Color/Graphics) is in use. If the request is to turn the cursor on, the default cursor
size is set. If the request is to turn the cursor off, bit 5 of the high-order byte of
the CX register must be turned on.

Modification

If you have IBM's Enhanced Color/Graphics adapter (EGA), change the line denoted
by {Mod. #1} to the following:

```
Reg.CX := $0C0D
```

This sets the cursor to the correct default shape for this adapter.

GrCursor

Name:	*GrCursor*
Type:	*Procedure*
Purpose:	*To position the cursor on a graphics screen*
Calling Sequence:	GrCursor(XGraphic, YGraphic, XTextOffset, YTextOffset)

Description

Although text and graphics can be freely mixed in Turbo, moving the (invisible) cursor around a graphics screen is inconvenient. It would be nice to position text on a graphics screen with the same coordinate system used to position the graphics. GrCursor provides this capability.

Input

XGraphic　integer　Horizontal (X) position on a graphics screen in the current graphics units

YGraphic　integer　Vertical (Y) position on a graphics screen in the current graphics units

XTextOffset integer　Number of text-character positions to move the cursor in the X direction relative to the location defined by XGraphic and YGraphic. The number can be negative (a move to the left), zero (no move), or positive (a move to the right).

YTextOffset integer　Number of text-character positions to move the cursor in the Y direction relative to the location defined by XGraphic and YGraphic. The number can be negative (an upward move), zero (no move), or positive (a downward move).

The computer should be in one of Turbo's graphics modes when you invoke this procedure.

Output

The invisible graphics cursor is moved to the position on the screen defined by the graphics coordinates XGraphic and YGraphic. If XTextOffset or YTextOffset (or both) is nonzero, the cursor location is adjusted the appropriate number of character positions. (Subsequent text displayed with a write statement is written at this cursor location.)

Limitations and Error Conditions

No range checking on the graphic coordinates occurs. If the requested location is outside the acceptable graphics domain, the cursor does not move at all.

The cursor positioning does not respect graphics windows but does accommodate regular text windows. If your application uses one type of window, you must also set the other type appropriately in order to achieve compatible results with this procedure.

Be sure that the computer is in one of the graphics modes before you call GrCursor.

Sample Usage

```
program SampleUsageOfGrCursor;

var
    XGraphic, YGraphic, XTextOffset, YTextOffset : integer;
    LeftX, RightX                                : integer;

{$I GrCursor.PSL}

BEGIN
    LeftX    := 119;
    RightX   := 450;
    YGraphic := 100;
    hires;
    hirescolor(white);
    draw(LeftX, YGraphic, RightX, YGraphic, white);
    XGraphic := (LeftX + RightX) div 2;
    XTextOffset := -2;
    YTextOffset := 2;
    GrCursor(XGraphic, YGraphic, XTextOffset, YTextOffset);
    write('Below');
    GrCursor(LeftX, YGraphic, -1, 0);
    write('L');
    GrCursor(RightX, YGraphic, 1, 0);
    write('R')
END.
```

This sample program draws a straight line on a high-resolution graphics screen and then does some simple text labeling relative to the line. An L is placed at the left end of the line, an R at the right end, and the word *Below* under the line. Figure 3.2 shows the result.

Fig. 3.2. *A demonstration of* GrCursor.

Subprogram Listing of GrCursor.PSL

```
procedure GrCursor(XGraphic, YGraphic, XTextOffset,
                   YTextOffset: integer);

var
   XText, YText: integer;

begin
   XText := trunc(XGraphic / 8.0) + 1 + XTextOffset;
   YText := trunc(YGraphic / 8.0) + 1 + YTextOffset;
   gotoxy(XText, YText)
end;
```

Variables

XText   The X location of the cursor in text units

YText   The Y location of the cursor in text units

Discussion

Actually, a cursor exists while the computer is in one of Turbo's graphics modes. You just can't see the cursor. It's as if a normal text screen were superimposed over your active video screen. You can move the cursor around with gotoxy statements and also display text with write statements. In high-resolution graphics (hires), the text screen is 80 characters wide by 25 characters high. In medium-resolution graphics (graphmode or graphcolormode), the text screen is 40 characters wide by 25 characters high.

Each character position maps into an 8-by-8 square of graphics pixels on the video screen. You can't quite display a text character "anywhere" on the screen because the character must be confined to one of the 8-by-8 squares located at fixed positions on the video screen.

GrCursor positions the cursor at the text-character "square" that contains the pixel specified by XGraphic and YGraphic. Because each of these text character squares contains 64 pixels, any pair of values for XGraphic and YGraphic that specifies a point within the same square results in the same cursor location.

The procedure works equally well with high- or medium-resolution graphics. Just be sure that you use the graphics coordinates appropriate for the current graphics mode.

Modifications

None

GraphBox

> **Name:** *GraphBox*
>
> **Type:** *Procedure*
>
> **Purpose:** *To draw boxes (with shading) while the computer is in any graphics mode*
>
> **Calling Sequence:** GraphBox(UpLeftX, UpLeftY, LoRightX, LoRightY, Color, ShadingType, Density)

Description

GraphBox draws a rectangular graphics box while the computer is in one of Turbo's graphics modes. This procedure is useful for framing, drawing bar charts, and many other graphics effects. You define the location and size of the box by specifying the graphics coordinates of the box's upper left and lower right corners. You can draw any of several different types of shading inside the box. The subprogram is fully compatible with any of Turbo's graphics modes, color settings, and windows.

Input

UpLeftX   integer   X location of the upper left corner of the box in the standard coordinates of the currently active graphics mode

UpLeftY	integer	Y location of the upper left corner
LoRightX	integer	X location of the lower right corner
LoRightY	integer	Y location of the lower right corner
Color	integer	Graphing color. Its specification depends on the active graphics mode. In medium-resolution graphics (graphmode or graphcolormode), Color can be from 0 to 3, indicating a color drawn from the active palette. In high-resolution graphics (hires), Color can be from 0 to 15. See the Turbo manual.
ShadingType	integer	The type of interior shading, namely

0	No shading (empty box)
1	Filled box
2	Horizontal shading
3	Vertical shading
4	Diagonal shading (up to right)
5	Diagonal shading (down to right)

Density	integer	The density of the interior shading in terms of the number of pixels between shading lines. Density has meaning when ShadingType is 2 through 5.

UpLeftX, UpLeftY, LoRightX, and LoRightY are relative to any active graphics window. Coordinate locations follow the Turbo standard of X increasing to the right and Y increasing downward. The upper left corner of the active window is always UpLeftX = 0 and UpLeftY = 0.

The computer should be in one of Turbo's graphics modes when you call GraphBox.

Output

GraphBox draws a rectangular graphics box at the specified location. The size, shading, and color of the box are determined by the input variables.

Limitations and Error Conditions

GraphBox does some range checking on the box coordinates. UpLeftX must be at least 0 but no more than LoRightX. UpLeftY must be at least 0 but no more than LoRightY. The procedure is bypassed with no effect if one of these conditions is violated. If UpLeftX equals LoRightX or if UpLeftY equals LoRightY, a line results instead of an enclosed box. No checks are made for any locations outside the active window (default or user-defined). The box is clipped by the window boundary if you attempt to draw a line through this boundary.

Color works according to the active graphics mode. Modulo arithmetic corrects values outside the expected color range. Resulting colors are hardware dependent. See the Discussion section.

If ShadingType is negative or greater than 5, an empty square results (as if ShadingType were 0). Density is irrelevant if ShadingType is 0 or 1. If Density is less than 1 when ShadingType is 2 through 5, an empty square results. If Density is 1 when ShadingType is 2 through 5, a filled square results (as if ShadingType were 1).

No visible effect occurs if the computer is not in one of the graphics modes.

Sample Usage

```
program SampleUsageOfGraphBox;

var
   UpLeftX, UpLeftY, LoRightX, LoRightY   : integer;
   Color, ShadingType, Density, J, DeltaX : integer;

{$I GraphBox.PSL}

BEGIN
   graphmode;
   DeltaX    := 50;
   UpLeftY   := 30;
   LoRightY  := 150;
   Color     := 3;
   Density   := 5;
   palette(1);
   for J := 0 to 5 do
      begin
         ShadingType := J;
         UpLeftX     := J * DeltaX;
         LoRightX    := UpLeftX + DeltaX;
         UpLeftY     := LoRightY - 50 - J * 10;
         GraphBox(UpLeftX, UpLeftY, LoRightX, LoRightY,
                        Color, ShadingType, Density);
      end
END.
```

Using Turbo's `graphmode`, this sample program demonstrates the different types of shading produced by `GraphBox`. Figure 3.3 shows the result.

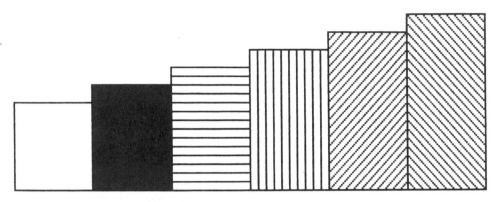

Fig. 3.3. *A demonstration of* GraphBox.

Subprogram Listing of GraphBox.PSL

```
procedure GraphBox(UpLeftX, UpLeftY, LoRightX, LoRightY,
                   Color, ShadingType, Density: integer);

var
   X, Y, Delta: integer;

   procedure DoItUp(X, Y: integer);

   begin
      Delta := LoRightX - X;
      if Y - UpLeftY < Delta then
         Delta := Y - UpLeftY;
      Draw(X, Y, X + Delta, Y - Delta, Color)
   end;

   procedure DoItDown(X, Y: integer);

   begin
      Delta := X - UpLeftX;
      if Y - UpLeftY < Delta then
         Delta := Y - UpLeftY;
      Draw(X, Y, X - Delta, Y - Delta, Color)
   end;
```

```
begin
    if (UpLeftX < 0) or (LoRightX < UpLeftX) or (UpLeftY < 0) or
                        (LoRightY < UpLeftY) then
        exit;
    draw(UpLeftX, UpLeftY, LoRightX, UpLeftY, Color);
    draw(UpLeftX, UpLeftY, UpLeftX, LoRightY, Color);
    draw(UpLeftX, LoRightY, LoRightX, LoRightY, Color);
    draw(LoRightX, UpLeftY, LoRightX, LoRightY, Color);
    case ShadingType of
        1: for X := UpLeftX to LoRightX do
               draw(X, UpLeftY, X, LoRightY, Color);
        2: begin
               if Density < 1 then
                   exit;
               Y := LoRightY - Density;
               while Y > UpLeftY do
                   begin
                       draw(UpLeftX, Y, LoRightX, Y, Color);
                       Y := Y - Density
                   end
           end;
        3: begin
               if Density < 1 then
                   exit;
               X := UpLeftX + Density;
               while X < LoRightX do
                   begin
                       draw(X, UpLeftY, X, LoRightY, Color);
                       X := X + Density
                   end
           end;
        4: begin
               if Density < 1 then
                   exit;
               X := UpLeftX;
               Y := LoRightY;
               repeat
                   DoItUp(X, Y);
                   Y := Y - Density
```

```
               until
                  Y <= UpLeftY;
               Y := LoRightY;
               while X < LoRightX do
                  begin
                     DoItUp(X, Y);
                     X := X + Density
                  end
            end;
         5: begin
               if Density < 1 then
                  exit;
               X := LoRightX;
               Y := LoRightY;
               repeat
                  DoItDown(X, Y);
                  Y := Y - Density
               until
                  Y <= UpLeftY;
               Y := LoRightY;
               while X > UpLeftX do
                  begin
                     DoItDown(X, Y);
                     X := X - Density
                  end
            end
      end
end;
```

Variables

X	Current X location in graphics coordinates
Y	Current Y location in graphics coordinates
Delta	Difference between two graphics coordinates

Discussion

You can obtain many different effects by taking advantage of the shading options. Stacked-bar charts are one example. When two boxes of the same width are placed side by side, the two diagonal shadings will line up on the common vertical border. This creates a pleasing "herringbone" pattern.

Colors appear different on various display monitors. Usually color rendition is better on RGB monitors than on those using composite video. Even black-and-white monitors are affected in different ways by the color selections. Experiment with the color options (including background color) to determine the most pleasing effects for your needs.

Modifications

None

DoXAxis

> **Name:** *DoXAxis*
>
> **Type:** *Procedure*
>
> **Purpose:** *To draw a horizontal x-axis for a subsequent graph*
>
> **Calling Sequence:** DoXAxis(XOrigin, YOrigin, XAxisL, NumSegsX,
> SubTicksX, Color)

Description

DoXAxis draws a horizontal x-axis while the computer is in any of Turbo's graphics modes. This procedure coordinates with other subprograms to facilitate the drawing of graphs and histograms. Input parameters control the location of the axis, its length, and the appearance of tick marks. DoXAxis is fully compatible with any of Turbo's graphics modes, color settings (if applicable), and windows.

Input

XOrigin	integer	X location of the axis origin (that is, the left boundary of the axis) in the standard coordinates of the active graphics mode
YOrigin	integer	Y location of the axis origin
XAxisL	integer	Length of the axis in standard units of the active graphics mode
NumSegsX	integer	The number of equal segments in which to divide the axis. Each of these segments is delineated with a pair of primary tick marks. (Including the first and last marks, the total number of tick marks is NumSegsX + 1.) If the axis has no tick marks, NumSegsX is zero.

SubTicksX	integer	The number of secondary tick marks to draw between each pair of primary tick marks
Color	integer	Graphing color. Its specification depends on the active graphics mode. In medium-resolution graphics (graphmode or graphcolormode), Color can be from 0 to 3, indicating a color drawn from the active palette. In high-resolution graphics (hires), Color can be from 0 to 15 (or the predefined descriptive constants). See the Turbo manual.

XOrigin and YOrigin are relative to any active graphics window. The computer should be in one of Turbo's graphics modes when you call DoXAxis.

Output

In the color specified, a horizontal line is drawn beginning at X = XOrigin and Y = YOrigin. The line extends XAxisL units in the positive X direction (toward the right). Primary and secondary tick marks are drawn if indicated by the input parameters. XOrigin, YOrigin, and XAxisL are in the units of the active graphics mode.

Limitations and Error Conditions

The procedure is bypassed with no effect if XAxisL is zero or negative. Only a straight horizontal line is drawn if NumSegsX is nonpositive. (In other words, no tick marks are drawn.) Primary (but no secondary) tick marks are drawn if SubTicksX is less than 1.

If XAxisL is not an exact integral multiple of NumSegsX, the X locations of the primary tick marks may not be exact integers. For graphics, however, exact integers are required. In such cases, the X locations of the tick marks are rounded to the nearest integer. Similarly, the X locations of secondary tick marks are rounded if necessary. Some nonuniform spacing of tick marks may result.

Color works according to the active graphics mode. Modulo arithmetic corrects values outside the expected color range. Resulting colors are hardware dependent. See the Discussion section.

If you try to extend the axis past the current window (either a user-defined window or the default window of the whole screen), the axis is "clipped," but no fatal error results.

No visible effect occurs if the computer is not in one of the graphics modes.

Sample Usage

```
program SampleUsageOfDoXAxis;

const
   Color = white;

var
   XOrigin, YOrigin, XAxisL, NumSegsX, SubTicksX: integer;

{$I DoXAxis.PSL}

BEGIN
   hires;
   graphbackground(black);   ·
   hirescolor(white);
   writeln('Sample X-Axes');
   XOrigin    := 50;
   YOrigin    := 20;
   XAxisL     := 500;
   NumSegsX   := 10;
   SubTicksX := 0;
   DoXAxis(XOrigin, YOrigin, XAxisL, NumSegsX, SubTicksX, Color);
   DoXAxis(XOrigin, 60, XAxisL, NumSegsX, 3, Color);
   DoXAxis(XOrigin, 100, 360, 2, 0, Color);
   DoXAxis(XOrigin, 140, 360, 2, 11, Color);
   DoXAxis(XOrigin, 180, 300, 0, 0, Color)
END.
```

This sample program demonstrates a few of the possible y=axis that DoYAxis can produce. Figure 3.5 shows the result.

Sample X-Axes

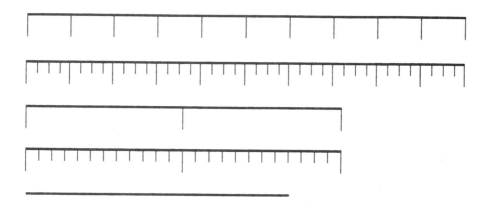

Fig. 3.4. *A demonstration of* DoXAxis.

Subprogram Listing of DoXAxis.PSL

```
procedure DoXAxis(XOrigin,  YOrigin,  XAxisL,  NumSegsX,
                  SubTicksX,  Color:  integer);

const
   BigTickSize   = 10;                                  {Mod. #1}
   SmallTickSize = 5;                                   {Mod. #2}

var
   X, J, K : integer;
   Temp    : real;

begin
   draw(XOrigin, YOrigin, XOrigin + XAxisL, YOrigin, Color);
   if NumSegsX > 0 then
      for J := 0 to NumSegsX do
         begin
            Temp := XAxisL / NumSegsX * J;
            X    := XOrigin + round(Temp);
            draw(X, YOrigin, X, YOrigin + BigTickSize, Color);
```

```
            if (SubTicksX > 0) and (J < NumSegsX) then
                for K := 1 to SubTicksX do
                    begin
                        Temp := XAxisL / NumSegsX / (SubTicksX + 1);
                        X    := X + round(Temp);
                        draw(X, YOrigin, X, YOrigin +
                                        SmallTickSize, Color)
                    end
            end
end;
```

Variables

BigTickSize	The length of the primary tick marks in units of the active graphics mode
SmallTickSize	The length of the secondary tick marks in units of the active graphics mode
X	Current X position in graphics units
J, K	Loop indices
Temp	Temporary real variable for the spacing between tick marks. This value is rounded if it's not an exact integer.

Discussion

Don't overlook the value of the secondary tick marks for enhancing the readability of your eventual graph. As an example, for monthly data, you might use the primary tick marks to represent years and set SubTicksX equal to 11. This creates 12 subdivisions (corresponding to the months) within each year.

If you use color, be aware that colors appear different on various monitors. You will probably have to experiment with the color options (including background color) to determine what best suits your needs.

Modifications

1. In the line denoted by {Mod. #1}, the constant BigTickSize controls the length of each primary tick mark. You may change the default setting of 10 to a larger or smaller (positive) integer. Larger values lengthen each tick mark, and smaller values shorten each one.

2. Similarly, the constant SmallTickSize controls the length of each secondary tick mark. To control the length of each secondary tick mark, adjust the constant's default setting of 5.

DoYAxis

> **Name:** *DoYAxis*
>
> **Type:** *Procedure*
>
> **Purpose:** *To draw a vertical y-axis for a subsequent graph*
>
> **Calling Sequence:** DoYAxis(XOrigin, YOrigin, YAxisL, NumSegsY,
>   SubTicksY, Color)

Description

DoYAxis draws a vertical y-axis while the computer is in any of Turbo's graphics modes. This procedure coordinates with other subprograms to facilitate the drawing of graphs and histograms. Input parameters control the location of the axis, its length, and the appearance of tick marks. DoYAxis is fully compatible with any of Turbo's graphics modes, color settings (if applicable), and windows.

Input

XOrigin	integer	X location of the axis origin (that is, the lower boundary of the axis) in the standard coordinates of the active graphics mode
YOrigin	integer	Y location of the axis origin
YAxisL	integer	Length of the axis in standard units of the active graphics mode
NumSegsY	integer	The number of equal segments in which to divide the axis. Each of these segments is delineated with a pair of primary tick marks. (Including the first and last marks, the total number of tick marks is NumSegsY + 1.) If the axis has no tick marks, NumSegsY is zero.
SubTicksY	integer	The number of secondary tick marks to draw between each pair of primary tick marks

Color   integer   Graphing color. Its specification depends on the
                            active graphics mode. In medium-resolution graphics
                            (graphmode or graphcolormode), Color can be from
                            0 to 3, indicating a color drawn from the active
                            palette. In high-resolution graphics (hires), Color
                            can be from 0 to 15 (or the predefined descriptive
                            constants). See the Turbo manual.

XOrigin and YOrigin are relative to any active graphics window. The computer
should be in one of Turbo's graphics modes when you call DoYAxis.

Output

In the color specified, a vertical line is drawn beginning at X = XOrigin and Y =
YOrigin. The line extends YAxisL units in the Y direction toward the top of the
screen. Primary and secondary tick marks are drawn if indicated by the input parameters. XOrigin, YOrigin, and YAxisL are in the units of the active graphics mode.

Limitations and Error Conditions

The procedure is bypassed with no effect if YAxisL is zero or negative. Only a
straight vertical line is drawn if NumSegsY is nonpositive. (In other words, no tick
marks are drawn.) Primary (but no secondary) tick marks are drawn if SubTicksY
is less than 1.

If YAxisL is not an exact integral multiple of NumSegsY, the Y locations of the primary
tick marks may not be exact integers. For graphics, however, exact integers are
required. In these cases, the Y locations of the tick marks are rounded to the nearest
integer. Similarly, the Y locations of secondary tick marks are rounded if necessary.
Some nonuniform spacing of tick marks may result.

Color works according to the active graphics mode. Modulo arithmetic corrects
values outside the expected color range. Resulting colors are hardware dependent.
See the Discussion section of DoXAxis.

If you try to extend the axis past the current window (either a user-defined window
or the default window of the whole screen), the axis is "clipped," but no fatal error
results.

No visible effect occurs if the computer is not in one of the graphics modes.

Sample Usage

```
program SampleUsageOfDoYAxis;

const
   Color = white;

var
   XOrigin, YOrigin, YAxisL, NumSegsY, SubTicksY: integer;

{$I DoYAxis.PSL}

BEGIN
   hires;
   graphbackground(black);
   hirescolor(white);
   writeln('Sample Y-Axes' );
   XOrigin   := 100;
   YOrigin   := 180;
   YAxisL    := 144;
   NumSegsY  := 6;
   SubTicksY := 0;
   DoYAxis(XOrigin, YOrigin, YAxisL, NumSegsY, SubTicksY, Color);
   DoYAxis(200, YOrigin, YAxisL, NumSegsY, 3, Color);
   DoYAxis(300, YOrigin, 96, 2, 0, Color);
   DoYAxis(400, YOrigin, 96, 2, 7, Color);
   DoYAxis(500, YOrigin, 70, 0, 0, Color)
END.
```

This sample program demonstrates a few of the possible y-axis that DoYAxis can produce. Figure 3.5 shows the result.

Sample Y-Axes

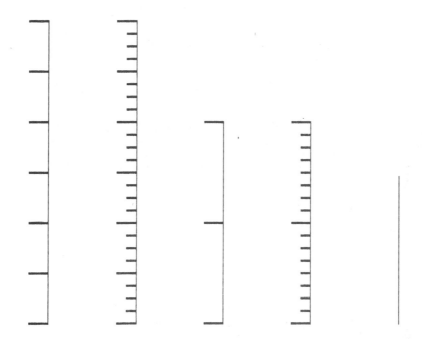

Fig. 3.5. *A demonstration of* DoYAxis.

Subprogram Listing of DoYAxis.PSL

```
procedure DoYAxis(XOrigin, YOrigin, YAxisL, NumSegsY,
                  SubTicksY, Color: integer);

const
  BigTickSize   = 22;                              {Mod. #1}
  SmallTickSize = 11;                              {Mod. #2}

var
  Y, J, K : integer;
  Temp    : real;
```

```
begin
   draw(XOrigin, YOrigin, XOrigin, YOrigin - YAxisL, Color);
   if NumSegsY > 0 then
      for J := 0 to NumSegsY do
         begin
            Temp := YAxisL / NumSegsY * J;
            Y    := YOrigin - round(Temp);
            draw(XOrigin, Y, XOrigin - BigTickSize, Y, Color);
            if (SubTicksY > 0) and (J < NumSegsY) then
               for K := 1 to SubTicksY do
                  begin
                     Temp := YAxisL / NumSegsY / (SubTicksY + 1);
                     Y    := Y - round(Temp);
                     draw(XOrigin, Y, XOrigin - SmallTickSize,
                                      Y, Color)
                  end
         end
end;
```

Variables

BigTickSize	The length of the primary tick marks in units of the active graphics mode
SmallTickSize	The length of the secondary tick marks in units of the active graphics mode
Y	Current Y position in graphics units
J, K	Loop indices
Temp	Temporary real variable for the spacing between tick marks. This value is rounded if it's not an exact integer.

Discussion

The comments in the Discussion section of the DoXAxis subprogram are applicable here.

Depending on your screen, the usual problem of aspect ratios in PC video graphing arises with DoYAxis and DoXAxis. You may note that the length of primary tick marks (in pixels) is not the same in the two subprograms. (In other words, BigTickSize has a different value in each subprogram.) This difference is necessary to coordinate the physical length of tick marks drawn on the screen. If BigTickSize has the same value in each subprogram, the x-axis primary tick marks are physically longer than the y-axis primary tick marks. In the two subprograms, `BigTickSize` is set to look appropriate with high-resolution graphics (`hires`) and typical screens. The same comments apply to the secondary tick marks and `SmallTickSize`. See the Modifications section.

Modifications

1. In the line denoted by {Mod. #1}, the constant `BigTickSize` controls the length of each primary tick mark. You may change the default setting of 22 to a larger or smaller (positive) integer. Larger values lengthen each tick mark, and smaller values shorten each one. For medium-resolution graphics (`graphmode` or `graphcolormode`), try

   ```
   BigTickSize = 11;
   ```

2. Similarly, the constant `SmallTickSize` controls the length of each secondary tick mark. To control the length of each secondary tick mark, adjust this variable's default setting of 10. For medium-resolution graphics, try

   ```
   SmallTickSize = 5;
   ```

AnnXAxis

Name:	*AnnXAxis*
Type:	*Procedure*
Purpose:	*To annotate a horizontal x-axis for a subsequent graph*
Calling Sequence:	AnnXAxis(XOrigin, YOrigin, XAxisL, NumSegsX, XTextArr, Mid)

Description

This procedure provides the textual annotation for the x-axis of a graph. (The axis itself can be drawn with DoXAxis.) AnnXAxis labels tick marks and displays a title for the whole axis. The annotations can be centered below the tick marks or between them. Input parameters work with DoXAxis to provide a consistent set of specifications for the x-axis. AnnXAxis is fully compatible with Turbo's high- or medium-resolution graphics modes.

Input

XOrigin	integer	X location of the axis origin (that is, the left boundary of the axis) in the standard coordinates of the active graphics mode
YOrigin	integer	Y location of the axis origin
XAxisL	integer	Length of the axis in standard units of the active graphics mode
NumSegsX	integer	Number of equal segments in which to divide the axis. Each of these segments is delineated with a pair of primary tick marks. (Including the first and last marks, the total number of tick marks is NumSegsX + 1.) If the axis has no tick marks, NumSegsX is zero.
XTextArr	string	Array containing the string annotations to place on the axis. Element zero contains the label for the whole axis. The succeeding elements contain the labels for the primary tick marks. A null string in any element suppresses that annotation.
Mid	boolean	Variable that indicates where the tick mark annotations should be located. If Mid is true, the annotations are centered in the spaces between the tick marks. If Mid is false, the annotations are centered below the tick marks.

AnnArrayType must be declared in a global type declaration, preferably with additional global declarations. The following lines use the numbers 100 and 80 as examples; your values may be different.

```
const
   MaxNumAxisAnn = 100;

type
   AxisAnnSize  = string[80];
   AnnArrayType = array[0..MaxNumAxisAnn] of AxisAnnSize;
```

The parameters XOrigin, YOrigin, XAxisL, and NumSegsX are identical to their counterparts in DoXAxis. These parameters are meant to work compatibly between the two subprograms, and they have identical meanings in each subprogram.

XOrigin and YOrigin are relative to any active graphics window. The computer should be in one of Turbo's graphics modes when you call AnnXAxis.

Output

After DoXAxis displays the physical axis (with tick marks) on the screen, AnnXAxis provides the textual labeling for the axis. If Mid is false, a centered label is placed below each primary tick mark. If Mid is true, each label is centered in the space between tick marks. See the Discussion section.

The axis title, if present, is centered with respect to the entire axis and placed below the other annotations.

All annotations are located relative to XOrigin, YOrigin, and XAxisL. If these parameters are identical in both DoXAxis and AnnXAxis, the physical axis and its labeling are compatible.

Limitations and Error Conditions

If NumSegsX is zero (or negative), no labeling of the tick marks is done. If XAxisL is zero, all annotations are superimposed just below XOrigin.

Although text can be freely mixed with graphics in Turbo, there are some restrictions on the location of text relative to specific graphics lines. See the Discussion section.

This subprogram respects regular text windows but does not accommodate graphing windows. If you use any windows, be sure to set window and graphwindow compatibly. If you try to extend an annotation outside the current text window, part of the annotation is displaced.

Annotations are drawn even if the computer is not in a graphics mode. Of course, AnnXAxis is meant to be used with DoXAxis, which requires a graphics mode.

Sample Usage

```
program SampleUsageOfAnnXAxis;

const
   MaxNumAxisAnn = 100;

type
   AxisAnnSize  = string[80];
   AnnArrayType = array[0..MaxNumAxisAnn] of AxisAnnSize;

var
   XOrigin,. YOrigin, XAxisL, NumSegsX, J : integer;
   XTextArr                               : AnnArrayType;
   Mid                                    : boolean;
```

```
{$I AnnXAxis.PSL}

procedure DrawAxis(XOrigin, YOrigin, XAxisL, NumSegsX: integer);

var
   X, J: integer;

begin
   draw(XOrigin, YOrigin, XOrigin + XAxisL, YOrigin, white);
   for J := 0 to NumSegsX do
      begin
         X := XOrigin + J * XAxisL div NumSegsX;
         draw(X, YOrigin, X, YOrigin + 10, white)
      end
end;

BEGIN
   hires;
   writeln('Sample Annotation on X-Axes');
   XOrigin   := 50;
   YOrigin   := 46;
   XAxisL    := 480;
   NumSegsX := 6;
   Mid       := false;
   for J := 1 to 7 do
      str(100 * (J - 1):1, XTextArr[J]);
   XTextArr[0] := 'Production Capacity (Units per Day)';
   DrawAxis(XOrigin, YOrigin, XAxisL, NumSegsX);
   AnnXAxis(XOrigin, YOrigin, XAxisL, NumSegsX, XTextArr, Mid);
   XTextArr[0] := 'Fiscal Year (First Quarter)';
   XTextArr[1] := 'Mar';
   XTextArr[2] := 'Apr';
   XTextArr[3] := 'May';
   DrawAxis(XOrigin, 140, 240, 3);
   AnnXAxis(XOrigin, 140, 240, 3, XTextArr, true)
END.
```

This sample program demonstrates a few of the possible axis annotations that AnnXAxis can produce. Figure 3.6 shows the result.

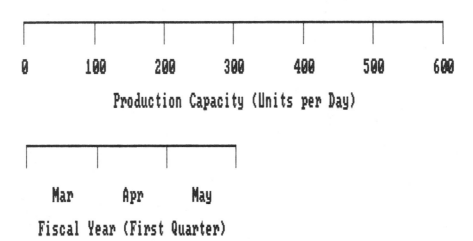

Fig. 3.6. *A demonstration of* AnnXAxis.

Subprogram Listing of AnnXAxis.PSL

```
procedure AnnXAxis(XOrigin, YOrigin, XAxisL, NumSegsX: integer;
                   XTextArr: AnnArrayType; Mid: boolean);

const
    YOffset1 = 4;                                    {Mod. #1}
    YOffset2 = 6;                                    {Mod. #2}
    XOffset1 = 0;                                    {Mod. #3}
    XOffset2 = 0;                                    {Mod. #4}

var
    TextLength, XText, YText, J, NumToDo : integer;
    Spacing, RealXGraphic                : real;

begin
    if NumSegsX > 0 then
        begin
            Spacing := XAxisL / NumSegsX;
            if Mid then
                NumToDo := NumSegsX
```

```
        else
            NumToDo := NumSegsX + 1;
        for J := 1 to NumToDo do
            begin
                TextLength := length(XTextArr[J]);
                if TextLength > 0 then
                    begin
                        RealXGraphic := XOrigin - (TextLength - 1) *
                                        4.0 + (J - 1) * Spacing;
                        if Mid then
                            RealXGraphic := RealXGraphic + Spacing /
                                            2.0;
                        XText := trunc(RealXGraphic / 8.0) +
                                        1 + XOffset1;
                        YText := trunc(YOrigin / 8.0) + YOffset1;
                        gotoxy(XText, YText);
                        write(XTextArr[J])
                    end
            end
    end;
    TextLength := length(XTextArr[0]);
    if TextLength > 0 then
        begin
            RealXGraphic := XOrigin + XAxisL / 2.0 -
                            4.0 * (TextLength - 1);
            XText := trunc(RealXGraphic / 8.0) + 1 + XOffset2;
            YText := trunc(YOrigin / 8.0) + YOffset2;
            gotoxy(XText, YText);
            write(XTextArr[0])
        end;
    gotoxy(1, 1)
end;
```

Variables

TextLength	The length (number of characters) of one of the elements of the array XTextArr
XText	X location in text units for the cursor
YText	Y location in text units for the cursor
J	Looping index

NumToDo	Number of annotations required for the tick mark labeling. This number depends on Mid. See the Discussion section.
Spacing	Number of graphics pixels separating each pair of primary tick marks
RealXGraphic	Temporary X location in graphics units

Discussion

AnnXAxis takes advantage of the fact that Turbo can mix text with graphics while the computer is in one of the graphics modes. Each text character occupies an 8-by-8 pixel square on the graphics screen. Thus, in hires mode, the 80-by-25 character grid can be thought of as superimposed over the 640-by-200 pixel graphics grid. A text character, however, cannot quite be "anywhere" on the graphics grid. Each character is confined to one of the 2,000 (80 times 25) character squares. Thus, if a tick mark is located near the edge of one of these 8-by-8 pixel text squares, the labeling appears slightly off center. This can be corrected by adjusting XOrigin, YOrigin, and/or XAxisL appropriately with the call to DoXAxis. (The idea is to have DoXAxis shift the axis location slightly so that the call to AnnXAxis can exactly center the annotations.)

Depending on Mid, the number of elements required in the XTextArr array varies. When Mid is false, there is one label for each primary tick mark. Since the number of primary tick marks is NumSegsX + 1, the number of elements in XTextArr should also be NumSegsX + 1. (Recall that element zero of XTextArr is reserved for the label for the whole axis.) When Mid is true, the labels appear between the tick marks. In this case, the number of annotations is only NumSegsX.

If you use crowded tick marks or if your annotations are lengthy, you may find that adjacent annotations overlap. This overlapping can be corrected by assigning null strings to the TextArr elements you want to blank out. For example, a null string assigned to every other element causes only every other tick mark to be annotated. You can experiment with different configurations.

Modifications

1. The constant YOffset1 controls how many text-character positions the tick mark annotations appear below the x-axis. (Recall that positive numbers are downward, and negative numbers are upward.) To move the labeling up or down, change this constant's value in the line denoted by {Mod. #1} to any integer.

2. The constant YOffset2 controls how far the label for the whole x-axis appears below the axis. You may change this constant's value in the line denoted by {Mod. #2} to any integer.

3. Tick mark annotations are nominally centered either directly below the tick marks or in the spaces between them (depending on Mid). If you want to move the annotations left or right, change the value of the constant XOffset1 to any integer. A positive value is a move to the right, and a negative value is a move to the left. This way, you can accomplish special positioning of the labels (such as left-adjusting them).

4. XOffset2 moves the location of the label for the whole axis left or right, from its nominally centered value. You may change this constant to any integer.

AnnYAxis

> **Name:** *AnnYAxis*
>
> **Type:** *Procedure*
>
> **Purpose:** *To annotate a vertical y-axis for a subsequent graph*
>
> **Calling Sequence:** AnnYAxis(XOrigin, YOrigin, YAxisL, NumSegsY, YTextArr, Mid)

Description

This procedure provides the textual annotation for the y-axis of a graph. (The axis itself can be drawn with DoYAxis.) AnnYAxis labels tick marks and displays a title for the whole axis. The annotations are drawn horizontally and placed to the left of the tick marks. Annotations can be centered either even with the tick marks or in the spaces between the pairs of tick marks. Input parameters work with DoYAxis to provide a consistent set of specifications for the y-axis. AnnYAxis is fully compatible with Turbo's high- or medium-resolution graphics modes.

Input

XOrigin	integer	X location of the axis origin (that is, the bottom of the axis) in the standard coordinates of the active graphics mode
YOrigin	integer	Y location of the axis origin
YAxisL	integer	Length of the axis in standard units of the active graphics mode
NumSegsY	integer	Number of equal segments in which to divide the axis. Each of these segments is delineated with a pair of primary tick marks. (Including the first

and last marks, the total number of tick marks is NumSegsY + 1.) If the axis has no tick marks, NumSegsY is zero.

YTextArr	string	Array containing the string annotations to place on the axis. Element zero contains the label for the whole axis. The succeeding elements contain the labels for the primary tick marks. A null string in any element suppresses that annotation.
Mid	boolean	Variable that indicates where the tick mark annotations should be located. If Mid is true, the annotations are centered in the spaces between the tick marks. If Mid is false, the annotations are centered even with the tick marks.

AnnArrayType must be declared in a global type declaration, preferably with additional global declarations. In the following lines, numbers 100 and 80 are examples; your values may be different.

```
const
   MaxNumAxisAnn = 100;

type
   AxisAnnSize  = string[80];
   AnnArrayType = array[0..MaxNumAxisAnn] of AxisAnnSize;
```

The parameters XOrigin, YOrigin, YAxisL, and NumSegsY are identical to their counterparts in DoYAxis. These parameters are meant to work compatibly between the two subprograms, and they have identical meanings in each subprogram.

XOrigin and YOrigin are relative to any active graphics window. The computer should be in one of Turbo's graphics modes when you call AnnYAxis.

Output

After DoYAxis displays the physical axis (with tick marks) on the screen, AnnYAxis provides the textual labeling for the axis. If Mid is false, a centered label is placed vertically, even with each primary tick mark. If Mid is true, each label is centered in the space between the tick marks. (See the Discussion section.)

The axis title, if present, is centered with respect to the entire axis and displayed vertically from the top down. The title is placed to the left of the other annotations.

All annotations are located relative to XOrigin, YOrigin, and YAxisL. If these parameters are identical in both DoYAxis and AnnYAxis, the physical axis and its labeling are compatible.

Limitations and Error Conditions

If NumSegsY is zero (or negative), no labeling of the tick marks is done. If YAxisL is zero, all annotations are superimposed just to the left of YOrigin.

Although text can be freely mixed with graphics in Turbo, there are some restrictions on the location of text relative to specific graphics lines. See the Discussion section.

This subprogram respects regular text windows but does not accommodate graphing windows. If you use any windows, be sure to set both window and graphwindow compatibly. If you try to extend an annotation outside the current text window, part of the annotation is displaced.

Annotations are drawn even if the computer is not in a graphics mode. Of course, AnnYAxis is meant to be used with DoYAxis, which requires a graphics mode.

Sample Usage

```
program SampleUsageOfAnnYAxis;

const
   MaxNumAxisAnn = 100;

type
   AxisAnnSize  = string[80];
   AnnArrayType = array[0..MaxNumAxisAnn] of AxisAnnSize;

var
   XOrigin, YOrigin, YAxisL, NumSegsY, J : integer;
   YTextArr                              : AnnArrayType;
   Mid                                   : boolean;

{$I AnnYAxis.PSL}

procedure DrawAxis(XOrigin, YOrigin, YAxisL, NumSegsY: integer);

var
   Y, J: integer;
```

```
begin
   draw(XOrigin, YOrigin, XOrigin, YOrigin - YAxisL, white);
   for J := 0 to NumSegsY do
      begin
         Y := YOrigin - J * YAxisL div NumSegsY;
         draw(XOrigin, Y, XOrigin - 22, Y, white)
      end
end;

BEGIN
   hires;
   writeln('Sample Annotation on Y-Axes');
   XOrigin  := 150;
   YOrigin  := 187;
   YAxisL   := 160;
   NumSegsY := 5;
   Mid      := false;
   for J := 1 to 6 do
      str(25 * (J - 1):1, YTextArr[J]);
   YTextArr[0] := 'Units Shipped';
   DrawAxis(XOrigin, YOrigin, YAxisL, NumSegsY);
   AnnYAxis(XOrigin, YOrigin, YAxisL, NumSegsY, YTextArr, Mid);
   YTextArr[0] := 'Year';
   YTextArr[1] := '1983';
   YTextArr[2] := '1984';
   YTextArr[3] := '1985';
   YTextArr[4] := '1986';
   DrawAxis(450, YOrigin, 128, 4);
   AnnYAxis(450, YOrigin, 128, 4, YTextArr, true)
END.
```

This sample program demonstrates a few of the possible axes annotations that AnnYAxis can produce. Figure 3.7 shows the result.

Sample Annotation on Y-Axes

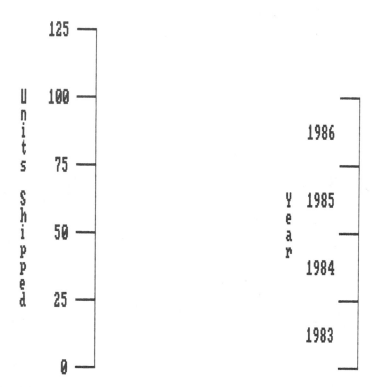

Fig. 3.7. *A demonstration of* AnnYAxis.

Subprogram Listing of AnnYAxis.PSL

```
procedure AnnYAxis(XOrigin, YOrigin, YAxisL, NumSegsY: integer;
                YTextArr: AnnArrayType; Mid: boolean);

const
   XOffset1 = -3;                                      {Mod. #1}
   XOffset2 = -9;                                      {Mod. #2}
   YOffset1 = 0;                                       {Mod. #3}
   YOffset2 = 0;                                       {Mod. #4}

var
   TextLength, XText, YText, J, NumToDo : integer;
   Spacing, RealXGraphic, RealYGraphic  : real;
```

```
begin
   if NumSegsY > 0 then
      begin
         Spacing := YAxisL / NumSegsY;
         if Mid then
            NumToDo := NumSegsY
         else
            NumToDo := NumSegsY + 1;
         for J := 1 to NumToDo do
            begin
               TextLength := length(YTextArr[J]);
               if TextLength > 0 then
                  begin
                     RealXGraphic := XOrigin - TextLength * 8.0;
                     XText := trunc(RealXGraphic / 8.0) +
                                    1 + XOffset1;
                     RealYGraphic := YOrigin - Spacing * (J - 1);
                     if Mid then
                        RealYGraphic := RealYGraphic - Spacing /
                                        2.0;
                     YText := trunc(RealYGraphic / 8.0) +
                                    1 + YOffset1;
                     gotoxy(XText, YText);
                     write(YTextArr[J])
                  end
            end
      end;
   TextLength := length(YTextArr[0]);
   if TextLength > 0 then
      begin
         XText := trunc(XOrigin / 8.0) + XOffset2;
         RealYGraphic := YOrigin - YAxisL / 2.0 -
                    4.0 * (TextLength - 1);
         YText := trunc(RealYGraphic / 8.0) + YOffset2;
         for J := 1 to TextLength do
            begin
               gotoxy(XText, YText + J);
               write(YTextArr[0][J])
            end
      end;
   gotoxy(1, 1)
end;
```

Variables

TextLength	The length (number of characters) of one of the elements of the array YTextArr
XText	X location in text units for the cursor
YText	Y location in text units for the cursor
J	Looping index
NumToDo	Number of annotations required for the tick mark labeling. This number depends on Mid. See the Discussion section.
Spacing	Number of graphics pixels separating each pair of primary tick marks
RealXGraphic	Temporary X location in graphics units
RealYGraphic	Temporary Y location in graphics units

Discussion

In the Discussion section of AnnXAxis, the comments pertaining to text and graphics mixing, the relationship between Mid and NumSegsX (or NumSegsY), and the use of null strings in XTextArr (or YTextArr) are relevant here. See that explanation.

Possible crowding of an annotation is a more serious problem in AnnYAxis than in AnnXAxis. Crowding may occur because only 25 text characters are available vertically, but 80 text characters are available horizontally (in hires). Because the label for the whole y-axis is displayed vertically, a practical limit for its string length is 20 characters. The tick mark annotations are displayed horizontally; be sure that there is enough room for them between the y-axis and the left edge of the screen. See the Modifications section.

Modifications

1. The integer constant XOffset1 controls how many text-character positions each tick mark annotation appears to the left of the y-axis. Measurement is from the y-axis to the center of each annotation. To move the labeling left or right, you can change the value of XOffset1 in the line denoted by {Mod. #1}. (Recall that increasing XOffset1 moves the annotations toward the right, and decreasing XOffset1 moves the annotations toward the left.) You may want to change this constant's value if your labels are long.

2. The constant XOffset2 controls how far (in text characters) the label for the whole y-axis appears to the left of the y-axis. You may change this constant's value in the line denoted by {Mod. #2} to any integer.

3. A tick mark annotation is nominally centered either even with the tick marks or in the space between them (depending on Mid). If you want to move the annotations up or down, change the value of the constant YOffset1 to any integer. A positive value is a move downward, and a negative value is a move upward. Thus, you can accomplish special noncentered positioning of the labels.

4. YOffset2 moves the location of the label for the whole axis up or down from its nominally centered value. You may change this constant to any integer.

AxisText

> **Name:** *AxisText*
>
> **Type:** *Procedure*
>
> **Purpose:** *To fill a text array with strings suitable for numeric axes annotations*
>
> **Calling Sequence:** AxisText(TextArr, NumSegs, LowVal, HighVal, RealFormat)

Description

Both the subprograms AnnXAxis and AnnYAxis require a string array (XTextArr and YTextArr, respectively) for storing the textual annotations for the axes tick marks. If these annotations are numeric, AxisText can automatically supply the strings needed for these arrays. For input, AxisText needs the numeric values at each end of the axis, the number of segments the axis is divided into, and the form (real or integer) for the annotations. The subprogram then stores in an array the appropriate strings for later use by AnnXAxis or AnnYAxis.

Input

NumSegs	integer	The number of segments on the axis. AxisText generates NumSegs + 1 strings. See the Discussion section.
LowVal	real	The numeric value at one end of the axis. (LowVal corresponds to the left end of an x-axis or to the bottom of a y-axis.)

HighVal   real   The numeric value at the other end of the axis.
                        (HighVal corresponds to the right end of an x-axis
                        or to the top of a y-axis.)

RealFormat   boolean   The type of string format produced. If RealFormat is
                        true, real number strings are produced. If RealFormat
                        is false, integer number strings are produced.

MaxNumAxisAnn and AnnArrayType must be declared in global const and type declarations. Preferably, AxisAnnSize is also declared globally as shown in the following
lines, but this declaration is not required. The numbers 100 and 80 are examples;
your values may be different.

```
const
   MaxNumAxisAnn = 100;

type
   AxisAnnSize  = string[80];
   AnnArrayType = array[0..MaxNumAxisAnn] of AxisAnnSize;
```

Output

TextArr   string   Array of the resulting numeric values expressed as
                        strings. The first element contains LowVal in string
                        form. The NumSegs + 1 element contains HighVal in
                        string form. Intermediate elements, if any, contain
                        equally spaced values between LowVal and HighVal.

Limitations and Error Conditions

If NumSegs is less than 1 or greater than MaxNumAxisAnn, the procedure is bypassed
with no effect.

If RealFormat is false (indicating that integer number strings are desired), the
absolute values of LowVal and HighVal must not be greater than 32767. If the
absolute value of a number to be converted to an integer string is greater than
32767, the value 0 (zero) is returned instead.

If necessary, numbers are rounded to fit the format specifications. See the Discussion
and Modification sections for additional details regarding the limitations of real and
integer formats.

Sample Usage

```
program SampleUsageOfAxisText;

const
   MaxNumAxisAnn = 100;

type
   AxisAnnSize  = string[80];
   AnnArrayType = array[0..MaxNumAxisAnn] of AxisAnnSize;

var
   TextArr           : AnnArrayType;
   LowVal, HighVal : real;
   NumSegs, J        : integer;
   RealFormat        : boolean;

{$I AxisText.PSL}

BEGIN
   NumSegs    := 6;
   LowVal     := -1.0;
   HighVal    := 2.00;
   RealFormat := true;
   AxisText(TextArr, NumSegs, LowVal, HighVal, RealFormat);
   writeln('Axis annotations in real format');
   for J := 1 to NumSegs + 1 do
      writeln(TextArr[J]);
   writeln;
   AxisText(TextArr, 4, 0, 100, false);
   writeln('Axis annotations in integer format');
   for J := 1 to 5 do
      writeln(TextArr[J])
END.
```

Running this test program produces the following output:

```
Axis annotations in real format
-1.00
-0.50
0.00
0.50
1.00
1.50
2.00

Axis annotations in integer format
0
25
50
75
100
```

Subprogram Listing of AxisText.PSL

```pascal
procedure AxisText(var TextArr: AnnArrayType; NumSegs: integer;
                   LowVal, HighVal: real; RealFormat: boolean);

var
   Interval, RealVal : real;
   IntVal, J         : integer;

begin
   if not (NumSegs in [1..MaxNumAxisAnn]) then
      exit;
   Interval := (HighVal - LowVal) / NumSegs;
   for J := 0 to NumSegs do
      begin
         RealVal := LowVal + J * Interval;
         if RealFormat then
            str(RealVal:1:2, TextArr[J + 1])          {Mod. #1}
         else
```

```
        begin
            if abs(RealVal) > 32767.0 then
                IntVal := 0
            else
                IntVal := round(RealVal);
            str(IntVal:1, TextArr[J + 1])
        end
    end
end;
```

Variables

Interval	(HighVal - LowVal) divided by NumSegs
RealVal	A real number value to be converted into a string and later stored in TextArr
IntVal	RealVal converted to an integer
J	Looping index

Discussion

For most graphs and bar charts, at least one axis is numeric. This subprogram provides a convenient way to store the string annotations for such axes for later use by AnnXAxis or AnnYAxis. The parameters in AxisText are designed for compatibility with AnnXAxis and AnnYAxis. Table 3.1 shows how the critical variables correspond in these three subprograms.

Table 3.1
Corresponding Variables in the Axes Subprograms

procedure AxisText	*procedure* AnnXAxis	*procedure* AnnYAxis
TextArr	XTextArr	YTextArr
NumSegs	NumSegsX	NumSegsY

(For the following paragraph, some knowledge of how AnnXAxis and AnnYAxis work is assumed. See those subprograms for details.)

AxisText produces NumSegs + 1 elements in the TextArr because that is what AnnXAxis and AnnYAxis expect when the tick marks are annotated. (There are

NumSegs + 1 tick marks.) If, however, the eventual annotations are to be located between the tick marks, the number of annotations required is only NumSegs. In this case, you can "trick" AxisText into producing the correct number of annotations by setting NumSegs one less than NumSegsX (or NumSegsY).

LowVal can be less than HighVal. If so, the resulting annotations are in descending sequence.

In integer mode, the strings are whatever length is required to express the resulting number. Truncation may be necessary in real mode, however. See the Modification section.

Modification

For real numbers, the format can be whatever you want. Our default setting is fixed format with two digits to the right of the decimal point. You may change this setting to any real-number format right after RealVal in the line denoted by {Mod. #1}.

4

Creating Screen Displays

The previous chapter deals with creating graphics effects. This chapter presents subprograms that assist you with displaying standard text on the screen.

Tab and TabXY are cursor-movement functions you can use in a write or writeln statement. Tab moves the cursor to a specified location on the current line, and TabXY moves the cursor anywhere on the screen. These functions ease the sometimes difficult task of aligning screen output in neat columns. For high-speed screen output, you can try ShowFast, which displays screen output about 10 times faster than Turbo's write or writeln. Finally, ShowArr and Show2Arr display the contents of one- and two-dimensional arrays, respectively.

Tab

> **Name:** *Tab*
>
> **Type:** char *function*
>
> **Purpose:** *To move the cursor to a specified column*
>
> **Calling Sequence:** Tab(TabCol)

Description

Tab moves the cursor to a specified column in the current line. Because Turbo doesn't provide such a feature, you can use this function in a write or writeln statement. Turbo's gotoxy procedure enables you to move the cursor anywhere you want, but gotoxy cannot be used in write or writeln. If you need to display columnar output on the screen, especially output containing variable-length text strings, then Tab is an easy way to move the cursor to the required columns.

Input

TabCol	integer	The column number (1–79) where the cursor is to be moved

Output

Tab	char	The function Tab returns a char value of ASCII 8 (backspace). The backspace aids in moving the cursor to the specified column when you use Tab in a write or writeln statement. See the Discussion section.

Limitations and Error Conditions

TabCol must be in the range from 1 to 79. The number is assumed to be 1 if it is less than 1, or 79 if it is greater than 79. The current cursor position does not matter, nor does it matter whether any text is already on the current screen line. This subprogram works for screen output only. If you use Tab with a write or writeln statement directed to the printer or a disk file, a single character with the value ASCII 8 (backspace) is sent to the printer or disk file, and the cursor is moved to position TabCol + 1 of the current screen line.

Sample Usage

```
program SampleUsageOfTab;

var
   TabCol: integer;

{$I Tab.PSL}

BEGIN
   TabCol := 15;
   writeln(' 12345678901234567890 - "Ruler" line' );
   writeln('First line', Tab(TabCol), 'X' );
   writeln('Second line', Tab(TabCol), 'Y' );
   writeln('abcdefghij', Tab(6), 'Z' )
END.
```

In the following program output, the first line is a "ruler" line, indicating column numbers in the other lines. The next two lines show how Tab moves the cursor to a fixed column (15) after displaying variable-length string data. The last line demonstrates how the cursor can be moved over data already on the same line.

```
12345678901234567890 - "Ruler" line
First line    X
Second line   Y
abcdeZghij
```

Subprogram Listing of Tab.PSL

```
function Tab(TabCol: integer): char;

begin
   if TabCol > 79 then
      TabCol := 79
   else
      if TabCol < 1 then TabCol := 1;
   gotoxy(TabCol + 1, wherey);
   Tab := #8
end;
```

Variables

None

Discussion

Displaying data in nice even columns can sometimes be quite awkward. Suppose that you are displaying one or more small fields in many different lines on the screen. For all the lines, you want to display something starting in, say, column 72. Without the Tab function, you can accomplish this task in several unwieldy ways. For instance, you can display your first few fields and then display the appropriate number of blank spaces until you reach column 72. Or you can end your write statement after the first fields, use the gotoxy procedure to move the cursor to column 72, and then use another write. A much simpler way, however, is to use the Tab function. The code will look something like this:

```
writeln(A, B, Tab(72), C);
```

Because Turbo does not allow the use of a procedure from within the built-in write (or writeln) procedure, we got a little tricky in creating Tab. Turbo does allow a function within write. We therefore used a char function that displays a cursor-movement character rather than a visible character or number. We moved the cursor out one position beyond the `TabCol` position and then set the `Tab` function value to the backspace character so that `write` moves the cursor backward to the position you specify. Because of this approach, the maximum allowable value for `TabCol` is 79, not 80.

Another function that would be handy in Turbo is `Space`. Suppose that you are displaying two variables and you want to leave N spaces between them. If a space function existed, you could use the code

```
writeln(A, Space(N), B);
```

We would have included such a function in this book, but you can just as easily get the same effect from standard Turbo commands by writing a null string (two consecutive apostrophes) followed by a length variable, as in

```
writeln(A, '' :N, B);
```

This technique has the advantage of working equally well for printer, disk, or screen output.

Modifications

None

TabXY

> **Name:** *TabXY*
>
> **Type:** char *function*
>
> **Purpose:** *To move the cursor to a specified column and row*
>
> **Calling Sequence:** `TabXY(TabCol, TabRow)`

Description

`TabXY` moves the cursor on the screen to both the column and the row you specify. Like `Tab`, `TabXY` can be used in a `write` or `writeln` statement because Turbo doesn't provide such a feature. Turbo's `gotoxy` procedure enables you to move the cursor anywhere you want, but `gotoxy` cannot be used in `write` or `writeln`. You will often find it simpler to use `TabXY` to position the cursor on the screen than to use numerous paired `write` and `gotoxy` statements.

Input

TabCol	integer	The column number (1–79) where the cursor is to be moved
TabRow	integer	The row number (1–25) where the cursor is to be moved

Output

TabXY	char	The function TabXY returns a char value of ASCII 8 (backspace). The backspace aids in moving the cursor to the specified column when TabXY is used in a write or writeln statement. See the Discussion section.

Limitations and Error Conditions

TabCol must be in the range from 1 to 79. The number is assumed to be 1 if it is less than 1, or 79 if it is greater than 79. Similarly, TabRow must be in the range from 1 to 25. The number is assumed to be 1 if it is less than 1, or 25 if it is greater than 25. The current cursor position makes no difference, nor does it matter whether any text is already on the screen. This subprogram works for screen output only. If TabXY is used with a write or writeln statement directed to the printer or a disk file, a single character with the value ASCII 8 (backspace) is sent to the printer or disk file, and the cursor is moved to column TabCol + 1 and row TabRow on the screen.

Sample Usage

```
program SampleUsageOfTabXY;

{$I TabXY.PSL}

BEGIN
   clrscr;
   writeln('12345678901234567890');
   writeln(TabXY(1,2), '2', TabXY(1,3), '3', TabXY(1,4), '4');
   writeln(TabXY(5,4), 'X', TabXY(2,3), 'Y', TabXY(12,2), 'Z');
   writeln(TabXY(1,5), 'Done')
END.
```

In the following program output, the first line is a "ruler" line, indicating column numbers in the other lines. The second `writeln` statement of the sample program displays the row numbers for rows 2 through 4. The third `writeln` statement displays X, Y, and Z at various screen locations, using `TabXY` to move the cursor. The last `writeln` moves the cursor below the area previously used and displays `Done`.

```
12345678901234567890
2               Z
3Y
4    X
Done
```

Subprogram Listing of TabXY.PSL

```pascal
function TabXY(TabCol, TabRow: integer): char;

begin
   if TabCol > 79 then
      TabCol := 79
   else
      if TabCol < 1 then TabCol := 1;
   if TabRow > 25 then
      TabRow := 25
   else
      if TabRow < 1 then TabRow := 1;
   gotoxy(TabCol + 1, TabRow);
   TabXY := #8
end;
```

Variables

None

Discussion

The Discussion section for `Tab` explains its benefits and the reasons why it is written in a slightly tricky way. Those comments are applicable here also, except that `TabXY` adds the capability of row movement. As with `Tab`, the coding method for `TabCol` limits the maximum allowable value to 79, not 80.

Modifications

None

ShowFast

> **Name:** *ShowFast*
>
> **Type:** *Procedure*
>
> **Purpose:** *To display a string of text on the screen at high speed*
>
> **Calling Sequence:** ShowFast(Message, Column, Row)

Description

The ShowFast subprogram displays on the screen a string of text in roughly 1/10 the time required by write or writeln. Although write and writeln are fast enough for most purposes, a faster display is sometimes needed. If you use write or writeln to fill the screen with text, the time required is about 2.0 seconds with the Monochrome Adapter or about 2.5 seconds with the Color/Graphics Adapter. If you use ShowFast, filling the screen takes about 0.2 seconds in either case.

Input

Message	string	The string of text you want to display on the screen
Column	integer	The column number (1–80) where you want the displaying to begin
Row	integer	The row number (1–25) where you want the displaying to begin

In addition, you must specify in the main program the following global type declaration:

```
type
   String255 = string[255];
```

Output

The output of this subprogram is text displayed on the screen, beginning in the column and row you specify and continuing for the length of Message.

Limitations and Error Conditions

Message can be any legal string, from 0 (zero) to 255 characters long. Column and Row must be within the ranges shown previously (1–80 and 1–25, respectively), but no range checking is done by the subprogram. Nor is checking done to determine whether the message extends beyond the end of the screen. (ShowFast does not scroll the screen if the message extends beyond column 80 of row 25; the subprogram continues putting the text into memory areas beyond the end of the screen.) You must be certain to check that the starting location and length of the message string are valid. If you don't, the results may be unpredictable. The cursor position is not changed by ShowFast. You must move the cursor yourself (with gotoxy) if you plan to use write or writeln to put more output on the same screen used by ShowFast. This subprogram was tested on a standard IBM Personal Computer using both the Monochrome Adapter and the Color/Graphics Adapter in 80-column text mode. The subprogram should work on other compatible computers that use the same screen memory locations, but verification is up to you.

Sample Usage

```
program SampleUsageOfShowFast;

type
   String255 = string[255];

var
  Message : String255;
  J       : integer;

{$I ShowFast.PSL}

BEGIN
   clrscr;
   delay(2000);
   Message := 'These lines were displayed by Turbo''s "writeln"';
   for J := 1 to 24 do
      writeln(Message);
   delay(5000);
   clrscr;
   delay(2000);
   Message := 'These lines were displayed by TPPL''s "ShowFast"';
   for J := 1 to 24 do
      ShowFast(Message, 1, J);
   delay(5000);
   gotoxy(1,24)
END.
```

This sample program fills the screen with messages in two different ways. You can compare the times required for each method. First, the program clears the screen, pauses for 2 seconds, and displays this message on lines 1 through 24, using writeln:

```
These lines were displayed by Turbo's "writeln"
```

Then the program pauses for 5 seconds, clears the screen, pauses for 2 more seconds, and displays this message on lines 1 through 24, using ShowFast:

```
These lines were displayed by TPPL's "ShowFast"
```

Subprogram Listing of ShowFast.PSL

```
procedure ShowFast(Message: String255; Column, Row: integer);

var
    VidLoc, Offset : integer;
    Pointer        : byte;

begin
    if mem[0:$449] = 7 then
       VidLoc := $B000
    else
       VidLoc := $B800;
    Offset := (Row - 1) * 80 + Column - 1;
    Offset := Offset + Offset;
    for Pointer := 1 to length(Message) do
       mem[VidLoc : Offset + Pointer + Pointer - 2] :=
                  ord(Message[Pointer])
end;
```

Variables

VidLoc	integer	The segment address of the start of video memory. For the Monochrome Adapter, the address is hex B000. For the Color/Graphics Adapter, the address is hex B800.
Offset	integer	The number of bytes into the screen memory area where the current character is to be placed. For the first 5 screen locations, Offset is 0, 2, 4, 6, and 8.

| Pointer | byte | A pointer to the current character in the `Message` string being placed on the screen |

Discussion

An IBM PC uses memory-mapped displays. This means that the text you see on the screen is a copy of the text encoded in a certain area of the computer's memory. `ShowFast` gains its speed by putting directly into the appropriate memory locations the text to be displayed instead of taking the longer (and slower) path used by `write` and `writeln`. Beware of the dangers of this fast approach! If other computers (from IBM or other manufacturers) change the memory areas they use, or change the indicator at location hex 449 (indicating that the Monochrome Adapter is in use if the contents are equal to 7, or the Color/Graphics Adapter otherwise), then this subprogram will no longer work correctly. By the same token, `ShowFast` is based on the scheme of 2 bytes (a data byte followed by an attribute byte) representing each screen position. `ShowFast` puts the data bytes into every other memory location, skipping over the attribute bytes. If this scheme is altered, the subprogram will fail. But given these caveats, `ShowFast` can be useful in many instances when a faster display is necessary. For example, you can use `ShowFast` to avoid sluggish response when you're paging through screens full of data.

Modifications

None

ShowArr

Name:	*ShowArr*
Type:	*Procedure*
Purpose:	*To display a numeric array's contents on the screen*
Calling Sequence:	`ShowArr(NumArray, Count)`

Description

This procedure displays on the screen the elements of a `real` array. If there are more elements in the array than there are lines on the screen, `ShowArr` waits for you to press a key to continue after displaying each full screen.

Input

NumArray   real   Array in which data is stored

Count   integer   Number of elements to be displayed

In addition, you must specify in your main program the following global `type` declaration, preferably using the global `const` declaration shown. The number 50 is an example; the size of your array may differ.

```
const
   ArraySize = 50;

type
   ArrayType = array[1..ArraySize] of real;
```

Output

No changes are made to the array's contents or Count. The contents of the array are displayed on the screen in the format shown in the Sample Usage section that follows.

Limitations and Error Conditions

Count must be greater than zero; otherwise, the subprogram exits without displaying anything.

Sample Usage

```
program SampleUsageOfShowArr;

const
   ArraySize = 50;

type
   ArrayType = array[1..ArraySize] of real;              {Mod. #4}

var
   NumArray : ArrayType;
   Count    : integer;

{$I ShowArr.PSL}
```

```
BEGIN
   NumArray[1] := 5;
   NumArray[2] := -24.67;
   NumArray[3] := -0.000314;
   Count := 3;
   ShowArr(NumArray, Count)
END.
```

Following is the output of this test program:

```
1     5.0000000000E+00
2    -2.4670000000E+01
3    -3.1400000000E-04
** Press a key to continue **
```

Subprogram Listing of ShowArr.PSL

```
procedure ShowArr(NumArray: ArrayType; Count: integer);

const
   Rows = 20;                                        {Mod. #1}
   Gap = ' ';                                        {Mod. #2}

var
   J: integer;

begin
   if Count < 1 then exit;
   clrscr;
   for J := 1 to Count do
      begin
         writeln(J:4, Gap, NumArray[J]);             {Mod. #3}
         if (J mod Rows = 0) or (J = Count) then
            begin
               writeln('** Press a key to continue **');
               repeat until keypressed;
               clrscr
            end
      end
end;
```

Variables

Rows	Number of rows (lines) that may be displayed on one screen
Gap	Two blank spaces, used in separating the display of the element number from the contents of the array element
J	Subscript that varies from 1 to Count, indicating the current element being displayed

Discussion

The logic of a subprogram to display all the elements in an array should be so straightforward that the subprogram would be almost trivial. A single executable statement like the following should be just about enough:

```
for J := 1 to Count do writeln(NumArray[J]);
```

Indeed, in many circumstances this *is* enough. Often, though, just a little more is needed. ShowArr takes two extra steps: (1) displays the element number to the left of each element's contents, and (2) pauses after each 20 elements (and at the end of the list) so that you can see the output before it scrolls off the screen. The subprogram remains quite simple, yet you may be surprised to see how complicated some programmers make such a thing.

Modifications

1. To change the number of rows (lines) displayed on each screen before waiting for a key to be pressed, change 20 in the statement indicated by {Mod. #1} to any integer from 1 to 23.

2. To change the spacing between the element number and its contents on each line, change the number of spaces between apostrophes in the statement indicated.

3. Change the format of each element's contents from exponential (floating point) notation to fixed-decimal notation by changing the indicated statement to something like this:

```
writeln(J:4, Gap, NumArray[J]:16:8);
```

See the Turbo manual for details about formatting real numbers.

4. To use this subprogram to display the contents of integer arrays rather than real ones, change the global type declaration to

```
type
        ArrayType = array[1..ArraySize] of integer;
```

Show2Arr

Name:	*Show2Arr*
Type:	*Procedure*
Purpose:	*To display a two-dimensional array's contents on the screen*
Calling Sequence:	Show2Arr(Num2Array, RowCount, N, M, Columns)

Description

This procedure displays on the screen the elements of a two-dimensional real array. If there are more elements in the array than there are lines on the screen, Show2Arr pauses after the screen fills and waits until you press a key before continuing.

Input

Num2Array	real	Array in which data is stored
RowCount	integer	Number of rows of elements to be displayed
N	integer	Width of the field for displaying each element with Turbo's write procedure. If the width is 0 (zero), floating-point format is used.
M	integer	Number of digits to be displayed to the right of the decimal point for each element
Columns	integer	Number of columns of output to be displayed on the screen

In addition, you must specify in the main program the following global const and type declarations in order to define the array. RowSize, which is the maximum number of rows the array can contain, is not required. But for compatibility with other subprograms, RowSize is recommended as the way to define Array2Type. The numbers 2 and 100 are examples; the size of your array may differ.

```
const
   ColSize = 2;
   RowSize = 100;

type
   Array2Type = array[1..RowSize, 1..ColSize] of real;
```

Output

No changes are made to the array's contents or to the other variables passed to the subprogram. The contents of the array are displayed on the screen in one of the formats shown in the Sample Usage section, depending on whether N is zero or the width of a write field.

Limitations and Error Conditions

RowCount and Columns must be greater than zero, and N and M must be nonnegative. Otherwise, the subprogram beeps, then displays the error message **Parameter error in Show2Arr **, and then exits. Your responsibility is to provide reasonable values for N, M, and Columns. See the Discussion section for more details.

Sample Usage

```
program SampleUsageOfShow2Arr;

const
   ColSize = 2;
   RowSize = 100;

type
   Array2Type = array[1..RowSize, 1..ColSize] of real;

var
   Num2Array                : Array2Type;
   RowCount, N, M, Columns  : integer;

{$I Show2Arr.PSL}
```

```
BEGIN
   Num2Array[1,1] := 1.01;   Num2Array[1,2] := 22.7;
   Num2Array[2,1] := 3.4;    Num2Array[2,2] := -42.0;
   Num2Array[3,1] := -0.05;  Num2Array[3,2] := -6666.66;
   RowCount := 3;
   N := 8;  M := 2;  Columns := 2;
   Show2Arr(Num2Array, RowCount, N, M, Columns);
   N := 0;
   Show2Arr(Num2Array, RowCount, N, M, 2)
END.
```

The output of the sample program is a screen containing this first group of lines and then, after a key is pressed, the second group:

```
   [1,1]    1.01     [1,2]    22.70
   [2,1]    3.40     [2,2]   -42.00
   [3,1]   -0.05     [3,2]-6666.66
   ** Press a key to continue **


   [1,1]  1.0100000000E+00     [1,2]   2.2700000000E+01
   [2,1]  3.4000000000E+00     [2,2]  -4.2000000000E+01
   [3,1] -5.0000000000E-02     [3,2]  -6.6666600000E+03
   ** Press a key to continue **
```

Subprogram Listing of Show2Arr.PSL

```
procedure Show2Arr(Num2Array: Array2Type;
                   RowCount, N, M, Columns: integer);

const
   Rows = 24;                                        {Mod. #1}

var
   J, K, LastElement, PageSize, ElementCount, ColWidth,
      NumOnPage: integer;

begin
   if (RowCount < 1) or (N < 0) or (M < 0) or (Columns < 1) then
      begin
         writeln(' ** Parameter error in Show2Arr **', chr(7));
         exit
      end;
```

```
   LastElement  := RowCount * ColSize;
   PageSize     := Rows * Columns;
   ElementCount := 0;
   NumOnPage    := 0;
   if N = 0 then
      ColWidth := 27
   else
      ColWidth := N + 9;                                        {Mod. #2}
   clrscr;
   for J := 1 to RowCount do
      begin
         for K := 1 to ColSize do
            begin
               gotoxy((NumOnPage mod Columns) * ColWidth + 1,
                     (NumOnPage div Columns) + 1);
               write('[', J, ',', K, ']');                    {Mod. #2}
               if N = 0 then
                  write(Num2Array[J,K])
               else
                  write(Num2Array[J,K]:N:M);
               ElementCount := ElementCount + 1;
               NumOnPage := ElementCount mod PageSize;
               if (NumOnPage = 0) or
                  (ElementCount = LastElement) then
                  begin
                     writeln;
                     write('** Press a key to continue **');
                     repeat until keypressed;
                     if ElementCount <> LastElement then
                        clrscr
                     else
                        writeln
                  end
            end
      end
end;
```

Variables

Rows	Number of rows (lines) that may be displayed on one screen
J	Subscript that varies from 1 to RowCount, indicating the current row being displayed
K	Subscript that varies from 1 to ColSize, indicating the column of the array (not the screen) being displayed
LastElement	Total number of elements in the array
PageSize	Total number of elements that fit on one screen
ElementCount	Counter indicating how many elements have been shown. Because the counter begins with the number 0 (zero), ElementCount represents the next element to be shown, not the current one.
ColWidth	Width of each column. The width is based on the value of N.
NumOnPage	Counter indicating how many elements have been shown on the current screen. NumOnPage ranges from zero to PageSize - 1.

Discussion

A number of ways are available for displaying on the screen the contents of a two-dimensional array. This subprogram provides one way, allowing you some control with the parameters you provide. The Modifications section suggests some changes to this method. The intent is to make the subprogram easily understood yet flexible enough so that you can apply it in different circumstances.

Columns can be any integer from 1 to 8, depending on what value you provide for N. If N is zero, you are requesting that your values be displayed in floating-point format, and Columns should be no larger than 3. If N is greater than zero, Columns should be no larger than 80/(N + 9).

The main for-do loops increment J and K through each row and column in the array. The other variables and constants keep track of where each element goes on the screen and whether the screen is full yet.

Modifications

1. To change the number of rows (lines) displayed on each screen before waiting for a key to be pressed, change the value in the statement indicated by {Mod. #1}. Rows can be any integer from 1 to 24.

2. Eliminate the display of the element numbers by deleting the second line indicated by {Mod. #2}. Then, if you like, change the first line indicated by {Mod. #2} to

   ```
   ColWidth := N + 1;
   ```

   This allows more columns to be displayed on each screen. With this second change, Columns should be no larger than 80/(N + 1).

5

Using the Printer

Routing normal text to a printer is straightforward in Turbo. You simply use the preassigned file lst in your write and writeln statements, as explained in the Turbo manual.

In this chapter are subprograms that create nonstandard effects with your printer. Three of the programs print text in a special way. You can get underscored text with UnderSc, boldfaced text with BoldFace, or overstruck text with StrikeOv.

NewPage form-feeds the printer. This causes the current page to eject and the next page to be positioned for printing (assuming that you are using continuous-roll or fan-feed paper).

Finally, PrtSc makes a printed copy of the current screen contents. This task is the same one accomplished by the Shift-PrtSc key combination, but here it is done within a Turbo program. Graphics screen images can be produced if your printer supports a graphics-emulation mode.

The subprograms use standard printer ASCII codes to accomplish special effects. These codes are supported almost universally by today's hardware. The subprograms should work with all of the popular printers.

UnderSc

> **Name:** *UnderSc*
>
> **Type:** char *function*
>
> **Purpose:** *To print underscored text*
>
> **Calling Sequence:** UnderSc(WorkStr)

Description

UnderSc enables the printer to underscore printed text. The function is designed for use inside a write or writeln statement directed to the printer through Turbo's preassigned lst file. Underscored text can be freely mixed with nonunderscored text in the same write statement.

Input

WorkStr   string   The text to be printed and underscored. It can be
                          specified as a string variable (of any string type) or
                          as a text literal.

In addition, the following global type declaration must appear in your main program:

```
type
  String255 = string[255];
```

Output

WorkStr is printed and underscored on the printer.

Limitations and Error Conditions

If WorkStr is null, a space character followed by a backspace is sent to the printer. This creates no net effect unless the printer is positioned at its last print position before the call to UnderSc.

If UnderSc is used in a write statement not directed to the printer (that is, without the lst file designation in the write statement), WorkStr is still routed to the printer. Subsequent text in the same write statement is also sent to the printer.

The printer must be on-line, or the system pauses to wait for the printer to come on-line.

Sample Usage

```
program SampleUsageOfUnderSc;

type
  String255 = string[255];
  StringType = string[20];
```

```
var
   WorkStr  : StringType;
   AreaCode : integer;

{$I UnderSc.PSL}

BEGIN
   writeln(lst, 'Respond ', UnderSc('immediately'), ' please.');
   writeln(lst);
   AreaCode := 212;
   str(AreaCode, WorkStr);
   writeln(lst, 'Call Dave at area code ', UnderSc(WorkStr));
   writeln(lst);
   str(pi:8:6, WorkStr);
   writeln(lst, 'Pi = ', UnderSc(WorkStr), ' approximately')
END.
```

Figure 5.1 shows the result of running this program with an EPSON MX™-80 printer attached to a standard IBM PC.

```
Respond immediately please.

Call Dave at area code 212

Pi = 3.141593 approximately
```

Fig. 5.1. *The program output illustrating the use of* UnderSc.

Subprogram Listing of UnderSc.PSL

```
function UnderSc(WorkStr: String255): char;

var
   J, WorkLen: byte;

begin
   write(lst, WorkStr);
   WorkLen := length(WorkStr);
   for J := 1 to WorkLen do
      write(lst, #8);
```

```
    for J := 1 to WorkLen do
       write(lst, #95);
    if WorkLen = 0 then
       begin
          write(lst, #32);
          UnderSc := #8
       end
    else
       begin
          write(lst, #8);
          UnderSc := #32
       end
end;
```

Variables

J   Loop index

WorkLen   The string length of WorkStr

Discussion

In the following comments, references to Turbo's write statement apply to writeln as well.

UnderSc is intended for use with write statements directed to the printer. Each write statement should send output to the printer through Turbo's preassigned lst file. That is, the write statements should begin like this:

```
   write(lst,
```

Except for the underscoring, the operation of each write statement is normal. Print head positions retain their expected values, and nonunderscored text can be freely mixed with the underscored text. See the Sample Usage program for some examples.

UnderSc accepts only string arguments. You can, however, get the value of a real or integer variable underscored. Use Turbo's str procedure to convert the value of your numeric variable (or constant) to a string (using format descriptors if you want). The call to str precedes the call to UnderSc. Then use UnderSc as usual. The Sample Usage program demonstrates this technique.

The normal ASCII codes for backspace (#8), underscore (#95), and space (#32) are used. Nearly all of today's popular printers support these codes, and UnderSc should work on almost any system.

The method UnderSc uses is interesting. The "natural" way to design UnderSc is as a procedure instead of a function; unfortunately, procedures cannot be called within write statements. Functions can, however. To achieve underscoring, you must therefore design UnderSc as a function. A problem arises in that any function must return a value. Any value returned by UnderSc is sent to the printer (causing undesirable print).

You can use a trick to achieve the desired effect. Once "inside" the UnderSc subprogram, you can call procedures. Thus, write statements directed to the printer (through Turbo's standard lst file) are used by UnderSc. WorkStr is printed, the appropriate number of backspaces are issued, and underscores are printed. Next, one extra backspace character is "printed." UnderSc then returns a space character (#32) as its char functional output, causing the original write statement to print one blank character. This positions the print head exactly where you want it with the correct underscoring accomplished. (If WorkStr is null, the algorithm is slightly modified.)

Modifications

None

BoldFace

Name:	*BoldFace*
Type:	char *function*
Purpose:	*To print boldfaced text*
Calling Sequence:	BoldFace(WorkStr)

Description

BoldFace enables the printer to print boldfaced text. The function is designed for use inside a write or writeln statement directed to the printer through Turbo's preassigned lst file. Boldfaced text can be freely mixed with regular text in the same write statement.

Input

WorkStr   string   The text to be printed in boldface. The text can be specified as a string variable (of any string type) or as a text literal.

In addition, the following global `type` declaration must appear in your main program:

```
type
   String255 = string[255];
```

Output

`WorkStr` is printed in boldface on the printer.

Limitations and Error Conditions

If `WorkStr` is null, a space character followed by a backspace is sent to the printer. This creates no net effect unless the printer is positioned at its last print position before the call to `BoldFace`.

If you use `BoldFace` in a `write` statement not directed to the printer (that is, without the `lst` file designation in the `write` statement), `WorkStr` is still routed to the printer. Subsequent text in the same `write` statement is also sent to the printer.

The printer must be on-line, or the system pauses to wait for the printer to come on-line.

Sample Usage

```
program SampleUsageOfBoldFace;

type
   String255  = string[255];
   StringType = string[20];

var
   WorkStr: StringType;

{$I BoldFace.PSL}

BEGIN
   WorkStr := 'Wednesday';
   writeln(lst, 'It is due ', BoldFace(WorkStr), ' by noon.');
   writeln(lst);
   writeln(lst, 'This line ends with ', BoldFace('boldface.'));
   writeln(lst);
   str(memavail, WorkStr);
   writeln(lst, BoldFace(WorkStr), ' paragraphs left on heap.')
END.
```

Figure 5.2 shows the result of running this program with an EPSON MX-80 printer attached to a standard IBM PC.

It is due Wednesday by noon.

This line ends with boldface.

23572 paragraphs left on heap.

Fig. 5.2. *The program output illustrating the use of* BoldFace.

Subprogram Listing of BoldFace.PSL

```
function BoldFace(WorkStr: String255): char;

const
   NumReps = 1;                                           {Mod. #1}

var
   J, K, WorkLen: byte;

begin
   write(lst, WorkStr);
   WorkLen := length(WorkStr);
   for J := 1 to NumReps do
      begin
         for K := 1 to WorkLen do
            write(lst, #8);
         write(lst, WorkStr);
      end;
   if WorkLen = 0 then
      begin
         write(lst, #32);
         BoldFace := #8
      end
   else
      begin
         write(lst, #8);
         BoldFace := #32
      end
end;
```

Variables

NumReps	Number of times to overprint WorkStr
J, K	Loop indices
WorkLen	The string length of WorkStr

Discussion

In the following comments, references to Turbo's write statement apply to writeln as well.

BoldFace is intended for use with write statements directed to the printer. Each write statement should send output to the printer through Turbo's preassigned lst file. That is, the write statements should begin like this:

```
write(lst,
```

Except for the boldfacing, the operation of each write statement is normal. Print head positions retain their expected values, and regular text can be freely mixed with the boldfaced text. See the Sample Usage program for some examples.

BoldFace accepts only string arguments. You can, however, get the value of a real or integer variable boldfaced. Use Turbo's str procedure to convert the value of your numeric variable (or constant) to a string (using format descriptors if you want). The call to str precedes the call to BoldFace. Then use BoldFace as usual.

The normal ASCII codes for backspace (#8) and space (#32) are used. Nearly all of today's popular printers support these codes, and BoldFace should work on almost any system.

BoldFace works by printing the desired text, backspacing, and then printing the text again. A programming trick was used in order to call BoldFace within a write statement. This trick is explained in the Discussion section for UnderSc.

Modification

Minimally, boldfaced text is produced by a single overprinting. If you need darker text, you may try additional overprintings to see the effect on your printer. The number of overprintings is controlled by the constant NumReps in the line denoted by {Mod. #1}. You may make NumReps any positive integer.

StrikeOv

> **Name:** *StrikeOv*
>
> **Type:** char *function*
>
> **Purpose:** *To print overstruck text*
>
> **Calling Sequence:** StrikeOv(WorkStr)

Description

StrikeOv enables the printer to print text and then strike it out by overprinting hyphens. Overprinted text is necessary in many legal documents. StrikeOv is designed for use inside a write or writeln statement directed to the printer through Turbo's preassigned lst file. Overstruck text can be freely mixed with regular text in the same write statement.

Input

WorkStr   string   The text to be printed and overstruck. It can be
                            specified as a string variable (of any string type) or
                            as a text literal.

In addition, the following global type declaration must appear in your main program:

```
type
   String255 = string[255];
```

Output

WorkStr is printed and overstruck on the printer.

Limitations and Error Conditions

If WorkStr is null, a space character followed by a backspace is sent to the printer. This creates no net effect unless the printer is positioned at its last print position before the call to StrikeOv.

If you use StrikeOv in a write statement not directed to the printer (that is, without the lst file designation in the write statement), WorkStr is still routed to the printer. Subsequent text in the same write statement is also sent to the printer.

The printer must be on-line, or the system pauses to wait for the printer to come on-line.

Sample Usage

```pascal
program SampleUsageOfStrikeOv;

type
   String255 = string[255];
   StringType = string[20];

var
   WorkStr: StringType;

{$I StrikeOv.PSL}

BEGIN
   writeln(lst, 'JOHNSON ', StrikeOv('AND JONES'), ' ALLEGEDLY');
   writeln(lst);
   str(1991, WorkStr);
   writeln(lst, 'Design is due in ', StrikeOv(WorkStr), ' 1989')
END.
```

Figure 5.3 shows the result of running this program with an EPSON MX-80 printer attached to a standard IBM PC.

```
JOHNSON AND-JONES ALLEGEDLY

Design is due in 1991 1989
```

Fig. 5.3. *The program output illustrating the use of* StrikeOv.

Subprogram Listing of StrikeOv.PSL

```pascal
function StrikeOv(WorkStr: String255): char;

var
   J, WorkLen: byte;

begin
   write(lst, WorkStr);
   WorkLen := length(WorkStr);
   for J := 1 to WorkLen do
      write(lst, #8);
```

```
    for J := 1 to WorkLen do
        write(lst, #45);                                    {Mod. #1}
    if WorkLen = 0 then
        begin
            write(lst, #32);
            StrikeOv := #8
        end
    else
        begin
            write(lst, #8);
            StrikeOv := #32
        end
end;
```

Variables

J	Loop index
WorkLen	The string length of WorkStr

Discussion

In the following comments, references to Turbo's write statement apply to writeln as well.

StrikeOv is intended for use with write statements directed to the printer. Each write statement should send output to the printer through Turbo's preassigned lst file. That is, the write statements should begin like this:

```
write(lst,
```

Except for the overprinting, the operation of each write statement is normal. Print head positions retain their expected values, and regular text can be freely mixed with the overstruck text. See the Sample Usage program for some examples.

StrikeOv accepts only string arguments. You can, however, get the value of a real or integer variable overprinted. Use Turbo's str procedure to convert the value of your numeric variable (or constant) to a string (using format descriptors if you want). The call to str precedes the call to StrikeOv. Then use StrikeOv as usual. The Sample Usage program demonstrates this technique.

The normal ASCII codes for backspace (#8), hyphen (#45), and space (#32) are used. Almost all of today's popular printers support these codes, and StrikeOv should work on almost any system.

The same trick explained in UnderSc is used to accomplish the overprinting. See the Discussion section of UnderSc for details.

Modification

Instead of using hyphens, you may want to overprint with some other character. Just change the ASCII code from #45 (hyphen) to whatever character you want. Make this change in the line denoted by {Mod. #1}.

NewPage

Name:	*NewPage*
Type:	*Procedure*
Purpose:	*To cause the printer to eject to the next page*
Calling Sequence:	NewPage

Description

This procedure causes the printer to form-feed continuous paper so that subsequent printing begins at the top of the next page.

Input

None

Output

The printer ejects the current page and positions the next page for printing.

Limitations and Error Conditions

NewPage works as intended only on printers using continuous-roll or fan-feed paper. The printer must be on-line, or the system pauses to wait for the printer to come on-line.

Sample Usage

```
program SampleUsageOfNewPage;

{$I NewPage.PSL}

BEGIN
   writeln(lst, 'Printing on top of page 1');
   writeln(lst, 'Printing on second line of page 1');
   NewPage;
   writeln(lst, 'Printing on top of page 2')
END.
```

Running this test program causes the following two lines to print on the current page in the printer:

```
Printing on top of page 1
Printing on second line of page 1
```

The current page is then ejected, and the printer form-feeds the paper. The following line is then printed at the top of the new page:

```
Printing on top of page 2
```

Subprogram Listing of NewPage.PSL

```
procedure NewPage;

begin
   writeln(lst, #12)                                    {Mod. #1}
end;
```

Variables

None

Discussion

This procedure is useful when you are printing reports or other documents that need to be adjusted to new pages.

Modification

Almost all of today's printers use ASCII 12 (decimal) as the form-feed character. If you have a printer that doesn't conform to this standard, change the #12 in the line indicated by {Mod. #1} to the value required for a form feed.

PrtSc

> **Name:** *PrtSc*
>
> **Type:** *Procedure*
>
> **Purpose:** *To print a copy of the current screen contents*
>
> **Calling Sequence:** PrtSc

Description

By pressing the Shift-PrtSc keys on an IBM PC, you send to the printer an image of the current screen. PrtSc does the same thing from within a Turbo program. A "snapshot" copy of the current screen is printed. You can use PrtSc for graphics images as well as for regular text. See the Discussion section.

Input

None

Output

A copy of the current screen contents is routed to the printer and printed.

Limitations and Error Conditions

The printer must be on-line, or the system pauses to wait for the printer to come on-line.

Sample Usage

```
program SampleUsageOfPrtSc;

{$I PrtSc.PSL}

BEGIN
   clrscr;
   writeln('This is line number 1');
   writeln('This is line number 2');
   gotoxy(1, 10);
   writeln('This is line number 10');
   PrtSc;
   writeln('This should not print on the printer')
END.
```

The results of this sample program are shown in figures 5.4 and 5.5. Figure 5.4 shows the output on the line printer, and figure 5.5 shows how the screen appears. Notice the additional line seen on the screen but not on the printer. This line does not appear on the printer because the call to PrtSc is made before the line is displayed.

```
This is line number 1
This is line number 2



This is line number 10
```

Fig. 5.4. *The output of the* PrtSc *demonstration program as it appears on the printer.*

```
This is line number 1
This is line number 2


This is line number 10
This should not print on the printer
```

Fig. 5.5. *The output of the* PrtSc *demonstration program as it appears on the screen.*

Subprogram Listing of PrtSc.PSL

```
procedure PrtSc;

type
   RegList = record
      AX, BX, CX, DX, BP, SI, DI, DS, ES, Flags: integer
   end;

var
   Reg: RegList;

begin
   intr($5, Reg)
end;
```

Variables

None

Discussion

You can use this subprogram to create images of a graphics screen while your program is in one of Turbo's graphics modes. To create such images, you need the proper hardware and software. You must be running DOS V2.0 or higher. From DOS, you must execute the program GRAPHICS.COM before you enter Turbo. GRAPHICS.COM is supplied by IBM with DOS V2.0 and higher. This program enables the normal Shift-PrtSc key sequence to work with graphics screens. In addition, your printer must be capable of a graphics mode. The IBM 80 CPS Graphics Printer and compatibles (including most EPSON printers) have this capability.

PrtSc works by generating the system's Shift-PrtSc function through a ROM BIOS call. In Turbo, the intr procedure invoking interrupt 5 performs this task.

Modifications

None

6

Manipulating Disk Files

Disk configuration is a critical element in any computer system. Data cannot remain in RAM (random-access memory) forever, and most people who use a computer for any practical purpose find that they give their disk drive(s) a heavy workout. This chapter presents a dozen subprograms to help you make good use of your disks.

First, a word about the *filespec* is necessary. A filespec (file specification) is a semi-official term that sometimes refers to a disk drive and file name and at other times includes the directory path to get to the file. As the term is used here, a filespec consists of four elements (of which three are optional) in the form D:\PATH\FILENAME.EXT. The D: specifies the disk drive, which is either A: or B: for floppy disks, or generally C: for a fixed disk. The \PATH\ is the subdirectory route through which DOS finds the file. If you never use subdirectories, you can omit the path and the surrounding backslashes. The FILENAME and .EXT make up the actual name of the disk file, following the rules in the DOS manual. Only the FILENAME portion of a filespec is required; D: and \PATH\ are needed only if the current default disk drive and path do not lead to your file, and .EXT is needed only if your file was named with an extension. Most of the programs in this chapter use a filespec in one form or another.

The subprogram DiskSp deals with an entire disk (not just one file) and reveals how much space is available on that disk. VerDisk is also global rather than file oriented; it sets the DOS disk verify switch on or off.

ShowDir and NextFile work with a disk directory. ShowDir displays a directory's contents, and NextFile finds in the directory the next file name subject to your specifications. FileInfo and FileDel deal with a single disk file. FileInfo obtains information about a disk file (size, date and time updated, and attributes). FileDel provides a simple way to delete a file.

The remaining six subprograms save and load disk files from and to three types of arrays: (1) one-dimensional real or integer (SaveArr and LoadArr), (2) two-dimensional real (Save2Arr and Load2Arr), and (3) text or string (SaveTxt and LoadTxt).

DiskSp

> **Name:** *DiskSp*
>
> **Type:** *Procedure*
>
> **Purpose:** *To determine how much disk space is available*
>
> **Calling Sequence:** DiskSp(DiskNum, BytesFree, BytesCluster, BytesCap)

Description

DiskSp uses a DOS function call to determine the number of bytes of free space available on the disk in the drive you specify, as well as the size of a cluster in bytes and the capacity of the disk in bytes. These values are useful indicators of the current status of a disk and are quite handy in many types of programs that store and track disk data.

Input

DriveNum	integer	The drive number of the disk you are inquiring about. Zero indicates the default disk drive, 1 indicates drive A, 2 indicates drive B, and so on.

Output

BytesFree	real	The number of bytes free (unused) on the disk
BytesCluster	real	The number of bytes in a cluster (allocation unit) on the disk
BytesCap	real	The capacity of the disk in bytes (that is, the number of clusters times the size of each cluster)

Limitations and Error Conditions

DriveNum must indicate a legal disk drive on your computer. Otherwise, all three output values are set to -1 to indicate an error. Legal values for DriveNum are theoretically 0 through 255. On a computer with two floppy disk drives, legal values are 0, 1, and 2. However, because only the low-order byte of DriveNum indicates the disk drive number, any value is acceptable if its low-order byte is a legal number. For example, 257 and 513 are the same as 1, and 258 and 514 are the same as 2.

Sample Usage

```
program SampleUsageOfDiskSp;

var
   DriveNum: integer;
   BytesFree, BytesCluster, BytesCap: real;

{$I DiskSp.PSL}

BEGIN
   DriveNum := 0;
   DiskSp(DriveNum, BytesFree, BytesCluster, BytesCap);
   if BytesCap > 0.0 then
      begin
         writeln('For disk drive number ', DriveNum);
         writeln(BytesFree:9:0,    ' bytes free space');
         writeln(BytesCluster:9:0, ' bytes per cluster');
         writeln(BytesCap:9:0,     ' bytes disk capacity')
      end
   else
      writeln('** Error - illegal DiskSp request **')
END.
```

With our original Turbo Pascal compiler disk (Version 3.01A) in the default disk drive, this sample program produces the following output (your Turbo disk may be different, perhaps because of changes in the READ.ME file):

```
For disk drive number 0
158720 bytes free space
  1024 bytes per cluster
362496 bytes disk capacity
```

Subprogram Listing of DiskSp.PSL

```
procedure DiskSp(DriveNum: integer; var BytesFree, BytesCluster,
              BytesCap : real);

type
   RegList = record
      AX, BX, CX, DX, BP, SI, DI, DS, ES, Flags: integer
   end;

var
   Reg: RegList;

begin
   Reg.DX := DriveNum;
   Reg.AX := $3600;
   msdos(Reg);
   if Reg.AX = $FFFF then
      begin
         BytesFree    := -1.0;
         BytesCluster := -1.0;
         BytesCap     := -1.0
      end
   else
      begin
         BytesCluster := 1.0 * Reg.AX * Reg.CX;
         BytesFree    := BytesCluster * Reg.BX;
         BytesCap     := BytesCluster * Reg.DX
      end
end;
```

Variables

Reg   A record containing the standard IBM PC register names.
                             Reg is used to pass values to and from Turbo's msdos
                             procedure.

Discussion

This subprogram uses DOS function call 36 (hex) to retrieve information. The
cluster is the fundamental allocation unit of DOS. If the cluster size is 1,024 bytes
(as it is for double-sided floppy disks), then the smallest space a file uses is 1,024

bytes, even if the file is only 50 bytes long. To determine the number of bytes of free space, DiskSp multiplies the number of clusters available by the cluster size. Note that a disk actually has more free space than this calculation indicates, because each file generally has some free space available in its last cluster. This "phantom" free space, however, is available only if you expand the file a little (without going beyond that last cluster boundary) or if you combine several small files into one large file, thus trading several partially empty clusters for one.

Modifications

None

VerDisk

Name:	*VerDisk*
Type:	*Procedure*
Purpose:	*To turn the DOS disk verification switch on or off*
Calling Sequence:	VerDisk(Verify)

Description

This subprogram turns the DOS "verify" switch on or off, depending on whether the Verify parameter is true or false. The same actions can be done with the DOS VERIFY command, but VerDisk provides a method of setting this switch from a Pascal program. The verify switch is off by default. Turning the switch on causes DOS to perform a verify operation after each disk write, thus checking that the written data is correctly recorded.

Input

Verify   boolean   Setting for the verify switch. A true value causes the switch to be set on. A false value causes the switch to be set off.

Output

Disk verification is activated or deactivated as requested. No variables are changed.

Limitations and Error Conditions

In the disk-verify operation, DOS does not actually reread the data just written on disk and compare that data with the data in memory. Instead, the verify operation looks for a mismatch of the cyclic redundancy checks (CRC), which do not match if data was incorrectly recorded. Although such errors occur rarely (and the verification process lengthens disk writing time), some people like to be cautious with certain critical data. Turning the verify switch on is one way to be cautious. Once set on, disk verification remains on until it is turned off by either the DOS VERIFY command or a program that invokes the same DOS call used by VerDisk.

Sample Usage

```
program SampleUsageOfVerDisk;

var
   Verify: boolean;

{$I VerDisk.PSL}

BEGIN
   Verify := true;
   VerDisk(Verify);
   if Verify then
      writeln('Disk verify is now on')
   else
      writeln('Disk verify is now off')
END.
```

This program turns disk verification on (even if it is already on) and displays the following message:

```
Disk verify is now on
```

Subprogram Listing of VerDisk.PSL

```
procedure VerDisk(Verify: boolean);

type
   RegList = record
      AX, BX, CX, DX, BP, SI, DI, DS, ES, Flags: integer
   end;
```

```
var
   Reg: RegList;

begin
   Reg.DX := $0000;
   if Verify then
      Reg.AX := $2E01
   else
      Reg.AX := $2E00;
   msdos(Reg)
end;
```

Variables

Reg   A record containing the standard IBM PC register names.
                             Reg is used to pass values to Turbo's msdos procedure.

Discussion

See both the Description section and the Limitations and Error Conditions section.

Modifications

None

ShowDir

> **Name:** *ShowDir*
>
> **Type:** *Procedure*
>
> **Purpose:** *To display a directory or subdirectory on the screen*
>
> **Calling Sequence:** ShowDir(FileSpec, Attr)

Description

Depending on the file specification and attribute characteristics, the entries (file names) in an MS-DOS® (or PC DOS) disk directory or subdirectory are displayed on the screen, five entries per line. You can specify the default disk drive and directory, or another drive and subdirectory of your choice. You can specify all files, including system and hidden files, or only normal file entries. The global characters * and ? are allowed in the file name and extension portion of the filespec. DOS V2.0 or higher is required.

Input

FileSpec   string   A standard DOS filespec in the form
                          D:\PATH\FILENAME.EXT, indicating the files you want
                          displayed. The current directory is assumed if the
                          disk drive (D:) and path are omitted. Global
                          characters (? and *) may be used in the file name
                          and extension. The path portion of FileSpec cannot
                          exceed 63 characters, and the total length of
                          FileSpec cannot exceed 79 characters.

Attr   byte   A byte with bits set to indicate the attributes of the
                          files you want displayed, as explained in two places
                          in the IBM DOS V2.0 manual (other versions of DOS
                          may have the explanations elsewhere): (1) Appendix
                          C, where the "file attribute" is explained in the DOS
                          Disk Directory section, and (2) Appendix D, in the
                          discussion of DOS function call 11 hex. Zero
                          indicates only "normal" files (no hidden or system
                          files and no subdirectories). Hex 10 adds
                          subdirectories. Hex 16 shows normal, hidden, and
                          system files, plus subdirectories. Hex 10 is usually
                          what you will want.

In addition, you must code in your main program the following global type declaration:

```
type
   String80 = string[80];
```

Output

The entries in the specified directory or subdirectory are displayed on the screen in five columns. Subdirectory names, if requested by Attr, are indicated with [D] before the name.

Limitations and Error Conditions

The starting message ** Directory listing for [FileSpec] ** is always displayed. If the specified directory or subdirectory is empty or does not exist, or if no files match the FileSpec and Attr requirements, then the message ** No filenames found. ** is displayed, and the subprogram terminates. Otherwise, the terminating message is ** End of directory listing. **. DOS V2.0 or higher is required for this subprogram.

Sample Usage

```
program SampleUsageOfShowDir;

type
   String80 = string[80];

var
   FileSpec : String80;
   Attr     : byte;

{$I ShowDir.PSL}

BEGIN
   FileSpec := '*.*';
   Attr     := $10;
   ShowDir(FileSpec, Attr);
   writeln('- - - - -');
   FileSpec := 'B:\MONTHLY.DAT\*.*';
   ShowDir(FileSpec, Attr)
END.
```

If a test disk is in the default disk drive (B:) and the root directory is set as the current directory, the Sample Usage program first displays the root directory, then a subdirectory. A line of five hyphens is displayed between the two directory listings.

```
** Directory listing for *.*
INDEX.DAT        [D]MONTHLY.DAT  MONTH.PAS     ZPGM          Z
Z2               ZSUBPGMS.PAS    ZSUBPGMS.DAT  RECAP.DAT
** End of directory listing. **
- - - - -
** Directory listing for B:\MONTHLY.DAT\*.*
[D].             [D]..           JAN.DAT       FEB.DAT
** End of directory listing. **
```

Subprogram Listing of ShowDir.PSL

```
procedure ShowDir(FileSpec: String80; Attr: byte);

type
   RegList = record
      AX, BX, CX, DX, BP, SI, DI, DS, ES, Flags: integer
   end;

const
   Columns = 5;                                      {Mod. #1}

var
   J, ColSize : integer;
   Reg        : RegList;
   DTA        : array[1..43] of byte;

begin
   ColSize := 80 div Columns;                        {Mod. #2}
   Reg.DX := ofs(DTA);
   Reg.DS := seg(DTA);
   Reg.AX := $1A00;
   msdos(Reg);
   writeln('** Directory listing for ', FileSpec);
   FileSpec := FileSpec + chr(0);
   Reg.DX := ofs(FileSpec[1]);
   Reg.DS := seg(FileSpec[1]);
   Reg.CX := Attr;
   Reg.AX := $4E00;
   msdos(Reg);
   if lo(Reg.AX) <> 0 then
      begin
         writeln('** No filenames found. **');
         exit
      end;
   if DTA[22] and $10 <> 0 then write('[D]');
   J := 31;
   while DTA[J] <> 0 do
      begin
         write(chr(DTA[J]));
         J := J + 1
      end;
```

```
   repeat
      Reg.DX := ofs(DTA);
      Reg.DS := seg(DTA);
      Reg.AX := $4F00;
      msdos(Reg);
      if lo(Reg.AX) = 0 then
         begin
            if wherex > (Columns - 1) * ColSize + 1 then writeln;
            while (wherex mod ColSize) <> 1 do write(' ');
            if DTA[22] and $10 <> 0 then write(' [D]' );
            J := 31;
            while DTA[J] <> 0 do
               begin
                  write(chr(DTA[J]));
                  J := J + 1
               end
         end
   until lo(Reg.AX) <> 0;
   writeln;
   writeln(' ** End of directory listing. **' )
end;
```

Variables

Columns	Constant 5. This is the number of columns on the screen.
J	Subscript used to extract file name from DTA
ColSize	Size (width) of screen columns. With 5 columns, ColSize is 16.
Reg	Record of registers for use in calling the msdos procedure
DTA	Disk transfer area, as required by DOS function calls

Discussion

If you write a program that requires a user to enter a file name, you usually want the files in a directory to be displayed first. If your program processes an input file, the user needs to see the existing file names in order to choose the correct one. If your program creates an output file, the user needs to see the existing file names to be able to choose a new, nonduplicate name. This subprogram displays a directory by making use of several PC DOS function calls. First, the subprogram uses call hex 1A, telling DOS where the disk transfer area is. Then the subprogram turns the FileSpec string into an ASCIIZ string (a special kind of string required by some DOS function calls) by adding a zero byte at the end.

Function call 4E (hex) finds the first entry that matches the ASCIIZ string. If no match is found (indicated by a nonzero return code in the low-order byte of the AX register), a message is displayed, and the subprogram ends. If a match is found, the file name is returned by DOS, beginning in the 31st byte of the DTA. Then function call hex 4F is used to find all the remaining entries that match the request. Each matching file name is displayed in turn, five names per line, until no more names can be found.

Function calls 4E and 4F are available only in DOS V2.0 and higher. Earlier versions of DOS require the use of function calls hex 11 and 12 instead.

Modifications

1. The number of columns displayed on the screen can range from 1 to 5. Simply change the number in the line denoted by {Mod. #1}.

2. This subprogram assumes that you are using an 80-column display. To convert the subprogram to a 40-column display, change 80 to 40 in the line indicated by {Mod. #2}. You also need to use the first modification to indicate either one or two columns, unless you can be sure that all file names on your disks are short. (That is, no file names have more than nine characters for three columns, six characters for four columns, and four characters for five columns. These limitations are based on the assumption that directory entries may be specified. Otherwise, add three to the lengths.)

NextFile

> **Name:** *NextFile*
>
> **Type:** *Procedure*
>
> **Purpose:** *To find the name of the next file in a disk directory*
>
> **Calling Sequence:** NextFile(FileSpec, Attr, Code, Name)

Description

Depending on the FileSpec and Attr (attribute) you specify, the next matching file name in an MS-DOS (or PC DOS) disk directory or subdirectory is returned in Name. You can specify the default disk drive and directory, or the drive and subdirectory of your choice. You can use the global characters ? and *, as in DOS commands. DOS V2.0 or higher is required. NextFile is useful for scanning a disk directory to find files with certain names or characteristics.

Input

FileSpec	string	A standard DOS filespec in the form D:\PATH\FILENAME.EXT, indicating the files you want found. The disk drive (D:) and path are optional. The file name may contain ? and/or *. The total length of FileSpec cannot exceed 79 characters, and the path cannot exceed 63 characters. Details about paths and file names are in the DOS manual.
Attr	byte	A byte with bits set to indicate the attributes of the files you want found. For details, see the Input section of ShowDir. Zero indicates "normal" files only. Hex 10 includes subdirectories too. Hex 16 includes also hidden and system files.
Code	integer	A numeric value that indicates the action you want taken. Zero indicates that this is the first request (that is, find the first file). One indicates a subsequent request (find the next file).

In addition, you must code in your main program the following global type declarations:

```
type
   String80 = string[80];
   String15 = string[15];
```

Output

Code	integer	Code is set to 1 if a file name was found to match your request, or 2 otherwise.
Name	string	A 15-character (maximum) string with the name of the file found. This string includes a period between the 8-character name and the 3-character extension, if any. If the name is a directory entry, Name has [D] in the first 3 positions, followed by the directory name.

Limitations and Error Conditions

Code is set to 2 when no matching file name can be found, whether on the first request or subsequent requests. This subprogram sets up a DTA (data transfer area) into which DOS places the file name data. Your program cannot take any action, such as opening a file, between calls to NextFile if the action might change the DTA. If your main program affects the DTA between uses of NextFile (for example, by opening and reading from each file as you find matching names), use NextFile to save in an array all the matching file names. Then retrieve each file name from the array before opening the file. For an example of saving file names in an array, see the full program SortDir in Chapter 18.

Sample Usage

```
program SampleUsageOfNextFile;

type
   String80 = string[80];
   String15 = string[15];

var
   FileSpec : String80;
   Name     : String15;
   Attr     : byte;
   Code     : integer;

{$I NextFile.PSL}

BEGIN
   FileSpec := '*.*';
   Attr     := $10;
   Code     := 0;
   repeat
      NextFile(FileSpec, Attr, Code, Name);
      if Code = 1 then
         write(Name:16)
   until Code <> 1;
   writeln
END.
```

With a test disk in disk drive B (the default drive at the time), this sample program displays the following output:

```
INDEX.DAT  [D]MONTHLY.DAT      MONTH.PAS          ZPGM
```

Subprogram Listing of NextFile.PSL

```
procedure NextFile(FileSpec: String80; Attr: byte;
                  var Code: integer; var Name: String15);

type
   RegList = record
      AX, BX, CX, DX, BP, SI, DI, DS, ES, Flags: integer
   end;

var
   J   : integer;
   Reg : RegList;
   DTA : array[1..43] of byte;

begin
   if (Code < 0) or (Code > 1) then
      begin
         Code := -1;
         exit
      end;
   if Code = 0 then
      begin
         Reg.DX := ofs(DTA);
         Reg.DS := seg(DTA);
         Reg.AX := $1A00;
         msdos(Reg);
         FileSpec := FileSpec + chr(0);
         Reg.DX := ofs(FileSpec[1]);
         Reg.DS := seg(FileSpec[1]);
         Reg.CX := Attr;
         Reg.AX := $4E00;
         msdos(Reg);
         if lo(Reg.AX) <> 0 then
```

```
          begin
            Name := '';
            Code := 2;
            exit
          end;
      if DTA[22] and $10 <> 0 then
        Name := '[D]'                                {Mod. #1}
      else
        Name := '';
      J := 31;
      while DTA[J] <> 0 do
        begin
          Name := Name + chr(DTA[J]);
          J := J + 1
        end;
      Code := 1
    end
  else
    begin
      Reg.DX := ofs(DTA);
      Reg.DS := seg(DTA);
      Reg.AX := $4F00;
      msdos(Reg);
      if lo(Reg.AX) = 0 then
        begin
          if DTA[22] and $10 <> 0 then
            Name := '[D]'                            {Mod. #1}
          else
            Name := '';
          J := 31;
          while DTA[J] <> 0 do
            begin
              Name := Name + chr(DTA[J]);
              J := J + 1
            end;
          Code := 1
        end
      else
        begin
          Name := '';
          Code := 2
        end
    end
  end
end;
```

Variables

J	Subscript used to extract the file name from DTA
Reg	Record of registers for use in calling the msdos procedure
DTA	Disk transfer area, as required by DOS function calls

Discussion

NextFile uses the same DOS function calls that ShowDir uses. See the Discussion section of ShowDir for details.

Modification

NextFile indicates a directory entry with [D] in the first three characters of Name. Change [D] in the two indicated lines to any other string of one to three characters, or to null (two apostrophes with no space between) in order to eliminate any differentiation between directories and file names.

FileInfo

> **Name:** *FileInfo*
>
> **Type:** *Procedure*
>
> **Purpose:** *To obtain information about a specified disk file*
>
> **Calling Sequence:** FileInfo(FileSpec, FileBytes, Yr, Mon, Day, Hr, Min, Sec, AttrList)

Description

The FileInfo subprogram returns certain information about a disk file: the size of the file (in bytes), the date and time the file was last updated, and the attributes of the file. All this data is obtained from the disk directory through a DOS function call.

Input

FileSpec	string	A DOS file specification in the standard form D:\PATH\FILENAME.EXT. If the disk drive or path is omitted, the current default disk or current directory is used. The global characters * and ? can be used in

the file name, but they are not generally useful because the subprogram does not return the file name found. The intent of the subprogram is to obtain the information about a specific file.

In addition, you must specify in your main program the following global type declarations:

```
type
   String80 = string[80];
   String5  = string[5];
```

Output

FileBytes	real	The number of bytes in the disk file. This value is -1.0 if no file is found to match the FileSpec.
Yr	byte	The year the file was last updated (0–99)
Mon	byte	The month the file was last updated (1–12)
Day	byte	The day the file was last updated (0–31)
Hr	byte	The hour the file was last updated (0–23)
Min	byte	The minute the file was last updated (0–59)
Sec	byte	The second the file was last updated (0–58). Sec is always an even number.
AttrList	string	A five-byte string containing a character for each attribute the file may have. For ease of use, each attribute always occupies the same position in the string (in alphabetical sequence). In other words, A, if present, is always in the first position; D, if present, is always second, etc. Here are the meanings of the attributes:

A	The file's archive bit is set.
D	The file is a subdirectory.
H	This is a hidden file.
R	The file is read-only.
S	This is a system file.

Limitations and Error Conditions

If no match for `FileSpec` is found on disk, then `FileBytes` is set to -1.0, and the subprogram returns control to your main program; the other output values are invalid. The year of last update (`Yr`) is set to 80 through 99 for the years 1980 through 1999, and 0 through 99 for the years 2000 through 2099. (That's right, when the year 2080 comes, `FileInfo` will return the year 80 for a file, and you won't know whether that means 1980 or 2080. Feel free to write us a letter of complaint at that time.) In the time-of-day value, the number of seconds is saved by DOS as the number of 2-second intervals. Thus, the `Sec` value returned by `FileInfo` can be an even number only. `FileSpec` must be no more than 79 bytes long; the path portion cannot exceed 63 bytes.

Sample Usage

```
program SampleUsageOfFileInfo;

type
   String80 = string[80];
   String5  = string[5];

var
   FileSpec                   : String80;
   FileBytes                  : real;
   Yr, Mon, Day, Hr, Min, Sec : byte;
   AttrList                   : String5;

{$I FileInfo.PSL}

BEGIN
   repeat
     writeln('Enter FileSpec  (or [Enter] to end)');
     readln(FileSpec);
     if length(FileSpec) = 0 then exit;
     FileInfo(FileSpec, FileBytes, Yr, Mon, Day, Hr, Min, Sec,
              AttrList);
     if FileBytes < 0.0 then
       writeln(FileSpec, ' not found')
     else
```

```
        begin
           writeln('For FileSpec ', FileSpec);
           writeln(FileBytes:8:0, ' bytes file size');
           writeln(Yr, '-', Mon, '-', Day, ' last update date');
           writeln(Hr, ':', Min, ':', Sec, ' last update time');
           writeln('Attributes = ', AttrList)
        end;
     writeln('- - - - -')
  until length(FileSpec) = 0
END.
```

This sample program is handy to have available when you are running Turbo Pascal. The program provides a way to check the date and time you last updated the files you are working with. For the sample output that follows, the Turbo compiler disk (3.01A) is in disk drive A. The system files for PC DOS V2.0 are also on the disk. If you are using different versions of Turbo or PC DOS, your output will be somewhat different. In addition, if you have run the TINST utility on your Turbo disk, the date and time of that update will be reflected. Note the result of running FileInfo on the file IBMBIO.COM (which you normally don't see in a directory listing). The attributes show IBMBIO.COM to be a hidden, read-only, system file. In the sample output shown, the Enter key was pressed to end the program after the two file names TURBO.COM and IBMBIO.COM were processed.

```
Enter FileSpec  (or [Enter] to end)
A:TURBO.COM
For FileSpec A:TURBO.COM
   39671 bytes file size
85-4-17 last update date
20:14:36 last update time
Attributes = A
- - - - -
Enter FileSpec  (or [Enter] to end)
A:IBMBIO.COM
For FileSpec A:IBMBIO.COM
   4608 bytes file size
83-3-8 last update date
12:0:0 last update time
Attributes = A HRS
- - - - -
Enter FileSpec  (or [Enter] to end)
```

Subprogram Listing of FileInfo.PSL

```
procedure FileInfo(FileSpec: String80; var FileBytes: real;
                   var Yr, Mon, Day, Hr, Min, Sec: byte;
                   var AttrList: String5);

type
   RegList = record
      AX, BX, CX, DX, BP, SI, DI, DS, ES, Flags: integer
   end;
   FileData = record
      Reserved : array[1..21] of byte;
      Attr     : byte;
      Time, Date, SizeLo, SizeHi: integer
   end;

var
   Reg : RegList;
   DTA : array[1..43] of byte;
   FD  : FileData absolute DTA;

begin
   Reg.DX := ofs(DTA);
   Reg.DS := seg(DTA);
   Reg.AX := $1A00;
   msdos(Reg);
   FileSpec := FileSpec + chr(0);
   Reg.DX := ofs(FileSpec[1]);
   Reg.DS := seg(FileSpec[1]);
   Reg.CX := $16;
   Reg.AX := $4E00;
   msdos(Reg);
   if lo(Reg.AX) <> 0 then
      begin
         FileBytes := -1.0;
         exit
      end;
   FileBytes := lo(FD.SizeLo) + 256.0 * hi(FD.SizeLo) +
                65536.0   * lo(FD.SizeHi) +
                16777216.0 * hi(FD.SizeHi);
```

```
 Yr  := (hi(FD.Date) shr 1) + 80;
 if Yr > 99 then Yr := Yr - 100;
 Mon := lo(FD.Date) shr 5 + (hi(FD.Date) and $01 shl 3);
 Day := lo(FD.Date) and $1F;
 Hr  := hi(FD.Time) shr 3;
 Min := lo(FD.Time) shr 5 + (hi(FD.Time) and $07 shl 3);
 Sec := (lo(FD.Time) and $1F) shl 1;
 AttrList := '     ';              {5 blank spaces}
 if FD.Attr and $20 = $20 then AttrList[1] := 'A';
 if FD.Attr and $10 = $10 then AttrList[2] := 'D';
 if FD.Attr and $02 = $02 then AttrList[3] := 'H';
 if FD.Attr and $01 = $01 then AttrList[4] := 'R';
 if FD.Attr and $04 = $04 then AttrList[5] := 'S'
end;
```

Variables

Reg	A record containing the standard IBM PC register names. Reg is used to pass values to and from Turbo's msdos procedure.
DTA	An array for the DOS data transfer area, in which DOS places the file information on request
FD	A record that redefines the DTA, simplifying the processing of the file's size, date, time, and attributes

Discussion

To set up a data transfer area, FileInfo invokes DOS function call 1A (hex). The DTA is then used by call 4E (hex) to retrieve the directory data for the specified file name. Parts of this directory data are the file's size, date, time, and attribute information you want. Converting this information into numbers that Turbo Pascal can use is a little tricky. The file's size (FileBytes) is presented by DOS as a four-byte integer. The subprogram converts this integer into a real variable because Turbo doesn't support four-byte integers. The date and time of the last update require some strange-looking manipulation because DOS uses only a few bits of each byte to represent each component. Finally, the disk file's attributes are converted from five different bits in a single byte to the more convenient five-byte string AttrList.

Modifications

None

FileDel

> **Name:** *FileDel*
>
> **Type:** *Procedure*
>
> **Purpose:** *To delete a disk file*
>
> **Calling Sequence:** `FileDel(FileSpec, Code)`

Description

`FileDel` uses a DOS function call to delete the file indicated by `FileSpec`. If the deletion is successful, `Code` is set to zero. Turbo's `erase` procedure is another way to delete a file, but `FileDel` is easier to use.

Input

`FileSpec`   `string`   A DOS file specification in the standard form `D:\PATH\FILENAME.EXT`. If the disk drive or path is omitted, the current default disk or current directory is used. The global characters `*` and `?` cannot be used.

In addition, the following global `type` specification is required in your main program:

```
type
    String80 = string[80];
```

Output

`Code`   `integer`   A return code from the subprogram. Zero indicates that the specified file has been deleted. Other codes signify that no file has been deleted. If `Code` is 2, there is no such named file to delete. If `Code` is 5, the specified file cannot be deleted because access is denied. (That is, the file attribute indicates that the file is read-only.)

Limitations and Error Conditions

The FileSpec string cannot exceed 79 characters, of which the path portion can be no more than 63 characters. The global characters * and ? cannot be used in the file name because of a restriction imposed by the DOS function call this subprogram invokes.

Sample Usage

```
program SampleUsageOfFileDel;

type
   String80 = string[80];

var
   FileSpec : String80;
   Code     : integer;

{$I FileDel.PSL}

BEGIN
   FileSpec := 'A:TESTFILE.DEL';
   FileDel(FileSpec, Code);
   if Code = 0 then
      writeln('File ', FileSpec, ' deleted')
   else
      writeln(FileSpec, ' not deleted. Code = ', Code)
END.
```

This test program produces the first of the following two messages if a file named TESTFILE.DEL is found and deleted from the current directory of the disk in drive A, and the second message if there is no such file to delete:

```
File A:TESTFILE.DEL deleted
A:TESTFILE.DEL not deleted. Code = 2
```

Subprogram Listing of FileDel.PSL

```
procedure FileDel(FileSpec: String80; var Code: integer);

type
   RegList = record
      AX, BX, CX, DX, BP, SI, DI, DS, ES, Flags: integer
   end;

var
   Reg: RegList;

begin
   FileSpec := FileSpec + chr(0);
   Reg.DX    := ofs(FileSpec[1]);
   Reg.DS    := seg(FileSpec[1]);
   Reg.AX    := $4100;
   msdos(Reg);
   Code := lo(Reg.AX);
   if (Reg.Flags and $01) = 0 then
      Code := 0
end;
```

Variables

Reg   A record containing the standard IBM PC register names.
                            Reg is used to pass values to and from Turbo's msdos
                            procedure.

Discussion

FileDel makes use of DOS function call 41 (hex) to delete the specified file. There's
nothing tricky here. The subprogram simply sets up the FileSpec as an ASCIIZ
string (by adding a hex zero at the end of the string), sets up the registers as
required by DOS, and calls Turbo's msdos procedure. Then Code is set to the code
returned by DOS.

Modifications

None

SaveArr

> **Name:** *SaveArr*
>
> **Type:** *Procedure*
>
> **Purpose:** *To save an array's contents onto a disk file*
>
> **Calling Sequence:** SaveArr(NumArray, Count, Code)

Description

SaveArr prompts you for a filespec, creates a disk file with that name, and then saves onto that disk file the contents of the real array NumArray. The companion subprogram LoadArr can later load the data back into an array.

Input

NumArray   real   Array in which the data to be saved is stored

Count   integer   Number of elements occupied in the array

In addition, you must specify in your main program the following global const and type declarations. The number 250 is an example.

```
const
   ArraySize = 250;

type
   ArrayType = array[1..ArraySize] of real;
```

Output

Code   integer   Error code from DOS. If Code is zero, the file was
                         successfully saved on disk. Positive values are the
                         decimal equivalents of the I/O error codes in
                         Appendix G of the Turbo manual. Negative one (-1)
                         indicates that the user canceled the request to save
                         the array on disk.

SaveArr creates an output disk file, using the filespec you enter at the keyboard while running the subprogram. After successfully saving the file, SaveArr displays a message showing how many elements were written to the file.

Limitations and Error Conditions

If Count is less than 1, the subprogram is bypassed. If you enter a null filespec, Code is set to -1, and the rest of the subprogram is bypassed. If a file already exists with the same name you provide, the old file is replaced by the new file. If the file cannot be saved on disk, the subprogram beeps and displays Code with a message saying which I/O statement encountered the error (rewrite, write, or close). Code is the decimal equivalent of the hex I/O error number in Appendix G of the Turbo manual. For example, decimal 240 is hex F0, which indicates that the data area of the disk is full. (In other words, your files are too big.) Decimal 241 (hex F1) means that the directory is full. (That is, you have too many file names in the root directory, or the subdirectory does not exist.)

Sample Usage

```
program SampleUsageOfSaveArr;

const
   ArraySize = 250;

type
   ArrayType = array[1..ArraySize] of real;              {Mod. #1}

var
   NumArray    : ArrayType;
   Count, Code : integer;

{$I SaveArr.PSL}

BEGIN
   for Count := 1 to 5 do
      NumArray[Count] := sqrt(Count);
   Count := 5;
   SaveArr(NumArray, Count, Code);
   if Code <> 0 then
      writeln('Unsuccessful file save.')
END.
```

This sample program produces the following output on the screen if you provide **B:ARRAYTST.DAT** as the filespec:

```
** Enter filespec for output file, or **
** press [Enter] key to cancel.        **
B:ARRAYTST.DAT
** 5 elements written to file B:ARRAYTST.DAT
```

If the directory being used is full before you run the sample program, the output looks like this instead:

```
** Enter filespec for output file, or **
** press [Enter] key to cancel.        **
B:ARRAYTST.DAT
** I/O error number 241(decimal) **
** from rewrite in SaveArr.  Aborted.  **
Unsuccessful file save.
```

Subprogram Listing of SaveArr.PSL

```pascal
procedure SaveArr(var NumArray: ArrayType;
                  var Count, Code: integer);

var
   J         : integer;
   FileSpec  : string[80];
   TheFile   : file of real;                          {Mod. #1}

begin
   if Count < 1 then exit;
   writeln('** Enter filespec for output file, or **');
   writeln('** press [Enter] key to cancel.        **');
   readln(FileSpec);
   if length(FileSpec) = 0 then
      begin
         Code := -1;
         exit
      end;
   assign(TheFile, FileSpec);
   {$I-}
   rewrite(TheFile);
   Code := ioresult;
   if Code <> 0 then begin
      writeln(chr(7));
      writeln('** I/O error number ', Code, '(decimal) **');
```

```
         writeln('** from rewrite in SaveArr.  Aborted.    **');
         exit
         end;
 for J := 1 to Count do begin
       write(TheFile, NumArray[J]);
       Code := ioresult;
       if Code <> 0 then begin
          writeln(chr(7));
          writeln('** I/O error number ', Code, '(decimal) **');
          writeln('** from write in SaveArr.  Aborted.     **');
          exit
          end
       end;
    close(TheFile);
    Code := ioresult;
    if Code <> 0 then begin
       writeln(chr(7));
       writeln('** I/O error number ', Code, '(decimal) **');
       writeln('** from close in SaveArr.  Aborted.    **');
       exit
       end;
    {$I+}
    writeln('** ', Count, ' elements written to file ', FileSpec)
end;
```

Variables

J	Subscript variable
FileSpec	Standard file specification for the output disk file
TheFile	Internal file name in the subprogram

Discussion

Use this subprogram with LoadArr to transfer data between arrays in memory and disk files. If you have two-dimensional arrays, use Save2Arr and Load2Arr. To display the file names on disk before asking for the output file name, use the ShowDir subprogram in your main program just before invoking SaveArr.

Modification

To convert this subprogram for use with integer arrays, change real to integer in the indicated statements in both the subprogram and the sample program.

Save2Arr

> **Name:** *Save2Arr*
>
> **Type:** *Procedure*
>
> **Purpose:** *To save a two-dimensional array's contents onto a disk file*
>
> **Calling Sequence:** Save2Arr(Num2Array, RowCount, Code)

Description

SaveArr2 prompts you for a filespec, creates a disk file with that name, and then saves onto that disk file the contents of the two-dimensional real array. The companion subprogram Load2Arr can later load the data back into an array.

Input

Num2Array   real   Array in which data is stored

RowCount   integer   Number of rows of elements occupied in array

In addition, you must specify in your main program the following global const and type declarations. ColSize is the exact number of columns (the second dimension) and is required. RowSize is the maximum number of rows (first dimension) and is not required as a constant. RowSize is recommended, however, as the way to specify the type declaration. The numbers 2 and 100 are examples.

```
const
   ColSize = 2;
   RowSize = 100;

type
   Array2Type = array[1..RowSize, 1..ColSize] of real;
```

Output

Code   integer   Error code from DOS. If Code is zero, the file was successfully saved on disk. Positive values are the decimal equivalents of the I/O error codes in Appendix G of the Turbo manual. Negative one (-1) indicates that the user canceled the request to save the array on disk.

Save2Arr creates an output disk file, using the filespec you enter at the keyboard while running the subprogram. After successfully saving the file, Save2Arr displays a message showing how many rows were written to the file.

Limitations and Error Conditions

If RowCount is less than 1, the subprogram is bypassed. If you enter a null filespec, Code is set to -1, and the rest of the subprogram is bypassed. If a file already exists with the same name you provide, the old file is replaced by the new file. If the file cannot be saved on disk, the subprogram beeps and displays Code with a message saying which I/O statement encountered the error (rewrite, write, or close). Code is the decimal equivalent of the hex I/O error number in Appendix G of the Turbo manual. For example, decimal 240 is hex F0, indicating that the data area of the disk is full. Decimal 241 (hex F1) means that the directory is full.

Sample Usage

```
program SampleUsageOfSave2Arr;

const
   ColSize = 2;
   RowSize = 100;

type
   Array2Type = array[1..RowSize, 1..ColSize] of real;

var
   Num2Array          : Array2Type;
   RowCount, Code, J : integer;

{$I Save2Arr.PSL}

BEGIN
   for RowCount := 1 to 5 do
      for J := 1 to ColSize do
         Num2Array[RowCount, J] := RowCount * J;
   RowCount := 5;
   Save2Arr(Num2Array, RowCount, Code);
   if Code <> 0 then
      writeln('Unsuccessful file save.')
END.
```

This sample program fills Num2Array with values equal to the product of the two subscripts for each element. For example, element [1, 1] is 1 times 1, element [3, 2] is 3 times 2, etc. The program produces the following output on the screen if you provide **B:SAVE2TST.DAT** as a filespec. (See subprogram SaveArr for sample output with an error condition.)

```
** Enter filespec for output file, or **
** press [Enter] key to cancel.        **
B:SAVE2TST.DAT
** 5 sets of 2 element(s) written to file B:SAVE2TST.DAT **
```

Subprogram Listing of Save2Arr.PSL

```pascal
procedure Save2Arr(var Num2Array: Array2Type;
                   var RowCount, Code: integer);

var
   J, K     : integer;
   FileSpec : string[80];
   TheFile  : file of real;

begin
   if RowCount < 1 then exit;
   writeln('** Enter filespec for output file, or **');
   writeln('** press [Enter] key to cancel.        **');
   readln(FileSpec);
   if length(FileSpec) = 0 then
      begin
         Code := -1;
         exit
      end;
   assign(TheFile, FileSpec);
   {$I-}
   rewrite(TheFile);
   Code := ioresult;
   if Code <> 0 then begin
      writeln(chr(7));
      writeln('** I/O error number ', Code, ' (decimal) **');
      writeln('** from rewrite in Save2Arr.  Aborted.  **');
      exit
      end;
```

```
   for J := 1 to RowCount do begin
      for K := 1 to ColSize do begin
         write(TheFile, Num2Array[J,K]);
         Code := ioresult;
         if Code <> 0 then begin
            writeln(chr(7));
            writeln(' ** I/O error number ', Code, ' (dec.) **');
            writeln(' ** from write in Save2Arr.  Aborted. **');
            exit
            end
         end
      end;
   close(TheFile);
   Code := ioresult;
   if Code <> 0 then begin
      writeln(chr(7));
      writeln(' ** I/O error number ', Code, ' (decimal) **');
      writeln(' ** from close in Save2Arr.  Aborted.    **');
      exit
      end;
   {$I+}
   writeln(' ** ', RowCount, ' sets of ', Colsize,
           ' element(s) written to file ', FileSpec, ' **')
end;
```

Variables

J	Subscript variable for rows
K	Subscript variable for columns
FileSpec	File specification for the output disk file
TheFile	Internal file name in the subprogram

Discussion

Use this subprogram with Load2Arr to transfer data between arrays in memory and disk files. To enter the data into the array from the keyboard, use Key2Arr. If you have one-dimensional arrays, use SaveArr and LoadArr. To display the file names on disk before asking for the output filespec, use the ShowDir subprogram in your main program just before invoking Save2Arr.

Modifications

None

SaveTxt

> **Name:** *SaveTxt*
>
> **Type:** *Procedure*
>
> **Purpose:** *To save a* string *array's contents onto a text disk file*
>
> **Calling Sequence:** SaveTxt(TextArray, LineCount, Code)

Description

SaveTxt prompts you for a filespec, creates a disk file with that name, and then saves onto that disk file the contents of the string array. The companion subprogram LoadTxt can later load the data back into an array.

Input

TextArray   string   Array in which data is stored

LineCount   integer   Number of lines occupied in the array

In addition, the following global const and type declarations must be specified in your main program. Actually, TextSize (the maximum number of text lines) and LineSize (the maximum length of each line) are not required by this subprogram but are required by related subprograms, and these declarations are the recommended means of defining TextArrayType. The numbers 250 and 120 are examples.

```
const
   TextSize = 250;

type
   LineSize = string[120];
   TextArrayType = array[1..TextSize] of LineSize;
```

Output

Code   integer   Error code from DOS. If Code is zero, the file was successfully saved on disk. Positive values are the decimal equivalents of the I/O error codes in

Appendix G of the Turbo manual. Negative one (-1) indicates that the user canceled the request to save the array on disk.

SaveTxt creates an output disk file, using the filespec you enter at the keyboard while running the subprogram. After successfully saving the file, the subprogram displays a message showing how many lines were written to the text file.

Limitations and Error Conditions

If LineCount is less than 1, the subprogram is bypassed. If you enter a null filespec, Code is set to -1, and the rest of the subprogram is bypassed. If a file already exists with the same name you provide, the old file is replaced by the new one. If the file cannot be saved on disk, the subprogram beeps and displays Code with a message saying which I/O statement encountered the error (rewrite, write, or close). Code is the decimal equivalent of the hex I/O error number listed in Appendix G of the Turbo manual. For example, decimal 240 is hex F0, indicating that the data area of the disk is full. Decimal 241 (hex F1) means that the directory is full.

Sample Usage

```
program SampleUsageOfSaveTxt;

const
   TextSize = 250;                                          {Mod. #1}

type
   LineSize = string[120];                                  {Mod. #1}
   TextArrayType = array[1..TextSize] of LineSize;

var
   TextArray        : TextArrayType;
   LineCount, Code  : integer;

{$I SaveTxt.PSL}

BEGIN
   TextArray[1] := 'See the quick brown fox';
   TextArray[2] := 'jump over the lazy dog.';
   LineCount := 2;
   SaveTxt(TextArray, LineCount, Code);
   if Code <> 0 then
      writeln('Unsuccessful file save.')
END.
```

This sample program produces the following output on the screen if you provide
B:ARRAYTST.TXT as the filespec.

```
** Enter filespec for text output file, or **
** press [Enter] key to cancel.              **
B:ARRAYTST.TXT
** 2 text lines written to file B:ARRAYTST.TXT
```

Subprogram Listing of SaveTxt.PSL

```
procedure SaveTxt(var TextArray: TextArrayType;
               var LineCount, Code: integer);

var
   J        : integer;
   FileSpec : string[80];
   TextFile : text;

begin
   if LineCount < 1 then exit;
   writeln('** Enter filespec for text output file, or **');
   writeln('** press [Enter] key to cancel.              **');
   readln(FileSpec);
   if length(FileSpec) = 0 then
      begin
         Code := -1;
         exit
      end;
   assign(TextFile, FileSpec);
   {$I-}
   rewrite(TextFile);
   Code := ioresult;
   if Code <> 0 then begin
      writeln(chr(7));
      writeln('** I/O error number ', Code, ' (decimal) **');
      writeln('** from rewrite in SaveTxt.  Aborted.    **');
      exit
   end;
```

```
   for J := 1 to LineCount do begin
      writeln(TextFile, TextArray[J]);
      Code := ioresult;
      if Code <> Ø then begin
         writeln(chr(7));
         writeln('** I/O error number ', Code, '(decimal) **');
         writeln('** from write in SaveTxt.  Aborted.     **');
         exit
         end
      end;
   close(TextFile);
   Code := ioresult;
   if Code <> Ø then begin
      writeln(chr(7));
      writeln('** I/O error number ', Code, '(decimal) **');
      writeln('** from close in SaveTxt.  Aborted.     **');
      exit
      end;
   {$I+}
   writeln(LineCount, ' text lines written to file ', FileSpec)
end;
```

Variables

J	Subscript variable
FileSpec	File specification of the output disk file
TextFile	Internal file name in the subprogram

Discussion

Use this subprogram with LoadTxt to transfer text data between arrays in memory and disk files. Use KeyTxt to enter the data into the array. To display the file names on disk before asking for the output filespec, use the ShowDir subprogram in your main program just before invoking SaveTxt.

Modification

Modify the values of TextSize and LineSize to match the data you are working with. See LoadTxt for details.

LoadArr

> **Name:** *LoadArr*
>
> **Type:** *Procedure*
>
> **Purpose:** *To load an array from data saved in a disk file*
>
> **Calling Sequence:** LoadArr(NumArray, Count, Code)

Description

You are prompted for a filespec, and the contents of the disk file are loaded into a real array. The companion subprogram SaveArr can create the disk file.

Input

Count   integer   Number of elements occupied in the array before loading it. Although normally zero, Count can be set to 50, for example, causing LoadArr to begin loading into the 51st element of the array.

The subprogram prompts you for the input filespec. In addition, you must specify in your main program the following global const and type declarations. The number 250 is an example.

```
const
    ArraySize = 250;

type
    ArrayType = array[1..ArraySize] of real;
```

Output

NumArray   real   Array into which the data is loaded

Count   integer   The updated counter of the number of elements now in the array

Code   integer   Error code from DOS. If Code is zero, the file was successfully loaded from disk. Nonzero values indicate unsuccessful loading, as explained in the Limitations and Error Conditions section.

After successfully loading the file, the subprogram displays a message showing how many elements were loaded into the array.

Limitations and Error Conditions

The subprogram avoids run-time errors by turning off Turbo's I/O error checking through the {$I-} compiler option. If an error occurs, LoadArr displays the error code in decimal and passes it back to the main program, which you can design to abort or retry as you prefer. As in the SaveArr subprogram, the error number (if positive) is the decimal equivalent of the hex I/O error number in Appendix G of the Turbo manual. The most likely errors will occur if you try to load a file that was not created with SaveArr or equivalent logic. Negative error numbers are produced when the user decides to cancel the request by pressing the Enter key instead of entering a filespec (-1), or tries to load a disk file that has more entries than the array can hold (-2).

Sample Usage

```
program SampleUsageOfLoadArr;

const
   ArraySize = 250;

type
   ArrayType = array[1..ArraySize] of real;              {Mod. #1}

var
   NumArray       : ArrayType;
   Count, Code, J : integer;

{$I LoadArr.PSL}

BEGIN
   Count := 0;
   LoadArr(NumArray, Count, Code);
   if Code <> 0 then
      writeln('Unsuccessful file load. Code = ', Code)
   else
      for J := 1 to Count do
         writeln(J:4, NumArray[J]:14:10)
END.
```

This sample program produces the following output on the screen if you provide
B:ARRAYTST.DAT as the filespec and if the file is the same one that was created
by the sample program for SaveArr.

```
** Enter filespec of input file, or **
** press [Enter] key to cancel.      **
B:ARRAYTST.DAT
** 5 elements now in array. **
     1  1.0000000000
     2  1.4142135624
     3  1.7320508076
     4  2.0000000000
     5  2.2360679775
```

Subprogram Listing of LoadArr.PSL

```pascal
procedure LoadArr(var NumArray: ArrayType;
                  var Count, Code: integer);

var
   FileSpec : string[80];
   TheFile  : file of real;                           {Mod. #1}
   TooMany  : boolean;

begin
   repeat                                              {Mod. #2}
      writeln(' ** Enter filespec of input file, or **' );
      writeln(' ** press [Enter] key to cancel.      **' );
      readln(FileSpec);
      if length(FileSpec) = 0 then
         begin
            Code := -1;
            exit
         end;
      assign(TheFile, FileSpec);
      {$I-}
      reset(TheFile);
      Code := ioresult;
      if Code <> 0 then
```

```
            begin
                writeln(chr(7));
                writeln('** No file named ', FileSpec, ' found. **');
                writeln('** Try again. **')
            end
    until Code = 0;
    TooMany := false;
    while not eof(TheFile) do
        begin
            Count := Count + 1;
            if (Count > ArraySize) and (not TooMany) then
                begin
                    TooMany := true;
                    writeln(chr(7));
                    writeln('** File ', FileSpec, ' too big. **');
                    writeln('** Only 1st ', ArraySize, ' loaded. **');
                    Code := -2;
                    Count := Count - 1
                end;
            if not TooMany then
                begin
                    read(TheFile, NumArray[Count]);
                    Code := ioresult;
                    if Code <> 0 then
                        begin
                            writeln('** Error during disk read. **');
                            writeln('** Code = ', Code, '(decimal) **');
                            close(TheFile);
                            exit
                        end
                end
            else
                begin
                    close(TheFile);
                    exit
                end
        end;
    close(TheFile);
    writeln('** ', Count, ' elements now in array. **')
end;
```

Variables

FileSpec	Name of the file to read from disk, including drive and path, if necessary
TheFile	Internal file name in the subprogram
TooMany	boolean flag indicating whether too many elements for the array are in the disk file

Discussion

Use this subprogram with SaveArr to transfer data between arrays in memory and disk files. If you have two-dimensional arrays, use Save2Arr and Load2Arr.

Modifications

1. To convert this subprogram for use with integer arrays, change real to integer in the indicated statements in both the subprogram and the sample program.

2. To display the names of current disk files on the default disk drive before asking for the input filespec, insert the following statements after the statement indicated by {Mod. #2}:

   ```
   writeln('** Files in the default disk/directory are:' );
   ShowDir('', $10);
   ```

   You also need to add the global statements required by the ShowDir subprogram, as well as another include statement for ShowDir (that is, {$I ShowDir.PSL}) just before the statement already shown in the sample program. If you prefer, you can use ShowDir to display the directory from your main program instead of modifying the subprogram.

Load2Arr

Name: *Load2Arr*

Type: *Procedure*

Purpose: *To load a two-dimensional array from data saved in a disk file*

Calling Sequence: Load2Arr(Num2Array, RowCount, Code)

Description

You are prompted for a filespec (disk drive, path, and file name). The contents of the disk file are loaded into a two-dimensional `real` array. The companion subprogram `Save2Arr` can create the disk file.

Input

RowCount integer
Number of rows occupied in the array before loading it. Although normally zero, RowCount can be set to 50, for example, causing Load2Arr to begin loading into the 51st row of the array.

The subprogram prompts you for the input filespec. In addition, you must specify in your main program the following global `const` and `type` declarations. The numbers 2 and 100 are examples.

```
const
   ColSize = 2;
   RowSize = 100;

type
   Array2Type = array[1..RowSize, 1..ColSize] of real;
```

Output

Num2Array real
Array into which the data is loaded

RowCount integer
The updated counter of the number of rows now in the array

Code integer
Error code from DOS. If Code is zero, the file was successfully loaded from disk. Nonzero values indicate unsuccessful loading, as explained in the Limitations and Error Conditions section.

After successfully loading the file, the subprogram displays a message showing how many rows are now in the array.

Limitations and Error Conditions

Like LoadArr, Load2Arr displays any error code in decimal and passes it back to the main program, which you can design to abort or retry as you prefer. Error codes are passed in Code and are the same as those explained in LoadArr, with the additional code of -3 if end-of-file is reached without the last row being filled.

In that case, an error message is displayed, and RowCount includes the final (partial) row.

Sample Usage

```
program SampleUsageOfLoad2Arr;

const
   ColSize = 2;
   RowSize = 100;

type
   Array2Type = array[1..RowSize, 1..ColSize] of real;

var
   Num2Array            : Array2Type;
   RowCount, Code, J, K : integer;

{$I Load2Arr.PSL}

BEGIN
   RowCount := 0;
   Load2Arr(Num2Array, RowCount, Code);
   if Code <> 0 then
      writeln('Unsuccessful file load. Code = ', Code)
   else
      begin
         writeln('The contents of the file are');
         for J := 1 to RowCount do
            begin
               for K := 1 to ColSize do
                  write(Num2Array[J,K]:8:1);
               writeln
            end
      end
END.
```

This sample program produces the following output on the screen if you provide **B:SAVE2TST.DAT** as the filespec and if the file is the same one that was created by the sample program for Save2Arr.

```
** Enter filespec of input file, or **
** press [Enter] key to cancel.      **
B:SAVE2TST.DAT
** 5 sets of 2 element(s) now in array. **
The contents of the file are
        1.0      2.0
        2.0      4.0
        3.0      6.0
        4.0      8.0
        5.0     10.0
```

Subprogram Listing of Load2Arr.PSL

```pascal
procedure Load2Arr(var Num2Array: Array2Type;
                   var RowCount, Code: integer);


var
  J       : integer;
  FileSpec : string[80];
  TheFile : file of real;
  TooMany : boolean;

begin
  repeat
    writeln('** Enter filespec of input file, or **');
    writeln('** press [Enter] key to cancel.      **');
    readln(FileSpec);
    if length(FileSpec) = 0 then
      begin
        Code := -1;
        exit
      end;
    assign(TheFile, FileSpec);
    {$I-}
    reset(TheFile);
    Code := ioresult;
    if Code <> 0 then
      begin
        writeln(chr(7));
        writeln('** No file named ', FileSpec, ' found. **');
        writeln('** Try again. **')
      end
```

```
        until Code = Ø;
      TooMany := false;
      while not eof(TheFile) do
          begin
              RowCount := RowCount + 1;
              if (RowCount > RowSize) and (not TooMany) then
                  begin
                      TooMany := true;
                      writeln(chr(7));
                      writeln('** File ', FileSpec, ' too big. **');
                      writeln('** Only ', RowSize, ' rows loaded. **');
                      Code := -2;
                      RowCount := RowCount - 1
                  end;
              if not TooMany then begin
                  J := 1;
                  while (J <= ColSize) and
                        (not eof(TheFile)) do begin
                      read(TheFile, Num2Array[RowCount,J]);
                      Code := ioresult;
                      if Code <> Ø then
                          begin
                              writeln('** Error during disk read. **');
                              writeln('** Code = ', Code, '(decimal) **');
                              close(TheFile);
                              exit
                          end;
                      J := J + 1
                      end;
                  if (eof(TheFile)) and (J <= ColSize) then
                      begin
                          writeln('** Last row not full. **');
                          writeln('** Has ', J - 1, ' element(s). **');
                          Code := -3
                      end
                  end
              else
                  begin
                      close(TheFile);
                      exit
                  end
          end;
      close(TheFile);
      writeln('** ', RowCount, ' sets of ', ColSize,
              ' element(s) now in array. **')
  end;
```

Variables

J	Subscript variable for columns
FileSpec	Name of file (including drive and path, if necessary) to read from disk
TheFile	Internal file name in the subprogram
TooMany	boolean flag indicating whether more rows are in the disk file than fit in the array

Discussion

Use this subprogram with Save2Arr to transfer data between two-dimensional arrays in memory and disk files. If you have one-dimensional arrays, use SaveArr and LoadArr.

Modifications

None

LoadTxt

Name:	*LoadTxt*
Type:	*Procedure*
Purpose:	*To load a text (string) array from data saved in a text disk file*
Calling Sequence:	LoadTxt(TextArray, LineCount, Code)

Description

You are prompted for a filespec, and the contents of the disk file are loaded into a string array. The companion subprogram SaveTxt can create the disk file (after you type it in with KeyTxt), or you may create the file with a word processor, a spreadsheet, a data base manager, or the Turbo editor.

Input

LineCount   integer   Number of lines occupied in the array before loading
                        it. Although normally zero, LineCount can be set to
                        50, for example, causing LoadTxt to begin loading
                        into the 51st element of the array.

The subprogram prompts you for the input filespec. In addition, you must specify
in your main program the following global const and type declarations. The numbers 250 and 120 are examples; your values may differ. TextSize is the maximum
number of lines of text, and LineSize is the maximum length of each line.

```
const
   TextSize = 250;

type
   LineSize = string[120];
   TextArrayType = array[1..TextSize] of LineSize;
```

Output

TextArray   string   Array into which the data is loaded

LineCount   integer   The updated counter indicating the number of lines
                        now in the array

Code   integer   Error code from DOS. If Code is zero, the file was
                        successfully loaded from disk. Nonzero values
                        indicate unsuccessful loading, as explained in the
                        Limitations and Error Conditions section.

After successfully loading the file, the subprogram displays a message showing how
many lines have been loaded into the array.

Limitations and Error Conditions

LineSize cannot exceed Turbo's maximum string length of 255. Disk file lines that
exceed LineSize in length are truncated. The subprogram avoids run-time errors
by turning off Turbo's I/O error checking through the {$I-} compiler option. If
an error occurs, LoadTxt displays the error code in decimal and passes it back to
your main program, which you can design to abort or retry as you prefer. As in
the SaveTxt subprogram, the error number (if positive) is the decimal equivalent
of the hex I/O error number in Appendix G of the Turbo manual. Negative error
numbers are produced when the user decides to cancel the request by pressing

Enter instead of entering a filespec (-1), or tries to load a disk file that has more
lines than the array can hold (-2).

Sample Usage

```
program SampleUsageOfLoadTxt;

const
   TextSize = 250;                                              {Mod. #1}

type
   LineSize = string[120];                                      {Mod. #1}
   TextArrayType = array[1..TextSize] of LineSize;

var
   TextArray           : TextArrayType;
   LineCount, Code, J : integer;

{$I LoadTxt.PSL}

BEGIN
   LineCount := 0;
   LoadTxt(TextArray, LineCount, Code);
   if Code <> 0 then
      writeln('Unsuccessful text file load. Code = ', Code)
   else
      for J := 1 to LineCount do
         writeln(J:4, '=', TextArray[J])
END.
```

This sample program produces the following output on the screen if you provide
B:ARRAYTST.TXT as the filespec and if the file is the same one created by the
sample program for SaveTxt.

```
** Enter filespec of input text file, or **
** press [Enter] key to cancel.          **
B:ARRAYTST.TXT
** 2 lines now in text array. **
   1=See the quick brown fox
   2=jump over the lazy dog.
```

Subprogram Listing of LoadTxt.PSL

```pascal
procedure LoadTxt(var TextArray: TextArrayType;
                  var LineCount, Code: integer);

var
   FileSpec : string[80];
   TextFile : text;
   TooMany  : boolean;

begin
   repeat
     writeln('** Enter filespec of input text file, or **');
     writeln('** press [Enter] key to cancel.          **');
     readln(FileSpec);
     if length(FileSpec) = 0 then
        begin
           Code := -1;
           exit
        end;
     assign(TextFile, FileSpec);
     {$I-}
     reset(TextFile);
     Code := ioresult;
     if Code <> 0 then
        begin
           writeln(chr(7));
           writeln('** No file named ', FileSpec, ' found. **');
           writeln('** Try again. **')
        end
   until Code = 0;
   TooMany := false;
   while not eof(TextFile) do
      begin
         LineCount := LineCount + 1;
         if (LineCount > TextSize) and (not TooMany) then
            begin
               TooMany := true;
               writeln(chr(7));
               writeln('** File ', FileSpec, ' too big. **');
               writeln('** Only 1st ', TextSize, ' loaded. **');
               Code := -2;
               LineCount := LineCount - 1
            end;
```

```
        if not TooMany then
          begin
            readln(TextFile, TextArray[LineCount]);
            Code := ioresult;
            if Code <> 0 then
              begin
                writeln('** Error during disk read. **');
                writeln('** Code = ', Code, '(decimal) **');
                close(TextFile);
                exit
              end
          end
        else
          begin
            close(TextFile);
            exit
          end
    end;
  close(TextFile);
  writeln('** ', LineCount, ' lines now in text array. **')
end;
```

Variables

FileSpec	Name of file (including drive and path, if necessary) to read from disk
TextFile	Internal file name in the subprogram
TooMany	boolean flag indicating whether too many lines for the array are in the disk file

Discussion

Use this subprogram with SaveTxt to transfer data between arrays in memory and disk files. When the data is in memory, operate on the data with the string manipulation subprograms in this book.

Modification

Be sure to choose carefully the values that define the size of the string array! The appropriate statements are indicated by {Mod. #1} in the Sample Usage program. Remember that memory is a scarce resource, and the memory taken up by the array is (LineSize + 1) times TextSize. If you know that no lines in your text file are longer than 80 characters, for example, then by all means change LineSize to 80. This frees up 10,000 bytes of RAM for other uses.

7

Making Music and Other Sounds

The IBM PC is an amazing machine, but its sound capability is not its strongest feature. Unfortunately, you cannot adjust the volume of the PC speaker, which is limited to one voice in a single timbre. Still, you can get the speaker to play different frequencies (notes) and create some interesting effects.

Music is definitely possible. To paraphrase Mark Twain, "Music on the PC is better than it sounds." The PlayTune subprogram uses a "tune definition language" to play music specified with strings. This language is patterned after that used in the PLAY command from IBM's Advanced BASIC language (BASICA). If you have BASIC programs using PLAY, you can easily convert them to run with PlayTune. Tunes are specified through Turbo strings that command the speaker to play particular notes for certain durations. The language is fairly natural, with notes specified by their conventional letters. Once your tune has been created, you can save it on disk and recall your music for an encore. The PlayInit subprogram is used to initialize certain global variables for use by PlayTune.

Sound effects are possible too. SoundEff provides a "library" of nine different effects ranging from an alarm to a telegraph. Each sound can be modified for just the right effect. Beep creates repetitive beeping sounds for use as an alert, prompt, or warning.

PlayInit

> **Name:** *PlayInit*
>
> **Type:** *Procedure*
>
> **Purpose:** *To initialize global variables for playing music with the* PlayTune *procedure*
>
> **Calling Sequence:** PlayInit

Description

This procedure initializes global variables for subsequent use by PlayTune. Once PlayInit is called, PlayTune can play music you create with a special tune definition language. This language is modeled after that used in the PLAY statement from BASICA. (BASICA is IBM's Advanced BASIC. See the IBM BASIC manual for an explanation of the PLAY statement.) Tunes are specified by string expressions consisting of special commands. Most strings that work with BASICA's PLAY command work also with PlayTune. See the PlayTune documentation for the language definition.

Input

You must make the following global var declarations in your main program:

```
var
    PitchArray: array[1..120] of integer;
    BaseOctave, Octave, GenNoteType, Tempo, PlayFrac: byte;
```

Output

The global variables PitchArray, BaseOctave, Octave, GenNoteType, Tempo, and PlayFrac are set to default values for subsequent use by PlayTune.

Limitations and Error Conditions

None

Sample Usage

```
program SampleUsageOfPlayInit;

var
    PitchArray: array[1..120] of integer;
    BaseOctave, Octave, GenNoteType, Tempo, PlayFrac: byte;
    J, K: integer;

{$I PlayInit.PSL}
```

```
BEGIN
   PlayInit;
   writeln('Frequencies of the Natural Notes' :42);
   writeln;
   writeln('     C    D    E    F    G    A    B' );
   for J := 0 to 6 do
      begin
         for K := 1 to 7 do
            write(PitchArray[J * 7 + K + 2]:6);
         writeln('Octave' :10, J:2)
      end
END.
```

Running this test program produces the following output:

```
           Frequencies of the Natural Notes

        C    D    E    F    G    A    B
       33   37   41   44   49   55   62   Octave 0
       65   73   82   87   98  110  123   Octave 1
      131  147  165  175  196  220  247   Octave 2
      262  294  330  349  392  440  494   Octave 3
      523  587  659  698  784  880  988   Octave 4
     1047 1175 1319 1397 1568 1760 1976   Octave 5
     2093 2349 2637 2794 3136 3520 3951   Octave 6
```

Normally PlayInit is used only with PlayTune. Here, however, PlayInit is used to produce a chart of musical frequencies. These are the frequencies in Hz (cycles per second) for the natural notes (no sharps or flats) allowed in the tune definition language. Each frequency is rounded to the nearest integer. (See PlayTune for a complete description of the tune definition language.)

Subprogram Listing of PlayInit.PSL

```
procedure PlayInit;

const
   SharpOffset = 60;
   NextFreq    = 1.05946309436;

var
   RealFreq : array[1..7] of real;
   BaseFreq : real;
   J, K     : integer;

begin
   BaseOctave   := 0;                                  {Mod. #1}
   Octave       := 3;                                  {Mod. #2}
   GenNoteType  := 4;                                  {Mod. #3}
   Tempo        := 120;                                {Mod. #4}
   PlayFrac     := 7;                                  {Mod. #5}
   BaseFreq     := 27.5;
   for J := 0 to 7 do
      begin
         RealFreq[1] := BaseFreq;
         RealFreq[2] := RealFreq[1] * NextFreq * NextFreq;
         RealFreq[3] := RealFreq[2] * NextFreq;
         RealFreq[4] := RealFreq[3] * NextFreq * NextFreq;
         RealFreq[5] := RealFreq[4] * NextFreq * NextFreq;
         RealFreq[6] := RealFreq[5] * NextFreq;
         RealFreq[7] := RealFreq[6] * NextFreq * NextFreq;
         BaseFreq    := RealFreq[7] * NextFreq * NextFreq;
         for K := 1 to 7 do
            begin
               PitchArray[J * 7 + K] := round(RealFreq[K]);
               PitchArray[J * 7 + K + SharpOffset] :=
                         round(RealFreq[K] * NextFreq)
            end
      end
end;
```

Variables

SharpOffset	Subscript difference in the PitchArray between a natural note and its corresponding sharp note
NextFreq	Frequency ratio between two consecutive notes in an equal-tempered scale. (See the Discussion section.)
RealFreq	Array of the exact frequencies (real numbers) of the natural notes in a particular octave
BaseFreq	Frequency of the note A in the lowest octave
BaseOctave	Lowest octave allowed
Octave	The relative octave used in the subsequent music. The actual octave is Octave + BaseOctave.
GenNoteType	Default note type. A value of 1 corresponds to a whole note, 2 to a half note, 4 to a quarter note, etc.
Tempo	The musical tempo defined as the number of quarter notes in a minute
PlayFrac	Fraction of the time (in eighths) that the music plays for the duration of each note. A 1 means that the music plays the first 1/8 of the time, and a pause occurs the last 7/8 of the time. A 6 indicates music for 6/8 and a pause for 2/8. Normal music has PlayFrac at 7.
J, K	Loop indices
PitchArray	Array containing the frequencies of all the notes defined in the tune definition language

Discussion

The music language for PlayTune allows notes in 7 octaves (0 to 6). Each octave has a range from C to B. Middle C starts octave 3. (These settings correspond exactly to those of BASICA's PLAY command.)

The following is an (extremely) brief discussion of some music theory as it applies to PlayTune and PlayInit. A little musical knowledge is assumed although you don't need to absorb this information to be able to use PlayTune successfully.

The most common musical tunings, such as a piano tuning, use the equal-tempered scale. Here, the ratio of the frequencies between any two consecutive notes (including sharps and flats) is a constant. Each octave consists of 12 notes (C, C#, D, D#, E, F, F#, G, G#, A, A#, and B). Each flat is the exact same tone as the sharp of the next lower whole note. For example, B flat is the same note as A sharp. (B#, C flat, E#, and F flat are undefined because the intervals between B and C, and between E and F, are only half notes.)

The frequency of any note in one octave is half that of the same note in the next higher octave. Thus, the constant multiplier between consecutive notes is the twelfth root of 2. This explains the strange constant value for `NextFreq`.

To calibrate the scale, you need to specify one frequency exactly. The usual convention is that one A note has a frequency of exactly 440 Hz. Higher A notes are at 880 Hz, 1760 Hz, etc. Lower A notes are at 220 Hz, 110 Hz, 55 Hz, and 27.5 Hz. (This last value is the constant in `BaseFreq`.) No notes other than some A's have frequencies with exact integer values. Yet Turbo's `sound` command (and the PC's speaker) require tones to be played at integral frequencies. Thus, `PlayInit` uses `NextFreq` to calculate the real-number frequencies and round them to integer values as appropriate.

`PitchArray` stores these integer frequencies for the notes allowed in the music language. For ease of use by `PlayTune` and for programming convenience in `PlayInit`, `PitchArray` stores these notes according to a certain scheme. `PitchArray[1]` is the A at 27.5 Hz. The first 56 values in `PitchArray` are the consecutive natural notes ending with a B. (These values span 8 octaves.) For the natural notes, the music language of `PlayTune` uses only `PitchArray[3]` through `PitchArray[51]`. These include 7 complete octaves, each ranging from C to B.

The sharp of each note is contained in `PitchArray`, offset 60 elements from the corresponding natural note. For example, the sharp of the D at `PitchArray[4]` is found at `PitchArray[64]`. It follows that flats are offset 59 from their corresponding natural notes. (The "illegal" values of B# and E# result in C and F, respectively, as you might expect. But the "illegal" values of C flat and F flat result in C and F, respectively.)

Modifications

Each of the following modifications enables you to change a default value for one of the music parameters. `PlayTune` can later reset any of them at any time. For each modifiable variable, the range of legal values is shown. See `PlayTune` for a more complete explanation of what each of these parameters does. All parameters must be integers in the range indicated.

1. `BaseOctave` sets the lowest octave allowed. In `PlayTune` any resetting of the octave is relative to this base octave. Usually, `BaseOctave` is 0. Legal values are 0 to 6.

2. `Octave` defines the starting octave of the music. Legal values are 0 to 6.

3. GenNoteType indicates the type of notes to be played. Legal values are 1 to 64. A whole note is 1, a half note is 2, a quarter note is 4, etc.

4. Tempo sets the speed of the music as the number of quarter notes per minute. Legal values are 1 to 255. The default of 120 means that each quarter note plays for one-half second.

5. PlayFrac controls the fraction of time (in eighths) that the music plays for each note. Legal values are 1 to 7. The value of 7 means that the music plays for the first 7/8 of the note's allotted time and is off the last 1/8. See also the M commands in PlayTune.

PlayTune

Name: *PlayTune*

Type: *Procedure*

Purpose: *To play music, using a tune definition language*

Calling Sequence: PlayTune(TuneString)

Description

The tune definition language used to specify the music corresponds (almost) exactly to that of the PLAY command in BASICA. (BASICA is IBM's Advanced BASIC. See the IBM BASIC manual for an explanation of PLAY.) Tunes are specified by string expressions, as explained in the Discussion section. Most strings that work with BASICA's PLAY command work also with PlayTune

Input

TuneString string   Music specified according to the tune definition language. (See the Discussion section.)

In addition, you must make in your main program the following global type and var declarations:

```
type
   TuneType = string[255];

var
   PitchArray: array[1..120] of integer;
   BaseOctave, Octave, GenNoteType, Tempo, PlayFrac: byte;
```

Before PlayTune can be called the first time, your main program must call PlayInit so that values can be set for the global variables.

Output

PlayTune plays music from your computer's speaker according to your command strings. No messages are displayed.

Limitations and Error Conditions

Each string passed to PlayTune is limited to a length of 253 characters. (This limit is necessary because two dollar-signs added to the end of your string serve as a terminator and 255 characters are the maximum allowable string length.)

The values of the various music parameters remain intact between calls to PlayTune. Therefore, you can play long musical pieces through successive calls to PlayTune without any loss of continuity.

The alphabetic commands in each string must be in uppercase. If you have strings defined with (some) lowercase, use the ConvUp subprogram to convert the strings to uppercase.

So that PlayTune is as short and as fast as possible, no error checking of any kind is done during the processing of your strings, not even range checks on the numeric quantities. A value outside its correct range can cause fatal errors during execution. Unexpected string characters are skipped. Blanks are not allowed. Between prime commands, blanks are simply ignored. Their effect within a command, however, can cause the music to play incorrectly.

Even if your music string contains an error, PlayTune returns (with sound off) to your main program unless a fatal error occurs. No (illegal) strings should cause PlayTune to go into an infinite loop.

Sample Usage

```
program SampleUsageOfPlayTune;

type
   TuneType = string[255];

var
   PitchArray: array[1..120] of integer;
   BaseOctave, Octave, GenNoteType, Tempo, PlayFrac: byte;
   TunePart: TuneType;
```

```
{$I PlayInit.PSL}
{$I PlayTune.PSL}

BEGIN
   PlayInit;
   TunePart := 'DF#AL204DL405DDP4';
   PlayTune('T180DF#AL2AL404AAP4F#F#P403D');
   PlayTune('DF#AL2AL404AAP4GGP403C+');
   PlayTune('C#EBL2BL404BBP4GGP403C+');
   PlayTune('C#EBL2BL404BBP4F+F+P403D');
   PlayTune(TunePart);
   PlayTune('04AAP403D');
   PlayTune(TunePart);
   PlayTune('04BBP4EEGL8BP8MLB1L4MNG+AMLL205F#1');
   PlayTune('L4MND04F#MLL2F+MNL4EMLL2BMNL4A');
   PlayTune('DP8D8D4')
END.
```

This program plays the classic melody from *The Beautiful Blue Danube*, by Johann Strauss, Jr., in the key of D.

Subprogram Listing of PlayTune.PSL

```
procedure PlayTune(TuneString: TuneType);

const
   SharpOffset = 60;

var
   PlayTime, IdleTime, DotTime, NoteTime   : integer;
   NoteType, PitchIndex, Position, Number  : byte;
   Character, NextChar                     : char;
   OK                                      : boolean;

   procedure StripNumber(var ByteNumb: byte);

   var
      NumberLength : byte;
      CharValue    : char;
      Code, Numb   : integer;
```

```pascal
   begin  {embedded procedure StripNumber}
      NumberLength := 1;
      CharValue    := TuneString[Position + NumberLength];
      while CharValue in ['0'..'9'] do
         begin
            NumberLength := NumberLength + 1;
            CharValue    := TuneString[Position + NumberLength]
         end;
      NumberLength := NumberLength - 1;
      val(copy(TuneString, Position + 1, NumberLength),
             Numb, Code);
      ByteNumb := Numb;
      if NumberLength = 0 then
         OK := false
      else
         if Code = 0 then
            OK := true
         else
            OK := false;
      Position := Position + NumberLength + 1
   end;  {embedded procedure StripNumber}

   procedure DottedNote;

   begin  {embedded procedure DottedNote}
      Position := Position + 1;
      while TuneString[Position] = '.' do
         begin
            DotTime  := 3 * DotTime div 2;
            Position := Position + 1
         end
   end;  {embedded procedure DottedNote}

begin  {procedure PlayTune}
   TuneString := TuneString + '$$';
   Position   := 1;
   repeat
      NoteType  := GenNoteType;
      DotTime   := 1000;                              {Mod. #1}
      Character := TuneString[Position];
      case Character of
        'A'..'G' :
```

```
    begin
        PitchIndex := (ord(Character) - 64) + Octave * 7;
        if Character in ['A', 'B'] then
            PitchIndex := PitchIndex + 7;
        Position := Position + 1;
        NextChar := TuneString[Position];
        case NextChar of
            '#',
            '+',
            '-': begin
                    PitchIndex := PitchIndex + SharpOffset;
                    if NextChar = '-' then
                        PitchIndex := PitchIndex - 1;
                    StripNumber(Number);
                    if OK then
                        NoteType := Number;
                    Position := Position - 1;
                    DottedNote
                 end;
            '0'..'9':
                 begin
                    Position := Position - 1;
                    StripNumber(NoteType);
                    Position := Position - 1;
                    DottedNote
                 end;
            '.': begin
                    DotTime := 3 * DotTime div 2;
                    DottedNote
                 end
        end; {embedded case}
        NoteTime := round(DotTime / Tempo /
                        NoteType * 240);
        PlayTime := round(NoteTime * PlayFrac / 8);
        IdleTime := NoteTime - PlayTime;
        sound(PitchArray[PitchIndex]);
        delay(PlayTime);
        nosound;
        delay(IdleTime)
    end;
'L': StripNumber(GenNoteType);
```

```
    'M' : begin
            case TuneString[Position + 1] of
              'S' : PlayFrac := 6;              {Mod. #2}
              'N' : PlayFrac := 7;              {Mod. #2}
              'L' : PlayFrac := 8              {Mod. #2}
            end;
            Position := Position + 2
          end;
    'O' : begin
            StripNumber(Octave);
            Octave := Octave + BaseOctave
          end;
    'P' : begin
            StripNumber(NoteType);
            Position := Position - 1;
            DottedNote;
            IdleTime := DotTime div Tempo *
                        (240 div NoteType);
            delay(IdleTime)
          end;
    'S' : StripNumber(BaseOctave);
    'T' : StripNumber(Tempo)
    else Position := Position + 1
  end
until Character = '$';
nosound
end;  {procedure PlayTune}
```

Variables

Variables for the Procedure PlayTune

SharpOffset	Subscript difference in the PitchArray between a natural note and its corresponding sharp note
BaseOctave	Lowest octave allowed
Octave	The current octave relative to BaseOctave. That is, the actual octave is BaseOctave + Octave.
GenNoteType	Default note type. A value of 1 corresponds to a whole note, 2 to a half note, 4 to a quarter note, etc.

Tempo	The tempo of the music defined as the number of quarter notes in a minute
PlayFrac	Fraction of the time (in eighths) that the music plays for each note. A 1 means that the music plays the first 1/8 of the time, and a pause occurs the last 7/8 of the time. A 6 means music for 6/8 and a pause for 2/8. Normal music has PlayFrac at 7.
PitchArray	Array containing the frequencies (to the nearest integer) of all the notes defined in the tune definition language
PlayTime	Number of milliseconds that music is on for each note
IdleTime	Number of milliseconds that music is off for each note
DotTime	Time interval (in milliseconds) for one-half note at normal tempo augmented by dotted notes, if any
NoteTime	Number of milliseconds for each note. NoteTime is PlayTime + IdleTime.
NoteType	Type of note to play, using the same conventions as GenNoteType
PitchIndex	Index into PitchArray for the note to be played
Position	Current position in TuneString
Number	A number returned by StripNumber
Character	Character at TuneString[Position]
NextChar	Character at TuneString[Position + 1]
OK	boolean return flag from StripNumber. If OK is true, a number was found; if OK is false, no number was found.

Variables for the Embedded Procedure StripNumber

NumberLength	Length (in characters) of a substring from TuneString, containing a numeric quantity
CharValue	One character from the substring
Code	Code passed back by val
Numb	Integer number passed back from val
ByteNumb	Numb set to a byte variable

Discussion

TuneString consists of a series of concatenated commands. No separator is needed between commands. All alphabetic commands must be in uppercase. Unless specifically indicated otherwise, each command is exactly like the PLAY statement in BASICA.

A lowercase n after a command indicates that an integer number must immediately follow the alphabetic character as part of the same command.

The following are the primary commands for PlayTune:

A to G   (with optional #, +, or - following) Plays the note indicated. The # or + afterward indicates a sharp, and - indicates a flat.

L n   Sets the length for all notes that follow. L1 is a whole note, and L4 is a quarter note. That is, the actual note length is 1/n, in which the value of n may range from 1 to 64. L4 is the default.

    The length also may follow a particular note when you want to change the length of that note only. Thus, L4AB-16C indicates to play a quarter note A, a sixteenth note B flat, and a quarter note C.

MF   This is ignored. (It is music foreground in BASICA's PLAY.)

MB   This is ignored. (It is music background in BASICA's PLAY.)

MS   Music staccato. Each subsequent note plays 3/4 of the time specified by L and is off the last 1/4 of the time.

MN   Music normal. Each subsequent note plays 7/8 of the time specified by L and is off the last 1/8 of the time. MN is the default M command.

ML   Music legato. Each subsequent note plays the full period specified by L. (There is no delay between notes.)

O n   Sets the octave for subsequent notes relative to the base octave. In other words, the current octave is made equal to n plus the base octave. The resultant octave must be from 0 to 6. Thus, there are 7 octaves, each with a range from C to B. Middle C begins octave 3. The value of n must be from 0 to 6. The default is 3. (BASICA's PLAY does not contain base octaves. That is, the base octave is effectively 0 with PLAY.)

P n   Pauses or rests. The value of n may be from 1 to 64. The length of the pause is determined by n, as for the L command.

S n   Sets the scale or base octave for all succeeding O commands. Using S
        does not change the current octave. The value of n must be from 0
        to 6. The default is 0. (This command is an addition to BASICA's
        PLAY statement.)

T n   Adjusts the tempo for subsequent music. This command sets to n the
        number of quarter notes per minute. The value of n may range from
        32 to 255. The default is 120. A quarter note plays for one-half
        second.

In addition, a dot (or period) after a note specification causes the note to be played
as a dotted note. This means that its length is multiplied by 3/2. More than one
dot may appear after each note, each dot causing another 3/2 multiplier to the
total length. For example, L4C. . causes a C to be played 9/4 as long as a quarter
note. Dots can appear directly after a note even if a numeric length designator
appears (for example, A8.). Dots may also be used after a P command to extend
the pause length in the same manner.

The X command (play substring) and n=variable commands from BASICA's PLAY
are not implemented in PlayTune. No semicolons (or any other separators) are
needed between commands. Separators are simply ignored by PlayTune and have
no effect on the resulting music.

If your music contains repetitious phrases, set string variables to these specific
phrases. Then call PlayTune with the string variable name as the argument so that
you can play these phrases whenever you like.

If you're working from sheet music, it's usually a good idea to find the lowest note
and define that in octave 0. Then set your other octaves higher as required. You
can later scale everything up a few octaves with one S command at the beginning
of your music. If you make your initial O commands too high, you cannot lower
them with a call to S; you can only raise them.

PlayTune contains two embedded procedures. StripNumber removes a numeric
substring from TuneString. DottedNote processes dotted notes if any are present.

Modifications

1. You can set the tempo outside the range possible with the T command by
   adjusting the value of DotTime in the indicated line. DotTime is the number
   of milliseconds allotted to a half note at normal tempo (before any
   dotting). If you change DotTime to 250, for example, all music plays four
   times as fast as otherwise specified. DotTime must have a positive integer
   value.

2. The three lines indicated by {Mod. #2} define the musical envelopes for staccato, normal, and legato music. PlayFrac is the fraction of the time (in eighths) that the music plays during the time interval allowed for each note. In each of these three lines, PlayFrac must be set to an integer value from 1 to 8. You can experiment with values smaller than 6 to see the effect on your music. If you change normal music (the second of these three lines), put an early MN command in your music to override the default setting for normal music caused by PlayInit.

SoundEff

Name:	*SoundEff*
Type:	*Procedure*
Purpose:	*To play various sound effects through the computer's speaker*
Calling Sequence:	SoundEff(Effect, RelativePitch, NumberToDo)

Description

This procedure provides nine fundamental sound effects you can use to enhance your programs. In addition, three frequency ranges are available for each effect. You can have any effect continuously repeated any number of times. The net result is a powerful sound effects generator. SoundEff is meant for "serious" sound effects. For music, use PlayTune, and for simple beeping sounds, use Beep.

Input

Effect	Scalar	The sound effect desired. It must be one of the values in the declared scalar type EffectsList.
RelativePitch	Scalar	The desired frequency relative to the base frequency. RelativePitch must be one of the values in the declared scalar type PitchFreq, namely, LowPitch, MediumPitch, or HighPitch.
NumberToDo	integer	Number of times to repeat the sound effect

In addition, the following global type declarations must be made in your main program. They define the declared scalar types EffectsList and PitchFreq.

```
type
   EffectsList = (Alarm, Bounce, Coin, Crickets, Falling,
                  Siren, Telegraph, Zap, Zoom);
   PitchFreq   = (LowPitch, MediumPitch, HighPitch);
```

Output

The requested sound effect plays through the computer's speaker. No messages are displayed on the screen.

Limitations and Error Conditions

If NumberToDo is less than 1, the sound effect is still produced once.

Sample Usage

```
program SampleUsageOfSoundEff;

type
   EffectsList = (Alarm, Bounce, Coin, Crickets, Falling,
                  Siren, Telegraph, Zap, Zoom);
   PitchFreq   = (LowPitch, MediumPitch, HighPitch);

var
   Effect        : EffectsList;
   RelativePitch : PitchFreq;
   NumberToDo    : integer;

{$I SoundEff.PSL}

BEGIN
   randomize;
   clrscr;
   writeln('I hear the crickets at night by the pond.');
   SoundEff(Crickets, MediumPitch, 2);
   writeln('I dropped a penny on the floor.');
   SoundEff(Coin, HighPitch, 1);
   delay(500);
   Effect        := Alarm;
   RelativePitch := MediumPitch;
   NumberToDo    := 3;
```

```
   writeln('A police car is going by.');
   SoundEff(Effect, RelativePitch, NumberToDo);
   writeln('My gosh, there goes a spaceship!');
   SoundEff(Zoom, LowPitch, 1);
   writeln('I''m sending out a telegraph message about it.');
   SoundEff(Telegraph, MediumPitch, 2)
END.
```

Running this test program produces the following output on the screen:

```
I hear the crickets at night by the pond.
I dropped a penny on the floor.
A police car is going by.
My gosh, there goes a spaceship!
I'm sending out a telegraph message about it.
```

Of course, each of these five sound descriptions is accompanied by the appropriate sound effect on the speaker.

Subprogram Listing of SoundEff.PSL

```
procedure SoundEff(Effect: EffectsList; RelativePitch: PitchFreq;
                NumberToDo: integer);

var
   NumberDone, PitchFactor : integer;
   J, K, M, N              : integer;

   function AdjustedPitch(RawPitch: integer): integer;

   begin
      AdjustedPitch := RawPitch * PitchFactor div 2      {Mod. #2}
   end;

   procedure TurnOn(Frequency, DelayLength: integer);

   begin
      sound(AdjustedPitch(Frequency));
      delay(DelayLength)
   end;
```

```
          procedure TurnOff(DelayLength: integer);

          begin
             nosound;
             delay(DelayLength)
          end;

      begin  {procedure SoundEff}
          PitchFactor := ord(RelativePitch) + 1;                    {Mod. #1}
          NumberDone  := 0;
          repeat
             case Effect of
                 Alarm:      for J := 1 to 2 do
                                begin
                                    TurnOn(1000, 300);
                                    TurnOn(500, 300)
                                end;
                 Bounce:     for J := 17 downto 0 do
                                begin
                                    for K := 500 to 700 do
                                       sound(AdjustedPitch(K));
                                    TurnOff(J * 30)
                                end;
                 Coin:       for J := 20 downto 1 do
                                begin
                                    TurnOn(500, 40);
                                    TurnOff(J * 5)
                                end;
                 Crickets:   for J := 1 to 60 do
                                for K := 3 to 10 do
                                    TurnOn(2500 + random(1000), 5);
                 Falling:    for J := 50 downto 1 do
                                begin
                                    TurnOn(30 * J, 100);
                                    TurnOff(50)
                                end;
                 Siren:      begin
                                for K := 200 to 2300 do
                                    sound(AdjustedPitch(K));
                                TurnOff(100)
                                end;
```

```
        Telegraph: for J := 1 to 10 do
                      begin
                          TurnOn(600, 100);
                          TurnOff(30 + random(200))
                      end;
        Zap:        for J := 1 to 10 do
                      begin
                          K := 250 + J * 25;
                          for M := 1 to 3 do
                              begin
                                  for N := 1 to 30 - M * 2 do
                                      TurnOn(N + K + M * 2, 2);
                                  delay(5);
                                  K := K + 30
                              end;
                          nosound
                      end;
        Zoom:       begin
                        for J := 1 to 7000 do
                            sound(AdjustedPitch(J));
                        for J := 7000 downto 1 do
                            sound(AdjustedPitch(J))
                    end
      end;
      nosound;
      NumberDone := NumberDone + 1
   until
      NumberDone >= NumberToDo
end;   {procedure SoundEff}
```

Variables

NumberDone	The number of times the sound effect has been repeated
PitchFactor	Multiplicative factor that adjusts the sound frequency and therefore the pitch. (See the Modifications section.)
J, K, M, N	Loop indices

Discussion

When appropriate, sound effects greatly enhance your programs. Unfortunately, the sound-effects capability of the IBM PC is somewhat limited. The PC's speaker's volume cannot be adjusted, it is capable of only one voice, and it has just a modest frequency response.

Many different effects are possible, however. SoundEff contains a "library" of nine fundamental sounds. Each one can be altered by the RelativePitch and NumberToDo parameters. The nine sounds have identifying names: Alarm, Bounce, Coin, Crickets, Falling, Siren, Telegraph, Zap, and Zoom. Use your imagination when you try each of the sound effects. Some undoubtedly will suggest other things to you.

SoundEff contains an embedded function and two embedded procedures. AdjustedPitch adjusts the normal sound pitch according to the parameter RelativePitch. TurnOn and TurnOff turn on sound and turn off sound. Each procedure includes a parameter for pausing for a specified period of time before returning to the calling program.

Be sure to put a randomize statement in your main program before calling SoundEff. Some of the effects use the random number generator to create their sounds.

Modifications

1. Each sound effect has its standard (regular) frequency range. When RelativePitch equals MediumPitch, this regular frequency range is produced by SoundEff. When RelativePitch equals LowPitch or HighPitch, the frequency range is modified and the sound effect is changed somewhat. PitchFactor applies a multiplicative factor to the regular frequencies to accomplish these changes. By changing the formula in the line indicated by {Mod. #1}, you can make the frequency range a different function of RelativePitch. PitchFactor must be a positive integer.

2. For several of the nine sound effects, the function AdjustedPitch calculates frequency adjustments required by the particular sound effect. These frequency adjustments are expressed as a function of PitchFactor. (PitchFactor is calculated in the line indicated by {Mod. #1}.) The formula for calculating AdjustedPitch is in the line indicated by {Mod. #2}. You may want to change the 2 at the end of the line to some other integer.

3. You have unlimited possibilities in modifying the various sound effects. All effects include numeric constants, which can be adjusted. Experiment to see whether you can produce effects more to your tastes or needs. You may even add completely new effects to the case statement. If so, add their names to EffectsList.

Beep

Name: *Beep*
Type: *Procedure*
Purpose: *To sound beeping noises from the speaker*
Calling Sequence: Beep(NumberToDo, Pitch, Duration)

Description

Beep creates repetitive beeping sounds. These are useful as a prompt (for expected input), as an error warning, or as a general alert to the user. You can specify the number of beeps to make, as well as the pitch and duration of each beep. Modifiable default values are maintained for each of these parameters so that Beep can be called with simple arguments (all zeros) to achieve a known effect.

Input

NumberToDo	integer	Number of beeps to produce. If NumberToDo is zero or negative, the default setting is used.
Pitch	integer	The pitch (or frequency) of each beep in cycles per second. If Pitch is zero or negative, the default setting is used. (See PlayInit for the correspondence between different frequency values and the musical scale.)
Duration	integer	Time duration for sounding each beep expressed in milliseconds. If Duration is zero or negative, the default setting is used.

Output

The desired beeping is produced through the computer's speaker. No messages are displayed on the screen.

Limitations and Error Conditions

Be sure that you request beeps which are audible. An extremely high pitch, say, Pitch > 15000, is too high for the human ear (and probably not within the speaker's frequency response). Many PC speakers produce a simple click if you request a pitch in such a high range. In addition, an extremely quick sound, such as Duration < 5, cannot be accurately produced by most PC speakers. You will have to test these conditions on your particular computer because speakers vary from one computer to the next.

Sample Usage

```
program SampleUsageOfBeep;

var
    NumberToDo, Pitch, Duration: integer;

{$I Beep.PSL}

BEGIN
    NumberToDo := 5;
    Pitch      := 50;
    Duration   := 500;
    writeln('Here are 5 low-pitched beeps, each for 1/2 second.');
    Beep(NumberToDo, Pitch, Duration);
    delay(2000);
    writeln('Here is the default beeping.');
    Beep(0, 0, 0)
END.
```

Running this test program produces the following output on your screen:

```
Here are 5 low-pitched beeps, each for 1/2 second.
Here is the default beeping.
```

Of course, the appropriate beeping accompanies each message as it is displayed on the screen.

Subprogram Listing of Beep.PSL

```
procedure Beep(NumberToDo, Pitch, Duration: integer);

const
    DelayLength  = 200;                            {Mod. #1}
    DefaultNumb  = 3;                              {Mod. #2}
    DefaultPitch = 440;                            {Mod. #3}
    DefaultDur   = 250;                            {Mod. #4}
```

```
var
  J: integer;

begin
  if NumberToDo < 1 then
    NumberToDo := DefaultNumb;
  if Pitch < 1 then
    Pitch := DefaultPitch;
  if Duration < 1 then
    Duration := DefaultDur;
  if NumberToDo > 0 then
    for J := 1 to NumberToDo do
      begin
        sound(Pitch);
        delay(Duration);
        nosound;
        delay(DelayLength)
      end
end;
```

Variables

DelayLength	The delay time in milliseconds between the end of one beep and the beginning of the next beep
DefaultNumb	Default number of beeps to produce if NumberToDo is less than 1
DefaultPitch	Default pitch in cycles per second. This is the pitch used if Pitch is less than 1.
DefaultDur	Default time duration in milliseconds to sound each beep. This is the duration used if Duration is less than 1.
J	Loop index

Discussion

You don't need to use Beep if you need only one beep at the computer's standard pitch and duration. The following Turbo statement accomplishes this:

```
  write(#7)
```

Beep is useful when you want program control over the pitch and duration of each beep or over the number of beeps to produce.

If you have frequent use for beeping at a particular pitch, duration, and/or repetition rate, you can reset the default constants DefaultPitch, DefaultDur, and/or DefaultNumb. You can get any of the default values by calling Beep with a value of zero for the appropriate parameter. (See the Modifications section.)

Modifications

1. DelayLength is the pause time after each beeping noise. If NumberToDo is greater than 1, DelayLength is the time interval between beeps. This delay is also used after the last beep before the subprogram returns. Its current setting is 200 (1/5 of a second).

2. DefaultNumb is the number of beeps to produce if NumberToDo is zero or negative. If you change DefaultNumb to zero, the subprogram is bypassed completely (no beep is produced) when NumberToDo is less than 1.

3. DefaultPitch is the pitch to use if Pitch is zero or negative. The current setting of 440 for DefaultPitch produces an A note. (See PlayInit.)

4. DefaultDur is the time duration to sound each beep if Duration is zero or negative. The current value of 250 for DefaultDur produces a beep for 1/4 second.

8

Sorting

One of the great mysteries to beginning programmers is why there are so many different techniques to sort data into ascending (or descending) order. Why doesn't someone take the time to figure out which technique is best so that everyone can use it? Can't we get rid of all these sorting routines with the strange names—like bubble sort, selection sort, insertion sort, Shell's sort, heapsort, quicksort, radix sort, and countless others?

Life is not that simple, however. The truth is that virtually every sorting technique has some merit and is best in certain (sometimes obscure) cases. Entire books have been written discussing the trade-offs among various techniques and explaining how to sort efficiently.

In choosing a technique, you should consider many factors. Some of these are the amount of data to sort, the size of the sort key, the order of the data before the sort, the architecture of the computer being used, the capabilities and efficiencies of the language in which the sort is programmed, the characteristics of peripheral devices that may hold portions of the data during sorting, the size of working memory available, and the simplicity of the algorithm.

Included in this chapter are two sorting techniques that work well in a broad range of circumstances. Each sorting subprogram in our library uses one of these techniques. See the Discussion sections of SortSIR and SortHR for details about choosing between the "straight insertion" and the "heapsort" methods. The chapter contains eight subprograms: SortSIR and SortHR for one-dimensional real or integer arrays; SortSI2R and SortH2R for two-dimensional real arrays; SortSIT and SortHT for text (string) arrays; and SortSIRT and SortHRT for paired arrays, one real or integer, and the other one text.

SortSIR

> **Name:** *SortSIR*
>
> **Type:** *Procedure*
>
> **Purpose:** *To sort a* real *array, using the straight insertion technique*
>
> **Calling Sequence:** SortSIR(NumArray, Count)

Description

This subprogram sorts in ascending order the elements of a one-dimensional real array, using the straight insertion technique. You can modify the subprogram to sort an integer array (SortSII) or to sort in descending order. The sort is performed in place, meaning that no extra work storage is needed for the sort process.

Input

NumArray   real   Array to be sorted

Count   integer   The number of array elements to be sorted

In addition, you must specify in your main program the following global type declaration, preferably using the global const declaration shown (for compatibility with other subprograms). The number 250 is an example; your array size may differ.

```
const
    ArraySize = 250;

type
    ArrayType = array[1..ArraySize] of real;
```

Output

NumArray   real   The same array, now sorted

Limitations and Error Conditions

If Count is less than or equal to 1, the sort procedure is bypassed, no error message is displayed, and the normal beginning and ending messages do not appear. No other error checking is done. Your responsibility is to make sure that Count is accurate and does not exceed the size of the array (ArraySize). SortSIR works with a minimum of two elements; the maximum number of elements is limited

only by the data segment memory size and your patience in waiting. You may set
Count to less than ArraySize. Only the first Count elements are sorted.

Sample Usage

```
program SampleUsageOfSortSIR;

const
   ArraySize = 250;

type
   ArrayType = array[1..ArraySize] of real;                    {Mod. #1}

var
   NumArray : ArrayType;
   Count    : integer;

{$I SortSIR.PSL}

BEGIN
   NumArray[1] := 4.2;    NumArray[2] := 1.03;
   NumArray[3] := -2.3;   NumArray[4] := 4.17;
   Count := 4;
   SortSIR(NumArray, Count);
   writeln(NumArray[1]:6:2, NumArray[2]:6:2, NumArray[3]:6:2,
          NumArray[4]:6:2)
END.
```

Running the test program produces the following output on the screen:

```
Begin SortSIR
4 entries sorted
 -2.30  1.03  4.17  4.20
```

Subprogram Listing of SortSIR.PSL

```
procedure SortSIR(var NumArray: ArrayType; Count: integer);

var
   J, K       : integer;
   ThisValue : real;                                   {Mod. #1}

begin
   if Count <= 1 then exit;                            {Mod. #2}
   writeln('Begin SortSIR');                           {Mod. #3}
   for J := 2 to Count do
      begin
         ThisValue := NumArray[J];
         K := J - 1;
         while (ThisValue < NumArray[K]) and           {Mod. #4}
               (K > 0) do
            begin
               NumArray[K + 1] := NumArray[K];
               K := K - 1
            end;
         NumArray[K + 1] := ThisValue
      end;
   writeln(Count, ' entries sorted')                   {Mod. #3}
end;
```

Variables

J	Subscript variable that points to the array's current element to be inserted into the correct order
K	Subscript that points to the position below J where the current element is to be inserted
ThisValue	Contents of NumArray[J], the current element being sorted

Discussion

This sorting technique should be familiar to many cardplayers who put their hands in order by working from one end to the other. Imagine that you are playing bridge. To sort your hand of 13 cards, start with the second card from the left. If it is in the correct order compared to the first card, leave the second card where it is. Otherwise, exchange it with the first card. Now look at the third card. Compare it with the second and first cards and insert the third card where it belongs. If you continue with this procedure until you get to the 13th card, your hand will be in order. This method is called a straight insertion sort (see Section 5.2.1 of Donald E. Knuth's *The Art of Computer Programming*, Volume 3, *Sorting and Searching*) because a scan is made through the array, from low subscript to high, with each element being inserted in the correct place among the previous elements already sorted.

To sort an `integer` array, refer to modification 1 in the Modifications section. To sort in descending order rather than ascending, see modification 4. To sort text (a `string` array), use `SortSIT` (sort: straight insertion, text).

Dozens of sorting techniques are in use today, and each has its merits. The straight insertion technique is a good choice on two occasions: when you have only a small number of elements to sort (say, less than 30 or 40), or when you have an array that is nearly in the correct order. The straight insertion technique's other main advantage is that it uses minimal memory: the technique can be coded compactly and sorts the array in place. As the size of the array grows, however, the efficiency of the sort decreases rapidly if the beginning sequence is random.

Generally, when the number of elements to be sorted doubles, the sort time quadruples. This guideline applies to the actual number of elements sorted (that is, `Count`), not to the maximum size of the array specified by `ArraySize`. For this reason, you'll find the heapsort technique (`SortHR` for `real` arrays) much faster for large arrays in random sequence. But straight insertion is extremely efficient when your array is already nearly in order. Unlike many other techniques, straight insertion takes advantage of the previously existing sequence. Table 8.1 shows approximate sorting times for arrays filled with random real numbers and also for arrays with only one or two elements out of order. See Appendix D for details about the environment used for timings.

Table 8.1
Approximate `SortSIR` Timings
Time (in Seconds)

Count	Random Sequence	Almost in Sequence
25	0.1	<0.1
50	0.3	<0.1
100	1.0	0.1
200	4.0	0.2
400	16.0	0.3
800	63.0	0.5

Modifications

1. To sort an integer array instead of a real array, change the word real to integer in the global type declaration. Make the same change to the statement indicated by {Mod. #1} in the SortSIR Subprogram Listing. These modified lines will look like this:

   ```
   type
       ArrayType = array[1..ArraySize] of integer;

   ThisValue : integer;
   ```

   When you save this version to your disk library, name the file SortSII. You should change the name in the procedure statement also.

2. To eliminate checking whether Count is 2 or greater, remove the indicated statement. Because this change makes an insignificant difference in the sort's speed, though, the change is not recommended.

3. To eliminate displaying the messages at the beginning and end of the sort, delete the two indicated statements.

4. To change the sort from ascending to descending order (that is, with largest numbers first), change the less-than sign (<) to a greater-than sign (>) in the indicated statement.

SortHR

> **Name:** *SortHR*
>
> **Type:** *Procedure*
>
> **Purpose:** *To sort a* real *array, using the heapsort technique*
>
> **Calling Sequence:** SortHR(NumArray, Count)

Description

Like SortSIR, this subprogram sorts in ascending order the elements of a one-dimensional real array. SortHR, however, uses the heapsort technique, which is much faster except for very small arrays or those that are nearly in order. You can modify SortHR to sort an integer array (SortHI) or to sort in descending order. The sort is performed in place.

Input

NumArray	real	Array to be sorted
Count	integer	The number of array elements to be sorted

In addition, you must specify in your main program the following global type declaration, preferably using the global const declaration shown. The number 200 is an example.

```
const
   ArraySize = 200;

type
   ArrayType = array[1..ArraySize] of real;
```

Output

NumArray	real	The same array, now sorted

Limitations and Error Conditions

If Count is less than or equal to 1, the sort procedure is bypassed, but no error message is displayed. No other error checking is done. Your responsibility is to make sure that Count is accurate and does not exceed the size of the array (ArraySize). SortHR works with a minimum of two elements; the maximum number of elements is limited only by the memory size of the data segment. You may set Count to less than ArraySize. Only the first Count elements are sorted.

Sample Usage

```
program SampleUsageOfSortHR;

const
   ArraySize = 200;

type
   ArrayType = array[1..ArraySize] of real;            {Mod. #1}

var
   NumArray : ArrayType;
   Count, J : integer;

{$I SortHR.PSL}
```

```
BEGIN
   NumArray[1] := 47.19;
   NumArray[2] := 21.6;
   NumArray[3] := 3.14;
   NumArray[4] := 22.0;
   NumArray[5] := -12.7;
   Count := 5;
   SortHR(NumArray, Count);
   writeln('The sorted data =');
   for J := 1 to Count do writeln(NumArray[J]:8:2)
END.
```

This test program produces the following output on the screen:

```
The sorted data =
  -12.70
    3.14
   21.60
   22.00
   47.19
```

Subprogram Listing of SortHR.PSL

```
procedure SortHR(var NumArray: ArrayType; Count: integer);

label
   H1, H2, H3, H4, H5, H7, H8, H9;

var
   I, J, L, R : integer;
   ThisValue  : real;                          {Mod. #1}

begin
   if Count <= 1 then exit;
   H1: L := Count div 2 + 1;
       R := Count;
   H2: if L > 1 then
          begin
             L := L - 1;
             ThisValue := NumArray[L]
          end
```

```
        else
           begin
              ThisValue   := NumArray[R];
              NumArray[R] := NumArray[1];
              R := R - 1;
              if R = 1 then
                 begin
                    NumArray[1] := ThisValue;
                    exit                     {successful end of sort}
                 end
           end;
H3: J := L;
H4: I := J;
    J := J + J;
    if J > R then goto H8;
    if J = R then goto H7;
H5: if NumArray[J] < NumArray[J+1] then              {Mod. #2}
       J := J + 1;
H7: NumArray[I] := NumArray[J];
    goto H4;
H8: J := I;
    I := J div 2;
H9: if (ThisValue <= NumArray[I]) or                 {Mod. #2}
       (J = L) then
       begin
          NumArray[J] := ThisValue;
          goto H2
       end
    else
       begin
          NumArray[J] := NumArray[I];
          goto H8
       end
end;
```

Variables

I, J, L, R   Subscript variables used to keep track of the elements in NumArray while SortHR arranges it into a heap and then selects the elements in the correct order. (See the Discussion section.)

ThisValue   An element of NumArray, now being sorted

Discussion

After reading the Discussion section of SortSIR, you may identify with the bridge player who uses the straight insertion technique to arrange cards in a hand. An insertion sort is an intuitively appealing method. However, the same cannot be said of the heapsort technique used in SortHR. We'll be amazed if any cardplayer in the world uses this method, efficient as it may be.

Because of heapsort's complexity, the complete technique will not be described here. For details, see Section 5.2.3 of Knuth's *The Art of Computer Programming* (mandatory reading for any serious student of sorting techniques). Generally, the heapsort process is similar to that used in a tennis tournament. Start with a group of, say, 32 competitors. Play 16 matches and have the winners go on to the next level of the treelike structure to play again. Continue with this approach until only two players remain, who meet in the final round. The winner is considered the best player in the tournament, even though the winner played only five opponents, not all 31.

The heapsort technique organizes the array elements into a "heap." This is a carefully defined type of tree structure similar to the final "winner board" after a tennis tournament, except that the technique spells out the relative magnitudes of *all* participants by playing some extra matches you don't see in tennis tournaments. Then heapsort proceeds through the heap, selecting the elements in the desired order.

You may notice something rare in the SortHR coding: numerous Pascal labels are in the subprogram (H1, H2, etc.). Shouldn't you avoid labels in order to adhere to good structured programming techniques? Normally, yes. In this case, we thought it best to adopt the labels suggested by Knuth so that you can follow his heapsort discussion if you want. We also retained his subscript naming. Refer to Algorithm H and exercise 18 in Section 5.2.3 of Knuth's book.

Choose this heapsort-based subprogram over the straight insertion subprogram when conditions for the latter do not apply. That is, use SortHR when your array is large (more than 30 or 40 elements) and you can't depend on the array being nearly in order before the sort. Compare the timings in table 8.2 with those in table 8.1 to see why.

Although not true for straight insertion sorting, the average time for heapsorting random data is virtually the same as that for heapsorting data which is nearly in order. When Count is greater than about 20, SortHR runs faster than SortSIR, but the difference may not be enough to compensate for the increased size of the code unless Count is 50 or more, depending on the situation.

Heapsort is not the only sophisticated sorting technique that works well with large amounts of data. Other techniques, especially quicksort and Shell's sort, are often

Table 8.2
Approximate SortHR Timings
Time (in Seconds)

Count	Random Sequence
25	0.1
50	0.2
100	0.4
200	0.8
400	1.8
800	4.0
1600	8.7
3200	18.8

used. We chose heapsort because it is generally the most efficient technique that has all these attributes: it saves memory by sorting in place, it is reasonably short (allowing you to type it in easily and save memory), and it is not subject to wide fluctuations in sorting time because of the initial sequence of the data or internal sort parameters.

Modifications

1. To sort an integer array instead of a real array, change the word real to integer in the global type declaration. Make the same change to the statement indicated by {Mod. #1} in the SortHR Subprogram Listing. If you save this version to your disk library, name the version SortHI. Change the name in the procedure statement also.

2. To change the sort from ascending to descending order (that is, with largest numbers first), change the less-than sign (<) to a greater-than sign (>) in the first line indicated by {Mod. #2}. Change <= to >= in the second indicated statement.

SortSI2R

> **Name:** *SortSI2R*
>
> **Type:** *Procedure*
>
> **Purpose:** *To sort a two-dimensional real array, using the straight insertion technique*
>
> **Calling Sequence:** SortSI2R(Num2Array, RowCount, SortCol)

Description

SortSI2R sorts in ascending order a two-dimensional real array, just as SortSIR sorts a one-dimensional array. You specify which column contains the sort key. The sort is performed in place. A modification is included if you want to sort in descending order.

Input

Num2Array	real	Array to be sorted
RowCount	integer	The number of rows in the array to be sorted
SortCol	integer	The column number of the sort key

In addition, you must specify in your main program the following global type and const declarations. ColSize is the exact number of columns (the second dimension) and is required. RowSize is the maximum number of rows (first dimension) and is not required as a constant. Specifying RowSize, however, facilitates the type declaration and retains compatibility with other subprograms. The numbers 2 and 100 are examples.

```
const
   ColSize = 2;
   RowSize = 100;

type
   Array2Type = array[1..RowSize, 1..ColSize] of real;
```

Output

Num2Array	real	The same array, now sorted

Limitations and Error Conditions

If RowCount is less than or equal to 1, the sort procedure is bypassed, but no error message is displayed. No other error checking is done. Your responsibility is to make sure that RowCount and SortCol are accurate and do not exceed the bounds of the array. You may set RowCount to less than RowSize. Only the first RowCount elements are sorted.

Sample Usage

```
program SampleUsageOfSortSI2R;

const
   ColSize = 2;
   RowSize = 100;

type
   Array2Type = array[1..RowSize, 1..ColSize] of real;

var
   Num2Array                  : Array2Type;
   RowCount, SortCol, J, K : integer;

{$I SortSI2R.PSL}

BEGIN
   Num2Array[1,1] := 4.4;     Num2Array[1,2] := 64.0;
   Num2Array[2,1] := -1.0;    Num2Array[2,2] := 11.2;
   Num2Array[3,1] := 3.7;     Num2Array[3,2] := 27.3;
   Num2Array[4,1] := 2.3;     Num2Array[4,2] := 88.5;
   RowCount := 4;
   SortCol  := 1;
   SortSI2R(Num2Array, RowCount, SortCol);
   writeln('Here is the data, sorted on the first column.');
   for J := 1 to RowCount do
      begin
         for K := 1 to ColSize do
            write(Num2Array[J,K]:9:2);
         writeln
      end
END.
```

This test program produces the following output:

```
Here is the data, sorted on the first column.
    -1.00    11.20
     2.30    88.50
     3.70    27.30
     4.40    64.00
```

Subprogram Listing of SortSI2R.PSL

```
procedure SortSI2R(var Num2Array: Array2Type;
                   RowCount, SortCol: integer);

var
   J, K, T : integer;
   ThisRow : array[1..ColSize] of real;

begin
   if RowCount <= 1 then exit;
   for J := 2 to RowCount do
      begin
         for T := 1 to ColSize do
            ThisRow[T] := Num2Array[J, T];
         K := J - 1;
         while (ThisRow[SortCol] <                    {Mod. #1}
               Num2Array[K, SortCol])
               and (K > 0) do
            begin
               for T := 1 to ColSize do
                  Num2Array[K+1, T] := Num2Array[K, T];
               K := K - 1
            end;
         for T := 1 to ColSize do
            Num2Array[K+1, T] := ThisRow[T]
      end;
end;
```

Variables

J	Subscript variable that points to Num2Array's current row to be inserted in the correct order
K	Subscript that points to the position below J where the current row is to be inserted
T	Subscript for copying all the elements of one row into another
ThisRow	An array of ColSize elements that holds the row currently being sorted

Discussion

Refer to the Discussion sections of SortSIR and SortH2R for details about how a straight insertion sort works and for potential uses of a subprogram that sorts two-dimensional arrays.

When compared to SortSIR, SortSI2R takes about twice as long when ColSize is 2, and 4 to 7 times as long when ColSize is 10.

Modification

To change the sort from ascending to descending order (that is, with largest numbers first), change the less-than sign (<) to a greater-than sign (>) in the line indicated by {Mod. #1}.

SortH2R

> **Name:** *SortH2R*
>
> **Type:** *Procedure*
>
> **Purpose:** *To sort a two-dimensional* real *array, using the heapsort technique*
>
> **Calling Sequence:** SortH2R(Num2Array, RowCount, SortCol)

Description

SortH2R sorts a two-dimensional real array into ascending order. You specify which column contains the sort key. The sort is performed in place. See the Modification section if you want to sort in descending order.

Input

Num2Array	real	Array to be sorted
RowCount	integer	The number of rows in the array to be sorted
SortCol	integer	The column number of the sort key

In addition, you must specify in your main program the following global type and const declarations. ColSize is the exact number of columns (the second dimension) and is required. RowSize is the maximum number of rows (first dimension) and is not required as a constant. Specifying RowSize, however, facilitates the type declaration and retains compatibility with other subprograms. The numbers 2 and 100 are examples.

```
const
   ColSize = 2;
   RowSize = 100;

type
   Array2Type = array[1..RowSize, 1..ColSize] of real;
```

Output

Num2Array   real   The same array, now sorted

Limitations and Error Conditions

If RowCount is less than or equal to 1, the sort procedure is bypassed, but no error message is displayed. No other error checking is done. Your responsibility is to make sure that RowCount and SortCol are accurate and do not exceed the bounds of the array. You may set RowCount to less than RowSize. Only the first RowCount elements are sorted.

Sample Usage

```
program SampleUsageOfSortH2R;

const
   ColSize = 2;
   RowSize = 100;

type
   Array2Type = array[1..RowSize, 1..ColSize] of real;

var
   Num2Array                : Array2Type;
   RowCount, SortCol, J, K : integer;

{$I SortH2R.PSL}

BEGIN
   Num2Array[1, 1] := 4.4;    Num2Array[1, 2] := 64.0;
   Num2Array[2, 1] := -1.0;   Num2Array[2, 2] := 11.2;
   Num2Array[3, 1] := 3.7;    Num2Array[3, 2] := 27.3;
   Num2Array[4, 1] := 2.3;    Num2Array[4, 2] := 88.5;
   RowCount := 4;
```

```
   SortCol  := 1;
   SortH2R(Num2Array, RowCount, SortCol);
   writeln('Here is the data, sorted on the first column.');
   for J := 1 to RowCount do
      begin
         for K := 1 to ColSize do
            write(Num2Array[J,K]:9:2);
         writeln
      end
END.
```

This text program produces the following output:

```
Here is the data, sorted on the first column.
    -1.00    11.20
     2.30    88.50
     3.70    27.30
     4.40    64.00
```

Subprogram Listing of SortH2R.PSL

```
procedure SortH2R(var Num2Array: Array2Type;
                  RowCount, SortCol: integer);

label
   H1, H2, H3, H4, H5, H7, H8, H9;

var
   I, J, L, R, T : integer;
   ThisRow       : array[1..ColSize] of real;

begin
   if RowCount <= 1 then exit;
H1: L := RowCount div 2 + 1;
    R := RowCount;
H2: if L > 1 then
        begin
           L := L - 1;
           for T := 1 to ColSize do
              ThisRow[T] := Num2Array[L,T]
        end
```

```
        else
          begin
            for T := 1 to ColSize do
               ThisRow[T] := Num2Array[R, T];
            Num2Array[R] := Num2Array[1];
            R := R - 1;
            if R = 1 then
               begin
                 for T := 1 to ColSize do
                    Num2Array[1, T] := ThisRow[T];
                 exit                       {successful end of sort}
               end
          end;
H3: J := L;
H4: I := J;
    J := J + J;
    if J > R then goto H8;
    if J = R then goto H7;
H5: if Num2Array[J, SortCol] <                          {Mod. #1}
       Num2Array[J+1, SortCol] then J := J + 1;
H7: Num2Array[I] := Num2Array[J];
    goto H4;
H8: J := I;
    I := J div 2;
H9: if (ThisRow[SortCol] <=                              {Mod. #1}
          Num2Array[I, SortCol]) or (J = L) then
       begin
         for T := 1 to ColSize do
            Num2Array[J, T] := ThisRow[T];
         goto H2
       end
    else
       begin
         Num2Array[J] := Num2Array[I];
         goto H8
       end
end;
```

Variables

I, J, L, R	Subscript variables used in keeping track of rows in Num2Array while SortH2R arranges it into a heap and then selects the rows in the correct order. (See the Discussion section of SortHR.)
T	Subscript for copying all the elements of one row into another
ThisRow	An array of ColSize elements that holds the row currently being sorted

Discussion

Refer to SortHR's Discussion section for an explanation of the heapsort technique and its merits compared to those of other sorting methods.

A common use for SortH2R is to sort paired X-Y data into ascending order for the X values, after which the array is prepared for many other potential uses (binary searching, graphing, curve fitting, etc.). In such a case, ColSize is 2, and SortCol is 1, assuming that you put the X values in the first column and the Y values in the second column.

When compared to SortHR, SortH2R takes about 30 percent longer when ColSize is 2, 60 percent longer when ColSize is 4, 2.5 times longer when ColSize is 10, and 5 times longer when ColSize is 25.

Modification

To change the sort from ascending to descending order (that is, with largest numbers first), change the less-than sign (<) to a greater-than sign (>) in the first line indicated by {Mod. #1}. In the second indicated statement, change <= to >=.

SortSIT

> **Name:** *SortSIT*
>
> **Type:** *Procedure*
>
> **Purpose:** *To sort a text array, using the straight insertion technique*
>
> **Calling Sequence:** SortSIT(TextArray, LineCount, Position, Width)

Description

This procedure sorts in ascending order the elements in a text (string) array, using the straight insertion technique. You indicate the position and size of the sort key; it does not have to begin in the first position. Because the sort is performed in place, no extra work storage is needed during the sort process. The sequence for text is the ASCII sequence, in which uppercase text is distinguished from lowercase text. All uppercase text is lower in sequence than lowercase text. You may need to use ConvUp (or a similar procedure) to convert text data into uniform capitalization in order to get the sorting results you want.

Input

TextArray   string   Array to be sorted

LineCount   integer   number of lines in the array to be sorted

Position   integer   Starting position of the sort key in each string

Width   integer   Size of the sort key, in bytes

In addition, you must specify in your main program the following global type declarations, preferably using the global const declaration shown. TextSize is the maximum number of lines of text. LineSize is the maximum length of each line. The numbers 250 and 120 are examples.

```
const
   TextSize = 250;

type
   LineSize = string[120];
   TextArrayType = array[1..TextSize] of LineSize;
```

Output

TextArray   string   The same array, now sorted

Limitations and Error Conditions

If LineCount is less than or equal to 1, the sort procedure is bypassed, no error message is displayed, and the normal beginning and ending messages do not appear. No other error checking is done. Position must be in the range from 1 to 255. Otherwise, the subprogram will get run-time error 11 (hex) because of an invalid string index in Turbo's copy procedure. The sort key (which occupies locations Position through Position + Width - 1 of each string in the array) does not have

to be located either within the length of all the strings in the array, or even within
the length of LineSize. The portion of the sort key that extends beyond either the
string length or LineSize is equivalent to the null string, and sorts as if that portion
of the sort key were a low value. Only the first LineCount lines are sorted if
LineCount is less than the number of lines in the array.

Sample Usage

```
program SampleUsageOfSortSIT;

const
   TextSize = 250;

type
   LineSize = string[120];
   TextArrayType = array[1..TextSize] of LineSize;

var
   TextArray : TextArrayType;
   LineCount, Position, Width, J: integer;

{$I SortSIT.PSL}

BEGIN
   TextArray[1] := 'JOHNSON    192 LBS   73 IN';
   TextArray[2] := 'SMITH      167 LBS   70 IN';
   TextArray[3] := 'JONES      184 LBS   68 IN';
   LineCount := 3;
   Position  := 1;
   Width     := 10;
   SortSIT(TextArray, LineCount, Position, Width);
   for J := 1 to LineCount do writeln(TextArray[J]);
   Position := 11;
   Width    := 3;
   SortSIT(TextArray, LineCount, Position, Width);
   for J := 1 to LineCount do writeln(TextArray[J])
END.
```

This test program demonstrates how different sort keys cause the same array to
be sorted into two different sequences. The first sequence results from a sort key
of the first 10 bytes (name), and the second sequence results from a sort key of
bytes 11 through 13 (weight).

```
Begin SortSIT
3 lines sorted
JOHNSON    192 LBS  73 IN
JONES      184 LBS  68 IN
SMITH      167 LBS  70 IN
Begin SortSIT
3 lines sorted
SMITH      167 LBS  70 IN
JONES      184 LBS  68 IN
JOHNSON    192 LBS  73 IN
```

Subprogram Listing of SortSIT.PSL

```pascal
procedure SortSIT(var TextArray: TextArraytype;
                  LineCount, Position, Width: integer);

var
   J, K      : integer;
   ThisLine  : LineSize;

begin
   if LineCount <= 1 then exit;
   writeln('Begin SortSIT');                        {Mod. #1}
   for J := 2 to LineCount do
      begin
         ThisLine := TextArray[J];
         K := J - 1;
         while (Copy(ThisLine, Position, Width) <        {Mod. #2}
                Copy(TextArray[K], Position, Width)) and
               (K > 0) do
            begin
               TextArray[K + 1] := TextArray[K];
               K := K - 1
            end;
         TextArray[K + 1] := ThisLine
      end;
   writeln(LineCount, ' lines sorted')              {Mod. #1}
end;
```

Variables

J	Subscript variable that points to the array's current line to be inserted in the correct order
K	Subscript that points to the position below J where the current line is to be inserted
ThisLine	Contents of TextArray[J], the current line being sorted

Discussion

Refer to SortSIR's Discussion section for an explanation of SortSIT and other sorting techniques; the same principles apply. Timing estimates for SortSIT depend on the length of the strings and the sort key. Timings increase with larger arrays just as SortSIR timings do. Use SortHT for faster sorting of large string arrays that are not already nearly in order.

Modifications

1. To eliminate displaying the messages at the beginning and end of the sort, delete the two statements indicated by {Mod. #1}.

2. To change the sort from ascending to descending order (that is, with largest values first), change the less-than sign (<) to a greater-than sign (>) in the indicated statement.

SortHT

> **Name:** *SortHT*
>
> **Type:** *Procedure*
>
> **Purpose:** *To sort a text array, using the heapsort technique*
>
> **Calling Sequence:** SortHT(TextArray, LineCount, Position, Width)

Description

This procedure sorts in ascending order the elements in a text (string) array, using the heapsort technique. You indicate the position and size of the sort key; it does not have to begin in the first position. Because the sort is performed in place, no extra work storage is needed for the sort process. The sequence for text is the ASCII sequence, in which uppercase text is distinguished from lowercase text. All uppercase text is lower in sequence than lowercase text. You may need to use ConvUp (or a similar procedure) to convert text data into uniform capitalization in order to get the sorting results you want.

Input

TextArray	string	Array to be sorted
LineCount	integer	The number of lines in the array to be sorted
Position	integer	Starting position of the sort key in each string
Width	integer	The size of the sort key, in bytes

In addition, you must specify in your main program the following global type declarations, preferably using the global const declaration shown. TextSize is the maximum number of lines of text. LineSize is the maximum length of each line. The numbers 250 and 120 are examples; your numbers may differ.

```
const
    TextSize = 250;

type
    LineSize = string[120];
    TextArrayType = array[1..TextSize] of LineSize;
```

Output

TextArray	string	The same array, now sorted

Limitations and Error Conditions

Refer to the Limitations and Error Conditions section of SortSIT.

Sample Usage

```
program SampleUsageOfSortHT;

const
   TextSize = 10;

type
   LineSize = string[40];
   TextArrayType = array[1..TextSize] of LineSize;
```

```
var
   TextArray : TextArrayType;
   LineCount, Position, Width, J: integer;

{$I SortHT.PSL}

BEGIN
   TextArray[1] := 'JOHNSON    192 LBS   73 IN';
   TextArray[2] := 'SMITH      167 LBS   70 IN';
   TextArray[3] := 'JONES      184 LBS   68 IN';
   LineCount := 3;
   Position  := 1;
   Width     := 10;
   SortHT(TextArray, LineCount, Position, Width);
   writeln('The data sorted by name is');
   for J := 1 to LineCount do writeln(TextArray[J]);
   Position := 11;
   Width    := 3;
   SortHT(TextArray, LineCount, Position, Width);
   writeln('The data sorted by weight is');
   for J := 1 to LineCount do writeln(TextArray[J])
END.
```

This sample program produces the same output as that of the sample program for SortSIT, except that SortHT does not display beginning and ending messages. Instead, this sample program displays a message before each set of output.

```
The data sorted by name is
JOHNSON    192 LBS   73 IN
JONES      184 LBS   68 IN
SMITH      167 LBS   70 IN
The data sorted by weight is
SMITH      167 LBS   70 IN
JONES      184 LBS   68 IN
JOHNSON    192 LBS   73 IN
```

Subprogram Listing of SortHT.PSL

```
procedure SortHT(var TextArray: TextArrayType;
                 LineCount, Position, Width: integer);

label
   H1, H2, H3, H4, H5, H7, H8, H9;

var
   I, J, L, R : integer;
   ThisLine   : LineSize;

begin
   if LineCount <= 1 then exit;
   H1: L := LineCount div 2 + 1;
       R := LineCount;
   H2: if L > 1 then
          begin
             L := L - 1;
             ThisLine := TextArray[L]
          end
       else
          begin
             ThisLine := TextArray[R];
             TextArray[R] := TextArray[1];
             R := R - 1;
             if R = 1 then
                begin
                   TextArray[1] := ThisLine;
                   exit                      {successful end of sort}
                end
          end;
   H3: J := L;
   H4: I := J;
       J := J + J;
       if J > R then goto H8;
       if J = R then goto H7;
   H5: if copy(TextArray[J], Position, Width) <        {Mod. #1}
          copy(TextArray[J+1], Position, Width) then J := J + 1;
   H7: TextArray[I] := TextArray[J];
       goto H4;
   H8: J := I;
       I := J div 2;
```

```
H9: if (copy(ThisLine, Position, Width) <=          {Mod. #1}
        copy(TextArray[I], Position, Width)) or (J = L) then
      begin
        TextArray[J] := ThisLine;
        goto H2
      end
    else
      begin
        TextArray[J] := TextArray[I];
        goto H8
      end
end;
```

Variables

I, J, L, R   Subscript variables used in keeping track of lines in TextArray while SortHT arranges it into a heap and then selects the lines in the correct order. (See the Discussion section of SortHR.)

ThisLine   A line of TextArray, now being sorted

Discussion

Refer to SortHR's Discussion section, which briefly explains the heapsort technique and indicates when this technique is superior to straight insertion. As with SortSIT, timing estimates for SortHT depend on the length of your strings and the sort key. Timings increase with larger arrays just as SortHR timings do. The size of the sort key makes a small difference in the sort time, but the lengths of the strings make a big difference. For random 20-byte strings with a 10-byte sort key, sorting with SortHT takes about 2.5 times as long as sorting real numbers with SortHR.

Modification

To change the sort from ascending to descending order (that is, with largest values first), change the less-than sign (<) to a greater-than sign (>) in the first statement indicated by {Mod. #1}. Change <= to >= in the second statement indicated by {Mod. #1}.

SortSIRT

> **Name:** *SortSIRT*
>
> **Type:** *Procedure*
>
> **Purpose:** *To sort paired* real *and text arrays, using the straight insertion technique*
>
> **Calling Sequence:** SortSIRT(NumArray, TextArray, Count)

Description

This procedure sorts the elements in related real and text arrays into numerical order based on the real array. Two arrays that are related (that is, the value of an element in one array is associated with the same numbered element in the other array) are often called paired arrays. An example is an array of test scores (the real array) and a second array that has the associated student names (the text array). SortSIRT can sort these two arrays so that the test score array is in ascending order and the student name array continues to match, entry for entry, the test score array. The Modifications section shows how to change the subprogram to sort based on the text array instead.

As with the other subprograms in the SortSIxx family, SortSIRT uses the straight insertion technique. Refer to SortSIR and SortHR for details about which sort to use in a particular situation.

Input

NumArray	real	The real array to be sorted
TextArray	string	The associated text array
Count	integer	The number of paired elements (in the two arrays) to be sorted

In addition, you must specify in your main program the following global type declarations, preferably using the global const declaration shown. ArraySize is the maximum number of elements in each array. LineSize is the maximum length of each entry in the text array. The numbers 50 and 20 are examples.

```
const
   ArraySize = 50;

type
   LineSize      = string[20];
   TextArrayType = array[1..ArraySize] of LineSize;
   ArrayType     = array[1..ArraySize] of real;
```

Output

NumArray   real   The same real array, now sorted

TextArray   string   The same text array, now sorted to match NumArray

Limitations and Error Conditions

If Count is less than or equal to 1, the sort procedure is bypassed, but no error message is displayed. No other error checking is done. Only the first Count elements in each array are sorted if Count is less than the number of elements in the arrays.

Sample Usage

```
program SampleUsageOfSortSIRT;

const
   ArraySize = 50;

type
   LineSize      = string[20];
   TextArrayType = array[1..ArraySize] of LineSize;
   ArrayType     = array[1..ArraySize] of real;

var
   NumArray  : ArrayType;
   TextArray : TextArrayType;
   Count, J  : integer;

{$I SortSIRT.PSL}
```

```
BEGIN
   NumArray[1] := 84.4;   TextArray[1] := 'Anderson';
   NumArray[2] := 81.0;   TextArray[2] := 'Baker';
   NumArray[3] := 93.7;   TextArray[3] := 'Charles';
   NumArray[4] := 72.3;   TextArray[4] := 'Dinsdale';
   Count := 4;
   SortSIRT(NumArray, TextArray, Count);
   writeln('Here is the data, sorted numerically.');
   for J := 1 to Count do
      writeln(NumArray[J]:8:2, ' = ', TextArray[J])
END.
```

This program produces the following output:

```
Here is the data, sorted numerically.
   72.30 = Dinsdale
   81.00 = Baker
   84.40 = Anderson
   93.70 = Charles
```

Subprogram Listing of SortSIRT.PSL

```
procedure SortSIRT(var NumArray: ArrayType;
                   var TextArray: TextArrayType; Count: integer);

var
   J, K      : integer;
   ThisNum   : real;                                    {Mod. #1}
   ThisLine  : LineSize;

begin
   if Count <= 1 then exit;
   for J := 2 to Count do
      begin
         ThisNum  := NumArray[J];
         ThisLine := TextArray[J];
         K := J - 1;
         while (ThisNum < NumArray[K])              {Mod. #2, 3}
                and (K > 0) do
```

```
        begin
            NumArray[K+1]  := NumArray[K];
            TextArray[K+1] := TextArray[K];
            K := K - 1
        end;
        NumArray[K+1]  := ThisNum;
        TextArray[K+1] := ThisLine
    end
end;
```

Variables

J	Subscript variable that points to the two arrays' current elements to be inserted in the correct order
K	Subscript that points to the position below J where the current elements are to be inserted
ThisNum	Contents of NumArray[J], the current real number being sorted
ThisLine	Contents of TextArray[J], the current text element being sorted

Discussion

Refer to the Discussion section of SortSIR for an explanation of straight insertion sorting. Timing estimates for SortSIRT depend on the length of your strings and increase with larger arrays just as SortSIR timings do. Use SortHRT for faster sorting of large paired arrays that are not already nearly in order.

Modifications

1. If you have an integer array paired with a text array, change real to integer in the indicated statement. Change also real to integer in your global type definition.

2. To change the sort from ascending to descending order (that is, with largest values first), change the less-than sign (<) to a greater-than sign (>) in the indicated statement.

3. Change the subprogram so that the sort key is the text array, not the real array, by changing the indicated statement to

   ```
   while (ThisLine < TextArray[K])
   ```

Name this version SortSITR when you save it to your disk library. This change causes the entire text string, from first position to last, to be the sort key. If you like, you may combine this modification with the second one by using > instead of < in this line.

SortHRT

Name:	*SortHRT*
Type:	*Procedure*
Purpose:	*To sort paired* real *and text arrays, using the heapsort technique*
Calling Sequence:	SortHRT(NumArray, TextArray, Count)

Description

This procedure sorts the elements in related real and text arrays into numerical order based on the real array. The heapsort technique is used. See SortSIRT for details about paired arrays.

Input

NumArray   real   The real array to be sorted

TextArray   string   The associated text array

Count   integer   The number of elements in the arrays to be sorted

In addition, you must specify in your main program the following global type declarations, preferably using the global const declaration shown. ArraySize is the maximum number of elements in each array. LineSize is the maximum length of each entry in the text array. The numbers 100 and 20 are examples.

```
const
   ArraySize = 100;

type
   LineSize      = string[20];
   TextArrayType = array[1..ArraySize] of LineSize;
   ArrayType     = array[1..ArraySize] of real;
```

Output

NumArray	real	The same real array, now sorted
TextArray	string	The same text array, now sorted to match NumArray

Limitations and Error Conditions

If Count is less than or equal to 1, the sort procedure is bypassed, but no error message is displayed. No other error checking is done. Only the first Count elements in each array are sorted if Count is less than the number of elements in the arrays.

Sample Usage

```
program SampleUsageOfSortHRT;

const
   ArraySize = 100;

type
   LineSize      = string[20];
   TextArrayType = array[1..ArraySize] of LineSize;
   ArrayType     = array[1..ArraySize] of real;

var
   NumArray  : ArrayType;
   TextArray : TextArrayType;
   Count, J  : integer;

{$I SortHRT.PSL}

BEGIN
   NumArray[1] := 84.4;   TextArray[1] := 'Anderson';
   NumArray[2] := 81.0;   TextArray[2] := 'Baker';
   NumArray[3] := 93.7;   TextArray[3] := 'Charles';
   NumArray[4] := 72.3;   TextArray[4] := 'Dinsdale';
   Count := 4;
   SortHRT(NumArray, TextArray, Count);
   writeln('Here is the data, sorted numerically.');
   for J := 1 to Count do
      writeln(NumArray[J]:8:2, ' = ', TextArray[J])
END.
```

This sample program is the same one presented for SortSIRT and produces the same output:

```
Here is the data, sorted numerically.
    72.30 = Dinsdale
    81.00 = Baker
    84.40 = Anderson
    93.70 = Charles
```

Subprogram Listing of SortHRT.PSL

```pascal
procedure SortHRT(var NumArray: ArrayType;
                  var TextArray: TextArrayType; Count: integer);

label
   H1, H2, H3, H4, H5, H7, H8, H9;

var
   I, J, L, R : integer;
   ThisNum    : real;
   ThisLine   : LineSize;

begin
   if Count <= 1 then exit;
   H1: L := Count div 2 + 1;
       R := Count;
   H2: if L > 1 then
          begin
             L := L - 1;
             ThisNum  := NumArray[L];
             ThisLine := TextArray[L]
          end
        else
          begin
             ThisNum  := NumArray[R];
             ThisLine := TextArray[R];
             NumArray[R]  := NumArray[1];
             TextArray[R] := TextArray[1];
             R := R - 1;
             if R = 1 then
```

```
                        begin
                            NumArray[1]  := ThisNum;
                            TextArray[1] := ThisLine;
                            exit                    {successful end of sort}
                        end
                end;
H3: J := L;
H4: I := J;
    J := J + J;
    if J > R then goto H8;
    if J = R then goto H7;
H5: if NumArray[J] < NumArray[J+1] then              {Mod. #2,3}
        J := J + 1;
H7: NumArray[I]  := NumArray[J];
    TextArray[I] := TextArray[J];
    goto H4;
H8: J := I;
    I := J div 2;
H9: if (ThisNum <= NumArray[I])                      {Mod. #2,3}
            or (J = L) then
        begin
            NumArray[J]  := ThisNum;
            TextArray[J] := ThisLine;
            goto H2
        end
    else
        begin
            NumArray[J]  := NumArray[I];
            TextArray[J] := TextArray[I];
            goto H8
        end
end;
```

Variables

I, J, L, R	Subscript variables used to keep track of the arrays while SortHRT arranges them into the heap form and then extracts the data in the correct order. (See SortHR for details.)
ThisNum	Contents of NumArray[J], the current real number being sorted

ThisLine   Contents of TextArray[J], the current text element being
                  sorted

Discussion

Refer to the Discussion section of SortHR for an explanation of the heapsort technique. Timing estimates for SortHRT depend on the length of your strings and
increase with larger arrays just as SortHR timings do. Use SortSIRT for faster sorting
of small paired arrays and for large paired arrays that are nearly in order.

Modifications

1. If you have an integer array paired with a text array, change real to
   integer in the indicated statement. Change also real to integer in your
   global type definition.

2. To change the sort from ascending to descending order (that is, with
   largest values first), change the less-than sign (<) to a greater-than sign
   (>) in the first of the two indicated statements. Change >= to <= in the
   second statement.

3. Change the subprogram so that the sort key is the text array, not the
   real array, by changing the two indicated statements to

   H5: if TextArray[J] < TextArray[J+1] then
   H9: if (ThisLine <= TextArray[I])

   Name this version SortHTR when you save it in your disk library. This
   change causes the entire text string, from first position to last, to be the
   sort key. If you like, you may combine this modification with
   modification 2 by using > instead of < in the first line and >= instead of
   <= in the second line.

is found, the program displays the subscript and the contents of that array element. The following output shows two runs of the program. In the first run, a match was found. In the second run, no match was found.

```
   1=0.8  2=0.3  3=0.5  4=0.2  5=0.7  6=0.7  7=0.7  8=0.5
 Subscript match = 3  Entry = 0.5

   1=0.8  2=0.9  3=0.0  4=0.1  5=0.2  6=0.2  7=0.1  8=0.9
 No match found
```

Subprogram Listing of SchURSer.PSL

```pascal
procedure SchURSer(var NumArray: ArrayType; Count: integer;
                   Key: real; var Result: integer);     {Mod. #1}

var
   J: integer;

begin
   Result := -1;
   for J := 1 to Count do
      if NumArray[J] = Key then
         begin
            Result := J;
            exit
         end
end;
```

Variables

J   Subscript variable used to point to the current array element being compared to the key

Discussion

Just as there are dozens of sorting techniques, there are dozens of searching techniques, each of which may be best in certain circumstances. SchURSer performs a serial search of an unsorted (or unordered) array. In a serial search, each array element is examined in turn, starting with the first element and proceeding to the last. Because the array is unsorted, you cannot make assumptions about what the contents of the next element may be. Thus, if the search key doesn't match an array element, you must search the next element. If the array is sorted, you know

---

9

Searching

Searching through an array to find a particular entry is a problem that comes up often in a wide variety of computer programs. Whether the search is for the name that goes with an account number or for a mathematical table lookup, nearly all programmers occasionally have to write programs that search.

First, consider some introductory terminology. Think of how you look up a friend's phone number in a telephone directory. The friend's name is the *search key* or *key*. The phone book is the *array* or *table* in which you try to find a *match* or *hit* for your key. The entire listing for the friend (name, address, and phone number) is the *entry* or *array element*. (For large data processing applications, the array is often an entire *file* on disk, and each entry is called a *record*. These terms are not used in this chapter.) A conventional phone book is *sorted* by customer name. But if you have only a phone number and you need to find the name that goes with it, the phone book is *unsorted* for your search key. The only way you can find a match for the phone number key is to do a *serial* search of the entire phone book, from beginning to end. (We recommend that you call the number and ask whose it is instead.)

Because there are nearly as many searching techniques as there are sorting techniques, once again we have tried to select the techniques that work best in a wide range of circumstances yet are still reasonably short and simple. The simplest technique is a serial search through an unsorted array. SchURSer searches an unsorted array of `real` numbers (or `integers` with a modification), and SchUTSer searches an unsorted text (`string`) array.

The array you search may already be sorted, or you may want to sort it with one of the subprograms in the previous chapter if you need to search the array repeatedly. A sorted array can be searched more efficiently. The two subprograms provided for serially searching sorted arrays are SchSRSer for `real` arrays and SchSTSer for text arrays. For large arrays the binary searching technique is usually much faster. See SchSRBin for `real` arrays and SchSTBin for text arrays.

SchURSer

```
Name: SchURSer

Type: Procedure

Purpose: To search an unsorted real array serially

Calling Sequence: SchURSer(NumArray, Count, Key, Result)
```

Description

SchURSer searches a real array serially, looking for a match for the Key value. The sequence of the array elements does not matter. If a match is found, the subscript of the matching element is returned in Result. If no match is found, Result is set to -1. This technique is suitable for low-volume searching (that is, searching small arrays frequently, or searching larger arrays infrequently). For large arrays that require frequent searching, it may be better to sort the array with SortSIR or SortHR and to search with SchSRSer or SchSRBin. See the Discussion section for details.

Input

NumArray	real	The array to be searched
Count	integer	Number of elements in the array to be searched
Key	real	The search key to be matched against the array entries

In addition, you must specify in your main program the following global type declaration, preferably using the global const declaration shown (for compatibility with other subprograms). The number 250 is an example; your array size may differ.

```
const
   ArraySize = 250;

type
   ArrayType = array[1..ArraySize] of real;
```

Output

Result	integer	The subscript (or index) of the array element that is found to match Key. If no match is found, Result is set to -1.

Limitations and Error Conditions

Only elements 1 through Count of the array are searched, even if the array more elements in it. No error checking is done. Your responsibility is to make that Count is accurate and does not exceed the size of the array.

Sample Usage

```
program SampleUsageOfSchURSer;

const
   ArraySize = 250;

type
   ArrayType = array[1..ArraySize] of real;          {Mod. #1}

var
   NumArray      : ArrayType;
   Count, Result : integer;
   Key           : real;                             {Mod. #1}

{$I SchURSER.PSL}

BEGIN
   for Count := 1 to 8 do
      begin
         NumArray[Count] := int(random*10.0) / 10.0;
         write(Count:3, '=', NumArray[Count]:3:1)
      end;
   writeln;
   Count := 8;
   Key   := 0.5;
   SchURSer(NumArray, Count, Key, Result);
   if Result < 0 then
      writeln('No match found')
   else
      writeln('Subscript match = ', Result, '  Entry =',
              NumArray[Result]:4:1)
END.
```

This sample program fills the first 8 elements of the array with random multiples of 0.1 in the range from 0 to 0.9 and displays these values on the screen. The program then searches for the first element containing the value 0.5. When a match

that each element is larger than (or equal to) the previous one; therefore, you don't need to examine every element except in rare cases. See SchSRSer and SchSRBin if your array is already in order.

The SchURSer searching technique is efficient in certain cases. SchURSer is a good choice when the array size is small (no more than 10 to 20 elements) and nothing is known about the keys to be matched. This condition is especially true for the "one shot" array search, when you simply need to match a key against an array once. Fooling around with a more complicated technique isn't necessary. The unsorted serial search is certainly the simplest approach.

SchURSer is also useful when the array size is small to medium (medium is an intentionally vague term here) and you know that a high percentage of the keys will match a small number of the array elements. Because the array elements don't have to be in a certain sequence (unlike the other searching techniques in this book), you have the flexibility of putting the most frequently used values at the top of the array, where matches are found quickly. If, for example, the array values represent postal ZIP codes for a localized mailing list and three or four ZIP codes match over 95 percent of the searches, you should put those ZIP codes at the top of the list. The efficiency in searching for that 95 percent compensates for the inefficiency with the other searches, unless the array is huge.

Even if your array is fairly small, the frequency of your searching may make another technique better. If your array has 50 elements and you search it only twice before the program ends, use whatever subprogram is easiest for you (probably this one). The slowest of the techniques only takes about 1/100 of a second. But if your program needs to search the array 1,000 times or 100,000 times, you are probably better off if you sort the array and use SchSRBin or SchSRSer. Look at the sort and search timings to be sure.

The conclusion you should draw from this discussion is that you must know the characteristics of your data in order to choose the best searching method. Our intent here is to provide enough information about the subprograms in this book so that you can choose wisely. Sometimes your choice may be obvious; at other times, you may need to study your data and make some calculations.

Table 9.1 shows approximate searching times when SchURSer is used on arrays of different sizes. The worst-case time refers to the amount of time the search takes when Key does not match any array element. The average-case time refers to the search time for half the array. As mentioned earlier, you may greatly improve this average time by "stacking" the most frequently used search keys in the first few array elements. The timings are basically linear. In other words, if you have to search through only 1/10 of the array before finding a match, the time to do so is about 1/10 the time for the worst case. On the other hand, if many searches result in no matches at all, your average time will be much closer to the worst-case time. See Appendix D for details about the environment used for timings.

Table 9.1
Approximate SchURSer Timings

Time (in Seconds)

Count	Worst Case	Average Case
10	0.002	0.001
25	0.006	0.003
50	0.012	0.006
100	0.02	0.01
200	0.05	0.02
400	0.09	0.05
800	0.18	0.09
1600	0.37	0.18
3200	0.73	0.37
6400	1.46	0.73

Modification

To search an integer array instead of a real array, change real to integer in the indicated line. Make the same change in the two indicated lines in the Sample Usage program (or your own program). When saving this integer version to your disk library, name the version SchUISer. Change the name in the procedure statement also. Note that the Sample Usage program is not designed to work with integers.

SchSRSer

> **Name:** *SchSRSer*
>
> **Type:** *Procedure*
>
> **Purpose:** *To search a sorted real array serially*
>
> **Calling Sequence:**   SchSRSer(NumArray, Count, Key, Result)

Description

SchSRSer searches a previously sorted real array serially, looking for a match for the Key value. If a match is found, the subscript of the matching element is returned in Result. If no match is found, Result is set to -1. Because the array is in ascending order, the no-match condition occurs as soon as an array element is found that is larger than the search key. This technique is suitable for low-volume searching (that is, searching small arrays frequently, or searching larger arrays infrequently). For higher-volume searching, use the SchSRBin subprogram.

Input

NumArray	real	The array to be searched
Count	integer	Number of elements in the array to be searched
Key	real	The search key to be matched against the array entries

In addition, you must specify in your main program the following global type declaration, preferably using the global const declaration shown (for compatibility with other subprograms). The number 250 is an example; your array size may differ.

```
const
   ArraySize = 250;

type
   ArrayType = array[1..ArraySize] of real;
```

Output

Result	integer	The subscript (or index) of the array element that is found to match Key. If no match is found, Result is set to -1.

Limitations and Error Conditions

The array must be sorted into ascending order before you call SchSRSer, or incorrect processing may take place. (The first array element that exceeds Key causes SchSRSer to end without a match; such a condition can occur erroneously if the array is out of sequence.) Only elements 1 through Count of the array are searched, even if the array has more elements in it. No error checking is done. Your responsibility is to make sure that Count is accurate and does not exceed the size of the array.

Sample Usage

```
program SampleUsageOfSchSRSer;

const
   ArraySize = 250;

type
   ArrayType = array[1..ArraySize] of real;          {Mod. #1}

var
   NumArray        : ArrayType;
   Count, Result : integer;
   Key             : real;                            {Mod. #1}

{$I SchSRSer.PSL}

BEGIN
   for Count := 1 to 20 do
      NumArray[Count] := Count * Count;
   Count := 20;
   Key   := 100.0;
   SchSRSer(NumArray, Count, Key, Result);
   if Result < 0 then
      writeln('No match found')
   else
      writeln('Subscript match = ', Result, '  Entry =',
              NumArray[Result])
END.
```

This sample program fills the first 20 entries of the array with the squares of the numbers from 1 to 20 (that is, 1, 4, 9, 16, 25, . . . , 400). Then the program searches for the element that contains the value 100.0. When a match is found, the program displays the subscript and the contents of that array element:

```
Subscript match = 10  Entry =  1.0000000000E+02
```

Subprogram Listing of SchSRSer.PSL

```
procedure SchSRSer(var NumArray: ArrayType; Count: integer;
                   Key: real; var Result: integer);       {Mod. #1}

var
   J: integer;

begin
   Result := -1;
   for J := 1 to Count do
      if NumArray[J] >= Key then                          {Mod. #2}
         if NumArray[J] = Key then
            begin
               Result := J;
               exit
            end
         else
            exit
end;
```

Variables

J   Subscript variable that points to the array element being
                compared to the key

Discussion

See the Discussion section of SchURSer for an explanation of different searching techniques and suggestions about which technique to use. To search an integer array instead of a real array, or to search an array already sorted in descending order, see the Modifications section.

Table 9.2 shows approximate searching times when SchSRSer is used on arrays of different sizes. The worst-case time refers to the amount of time the search takes when Key is greater than or equal to the contents of the largest array element. The average-case time refers to the search time for half the array. For random data, this search technique takes the average-case time when no match is found (unlike SchURSer, which takes the worst-case time). Note that the average time rarely occurs in real-life situations; the real average time is usually different because the data in any practical application is seldom truly random. As with SchURSer, this subprogram yields quite linear timings—if you search only 1/10 of the array, then the time is about 1/10 the worst-case time.

Table 9.2

Approximate SchSRSer Timings

Time (in Seconds)

Count	Worst Case	Average Case
10	0.002	0.001
25	0.006	0.003
50	0.012	0.006
100	0.02	0.01
200	0.05	0.02
400	0.09	0.05
800	0.18	0.09
1600	0.37	0.18
3200	0.73	0.37
6400	1.46	0.73

Note that these times are the same as those shown for SchURSer. The difference is that this subprogram does not necessarily get its worst-case time when no match is found, but SchURSer does. With SchURSer, however, you may be able to place the most frequently matched elements near the top of the array (greatly reducing the search time) because sequential order is not necessary.

Modifications

1. To search an integer array instead of a real array, change real to integer in the indicated subprogram line. Make the same change in the two indicated lines in the Sample Usage program (or your own program). When saving this integer version to your disk library, name the version SchSISer. Change the name in the procedure statement also.

2. To change the subprogram so that it searches a descending array instead of an ascending one, change >= to <= in the indicated line.

SchSRBin

> **Name:** *SchSRBin*
>
> **Type:** *Procedure*
>
> **Purpose:** *To search a sorted real array, using a binary search*
>
> **Calling Sequence:** SchSRBin(NumArray, Count, Key, Result)

Description

SchSRBin searches a previously sorted `real` array, using a binary search. If a match is found, the subscript of the matching element is returned in `Result`. If no match is found, `Result` is set to -1. On randomly distributed data, the binary searching technique is much faster than serial techniques unless your array is extremely small.

Input

NumArray	real	The array to be searched
Count	integer	Number of elements in the array to be searched
Key	real	The search key to be matched against the array entries

In addition, you must specify in your main program the following global `type` declaration, preferably using the global `const` declaration shown (for compatibility with other subprograms). The number 250 is an example; your array size may differ.

```
const
   ArraySize = 250;

type
   ArrayType = array[1..ArraySize] of real;
```

Output

Result	integer	The subscript (or index) of the array element that is found to match Key. If no match is found, Result is set to -1.

Limitations and Error Conditions

The array must be sorted in ascending order before you call SchSRBin, or incorrect processing may take place. Only elements 1 through Count of the array are searched, even if the array has more elements in it. No error checking is done. Your responsibility is to make sure that Count is accurate and does not exceed the size of the array.

Sample Usage

```
program SampleUsageOfSchSRBin;

const
   ArraySize = 250;

type
   ArrayType = array[1..ArraySize] of real;                    {Mod. #1}

var
   NumArray        : ArrayType;
   Count, Result : integer;
   Key             : real;                                     {Mod. #1}

{$I SchSRBin.PSL}

BEGIN
   for Count := 1 to 21 do
      NumArray[Count] := Count * Count;
   Count := 21;
   Key    := 81.0;
   SchSRBin(NumArray, Count, Key, Result);
   if Result < 0 then
      writeln('No match found')
   else
      writeln('Subscript match = ', Result, '  Entry =',
              NumArray[Result])
END.
```

This sample program fills the first 21 entries of the array with the squares of the numbers from 1 to 21 (that is, 1, 4, 9, 16, 25, . . ., 441). Then the program searches for the element that contains the value 81.0. When a match is found, the program displays the subscript and the contents of that array element:

```
Subscript match = 9  Entry =  8.1000000000E+01
```

Subprogram Listing of SchSRBin.PSL

```
procedure SchSRBin(var NumArray: ArrayType; Count: integer;
                   Key: real; var Result: integer);      {Mod. #1}

var
   Low, High, J: integer;

begin
   Result := -1;
   Low    := 1;
   High   := Count;
   while High >= Low do
      begin
         J := (Low + High) div 2;
         if Key < NumArray[J] then
            High := J - 1
         else
            if Key > NumArray[J] then
               Low := J + 1
            else
               begin
                  Result := J;
                  exit
               end
      end
end;
```

Variables

Low	The subscript of the lowest element with which the search key can be matched
High	The subscript of the highest element with which the search key can be matched
J	Subscript variable that points to the array element being compared to the key

Discussion

The binary searching technique begins by examining the middle element of the array. If that element is larger than Key, everything above the midpoint is larger also, and only the elements below the midpoint need to be considered further. The next element considered is the one at the midpoint of the remaining elements. The binary search continues this way, eliminating half the remaining elements from consideration with each pass, until either a match is found or no possible matches remain. This approach results in many fewer comparisons than for serial searching techniques.

For randomly distributed data, SchSRBin is faster than SchURSer or SchSRSer in worst-case situations for arrays that are larger than approximately 8 elements. For the average case, the cutoff is about 15 elements. As the size of the array increases, the binary search becomes comparatively faster. Remember, however, that the two serial searching techniques can yield much better than average-case results, depending on the data. The results of the binary searching technique are seldom better than the average-case results. (The Discussion section of SchURSer has an explanation of different searching techniques and suggestions about which technique to use in a particular situation.)

Table 9.3 shows approximate searching times when SchSRBin is used on arrays of various sizes. The worst-case time refers to the amount of time the search takes when Key has no match in the array. The average-case time refers to the time required for finding a match in randomly distributed data. From these timings, you can obviously see that the binary search is by far the fastest of the three techniques in worst-case situations (about 10 times as fast for 200 elements, and 100 times as fast for 3,200 elements). Use the binary search unless you are searching extremely small arrays, or unless the other two techniques are close to best-case timings because of frequently found matches at the top of the array.

Table 9.3
Approximate SchSRBin Timings

Time (in Seconds)

Count	Worst Case	Average Case
10	0.002	0.002
25	0.003	0.002
50	0.003	0.003
100	0.004	0.003
200	0.004	0.004
400	0.005	0.004
800	0.005	0.005
1600	0.006	0.005
3200	0.006	0.006
6400	0.007	0.006

Modification

To search an `integer` array instead of a `real` array, change `real` to `integer` in the line indicated by {Mod. #1}. Make the same change in the two indicated lines in the Sample Usage program (or your own program). When saving this `integer` version to your disk library, name the version `SchSIBin`. Change the name in the `procedure` statement also.

SchUTSer

> **Name:** *SchUTSer*
>
> **Type:** *Procedure*
>
> **Purpose:** *To search an unsorted text (`string`) array serially*
>
> **Calling Sequence:** `SchUTSer(TextArray, LineCount, Position, TextKey, Result)`

Description

`SchUTSer` searches a text array serially. The array doesn't need to be sorted. If a match is found, the subscript of the matching element is returned in `Result`. If no match is found, `Result` is set to -1. If the text array is small and sorted, see `SchSTSer`. For high-volume searching, see `SchSTBin`.

Input

`TextArray`	`string`	The array to be searched
`LineCount`	`integer`	Number of text lines in the array to be searched
`Position`	`integer`	The starting position of the search key in each text line
`TextKey`	`string`	The search key to be matched against the text array entries

In addition, you must specify in your main program the following global `type` declarations, preferably using the global `const` declaration shown (for compatibility with other subprograms). `TextSize` is the maximum number of lines of text in the array. `LineSize` is the maximum length of each line. `TextArrayType` and `String255` are required by the subprogram. The numbers 100 and 25 are examples; your array size may differ.

```
const
   TextSize = 100;

type
   LineSize = string[25];
   TextArrayType = array[1..TextSize] of LineSize;
   String255 = string[255];
```

Output

Result   integer   The subscript (or index) of the array element that is
                        found to match TextKey. If no match is found,
                        Result is set to -1.

Limitations and Error Conditions

If TextKey is a null string, no match is returned. Only elements 1 through LineCount of the array are searched, even if the array has more elements in it. No error checking is done. Your responsibility is to make sure that LineCount is accurate and does not exceed the size of the array.

Sample Usage

```
program SampleUsageOfSchUTSer;

const
   TextSize = 100;

type
   LineSize = string[25];
   TextArrayType = array[1..TextSize] of LineSize;
   String255 = string[255];

var
   LineCount, Position, Result : integer;
   TextArray                   : TextArrayType;
   TextKey                     : String255;

{$I SchUTSer.PSL}
```

```
BEGIN
   TextArray[1] := 'CA California';
   TextArray[2] := 'AZ Arizona';
   TextArray[3] := 'AL Alabama';
   TextArray[4] := 'AR Arkansas';
   TextArray[5] := 'AK Alaska';
   LineCount := 5;
   Position  := 1;
   TextKey   := 'AZ';
   SchUTSer(TextArray, LineCount, Position, TextKey, Result);
   if Result < 0 then
      writeln('No match found')
   else
      writeln('Subscript match = ', Result, '  Entry = ',
             TextArray[Result])
END.
```

This sample program demonstrates how SchUTSer can perform a table lookup that converts a two-character postal abbreviation into the state's name. Only the first five states are included in this sample. The key is the state abbreviation, which starts in the first position of each text array element. Note that the state abbreviations are not sorted. This example is based on the assumptions that CA is the TextKey most often encountered and that AZ is the next most frequent key. These two states are therefore placed in the first two array positions to speed the search. (See the Discussion section.) After a match is found, the main program can use Turbo's copy function to extract the state's name, which starts in the fourth position of each array element. Output from the sample program is the following:

```
Subscript match = 2  Entry = AZ Arizona
```

Subprogram Listing of SchUTSer.PSL

```
procedure SchUTSer(var TextArray: TextArrayType;
                   LineCount, Position: integer;
                   TextKey: String255; var Result: integer);

var
   J, Width: integer;
```

```
begin
   Result := -1;
   Width := length(TextKey);
   if Width < 1 then exit;
   for J := 1 to LineCount do
      if copy(TextArray[J], Position, Width) = TextKey then
         begin
            Result := J;
            exit
         end
end;
```

Variables

J   Subscript variable that points to the array element being
             compared to the key

Width   The size (length) of the search key passed to the
             subprogram

Discussion

The trade-offs among various searching techniques are covered in the Discussion
sections of the first three subprograms in this chapter.

SchUTSer performs a serial search of an unsorted array and is therefore a twin of
SchURSer. SchUTSer is best for one-shot searches for which sorting the array before
searching is not worth the time and effort, for searches of extremely small arrays,
or for searches of larger arrays when you expect nearly all searches to find a match
in the first few array entries.

Use the timing tables for the first three subprograms in this chapter as guidelines
for the timings of the last three subprograms. Timings are less predictable for string
arrays than for real arrays because both the string lengths and the key lengths may
vary widely. However, the timings for these string techniques relate to each other
the same way the corresponding real number timings do.

Modifications

None

SchSTSer

> **Name:** *SchSTSer*
>
> **Type:** *Procedure*
>
> **Purpose:** *To search a sorted text (*string*) array serially*
>
> **Calling Sequence:** SchSTSer(TextArray, LineCount, Position, TextKey, Result)

Description

SchSTSer searches a previously sorted text array serially. If a match is found, the subscript of the matching element is returned in Result. If no match is found, Result is set to -1. For high-volume searching, see the SchSTBin subprogram.

Input

TextArray	string	The array to be searched
LineCount	integer	Number of text lines in the array to be searched
Position	integer	The starting position of the search key in each text line
TextKey	string	The search key that is to be matched against the text array entries

In addition, you must specify in your main program the following global type declarations, preferably using the global const declaration shown (for compatibility with other subprograms). TextSize is the maximum number of lines of text in the array. LineSize is the maximum length of each line. TextArrayType and String255 are required by the subprogram. The numbers 100 and 25 are examples; the size of your array may differ.

```
const
   TextSize = 100;

type
   LineSize = string[25];
   TextArrayType = array[1..TextSize] of LineSize;
   String255 = string[255];
```

Output

Result   integer   The subscript (or index) of the array element that is
                             found to match TextKey. If no match is found,
                             Result is set to -1.

Limitations and Error Conditions

The array must be sorted in ascending order before you call SchSTSer (using as
the sort key the same portion of each text line that is used as the search key). If
TextKey is a null string, no match is returned. Only elements 1 through LineCount
of the array are searched, even if the array has more elements in it. No error checking
is done. Your responsibility is to make sure that LineCount is accurate and does
not exceed the size of the array.

Sample Usage

```
program SampleUsageOfSchSTSer;

const
   TextSize = 100;

type
   LineSize = string[25];
   TextArrayType = array[1..TextSize] of LineSize;
   String255 = string[255];

var
   LineCount, Position, Result : integer;
   TextArray                   : TextArrayType;
   TextKey                     : String255;

{$I SchSTSer.PSL}

BEGIN
   TextArray[1] := 'AL Alabama';
   TextArray[2] := 'AK Alaska';
   TextArray[3] := 'AZ Arizona';
   TextArray[4] := 'AR Arkansas';
   TextArray[5] := 'CA California';
   LineCount := 5;
   Position  := 4;
```

```
    TextKey   := 'Arkansas';
    SchSTSer(TextArray, LineCount, Position, TextKey, Result);
    if Result < 0 then
        writeln('No match found')
    else
        writeln('Subscript match = ', Result, '  Entry = ',
                TextArray[Result])
END.
```

This sample program demonstrates the use of SchSTSer to perform a table lookup for converting a state name into a two-character postal abbreviation. (The SchUTSer sample converts in the opposite direction.) Only the first five states are included in this sample. The key is the state name, which starts in the fourth position of each text array element. Note that the array entries are in ascending alphabetical order depending on the state name (the search key in this example), not the abbreviation. After a match is found, the main program can use Turbo's copy function to extract the state abbreviation from the first two positions of the array element. The sample program's output is the following:

```
    Subscript match = 4  Entry = AR Arkansas
```

Subprogram Listing of SchSTSer.PSL

```
procedure SchSTSer(var TextArray: TextArrayType;
                   LineCount, Position: integer;
                   TextKey: String255; var Result: integer);

var
  J, Width: integer;

begin
  Result := -1;
  Width  := length(TextKey);
  if Width < 1 then exit;
  for J := 1 to LineCount do
    if copy(TextArray[J], Position, Width) >= TextKey then
      if copy(TextArray[J], Position, Width) = TextKey then
        begin
          Result := J;
          exit
        end
      else
        exit
end;
```

Variables

J	Subscript variable that points to the array element being compared to the key
Width	The size of the search key passed to the subprogram

Discussion

The trade-offs among various searching techniques are covered in the Discussion sections of the first three subprograms in this chapter. Because SchSTSer performs a serial search of a sorted array, SchSTSer is a twin of SchSRSer. Generally, the serial search of a sorted array is best for searching extremely small arrays (no more than 10 to 20 entries).

As mentioned in the Discussion section of SchUTSer, timings of string searches vary widely depending on the sizes of your strings and the sort key. For guidelines to the relative merits of each technique in different situations, you can use the timing tables of subprograms that search real arrays.

Modifications

None

SchSTBin

Name:	*SchSTBin*
Type:	*Procedure*
Purpose:	*To search a sorted text (string) array, using a binary search*
Calling Sequence:	SchSTBin(TextArray, LineCount, Position, TextKey, Result)

Description

SchSTBin searches a previously sorted text array, using a binary search. If a match for TextKey is found, the subscript of the matching element is returned in Result. If no match is found, Result is set to -1. On randomly distributed data, the binary searching technique is much faster than serial techniques unless the arrays are extremely small.

Input

TextArray	string	The array to be searched
LineCount	integer	Number of text lines in the array to be searched
Position	integer	The starting position of the search key in each text line
TextKey	string	The search key to be matched against the text array entries

In addition, you must specify in your main program the following global type declarations, preferably using the global const declaration shown (for compatibility with other subprograms). TextSize is the maximum number of lines of text in the array, and LineSize is the maximum length of each line. TextArrayType and String255 are required by the subprogram. The numbers 100 and 25 are examples; the size of your array may differ.

```
const
   TextSize = 100;

type
   LineSize = string[25];
   TextArrayType = array[1..TextSize] of LineSize;
   String255 = string[255];
```

Output

Result	integer	The subscript (or index) of the array element that is found to match TextKey. If no match is found, Result is set to -1.

Limitations and Error Conditions

The array must be sorted in ascending order before you call SchSTBin (using as the sort key the same portion of each text line that is used as the search key). If TextKey is a null string, no match is returned. Only elements 1 through LineCount of the array are searched, even if the array has more elements in it. No error checking is done. Your responsibility is to make sure that LineCount is accurate and does not exceed the size of the array.

Sample Usage

```
program SampleUsageOfSchSTBin;

const
   TextSize = 100;

type
   LineSize = string[25];
   TextArrayType = array[1..TextSize] of LineSize;
   String255 = string[255];

var
   LineCount, Position, Result : integer;
   TextArray                   : TextArrayType;
   TextKey                     : String255;

{$I SchSTBin.PSL}

BEGIN
   TextArray[1] := 'AL Alabama';
   TextArray[2] := 'AK Alaska';
   TextArray[3] := 'AZ Arizona';
   TextArray[4] := 'AR Arkansas';
   TextArray[5] := 'CA California';
   LineCount := 5;
   Position  := 4;
   TextKey   := 'Alaska';
   SchSTBin(TextArray, LineCount, Position, TextKey, Result);
   if Result < 0 then
      writeln('No match found')
   else
      writeln('Subscript match = ', Result, '  Entry = ',
              TextArray[Result])
END.
```

This sample program, like the one for SchSTSer, demonstrates the use of a table lookup for converting a state name into a two-character postal abbreviation. (The SchUTSer sample converts in the opposite direction.) Only the first five states are included in this sample. The key is the state name, which starts in the fourth position of each text array element. Note that the array entries are in ascending alphabetical order depending on the state name (the search key in this example), not the abbreviation. The sample program searches for a match for Alaska and then displays the entry found:

```
Subscript match = 2  Entry = AK Alaska
```

Subprogram Listing of SchSTBin.PSL

```
procedure SchSTBin(var TextArray: TextArrayType;
                   LineCount, Position: integer;
                   TextKey: String255; var Result: integer);

var
   Low, High, J, Width: integer;

begin
   Result := -1;
   Width  := length(TextKey);
   if Width < 1 then exit;
   Low    := 1;
   High   := LineCount;
   while High >= Low do
      begin
         J := (Low + High) div 2;
         if TextKey < copy(TextArray[J], Position, Width) then
            High := J - 1
         else
            if TextKey > copy(TextArray[J], Position, Width) then
               Low := J + 1
            else
               begin
                  Result := J;
                  exit
               end
      end
end;
```

Variables

Low	The subscript of the lowest entry with which a match is possible
High	The subscript of the highest entry with which a match is possible

J   Subscript variable that points to the array element being
                           compared to the key

Width   The size of the search key

Discussion

The trade-offs among various searching techniques are covered in the Discussion
sections of the first three subprograms in this chapter. SchSTBin, which performs
a binary search of a sorted array, is a twin of SchSRBin. With random data in which
a match is always found, a binary search is faster than a serial search if the array
size has more than approximately 15 elements. For worst-case searches, the binary
search is faster whenever the array contains more than about 8 elements.

As mentioned in the Discussion section of SchUTSer, timings vary widely for string
searching with different string and sort key sizes. For guidelines to the relative
merits of each technique in different situations, you can use the timing tables for
subprograms that search real arrays.

Modifications

None

10

Parsing

Parsing is the dissection of text strings into meaningful components. Typically, strings are searched for certain keywords or characters that have meaning in the current semantic context. The Turbo Pascal compiler includes a sophisticated parser that must interpret Pascal program syntax so that the compiler can generate appropriate machine code.

We use the term parsing to include what is generally referred to as *lexical scanning*. This is the process of searching through a string in order to construct its overall meaning. Individual components are interpreted one at a time for their meanings within the legal syntax. This is often done in "parsers" that process English commands. An adventure game is a good example of a program that includes a parser to process commands in English.

Parsers generally work in one of two ways. The first is to divide the source string into substrings at appropriate keywords. The substrings are then processed for further interpretation. The second method is to keep a pointer in the source string. A keyword check is performed at the pointer. When a keyword is found, its meaning is interpreted, and the pointer is updated.

This chapter provides six fundamental parsing subprograms. SplitD searches a string for a specific delimiter (of any length) and divides the string at the delimiter (if the delimiter is found). SplitCh searches a string for the occurrence of any single character delimiter from a set of delimiters you specify. Again, the string is split at a delimiter if one is found. SubStrD finds a substring bounded by two specified delimiters.

The remaining three subprograms are of the "pointer" type. Given an array of keywords, ParseKW detects whether the pointer is at one of the keywords. ParseRN detects whether the pointer points to a real number. And ParseIN checks for an integer number. Each of these subprograms "reports" what it finds and updates the pointer appropriately.

Capitalization is sometimes a stumbling block in the parsing process. Suppose that you have *begin* as a keyword. You want the parser to detect *BEGIN*, *Begin*, or even

BeGiN as valid. This problem is easily solved with ConvUp or ConvLow from Chapter 11. These two subprograms convert a string to all uppercase or lowercase letters. If you process each source string through ConvUp, for example, your keyword list for parsing needs to include only *BEGIN* for detecting any of the variants.

A minor inconvenience is associated with Turbo Pascal subprograms that pass strings as var parameters to and from main programs. Pascal demands strict type checking. In other words, the string type of the actual parameter in the main program must exactly match the formal parameter in the subprogram. We would like to design the subprograms as "black boxes" that require no internal coding changes for adoption by any particular main program. In an ideal world, you could then declare strings to be whatever type you wanted and still use any of the subprograms without modification.

Pascal is not this forgiving, however. (There is good reason, of course. The restrictions protect you from potentially referencing beyond the active string length.) A compromise is therefore necessary. Three primary "solutions" to this dilemma are possible.

The solution in our subprograms is to declare the string type globally in the main program, using the name expected by the subprogram. This solution always works and puts minimal demand on memory resources. The disadvantage is that each string in the main program must be declared with the correct type name (or one that matches the correct name in length).

A second solution is to use Turbo's {$V-} compiler directive, which permits the relaxation of strict type checking. You place the {$V-} directive in your main program before one of the subprograms is invoked. (You can restore the type checking with {$V+} right after the subprogram call.) This method permits you to declare variable strings of any type you want. The disadvantages are minor: you still need a global declaration for each string type that occurs in the subprogram, you may clobber good data with mismatched string references, and this compiler directive may work differently in future Turbo releases. Because we would like this book to persevere, it's the last concern that worries us.

The last solution is to use in your main programs work strings as temporary holding places for communication with the subprograms. You must declare an extra string type globally. A convenient choice is

```
String255 = string[255]
```

This declares a maximum-length string. You must globally equate to String255 the string type names used in the subprograms. You must also define some work strings in your main program to be this type. These work strings serve as buffers between the subprogram and the active data strings in your main program. The active strings can be of any string type. When you want to pass one of these strings to a subprogram, you first equate one of the work strings to the active string. You can then pass the work string to the subprogram, because the work string is of the correct type. Similarly, you use other work strings to receive strings back from the subprogram. You then equate your active string variables to the appropriate work strings. Two disadvantages of this approach are the extra coding required and the extra memory needed.

SplitD

> **Name:** *SplitD*
>
> **Type:** *Procedure*
>
> **Purpose:** *To divide a string at a specified delimiter*
>
> **Calling Sequence:** `SplitD(SourceStr, Delimiter, LeftPart, RightPart, Found)`

Description

SplitD provides a fundamental parsing capability for processing text strings. SplitD searches a source string left to right for the first occurrence of a given delimiter. If the delimiter is found, the source string is split into two output strings—the part to the left of the delimiter and the part to the right. The delimiter can be any length.

Input

SourceStr   string   The source string. It can be any length and may be specified as a variable or a literal in the calling statement. SourceStr's type must be declared globally as ParseType.

Delimiter   string   The delimiter. It can be any length and may be specified as a variable or a literal in the calling statement. Delimiter's type must be declared globally as DelimType.

The two string types, ParseType and DelimType, must be declared globally in the type block of the main program:

```
type
   ParseType = string[255];
   DelimType = string[20];
```

The lengths of 255 and 20 are examples; your maximum string lengths may differ.

Output

LeftPart   string   The substring from SourceStr to the left of Delimiter. LeftPart is set to the null string if Delimiter is not found in SourceStr. LeftPart is of type ParseType.

RightPart   string   The substring from SourceStr to the right of Delimiter. RightPart is set to the null string if Delimiter is not found in SourceStr. RightPart is of type ParseType.

Found   boolean   A flag that indicates whether Delimiter is found in SourceStr. If so, Found is true. If not, Found is false.

Limitations and Error Conditions

If either SourceStr or Delimiter (or both) is a null string, LeftPart and RightPart are null strings, and Found is false.

If the delimiter occurs more than once inside the source string, only the first (leftmost) occurrence is processed by SplitD. When the delimiter occurs at one end of the source string, LeftPart or RightPart (as appropriate) is null. If Delimiter and SourceStr are identical, Found is true, and both LeftPart and RightPart are null.

Sample Usage

```
program SampleUsageOfSplitD;

type
   ParseType = string[255];
   DelimType = string[20];

var
   SourceStr, LeftPart, RightPart : ParseType;
   Delimiter                      : DelimType;
   Found                          : boolean;
```

```
{$I SplitD.PSL}

BEGIN
   SourceStr := 'This is a test';
   Delimiter := 'is';
   SplitD(SourceStr, Delimiter, LeftPart, RightPart, Found);
   writeln(Found);
   if Found then
      writeln('Left part: >', LeftPart, '<      ',
              'Right part: >', RightPart, '<' );
   writeln;
   SplitD(SourceStr, ' is ', LeftPart, RightPart, Found);
   writeln(Found);
   if Found then
      writeln('Left part: >', LeftPart, '<      ',
              'Right part: >', RightPart, '<' );
   writeln;
   SplitD(SourceStr, 'test', LeftPart, RightPart, Found);
   writeln(Found);
   if Found then
      writeln('Left part: >', LeftPart, '<      ',
              'Right part: >', RightPart, '<' );
   writeln;
   SplitD('abcd', 'BC', LeftPart, RightPart, Found);
   writeln(Found)
END.
```

Running this test program produces the following output. The less-than (<) and greater-than (>) symbols are used here to delineate strings so that spaces, if present, can be seen more readily.

```
TRUE
Left part: >Th<      Right part: > is a test<

TRUE
Left part: >This<      Right part: >a test<

TRUE
Left part: >This is a <      Right part: ><

FALSE
```

Subprogram Listing of SplitD.PSL

```
procedure SplitD(SourceStr: ParseType; Delimiter: DelimType;
                 var LeftPart, RightPart: ParseType;
                 var Found: boolean);

var
   SourceLen, DelimLen, Position: byte;

begin
   SourceLen := length(SourceStr);
   DelimLen  := length(Delimiter);
   LeftPart  := '';
   RightPart := '';
   Found     := false;
   if (SourceLen = 0) or (DelimLen = 0) then
      exit;
   Position := pos(Delimiter, SourceStr);
   if Position > 0 then
      begin
         LeftPart  := copy(SourceStr, 1, Position - 1);
         RightPart := copy(SourceStr, Position + DelimLen,
                        SourceLen - Position - DelimLen + 1);
         Found     := true
      end
end;
```

Variables

SourceLen	The string length of SourceStr
DelimLen	The string length of Delimiter
Position	Current position in SourceStr

Discussion

This fundamental parsing subprogram has many possible applications in programs that process text strings. For a simple example, suppose that you are processing a series of names, each written as a last name, comma, space, and first name. If you make the delimiter a comma followed by a space, each name is divided into a last name and a first name.

Another possible use of SplitD occurs in "natural" language command processing. Suppose that you have a program which requests the user to input command strings like CREATE PLOT. The verb CREATE is an acceptable command in your language. Legal objects of this verb might be REPORT and FILE. If you make CREATE the delimiter, SplitD returns the object of the verb in RightPart. (The problem of uppercase and lowercase letters in this command syntax can be solved with the subprogram ConvUp in Chapter 11. See the introduction to this chapter and ConvUp in Chapter 11 for more details.)

Modifications

None

SplitCh

Name:	*SplitCh*
Type:	*Procedure*
Purpose:	*To divide a string at a delimiter from a set of character delimiters*
Calling Sequence:	SplitCh(SourceStr, DelimSet, LeftPart, RightPart, DelimChar, Found)

Description

A source string is searched left to right for the first occurrence of one of the delimiters specified in a delimiter set. If such a delimiter is found, the source string is split into two output strings—the part to the left of the delimiter and the part to the right. Each delimiter in the set must be a single character, but the set can contain any number of such characters (up to Turbo's maximum of 256).

Input

SourceStr   string   The source string. It can be any length and may be specified as a variable or a literal in the calling statement. SourceStr's type must be declared globally as ParseType.

DelimSet   char   The list of delimiters expressed as a set. Each element of the set is one character. The set can consist of any number of characters (up to 256) and may be specified as a variable or a literal in the calling statement. DelimSet's type must be declared globally as DelimSetType.

In addition, ParseType and DelimSetType must be declared global in the type block of your main program:

```
type
   ParseType    = string[255];
   DelimSetType = set of char;
```

The number 255 is an example. Your maximum string length may differ.

Output

LeftPart   string   The substring from SourceStr to the left of DelimChar. LeftPart is the null string if no delimiter match occurs in the source string. LeftPart is of type ParseType.

RightPart   string   The substring from SourceStr to the right of DelimChar. RightPart is the null string if no delimiter match occurs in the source string. RightPart is of type ParseType.

DelimChar   char   The first character from DelimSet found in SourceStr. If Found is false, DelimChar is chr(0).

Found   boolean A flag that indicates whether a delimiter is found in SourceStr. If so, Found is true. If not, Found is false.

Limitations and Error Conditions

If SourceStr is a null string, LeftPart and RightPart are null strings, Found is false, and DelimChar is set to chr(0).

If the source string contains more than one occurrence of a character in DelimSet, only the first (leftmost) occurrence is processed by SplitCh. When the delimiter occurs at one end of the source string, LeftPart or RightPart (as appropriate) is null. If SourceStr is a single character contained in DelimSet, Found is true, and both LeftPart and RightPart are null.

Sample Usage

```
program SampleUsageOfSplitCh;

type
   ParseType    = string[255];
   DelimSetType = set of char;

var
   SourceStr, LeftPart, RightPart: ParseType;
   DelimSet                      : DelimSetType;
   DelimChar                     : char;
   Found                         : boolean;

{$I SplitCh.PSL}

BEGIN
   SourceStr := 'It''s true!  The secret is mine.';
   DelimSet := ['.', '?', '!'];
   SplitCh(SourceStr, DelimSet, LeftPart, RightPart,
                   DelimChar, Found);
   if Found then
      writeln('First sentence: ', LeftPart);
   writeln;
   SplitCh('429Widgets', ['A'..'Z'], LeftPart, RightPart,
                                   DelimChar, Found);
   writeln('Number: ', LeftPart);
   writeln('Item:   ', DelimChar + RightPart)
END.
```

Running this test program produces the following output:

```
First sentence: It's true

Number: 429
Item:   Widgets
```

Subprogram Listing of SplitCh.PSL

```
procedure SplitCh(SourceStr: ParseType; DelimSet: DelimSetType;
                  var LeftPart, RightPart: ParseType;
                  var DelimChar: char; var Found: boolean);

var
   SourceLen, Position: integer;

begin
   SourceLen := length(SourceStr);
   LeftPart  := '';
   RightPart := '';
   DelimChar := chr(0);
   Found     := false;
   if (SourceLen = 0) then
      exit;
   Position := 0;
   repeat
      Position := Position + 1;
      if SourceStr[Position] in DelimSet then
         begin
            Found     := true;
            LeftPart  := copy(SourceStr, 1, Position - 1);
            DelimChar := SourceStr[Position];
            if Position < SourceLen then
               RightPart := copy(SourceStr, Position + 1,
                                    SourceLen - Position)
         end
   until
      Found or (Position = SourceLen)
end;
```

Variables

SourceLen	The string length of SourceStr
Position	Current position in SourceStr

Discussion

This subprogram is useful whenever you need to parse a string based on a range or collection of delimiters. For example, you can search for any uppercase letter, punctuation mark, numeral, etc.

Turbo's **set** type allows easy enumeration of delimiter ranges. Here are some set specifications to give you a few ideas:

```
LowercaseLetters := ['a'..'z'];
PunctuationChars := [',', '.', '!', '?', ';', ':'];
AnythingButSpace := [chr(0)..chr(255)] - [chr(32)];
RealNumberChars  := ['+', '-', '.', 'E', 'e', '0'..'9'];
```

The disadvantage of sets is that each set member is restricted to a single character. The SplitD subprogram handles a delimiter of any length but is restricted to one delimiter at a time.

DelimChar is the null character when no delimiter match is found. Be aware that a null string and a null character are different. A null string is a string devoid of any characters. When you use Turbo's built-in length function, a null string has a length of zero. A Turbo variable of type char consists of a single character. It always has a length of exactly 1, even if this single character is the "null" character created by chr(0). (You can include the null character in DelimSet, and this subprogram recognizes the null character if it occurs in SourceStr. In these contexts, the null character has a length of 1 and prints as a space with write statements.) If SourceStr is a null string, Found is always false. This holds even if DelimSet is empty ([]) or contains the null character ([chr(0)]).

Modifications

None

SubStrD

Name:	*SubStrD*
Type:	*Procedure*
Purpose:	*To find a substring bounded by two delimiters*
Calling Sequence:	SubStrD(SourceStr, DelimL, DelimR, ObjectStr, Position)

Description

SubStrD searches a source string left to right for the first occurrence of a given delimiter. If the delimiter is found, the search continues for the first occurrence of a second delimiter. If both delimiters are found, the substring bounded by the delimiters is returned. The two delimiters can be any length.

Input

SourceStr   string   The source string. It can be any length and may be specified in the argument list as a variable or a string literal. SourceStr's type must be declared globally as ParseType.

DelimL   string   The left (first) delimiter. It can be any length and may be specified as a variable or a literal in the calling statement. DelimL's type must be declared globally as DelimType.

DelimR   string   The right (second) delimiter. It can be any length and may be specified as a variable or a literal in the calling statement. DelimR's type must be declared globally as DelimType.

The two string types, ParseType and DelimType, must be declared globally in the type block of your main program:

```
type
   ParseType = string[255];
   DelimType = string[20];
```

The lengths 255 and 20 are examples; your string lengths may differ.

Output

ObjectStr   string   The substring from SourceStr, bounded by DelimL on the left and DelimR on the right. ObjectStr is set to the null string if the delimiters are not found in the source string. ObjectStr is of type ParseType.

Position   integer   If the delimiters are found, Position points to the character position in SourceStr where the first character of DelimL occurs. If the delimiters are not found (sequentially) in SourceStr, Position is set to 0 (zero).

Limitations and Error Conditions

Position is zero and ObjectStr is null if any of the following conditions is true: DelimL is null, DelimR is null, SourceStr is null or of length 1, or DelimL does not occur to the left of DelimR in the source string.

If more than one pair of the delimiters occur in SourceStr, only the leftmost substring bounded by both delimiters is processed. If the delimiters occur adjacent to each other, Position points to the first character of DelimL, and ObjectStr is null.

Sample Usage

```
program SampleUsageOfSubStrD;

type
   ParseType = string[255];
   DelimType = string[20];

var
   SourceStr, ObjectStr : ParseType;
   DelimL, DelimR       : DelimType;
   Position             : integer;

{$I SubStrD.PSL}

BEGIN
   SourceStr := 'Phone number is (213) 555-1212';
   DelimL    := '(';
   DelimR    := ')';
   SubStrD(SourceStr, DelimL, DelimR, ObjectStr, Position);
   writeln('Area code is ', ObjectStr);
   writeln('Found at position ', Position, ' in source string');
   writeln;
   SubStrD('Mr. John Doe', 'Mr. ', ' ', ObjectStr, Position);
   {Note the space character  *   * above each asterisk}
   writeln('The gentleman''s first name is ', ObjectStr)
END.
```

Running this test program produces the following output:

```
Area code is 213
Found at position 17 in source string

The gentleman's first name is John
```

Subprogram Listing of SubStrD.PSL

```
procedure SubStrD(SourceStr: ParseType; DelimL, DelimR:
                  DelimType; var ObjectStr: ParseType;
                  var Position: integer);

var
   SourceLen, LeftDLen, RightDLen, DelimLPos, DelimRPos: integer;

begin
   SourceLen := length(SourceStr);
   LeftDLen  := length(DelimL);
   RightDLen := length(DelimR);
   ObjectStr := '';
   Position  := 0;
   if (SourceLen < 2) or (LeftDLen = 0) or (RightDLen = 0) then
      exit;
   DelimLPos := pos(DelimL, SourceStr);
   if DelimLPos = 0 then
      exit;
   Delete(SourceStr, 1, DelimLPos + LeftDLen - 1);
   SourceLen := length(SourceStr);
   if SourceLen = 0 then
      exit;
   DelimRPos := pos(DelimR, SourceStr);
   if DelimRPos > 0 then
      begin
         Position  := DelimLPos;
         ObjectStr := copy(SourceStr, 1, DelimRPos - 1)
      end
end;
```

Variables

SourceLen	The string length of SourceStr
LeftDLen	The string length of the left delimiter
RightDLen	The string length of the right delimiter
DelimLPos	Position of the first character of DelimL in the source string

DelimRPos   Position of the first character of DelimR in the string
                     formed by deleting all text from the source string to the
                     left of and including DelimL

Discussion

The delimiters can be identical. This is true in many practical uses of SubStrD. For
example, a *word* is often defined as text bounded by a space on each side. If each
delimiter is made to be a space, SubStrD finds the first word in the text string.
(There are limitations to this simple approach, of course. If the leftmost character
of the source string is not a space, only an embedded word can be found. If two
or more spaces occur consecutively, the null string is returned.)

The output variable Position acts as a success or failure indicator. Position has
a positive value when the delimiters are found (success) and a zero value when
they are not found (failure). Does it seem more logical to have Position point to
the first character of the bounded substring instead of to the left delimiter? There
is a pathological case that precludes this alternative. When the two delimiters occur
juxtaposed, ObjectStr is legitimately the null string. But you can't point to the
character position of the null string. Therefore, Position points to the left delimiter.

Modifications

None

ParseKW

Name: *ParseKW*

Type: *Procedure*

Purpose: *To detect a keyword at a specific position in a string*

Calling Sequence: ParseKW(SourceStr, KWArray, KWCount, Position,
                                 KWIndex)

Description

Given a string array of keywords, ParseKW detects whether a source string contains
one of the keywords at a specified position. If so, the keyword is returned, and the
position variable is updated to point just beyond the keyword. The source string
and keywords can be any length. This subprogram is useful in "natural language"
command processing and many other applications.

Input

SourceStr	string	The source string. It can be any length and may be specified as a variable or a literal in the calling statement. SourceStr's type must be declared globally as ParseType.
KWArray	string	A string array containing the list of keywords. Each keyword can be any length. The array type must be declared globally as KWArrayType.
KWCount	integer	The number of active elements in KWArray. KWCount must be at least 1.
Position	integer	The position in SourceStr where a keyword match is looked for. Position must be at least 1 and no more than the length of SourceStr. Position must be specified as a variable and cannot be a literal.

In addition, the following global type declaration must appear in your main program. The numbers 255, 25, and 20 are examples. Your values may differ.

```
type
   ParseType  = string[255];
   KWArrayType = array[1..25] of string[20];
```

Output

Position	integer	Current position in SourceStr. Position retains its input value if no keyword match is found. Position is positioned at the first SourceStr character past the keyword if a match is found. If the end of the keyword coincides with the end of SourceStr, Position is set to 0 (zero).
KWIndex	integer	Array index of the matching keyword or 0 (zero) if no keyword is found

Limitations and Error Conditions

KWIndex is set to zero and the procedure is bypassed if any of the following conditions is true: KWCount is less than 1, SourceStr is null, or Position is less than 1 or greater than the length of SourceStr.

If KWCount is less than the number of elements in KWArray, only the first KWCount elements of the array are checked. Make sure that KWCount is not set higher than the actual number of elements in the array. Spurious matches are possible in this case.

The array of keywords is checked in ascending order. Be careful of ambiguity if your list of keywords contains similar strings. For example, suppose that DO appears in KWArray before DOODLE. Then DOODLE can never be detected because DO is always found first. Place DOODLE before DO to solve this potential problem.

Sample Usage

```
program SampleUsageOfParseKW;

type
   ParseType   = string[255];
   KWArrayType = array[1..25] of string[20];

var
   SourceStr                    : ParseType;
   KWArray                      : KWArrayType;
   KWCount, Position, KWIndex : integer;

{$I ParseKW.PSL}

BEGIN
   KWArray[1] := 'MOVE';
   KWArray[2] := 'CHANGE';
   KWArray[3] := 'COMPILE';
   KWArray[4] := 'DELETE';
   KWCount    := 4;
   SourceStr  := 'CHANGE PAPER IN THE PRINTER';
   Position   := 1;
   ParseKW(SourceStr, KWArray, KWCount, Position, KWIndex);
   if KWIndex > 0 then
      begin
         writeln('Keyword (', KWArray[KWIndex], ') found');
         writeln('Position in source string is now ', Position)
      end;
   writeln;
   ParseKW(SourceStr, KWArray, KWCount, Position, KWIndex);
   if KWIndex > 0 then
      writeln('Keyword ', KWIndex, ' found')
   else
      writeln('Keyword not found')
END.
```

Running this test program produces the following output:

```
Keyword (CHANGE) found
Position in source string is now 7

Keyword not found
```

Subprogram Listing of ParseKW.PSL

```pascal
procedure ParseKW(SourceStr: ParseType; var KWArray: KWArrayType;
                  KWCount: integer; var Position,
                  KWIndex: integer);

var
   TempStr             : ParseType;
   SourceLen, TempLen  : integer;
   Found               : boolean;

begin
   SourceLen := length(SourceStr);
   KWIndex   := 0;
   if (KWCount < 1) or not (Position in [1..SourceLen]) then
      exit;
   if Position > 1 then
      delete(SourceStr, 1, Position - 1);
   KWIndex := 0;
   repeat
      KWIndex := KWIndex + 1;
      TempStr := KWArray[KWIndex];
      TempLen := length(TempStr);
      Found   := (copy(SourceStr, 1, TempLen) = TempStr)
   until
      Found or (KWIndex = KWCount);
   if Found then
      begin
         Position := Position + TempLen;
         if Position > SourceLen then
            Position := 0
      end
   else
      KWIndex := 0
end;
```

Variables

TempStr	Temporary string (a copy of one of the keywords)
SourceLen	The string length of SourceStr
TempLen	The string length of TempStr
Found	boolean flag indicating whether or not a keyword match is found

Discussion

This kind of subprogram is a fundamental tool for lexical scanning. Suppose that you are writing a user interface that accepts "natural" language. (Examples are a compiler, adventure game, and input processor.) Your user is going to give commands from an allowable language. The interface must interpret these commands and take appropriate action.

Consider the legal commands used to have the form of a verb followed by an object. Assume that the legal verbs are "TURN ON ", "TURN OFF ", and "BEGIN ". (Note the terminating space for each verb.) These verbs are put in an array called Verbs. Another array called Object contains PRINTER and COLOR MONITOR. Your interface could contain code like this:

```
{ Verb and Object arrays are defined}
 Position := 1;
 ParseKW(SourceStr, Verbs, 3, Position, KWIndex);
 case KWIndex of
   0: writeln('What are you talking about?' );
   1: begin
         ParseKW(SourceStr, Object, 2, Position, NewIndex);
         case NewIndex of
           0: writeln('TURN ON what?' );
           1: writeln('I should TURN ON the PRINTER' );
           2: writeln('I should TURN ON the COLOR MONITOR' )
         end
      end;
   2: {similar code to above except now TURNing OFF};
   3: {similar code to above except now BEGINning}
 end;
```

Modifications

None

ParseRN

Name: *ParseRN*
Type: *Procedure*
Purpose: *To detect a real number at a specific position in a string*
Calling Sequence: ParseRN(SourceStr, Position, Found, RealValue)

Description

ParseRN examines a source string for a real number beginning at a specified string position. If such a number is found, the value of the number is returned, and a position variable is updated to the character in the source string just beyond the number. The source string can be any length.

Input

SourceStr   string   The source string. It can be any length and may be specified as a variable or a literal in the calling statement. SourceStr's type must be declared globally as ParseType.

Position   integer   The position in SourceStr where a real number is looked for. Position must be at least 1 and no more than the length of SourceStr. Position must also be specified as a variable and cannot be a literal.

In addition, the following global type declaration must appear in your main program:

```
type
    ParseType = string[255];
```

The number 255 is only an example. Your string length may differ.

Output

Position   integer   Current position in SourceStr. Position retains its input value if no legal real number is found. If a number is found, Position points to the first SourceStr character past the number. If the end of the number coincides with the end of SourceStr, Position is set to 0 (zero).

Found	boolean	A flag indicating whether a real number was found in SourceStr, beginning at the input value of Position. If so, Found is true. If not, Found is false.
RealValue	real	The real number found, if any. It is set to 0.0 if no number is found.

Limitations and Error Conditions

Found is false and RealValue is zero if the input value of Position is less than 1 or greater than the length of SourceStr.

Leading spaces are not allowed before or inside the number. The only characters used in Turbo's real numbers are the plus sign (+), the minus sign (-), the decimal point (.), the exponential indicator (E or e), and the 10 digits from 0 to 9. On input, Position must be pointing to one of these characters, or no number is detected.

The way Turbo (and this subprogram) interpret real number strings has several quirks. See the Discussion section.

Sample Usage

```
program SampleUsageOfParseRN;

type
   ParseType = string[255];

var
   SourceStr : ParseType;
   Position  : integer;
   Found     : boolean;
   RealValue : real;

{$I ParseRN.PSL}

BEGIN
   SourceStr := 'Rainfall is 4.52 inches';
   Position  := 13;
   ParseRN(SourceStr, Position, Found, RealValue);
   if Found then
      begin
         writeln('Number found is:', RealValue);
         writeln('New position is: ', Position)
      end;
```

```
   writeln;
   Position := 1;
   ParseRN('-3.28E39', Position, Found, RealValue);
   if Found then
      begin
         writeln('Number found is:', RealValue);
         writeln('New position is: ', Position)
      end
END.
```

Running this test program produces the following output:

```
Number found is:   4.52000000000E+00
New position is: 17

Number found is: -3.28000000000E+03
New position is: 8
```

Subprogram Listing of ParseRN.PSL

```
procedure ParseRN(SourceStr: ParseType; var Position: integer;
                  var Found: boolean; var RealValue: real);

var
   SourceLen, TrialLen, Code: integer;

begin
   SourceLen := length(SourceStr);
   RealValue := 0.0;
   Found     := false;
   if not (Position in [1..SourceLen]) then
      exit;
   TrialLen := SourceLen - Position + 1;
   repeat
      val(copy(SourceStr, Position, TrialLen), RealValue, Code);
      if Code > TrialLen then
         Code := TrialLen;
      if Code > 0 then
         TrialLen := Code - 1
   until
      (TrialLen = 0) or (Code = 0);
```

```
   if (Code = 0) then
      begin
         Found    := true;
         Position := Position + TrialLen;
         if Position > SourceLen then
            Position := 0
      end
end;
```

Variables

SourceLen	The string length of SourceStr
TrialLen	The string length of a substring from SourceStr
Code	Code returned from Turbo's built-in val procedure

Discussion

The interpretation of strings as numbers (especially real numbers) is a great mystery in Turbo. Evident are a few glaring inconsistencies in what constitutes a real number expression for use in an assignment statement, a constant, and the val procedure. We can design ParseRN to interpret strings any way we want. Because Turbo has the built-in val procedure and because ParseRN is likely to be used in environments invoking val, the easiest way to design ParseRN is to take advantage of val (instead of writing our own lexical interpreter for real numbers).

Two major surprises arise. The first is that val (and thus ParseRN) does not accept a plus sign leading a number although this is perfectly legal in an assignment statement. (A plus sign is OK after the exponential indicator.) If Position points to a plus sign, Found will automatically be false. You can solve this problem by explicitly checking for the plus sign in your main program before calling ParseRN. If you find a plus sign, increment Position by one.

The second surprise is that val accepts a real number beginning with a decimal point. This is specifically illegal in assignment statements. If you want consistency, you have to check explicitly for this case also. See the Limitations section of GetNumR (Chapter 2) for further explanation of real number representations with val.

Beware of some tricky cases with real numbers terminating before you might expect. The second example in the Sample Usage program is a good illustration. The exponent (39) is too large for a real number. The 3 is OK, but the 39 is not. Therefore, val balks at the 9 and uses the 3 as the whole exponent. Position is on the 9 when this example finishes.

Modifications

None

ParseIN

> **Name:** *ParseIN*
>
> **Type:** *Procedure*
>
> **Purpose:** *To detect an integer number at a specific position in a string*
>
> **Calling Sequence:** `ParseIN(SourceStr, Position, Found, IntValue)`

Description

`ParseIN` examines a source string for an integer number beginning at a specified string position. If an integer is found, the value of the number is returned, and a position variable is updated to the character in the source string just beyond the number. The source string can be any length.

Input

`SourceStr`	`string`	The source string. It can be any length and may be specified as a variable or a literal in the calling statement. `SourceStr`'s type must be declared globally as `ParseType`.
`Position`	`integer`	The position in `SourceStr` where an integer number is looked for. `Position` must be at least 1 and no more than the length of `SourceStr`. `Position` must be specified as a variable and cannot be a literal.

In addition, the following global `type` declaration must appear in your main program:

```
type
   ParseType = string[255];
```

The number 255 is an example. Your string length may differ.

Output

Position	integer	Current position in SourceStr. It retains its input value if no legal integer number is found. If such a number is found, Position points to the first SourceStr character past the number. If the end of the number coincides with the end of SourceStr, Position is set to 0 (zero).
Found	boolean	A flag indicating whether an integer number was found in SourceStr, beginning at the input value of Position. If so, Found is true. If not, Found is false.
IntValue	integer	The integer number found, if any. It is set to 0 (zero) if no number is found.

Limitations and Error Conditions

Found is false and IntValue is zero if the input value of Position is less than 1 or greater than the length of SourceStr. Leading spaces are not allowed before or inside the number. The only characters used in Turbo's integer numbers are the minus sign (-) and the 10 digits from 0 to 9. On input, Position must be pointing to one of these characters, or no number is detected.

The way Turbo (and this subprogram) interprets integer number strings has some quirks. See the Discussion section.

Sample Usage

```
program SampleUsageOfParseIN;

type
   ParseType = string[255];

var
   SourceStr : ParseType;
   Position  : integer;
   Found     : boolean;
   IntValue  : integer;

{$I ParseIN.PSL}
```

```
BEGIN
   SourceStr := 'WAREHOUSE 238 HAS THE LARGEST INVENTORY';
   Position  := 11;
   ParseIN(SourceStr, Position, Found, IntValue);
   if Found then
      begin
         writeln('Number found is: ', IntValue);
         writeln('New position is: ', Position)
      end;
   writeln;
   Position := 1;
   ParseIN('-45768', Position, Found, IntValue);
   if Found then
      begin
         writeln('Number found is: ', IntValue);
         writeln('New position is: ', Position)
      end
END.
```

Running this test program produces the following output:

```
Number found is: 238
New position is: 14

Number found is: -4576
New position is: 6
```

Subprogram Listing of ParseIN.PSL

```
procedure ParseIN(SourceStr: ParseType; var Position: integer;
                  var Found: boolean; var IntValue: integer);

var
   SourceLen, TrialLen, Code: integer;

begin
   SourceLen := length(SourceStr);
   IntValue  := 0;
   Found     := false;
   if not (Position in [1..SourceLen]) then
      exit;
```

```
    TrialLen := SourceLen - Position + 1;
    repeat
       val(copy(SourceStr, Position, TrialLen), IntValue, Code);
       if Code > TrialLen then
          Code := TrialLen;
       if Code > 0 then
          TrialLen := Code - 1
    until
       (TrialLen = 0) or (Code = 0);
    if (Code = 0) then
       begin
          Found      := true;
          Position := Position + TrialLen;
          if Position > SourceLen then
             Position := 0
       end
end;
```

Variables

SourceLen	The string length of SourceStr
TrialLen	The string length of a substring from SourceStr
Code	Code returned from Turbo's built-in val procedure

Discussion

This subprogram is the companion to ParseRN. ParseIN is used when integer numbers are expected. ParseRN is used for real numbers.

As explained in the Discussion section of ParseRN, there are pitfalls in using Turbo's built-in val procedure to interpret real numbers. You must also be careful in using val with integer numbers. The major surprise involves the plus sign. The built-in val procedure (and thus ParseIN) does not accept a plus sign leading a number although this is perfectly legal in an assignment statement. If Position points to a plus sign, Found is false. You can overcome this problem by explicitly checking for the plus sign in your main program before you call ParseIN. If you find a plus sign, increment Position by one. See the Limitations section of GetNumI (Chapter 2) for further explanation of integer number representations with val.

Beware of some tricky cases with integer numbers terminating before you might expect. The second example in the Sample Usage program is a good illustration. The number (-45768) is outside Turbo's integer number range. The -4576 is OK, but the 8 makes the expression too large for an integer number. Therefore, val balks at the 8 and uses -4576 as the whole number. Position is on the 8 when this example finishes. (If you anticipate your numbers being too large for integers, use ParseRN instead.)

Modifications

None

11

Converting

This chapter presents four short subprograms that perform useful manipulations of text strings. Two of the subprograms deal with conversion between hexadecimal and integer numbers. Turbo maps the hex numbers 0000 through FFFF into the integers 0 through 32767 followed by -32768 through -1. This mapping can lead to confusion, especially when you have to manipulate integers for memory address calculations. Because Turbo does not provide any way to display hexadecimal numbers, we have. IntToHex converts an integer number into a four-character hex string. The inverse function, HexToInt, converts a four-character hex string into an integer number.

ConvUp converts a text string into uppercase letters. Nonalphabetic characters are unaffected. This procedure provides a mechanism to "normalize" strings before they are interpreted by PlayTune or any of the searching or parsing routines. The companion subprogram, ConvLow, converts text strings to lowercase letters.

IntToHex

> **Name:** *IntToHex*
>
> **Type:** string *function*
>
> **Purpose:** *To convert an integer number into a four-character hex string*
>
> **Calling Sequence:** IntToHex(IntNum)

Description

This subprogram is a function that converts any integer number into a four-character hexadecimal string. Leading zeros, if any, are included in the hex string. With IntToHex, you can make some sense of the integer variables you use for address calculations. By displaying these variables in hex format, you avoid the confusion that comes from Turbo's mapping into the hex numbers 0000 through FFFF the integers 0 through 32767 followed by -32768 through -1.

Input

IntNum   integer   The integer number you want converted into a hexadecimal number. IntNum can be a variable or a literal constant.

In addition, you must specify in your main program the following global type declaration:

```
type
   String4 = string[4];
```

Output

IntToHex   string   The function IntToHex returns a four-character string that is the hexadecimal equivalent of IntNum.

Limitations and Error Conditions

None

Sample Usage

```
program SampleUsageOfIntToHex;

type
   String4 = string[4];

var
   IntNum: integer;

{$I IntToHex.PSL}

BEGIN
   writeln('Enter integer from -32768 to 32767 (0 to end)');
   repeat
      write('? ');
      readln(IntNum);
      writeln(IntNum, ' in decimal is hex ', IntToHex(IntNum))
   until IntNum = 0
END.
```

The following is sample output from the test program. You can use the values shown as test data.

```
Enter integer from -32768 to 32767 (0 to end)
? 122
122 in decimal is hex 007A
? -21555
-21555 in decimal is hex ABCD
? 32767
32767 in decimal is hex 7FFF
? -1
-1 in decimal is hex FFFF
? 4660
4660 in decimal is hex 1234
? 0
0 in decimal is hex 0000
```

Subprogram Listing of IntToHex.PSL

```pascal
function IntToHex(IntNum: integer): String4;

const
   HexChars: array[0..15] of char = '0123456789ABCDEF';

var
   Temp      : byte;
   TempStr   : string[2];

begin
   Temp      := hi(IntNum);
   TempStr   := HexChars[Temp shr 4] + HexChars[Temp and $0F];
   Temp      := lo(IntNum);
   IntToHex  := TempStr + HexChars[Temp shr 4] +
                          HexChars[Temp and $0F]
end;
```

Variables

HexChars	A typed constant char array containing the 16 hex characters (0–9 and A–F)
Temp	A work variable containing the byte currently being converted from IntNum

| TempStr | A work string containing the hex characters of the high-order byte of IntNum |

Discussion

All right, it's trivia quiz time. Here's the question: What is the result if you add one to an integer variable that has the value 32767? Take a minute to think. We'll even make it a multiple-choice question. Your choices are the following: (1) 32768, (2) overflow error, (3) -1, (4) -32767, or (5) none of the above.

Did you pick your answer? The correct answer is "none of the above." The result of 32767 + 1 is -32768. Because of the way Turbo implements integer variables, this operation is the equivalent of adding hex 7FFF and 1, which is hex 8000. And in two's complement notation, hex 8000 is decimal -32768.

The point of this diversion is that undesirable things can happen if you exceed Turbo's integer capacity. Be aware of these possibilities whenever you are manipulating integers, including dealing with computer addresses. If you write a program that displays the addresses of some critical internal data, some addresses will be negative if you display them as integer values. Because Turbo provides no means of displaying numbers in hexadecimal, you can use IntToHex to do the job.

Modifications

None

HexToInt

> **Name:** *HexToInt*
>
> **Type:** integer *function*
>
> **Purpose:** *To convert a hex string of one to four characters into an integer number*
>
> **Calling Sequence:** HexToInt(HexString)

Description

This subprogram, the opposite of IntToHex, is a function that converts a hexadecimal string of one to four characters into an integer number. With HexToInt, you can write a program that requests keyboard input of a hexadecimal number and converts it into an integer value for use in calculations or as an address.

Input

HexString   string   The one- to four-character hexadecimal string you
                         want converted into an integer number

In addition, you must specify in your main program the following global type
declaration:

```
type
   String4 = string[4];
```

Output

HexToInt   integer   The function HexToInt returns an integer number
                         equivalent to the hexadecimal string in HexString.

Limitations and Error Conditions

HexString must be one to four characters long (or a null string). All of the characters must be legal hex digits (0–9, A–F) or blank spaces. Letters must be uppercase. You can use the ConvUp subprogram to be sure that all letters are uppercase.
A blank space is treated as if it were a zero digit. Thus, leading blank spaces are
effectively ignored, but trailing or embedded blank spaces are treated as significant
zeros. For example, the string ' ABC' (one leading space) is treated as ' ØABC' , but
' ABC ' (one trailing space) is treated as ' ABCØ' . When an illegal character is found
(not 0–9, A–F, or a blank space), HexToInt returns zero as the integer number for
the hex string. You can change the illegal return value as shown in the Modifications
section.

Sample Usage

```
program SampleUsageOfHexToInt;

type
   String4 = string[4];

var
   HexString: String4;

{$I HexToInt.PSL}
```

```
BEGIN
   writeln('Enter 1 to 4 character hex number (FFFF to end)');
   repeat
      write('? ');
      readln(HexString);
      writeln(HexString, ' hex is decimal ', HexToInt(HexString))
   until HexString = 'FFFF'
END.
```

The following is sample output from this test program. You can use the values shown as test data. Note that the fourth number entered (**123R**) contains an illegal hex character and is converted into zero as a result.

```
Enter 1 to 4 character hex number (FFFF to end)
? ABCD
ABCD hex is decimal -21555
? 7FFF
7FFF hex is decimal 32767
? 7A
7A hex is decimal 122
? 123R
123R hex is decimal 0
? 1234
1234 hex is decimal 4660
? FFFF
FFFF hex is decimal -1
```

Subprogram Listing of HexToInt.PSL

```
function HexToInt(HexString: String4): integer;

var
   J, Total, Mult, Digit : integer;
   Temp                  : char;

begin
   Total := 0;
   Mult  := 1;
   for J := length(HexString) downto 1 do
```

```
      begin
        Temp := HexString[J];
        if ord(Temp) = 32 then Temp := '0';              {Mod. #1}
        if Temp in ['0'..'9', 'A'..'F'] then
           begin
              Digit := ord(Temp) - 48;
              if Digit > 9 then Digit := Digit - 7;
              Total := Total + Digit * Mult
           end
        else
           begin
              HexToInt := 0;                              {Mod. #2}
              exit
           end;
        Mult := Mult * 16
     end;
   HexToInt := Total
end;
```

Variables

J	The position within the string where the character currently being converted into hex is located
Total	The accumulated total of the value of HexToInt
Mult	The multiplier for each hex position (1 for the low-order position, 16 for the next position, 256 for the next position, and 4096 for the high-order position)
Digit	The numeric value of the hex digit being converted
Temp	The hex character being converted

Discussion

HexToInt scans the character string from right to left (low order to high order) one hex digit at a time, determining the numerical value of the hex digit and multiplying the digit by the appropriate power of 16 (1, 16, 256, or 4096). The sum of these values is the decimal equivalent of the hex character string.

Modifications

1. To make a blank space an illegal character instead of an implied zero, delete the line indicated by {Mod. #1}.

2. Change Ø in the indicated line in order to alter the output of HexToInt when an illegal character is found. Depending on your application, you may need to differentiate between an illegal zero and a legal one. We chose zero as the illegal value because zero is relatively easy to check in your main program. (That is, if HexString is all zeros, then the result is legal.) If you want, change the zero in the indicated line to -1 or 32767 or any valid integer value you choose.

ConvUp

> **Name:** *ConvUp*
>
> **Type:** *Procedure*
>
> **Purpose:** *To convert a string to uppercase letters*
>
> **Calling Sequence:** ConvUp(ConvString)

Description

This procedure converts to uppercase any lowercase letters in a string. Nonalphabetic characters are unchanged. ConvUp is useful as a preprocessor for strings before they are passed to one of the searching or parsing subprograms. ConvUp can be used also to rectify strings for PlayTune and HexToInt.

Input

ConvString   string   The string to be converted. It can be any length and must be specified as a variable in the calling statement.

In addition, you must specify in your main program the following global type declaration:

```
type
   string255 = string[255];
```

Output

ConvString   string   The same string, now converted. Any lowercase
letters are replaced by the equivalent uppercase
letters. Other characters are unchanged.

Limitations and Error Conditions

None

Sample Usage

```
program SampleUsageOfConvUp;

type
   String255 = string[255];

var
   ConvString: String255;

{$I ConvUp.PSL}

BEGIN
   ConvString := 'Give Jack $100.46';
   ConvUp(ConvString);
   writeln(ConvString)
END.
```

Running this test program produces the following output:

```
GIVE JACK $100.46
```

Subprogram Listing of ConvUp.PSL

```
procedure ConvUp(var ConvString: String255);

var
   J: byte;

begin
   for J := 1 to length(ConvString) do
      ConvString[J] := upcase(ConvString[J])
end;
```

Variables

J   Looping index

Discussion

A typical use of this subprogram is to rectify strings before a sort, search, or parse is performed on them. For example, suppose that your main program takes commands from the user in "natural" language. Let's say that your program needs to parse an input string at the keyword START. The problem is that your user may type *Start*, *start*, *START*, or even something like *StART*. An expedient approach is to run the input string through ConvUp before searching the string. Then you need to check only the converted string for START in order to cover all these possible cases.

Modifications

None

ConvLow

> **Name:** *ConvLow*
>
> **Type:** *Procedure*
>
> **Purpose:** *To convert a string to lowercase letters*
>
> **Calling Sequence:** ConvLow(ConvString)

Description

This procedure converts to lowercase any uppercase letters in a string. Nonalphabetic characters are unchanged. ConvLow is useful as a preprocessor for strings before they are passed to one of the searching or parsing subprograms.

Input

ConvString   string   The string to be converted. It can be any length and must be specified as a variable in the calling statement.

In addition, you must specify in your main program the following global type declaration:

```
type
    string255 = string[255];
```

Output

ConvString   string   The same string, now converted. Any uppercase letters are replaced by the equivalent lowercase letters. Other characters are unchanged.

Limitations and Error Conditions

None

Sample Usage

```
program SampleUsageOfConvLow;

type
   String255 = string[255];

var
   ConvString: String255;

{$I ConvLow.PSL}

BEGIN
   ConvString := 'Give Jack $100.46';
   ConvLow(ConvString);
   writeln(ConvString)
END.
```

Running this test program produces the following output:

```
give jack $100.46
```

Subprogram Listing of ConvLow.PSL

```
procedure ConvLow(var ConvString: String255);

var
   TestChar : char;
   J        : byte;

begin
   for J := 1 to length(ConvString) do
     begin
        TestChar := ConvString[J];
        if TestChar in ['A'..'Z'] then
           ConvString[J] := chr(ord(TestChar) + 32)
     end
end;
```

Variables

TestChar	Character from ConvString
J	Looping index

Discussion

Because lowercase letters are 32 positions higher than uppercase letters in the ASCII sequence, ConvLow simply adds 32 to the numeric representation of any uppercase letter in the string.

ConvLow is the companion subprogram to ConvUp. Each subprogram can be used in a similar way. See ConvUp for further explanation.

Modifications

None

12

Mathematics and Engineering

This chapter presents 15 subprograms for mathematicians and engineers. The emphasis is on practical numerical techniques required in a large variety of engineering problem solving. The subprograms can be grouped into five major subdivisions:

1. Library functions (hyperbolic functions, exponentiation)

2. Vector mathematics (three-dimensional vector products)

3. Matrix arithmetic (two-dimensional matrix manipulation)

4. Functional analysis (roots, derivatives, etc., of a function)

5. Differential equations (ordinary differential equation solver)

The library functions are `Power` and `HyperLib`. `CrossPr` and `DotPr` are the vector math subprograms. The matrix arithmetic set contains `MatShow`, `MatAdd`, `MatSub`, `MatMult`, `MatTrans`, `MatInv`, and `Determ`. Functional analysis subprograms consist of `Integral` (definite integrals), `Root` (real roots), and `Deriv` (derivatives). `DiffEqn` solves ordinary differential equations.

Taking advantage of Pascal's flexibility, we developed some tools in Turbo to facilitate representation of possibly awkward mathematical constructs. These tools include special data structures for vectors and matrices. We developed also a technique to express your own functions. Generally, subprograms in one subdivision can be easily linked together in your main programs to form cohesive units.

Turbo Pascal has two limitations that hinder us mildly. One is that array dimensions must be declared explicitly and stay fixed between main programs and subprograms. Suppose that you want a general matrix multiplication subprogram for your library. You need some way to pass the different array dimensions to the subprogram each time it is called. But Turbo doesn't permit such activity. (Turbo does not support conformant-array parameters, a feature designed to solve this problem. Only a few Pascal compilers implement these parameters.)

The second limitation is that Turbo does not allow passing to a subprogram the name of a function as a parameter. (Again, this is permitted in some Pascal compilers.) We wanted to do this in the functional analysis subprograms so that they could be written as general library routines.

Our solution to both problems is similar. We require certain global declarations in the main programs. (These declarations remain in force inside the subprograms.) Through careful global specifications in a few key places, only minimal programming changes are needed for new applications. These techniques are developed and explained in the appropriate subprogram write-ups.

Power

> **Name:** *Power*
>
> **Type:** real *function*
>
> **Purpose:** *To perform exponentiation of real numbers*
>
> **Calling Sequence:** Power(Number, Exponent)

Description

Power raises a positive number to any power.

Input

Number	real	Number on which to perform exponentiation. Number must be greater than zero but does not need to be an integer value.
Exponent	real	Exponent to which Number is raised. Exponent can be positive, negative, or zero but does not need to be an integer value.

Output

Power	real	The function Power returns Number raised to the Exponent power.

Limitations and Error Conditions

If Number is negative or zero, Power returns a value of zero. A fatal run-time error occurs if you try to calculate a result outside Turbo's real-number range. Results must be greater than 1.0E-38 and less than 1.0E+38.

Sample Usage

```
program SampleUsageOfPower;

var
   Number, Exponent, Result: real;

{$I Power.PSL}

BEGIN
   Number   := 2.0;
   Exponent := 5.0;
   Result   := Power(Number, Exponent);
   writeln(Number:4:2, ' to the', Exponent:5:2,
                       ' power is', Result:6:2);
   Result := Power(23.0, 1/3);
   writeln('Cube root of 23 is', Result)
END.
```

Running this test program produces the following output:

```
2.00 to the 5.00 power is 32.00
Cube root of 23 is  2.8438669798E+00
```

If Number and Exponent are set to 5 and -2 before you invoke Power, then Result is 0.04 afterward. If Number is -3 and Exponent is anything, Result is zero. If Number is zero and Exponent is anything, Result is zero. Note that Power can use input arguments that are variable names or numeric constants.

Subprogram Listing of Power.PSL

```
function Power(Number, Exponent: real): real;

begin
   if Number > 0.0 then                        {Mod. #1}
      Power := exp(Exponent * ln(Number))
   else                                        {Mod. #1, 2}
      Power := 0.0                             {Mod. #1, 3}
end;
```

Variables

None

Discussion

To implement exponentiation in any (positive) base, this function makes use of the natural (base e) functions exp and ln. Power allows the Pascal statement R := Power(X, Y) to be the equivalent of R = X ^ Y in BASIC for a positive X. Don't overlook the application of this function in calculating roots as well as powers. Turbo Pascal has the sqrt function for square roots, but Power calculates other roots also (cube roots when Exponent is 1/3, inverse fourth roots when Exponent is -0.25, etc.)

Modifications

1. To eliminate detection of the error condition, delete the three lines indicated by {Mod. #1}. This change slightly speeds up the calculation. (We recommend this modification only if you do error checking in your mainline program and you need increased speed because of high-volume use of Power.)

2. If you want to allow Number to be zero, add the following lines after the indicated else statement:

```
if (Number = 0.0) and (Exponent = 0.0) then
   Power := 1.0
else
```

3. To cause your program to end abnormally if Number is not positive (instead of simply returning a value of zero), change the line indicated by {Mod. #3} to

```
Power := Number / 0.0          {force error}
```

This change causes Power to divide by zero when the error condition occurs, forcing a run-time error. Generally, a better course of action is to display a descriptive message and then end normally, but sometimes a forced error is expedient during testing.

HyperLib

> **Name:** *HyperLib*
>
> **Type:** real *function*
>
> **Purpose:** *To calculate the hyperbolic functions sinh, cosh, and tanh*
>
> **Calling Sequence:** Sinh(Number), Cosh(Number), Tanh(Number)

Description

HyperLib is a minilibrary consisting of the three common hyperbolic functions sinh, cosh, and tanh. These functions are the hyperbolic sine, hyperbolic cosine, and hyperbolic tangent, respectively. HyperLib contains three separate subprograms. To invoke one, select Sinh, Cosh, or Tanh.

Input

Number	real	Argument of the hyperbolic function. Number can have any real value (positive, negative, or zero).

Output

Sinh	real	Function yielding the hyperbolic sine of Number
Cosh	real	Function yielding the hyperbolic cosine of Number
Tanh	real	Function yielding the hyperbolic tangent of Number

Limitations and Error Conditions

To prevent overflow, you must not set the absolute value of Number greater than 88.

Sample Usage

```
program SampleUsageOfHyperLib;

var
   Number, SinhResult, CoshResult, TanhResult: real;

{$I HyperLib.PSL}
```

```
BEGIN
   writeln('X':10, 'Sinh(X)':13, 'Cosh(X)':13, 'Tanh(X)':13);
   Number := -1.0;
   while Number <= 1.0 do
      begin
         SinhResult := Sinh(Number);
         CoshResult := Cosh(Number);
         TanhResult := Tanh(Number);
         writeln(Number:10:2, SinhResult:13:5, CoshResult:13:5,
                              TanhResult:13:5);
         Number := Number + 0.5
      end
END.
```

Running this test program produces the following abbreviated table of the hyperbolic functions:

```
       X      Sinh(X)      Cosh(X)      Tanh(X)
   -1.00     -1.17520      1.54308     -0.76159
   -0.50     -0.52110      1.12763     -0.46212
    0.00      0.00000      1.00000      0.00000
    0.50      0.52110      1.12763      0.46212
    1.00      1.17520      1.54308      0.76159
```

Subprogram Listing of HyperLib.PSL

```
function Sinh(Number: real): real;

begin                                          {Mod. #1}
   Sinh := (exp(Number) - exp(- Number)) / 2.0
end;

function Cosh(Number: real): real;

begin                                          {Mod. #1}
   Cosh := (exp(Number) + exp(- Number)) / 2.0
end;

function Tanh(Number: real): real;

begin
   Tanh := Sinh(Number) / Cosh(Number)
end;
```

Variables

None

Discussion

The hyperbolic functions are useful in various disciplines of engineering, applied mathematics, and pure mathematics. The Turbo function exp is used to define these functions.

Because tanh(X) = sinh(X) / cosh(X), the Tanh function has been implemented by invoking Sinh and Cosh. Thus, you must include all three functions from HyperLib if you plan to use Tanh. If you just need Sinh or Cosh, you can include only that function in your application.

The reciprocals of the functions in HyperLib are the hyperbolic cosecant, secant, and cotangent. You can add these and the inverse hyperbolic functions to HyperLib if you like. The functional definitions can be found in many math texts and other references. Appendix E of the IBM BASIC manual is one source you may already have.

Modification

The Sinh and Cosh functions cause numeric overflow if either is invoked when Number has an absolute value greater than 88. To avoid this overflow, insert the following five lines immediately after the begin statements indicated by {Mod. #1}:

```
if Number > 88.0 then
   Number := 88.0
else
   if Number < - 88.0 then
      Number := -88.0;
```

These lines cause the functions to return the largest real numbers (positive or negative as appropriate) possible with standard IBM Turbo Pascal precision.

CrossPr

> **Name:** *CrossPr*
>
> **Type:** *Procedure*
>
> **Purpose:** *To calculate the cross product of two vectors*
>
> **Calling Sequence:** CrossPr(VectorA, VectorB, VectorC)

Description

The cross product of two vectors is a vector. CrossPr calculates the cross product of two input vectors. All vectors are three-dimensional. They are mathematically specified in Cartesian coordinates with an X, a Y, and a Z component. In Turbo, a special record type is used to represent the vectors.

Input

VectorA   record   The first input vector. It consists of an X, a Y, and a Z component. Each component is a real number.

VectorB   record   The second input vector. It consists of an X, a Y, and a Z component. Each component is a real number.

The following global type declaration must be specified in your main program:

```
type
   VectorType =
      record
         X, Y, Z: real
      end;
```

This type declaration creates a special data type for representing each vector. See the Discussion section for details.

Output

VectorC   record   The cross product of VectorA and VectorB. VectorC consists of an X, a Y, and a Z component. Each component is a real number.

Limitations and Error Conditions

None

Sample Usage

```
program SampleUsageOfCrossPr;

type
   VectorType =
      record
         X, Y, Z: real
      end;
```

```
var
   VectorA, VectorB, VectorC: VectorType;

{$I CrossPr.PSL}

BEGIN
   VectorA.X := 1.5;   VectorA.Y := 2.0;   VectorA.Z := -1.0;
   VectorB.X := 3.0;   VectorB.Y := 4.0;   VectorB.Z := 5.0;
   CrossPr(VectorA, VectorB, VectorC);
   writeln('VectorA(X,Y,Z) = (', VectorA.X:7:2, VectorA.Y:7:2,
                                  VectorA.Z:7:2, ')');
   writeln('VectorB(X,Y,Z) = (', VectorB.X:7:2, VectorB.Y:7:2,
                                  VectorB.Z:7:2, ')');
   writeln('VectorC(X,Y,Z) = (', VectorC.X:7:2, VectorC.Y:7:2,
                                  VectorC.Z:7:2, ')')
END.
```

Running this test program produces the following output:

```
VectorA(X,Y,Z) = (   1.50    2.00   -1.00)
VectorB(X,Y,Z) = (   3.00    4.00    5.00)
VectorC(X,Y,Z) = (  14.00  -10.50    0.00)
```

Subprogram Listing of CrossPr.PSL

```
procedure CrossPr(VectorA, VectorB: VectorType;
                  var VectorC: VectorType);

begin
   VectorC.X := VectorA.Y * VectorB.Z - VectorA.Z * VectorB.Y;
   VectorC.Y := VectorA.Z * VectorB.X - VectorA.X * VectorB.Z;
   VectorC.Z := VectorA.X * VectorB.Y - VectorA.Y * VectorB.X
end;
```

Variables

None

Discussion

Vectors occur frequently in physics and engineering problems, especially in the area of force field kinetics. Vector attributes are a magnitude and a direction in three-dimensional space. With standard Cartesian coordinates, a vector is specified by three real numbers corresponding to its components in the X, Y, and Z directions.

For notational convenience, we developed the `record` data type `VectorType` to represent vectors. Each vector is specified by a record having three fields: X, Y, and Z. Each of these fields consists of a real number (positive, negative, or zero) that represents the appropriate vector component. Thus, you can reference the components of, say, `VectorSample` with the specifications `VectorSample.X`, `VectorSample.Y`, and `VectorSample.Z`. By the way, the field identifiers X, Y, and Z are unique only within the records in which they are defined. Therefore, you can still use X, Y, and Z as variable names in the same block(s) in which you use the records.

Given two input vectors, the resultant cross product has a magnitude equal to the product of the magnitudes of the two input vectors multiplied by the sine of the angle between them. The direction of the resultant vector is perpendicular to the plane containing the two input vectors. The order of the two input vectors is important because "A cross B" does not equal "B cross A" if A and B are the two original vectors. In fact, reversing the specification will result in a new resultant vector, with each component having a sign opposite from that of the old resultant vector. That is, (A X B) equals -(B X A), in which X is the conventional notation denoting the cross product.

Modifications

None

DotPr

Name:	*DotPr*
Type:	`real` *function*
Purpose:	*To calculate the dot product of two vectors*
Calling Sequence:	`DotPr(VectorA, VectorB)`

Description

The dot (or scalar) product is a single real number. The two input vectors are three-dimensional. They are mathematically specified in Cartesian coordinates with an X, a Y, and a Z component. In Turbo, a special `record` type is used to represent the vectors.

Input

VectorA	record	The first input vector. It consists of an X, a Y, and a Z component. Each component is a real number.
VectorB	record	The second input vector. It consists of an X, a Y, and a Z component. Each component is a real number.

The following global type declaration must be specified in your main program:

```
type
   VectorType =
      record
         X, Y, Z: real
      end;
```

This type declaration creates a special data type for representing each vector. See the Discussion section of the CrossPr subprogram for details.

Output

DotPr	real	The function DotPr returns the dot product (a scalar) of VectorA and VectorB.

Limitations and Error Conditions

None

Sample Usage

```
program SampleUsageOfDotPr;

type
   VectorType =
      record
         X, Y, Z: real
      end;

var
   VectorA, VectorB : VectorType;
   Result           : real;

{$I DotPr.PSL}
```

```
BEGIN
   VectorA. X := 1.5;   VectorA. Y := 2. 0;   VectorA. Z := -1. 0;
   VectorB. X := 3. 0;   VectorB. Y := 4. 0;   VectorB. Z := 5. 0;
   Result     := DotPr(VectorA, VectorB);
   writeln('VectorA(X, Y, Z) = (', VectorA. X:7:2, VectorA. Y:7:2,
                                    VectorA. Z:7:2, ')' );
   writeln('VectorB(X, Y, Z) = (', VectorB. X:7:2, VectorB. Y:7:2,
                                    VectorB. Z:7:2, ')' );
   writeln('Dot Product = ', Result:6:2)
END.
```

Running this test program produces the following output:

```
VectorA(X, Y, Z) = (   1.50    2. 00   -1. 00)
VectorB(X, Y, Z) = (   3. 00    4. 00    5. 00)
Dot Product =    7.50
```

Subprogram Listing of DotPr.PSL

```
function DotPr(VectorA, VectorB: VectorType): real;

begin
   DotPr := VectorA. X * VectorB. X + VectorA. Y * VectorB. Y +
            VectorA. Z * VectorB. Z
end;
```

Variables

None

Discussion

DotPr uses the same three-dimensional vector representation described in the Description and Discussion sections of the CrossPr subprogram. The identical record data structure VectorType is used also to make these two subprograms compatible in the same main program.

The dot product is a scalar quantity described by one real number. Thus, this subprogram is a function, whereas CrossPr (producing a vector) is a procedure.

The dot product is defined as the product of the magnitudes of the two input vectors multiplied by the cosine of the angle between them. Unlike the order of the input vectors for CrossPr, the order of the two input vectors is not important here because "A dot B" does equal "B dot A" if A and B are the two original input vectors.

Modifications

None

MatShow

> **Name:** *MatShow*
>
> **Type:** *Procedure*
>
> **Purpose:** *To display the contents of a matrix*
>
> **Calling Sequence:** MatShow(MatrixA)

Description

MatShow displays on the current output device (usually the screen) the values of a matrix. The matrix must be two-dimensional and square, and it must contain values of type real. MatShow is intended for simple fixed-format applications. See the more flexible subprogram Show2Arr (Chapter 4) for additional capability.

Input

MatrixA   real   An array containing the matrix to be displayed

The following global const and type declarations must be specified in your main program:

```
const
   MatrixSize = 3;

type
   MatrixType = array[1..MatrixSize, 1..MatrixSize] of real;
```

The constant MatrixSize defines the size of the square array. (That is, the value of MatrixSize is the number of elements on a main diagonal of your matrix.) MatrixSize can be any positive integer. The value 3 is used here only as an example.

Output

The elements of MatrixA are displayed on the current output device (normally the screen).

Limitations and Error Conditions

For this formatting, it is assumed that each element in your matrix has an absolute value less than 1,000,000 and that no more than two significant digits are to the right of each decimal point. If these restrictions are too severe, refer to the Modification section or the Show2Arr subprogram.

Sample Usage

```
program SampleUsageOfMatShow;

const
   MatrixSize = 3;

type
   MatrixType = array[1..MatrixSize, 1..MatrixSize] of real;

var
   MatrixA : MatrixType;
   I, J    : integer;

{$I MatShow.PSL}

BEGIN
   for I := 1 to MatrixSize do
      for J := 1 to MatrixSize do
         MatrixA[I,J] := I * J / 2.0;
   MatShow(MatrixA)
END.
```

Running this test program produces the following output:

```
   0.50      1.00      1.50
   1.00      2.00      3.00
   1.50      3.00      4.50
```

Subprogram Listing of MatShow.PSL

```
procedure MatShow(var MatrixA: MatrixType);

var
   I, J: integer;

begin
   for I := 1 to MatrixSize do
      begin
         for J := 1 to MatrixSize do
            write(MatrixA[I, J]:10:2);                {Mod. #1}
         writeln
      end;
   writeln
end;
```

Variables

I   Subscript pointing to the current row of the matrix being
                     referenced

J   Subscript pointing to the current column of the matrix
                     being referenced

Discussion

Two-dimensional matrices occur frequently in the solutions of mathematical and
engineering problems. We include several matrix manipulation subprograms in this
book. For all these subprograms, we have assumed that the matrices are square.
In the discussion of subsequent subprograms, however, we'll show how certain
nonsquare matrices can be accommodated.

MatShow displays the values of MatrixA in the conventional "square table" form.
One line of output displays the values of one row of the matrix. If you use MatShow
with a value of MatrixSize larger than 8, the subprogram will cause displayed output
from one row to "spill over" to the next line of output.

Turbo Pascal does not provide a convenient method of passing differently sized
arrays to the same subprogram. This means that the matrix dimension (MatrixSize)
must be declared globally. If your main program uses several arrays that differ in
size, you can use MatShow in two ways for different cases.

One way is to declare (in your main program) all the different sizes of your arrays. This necessitates setting multiple constants (for example, MatrixSizeA = 4, MatrixSizeB = 6, MatrixSizeC = 7, etc.) and using them in appropriate var declarations for each matrix. Then multiple copies of MatShow can be created (named MatShowA, MatShowB, MatShowC, etc.) when the variable MatrixSize becomes MatrixSizeA in MatShowA, MatrixSizeB in MatShowB, and so on. When you want to display a matrix, you'll have to know its size beforehand and invoke the correct procedure.

The second method is to set MatrixSize in your main program to the largest value required for any of your matrices. Then MatShow can be invoked for every matrix. Matrices of smaller than maximum size, however, are displayed with unpredictable values for the extraneous array elements.

Modification

Each matrix element is currently displayed with 10:2 format. This accommodates real numbers with an absolute value less than 1,000,000 and no more than two significant figures to the right of the decimal point. If this format is insufficient, you may change 10:2 to anything allowed for real numbers.

MatAdd

> **Name:** *MatAdd*
>
> **Type:** *Procedure*
>
> **Purpose:** *To add two matrices*
>
> **Calling Sequence:** MatAdd(MatrixA, MatrixB, MatrixC)

Description

MatAdd adds two matrices together and stores the result in a third matrix. All matrices are two-dimensional, square, and the same size. All of them contain values of type real.

Input

MatrixA	real	Array containing the first matrix to be summed
MatrixB	real	Array containing the matrix to be added to MatrixA

The following global const and type declarations must be specified in your main program:

```
const
   MatrixSize = 3;

type
   MatrixType = array[1..MatrixSize, 1..MatrixSize] of real;
```

The constant MatrixSize defines the size of the square arrays. (In other words, the value of MatrixSize is the number of elements on the main diagonal of each of your three matrices.) MatrixSize can be any positive integer. The value 3 is only an example.

Output

MatrixC   real   Array containing the sum of MatrixA and MatrixB

Limitations and Error Conditions

None

Sample Usage

```
program SampleUsageOfMatAdd;

const
   MatrixSize = 3;

type
   MatrixType = array[1..MatrixSize, 1..MatrixSize] of real;

var
   MatrixA, MatrixB, MatrixC : MatrixType;
   I, J                      : integer;

{$I MatAdd.PSL}
{$I MatShow.PSL}
```

```
BEGIN
   for I := 1 to MatrixSize do
      for J := 1 to MatrixSize do
         begin
            MatrixA[I,J] := I * J / 2.0;
            MatrixB[I,J] := I - J
         end;
   MatAdd(MatrixA, MatrixB, MatrixC);
   writeln('MatrixA =');   MatShow(MatrixA);
   writeln('MatrixB =');   MatShow(MatrixB);
   writeln('MatrixA + MatrixB =');   MatShow(MatrixC)
END.
```

Running this test program produces the following output:

```
   MatrixA =
          0.50        1.00        1.50
          1.00        2.00        3.00
          1.50        3.00        4.50

   MatrixB =
          0.00       -1.00       -2.00
          1.00        0.00       -1.00
          2.00        1.00        0.00

   MatrixA + MatrixB =
          0.50        0.00       -0.50
          2.00        2.00        2.00
          3.50        4.00        4.50
```

Subprogram Listing of MatAdd.PSL

```
procedure MatAdd(var MatrixA, MatrixB, MatrixC: MatrixType);

var
   I, J: integer;

begin
   for I := 1 to MatrixSize do
      for J := 1 to MatrixSize do
         MatrixC[I,J] := MatrixA[I,J] + MatrixB[I,J]
end;
```

Variables

I	Subscript pointing to the current row of the matrix being referenced
J	Subscript pointing to the current column of the matrix being referenced

Discussion

The mathematical definition of matrix addition requires that both input matrices be identical in size. They don't need to be square, however, as long as each matrix has the same number of rows and each matrix has the same number of columns. But the number of rows does not have to equal the number of columns.

You can use MatAdd to add two matrices that aren't square. To add the matrices, set MatrixSize to the number of rows or the number of columns, whichever is greater. This creates square matrices with extraneous rows or columns. (Some memory is thus wasted.) MatAdd works even though your matrices contain some unneeded elements. You must keep track of which parts of the square matrices are relevant. The numbers you get in the unneeded row(s) or column(s) will be unpredictable. You might want to set the extraneous array elements to zero in your input matrices before you invoke MatAdd. Then the resulting sum matrix will have zeros in the same (appropriate) locations. Therefore, the extraneous array elements will stand out more easily if you display the matrices with a procedure such as MatShow. Setting the unneeded elements to zero also avoids the small possibility of overflow that could result from adding two (unknown) large numbers.

Modifications

None

MatSub

Name:	*MatSub*
Type:	*Procedure*
Purpose:	*To subtract one matrix from another*
Calling Sequence:	MatSub(MatrixA, MatrixB, MatrixC)

Description

MatSub subtracts one matrix from another and stores the result in a third matrix. All matrices are two-dimensional, square, and the same size. All of them contain values of type real.

Input

MatrixA	real	Array containing the first matrix
MatrixB	real	Array containing the matrix to be subtracted from MatrixA

The following global const and type declarations must be specified in your main program:

```
const
   MatrixSize = 3;

type
   MatrixType = array[1..MatrixSize, 1..MatrixSize] of real;
```

The constant MatrixSize defines the size of the square arrays. (That is, the value of MatrixSize is the number of elements on the main diagonal of each of your three matrices.) MatrixSize can be any positive integer. The value 3 is only an example.

Output

MatrixC	real	Array containing the result of MatrixA - MatrixB

Limitations and Error Conditions

None

Sample Usage

```
program SampleUsageOfMatSub;

const
   MatrixSize = 3;

type
   MatrixType = array[1..MatrixSize, 1..MatrixSize] of real;
```

```
var
   MatrixA, MatrixB, MatrixC : MatrixType;
   I, J                      : integer;

{$I MatSub.PSL}
{$I MatShow.PSL}

BEGIN
   for I := 1 to MatrixSize do
     for J := 1 to MatrixSize do
        begin
           MatrixA[I,J] := I * J / 2.0;
           MatrixB[I,J] := I - J
        end;
   MatSub(MatrixA, MatrixB, MatrixC);
   writeln('MatrixA =');  MatShow(MatrixA);
   writeln('MatrixB =');  MatShow(MatrixB);
   writeln('MatrixA - MatrixB =');  MatShow(MatrixC)
END.
```

Running this test program produces the following output:

```
MatrixA =
       0.50      1.00      1.50
       1.00      2.00      3.00
       1.50      3.00      4.50

MatrixB =
       0.00     -1.00     -2.00
       1.00      0.00     -1.00
       2.00      1.00      0.00

MatrixA - MatrixB =
       0.50      2.00      3.50
       0.00      2.00      4.00
      -0.50      2.00      4.50
```

Subprogram Listing of MatSub.PSL

```
procedure MatSub(var MatrixA, MatrixB, MatrixC: MatrixType);

var
   I, J: integer;

begin
   for I := 1 to MatrixSize do
      for J := 1 to MatrixSize do
         MatrixC[I,J] := MatrixA[I,J] - MatrixB[I,J]
end;
```

Variables

I   Subscript pointing to the current row of the matrix being referenced

J   Subscript pointing to the current column of the matrix being referenced

Discussion

In the Discussion section of the MatAdd procedure, the comments pertaining to nonsquare matrices are equally valid for MatSub. Refer to that section for details.

Modifications

None

MatMult

> **Name:** *MatMult*
>
> **Type:** *Procedure*
>
> **Purpose:** *To multiply two matrices*
>
> **Calling Sequence:** MatMult(MatrixA, MatrixB, MatrixC)

Description

MatMult multiplies two matrices and stores the result in a third matrix. All matrices are two-dimensional, square, and the same size. All of them contain values of type real.

Input

MatrixA	real	Array containing the first matrix of the multiplication
MatrixB	real	Array containing the matrix that multiplies MatrixA

The following global const and type declarations must be specified in your main program:

```
const
   MatrixSize = 3;

type
   MatrixType = array[1..MatrixSize, 1..MatrixSize] of real;
```

The constant MatrixSize defines the size of the square arrays. (In other words, the value of MatrixSize is the number of elements on the main diagonal of each of your three matrices.) MatrixSize can be any positive integer. The value 3 is only an example.

Output

MatrixC	real	Array containing the result of MatrixA multiplied by MatrixB

Limitations and Error Conditions

None

Sample Usage

```
program SampleUsageOfMatMult;

const
   MatrixSize = 3;

type
   MatrixType = array[1..MatrixSize, 1..MatrixSize] of real;

var
   MatrixA, MatrixB, MatrixC : MatrixType;
   I, J                      : integer;

{$I MatMult.PSL}
{$I MatShow.PSL}

BEGIN
   for I := 1 to MatrixSize do
     for J := 1 to MatrixSize do
        begin
           MatrixA[I,J] := I * J / 2.0;
           MatrixB[I,J] := I - J
        end;
   MatMult(MatrixA, MatrixB, MatrixC);
   writeln('MatrixA =');  MatShow(MatrixA);
   writeln('MatrixB =');  MatShow(MatrixB);
   writeln('MatrixA * MatrixB =');  MatShow(MatrixC)
END.
```

Running this test program produces the following output:

```
MatrixA =
      0.50       1.00       1.50
      1.00       2.00       3.00
      1.50       3.00       4.50

MatrixB =
      0.00      -1.00      -2.00
      1.00       0.00      -1.00
      2.00       1.00       0.00
```

```
MatrixA * MatrixB =
       4.00        1.00       -2.00
       8.00        2.00       -4.00
      12.00        3.00       -6.00
```

Subprogram Listing of MatMult.PSL

```
procedure MatMult(MatrixA, MatrixB: MatrixType;
                  var MatrixC: MatrixType);

var
  I, J, K : integer;
  TempSum : real;

begin
  for I := 1 to MatrixSize do
    for J := 1 to MatrixSize do
      begin
        TempSum := 0.0;
        for K := 1 to MatrixSize do
          TempSum := TempSum + MatrixA[I,K] * MatrixB[K,J];
        MatrixC[I,J] := TempSum
      end
end;
```

Variables

I	Subscript pointing to the currently referenced row of MatrixA or MatrixC
J	Subscript pointing to the currently referenced column of MatrixB or MatrixC
K	Subscript pointing to the currently referenced column of MatrixA or the currently referenced row of MatrixB
TempSum	Temporary (partial) value of the multiplication

Discussion

Multiplication of two-dimensional matrices is defined only when the number of columns in the first matrix is equal to the number of rows in the second matrix. Of course, this compatibility is automatic when the two matrices are square.

You can use MatMult for nonsquare matrices by applying the technique explained in the Discussion section of the MatAdd subprogram. Refer to that section for details. We recommend filling the extraneous row(s) or column(s) with zeros.

Modifications

None

MatTrans

> **Name:** *MatTrans*
>
> **Type:** *Procedure*
>
> **Purpose:** *To transpose a matrix*
>
> **Calling Sequence:** MatTrans(MatrixA, MatrixB)

Description

MatTrans creates the transpose of a given matrix. The initial matrix and its transpose are two-dimensional, square, and the same size. They contain values of type real.

Input

MatrixA   real   Array containing the matrix to be transposed

The following global const and type declarations must be specified in your main program:

```
const
   MatrixSize = 3;

type
   MatrixType = array[1..MatrixSize, 1..MatrixSize] of real;
```

The constant MatrixSize defines the size of the square arrays. (That is, the value of MatrixSize is the number of elements on the main diagonal of your input matrix.) MatrixSize can be any positive integer. The value 3 is only an example.

Output

MatrixB   real   Array containing the transpose of MatrixA

Limitations and Error Conditions

None

Sample Usage

```
program SampleUsageOfMatTrans;

const
   MatrixSize = 3;

type
   MatrixType = array[1..MatrixSize, 1..MatrixSize] of real;

var
   MatrixA, MatrixB : MatrixType;
   I, J             : integer;

{$I MatTrans.PSL}
{$I MatShow.PSL}

BEGIN
   for I := 1 to MatrixSize do
     for J := 1 to MatrixSize do
        MatrixA[I,J] := I - J;
   MatTrans(MatrixA, MatrixB);
   writeln('MatrixA =');  MatShow(MatrixA);
   writeln('Transpose of MatrixA =');  MatShow(MatrixB)
END.
```

Running this test program produces the following output:

```
MatrixA =
      0.00     -1.00     -2.00
      1.00      0.00     -1.00
      2.00      1.00      0.00

Transpose of MatrixA =
      0.00      1.00      2.00
     -1.00      0.00      1.00
     -2.00     -1.00      0.00
```

Subprogram Listing of MatTrans.PSL

```
procedure MatTrans(MatrixA: MatrixType;
                   var MatrixB: MatrixType);

var
  I, J: integer;

begin
  for I := 1 to MatrixSize do
    for J := 1 to MatrixSize do
      MatrixB[J, I] := MatrixA[I, J]
end;
```

Variables

I
Subscript pointing to the currently referenced row of MatrixA and the currently referenced column of MatrixB

J
Subscript pointing to the currently referenced column of MatrixA and the currently referenced row of MatrixB

Discussion

You can create the transpose of a nonsquare matrix with MatTrans by using the technique presented in the Discussion section of the MatAdd subprogram. Refer to that section for details.

Modifications

None

MatInv

Name:	*MatInv*
Type:	*Procedure*
Purpose:	*To invert a matrix*
Calling Sequence:	MatInv(MatrixA, MatrixB, OK)

Description

MatInv inverts a matrix, if possible. The matrix must be two-dimensional and square, and it must contain values of type real.

Input

MatrixA real   Array containing the matrix to be inverted

The following global const and type declarations must be specified in your main program:

```
const
   MatrixSize = 3;

type
   MatrixType = array[1..MatrixSize, 1..MatrixSize] of real;
```

The constant MatrixSize defines the size of the square arrays. (That is, the value of MatrixSize is the number of elements on the main diagonal of the matrix to be inverted.) MatrixSize can be any positive integer. The value 3 is only an example.

Output

MatrixB real   Array containing the inverse of MatrixA

OK   boolean Result of the procedure. If OK is true, the inversion was successful; if OK is false, the inversion was unsuccessful.

Limitations and Error Conditions

Matrix inversion cannot be accomplished if the matrix is singular (has a determinant equal to zero). In such cases, the procedure terminates with OK set to false. The values in the array MatrixB are indeterminate.

The algorithm tests whether certain computational values have become zero. Because of round-off and truncation errors, however, a certain tolerance away from zero must be allowed in these values. The constant ErrorBound defines this tolerance limit. You should set it to a value about 10 orders of magnitude (Turbo's real-number precision) smaller than the absolute value of typical numbers in your input matrix. ErrorBound's current setting is appropriate for matrix elements of order unity. If your application uses much larger or much smaller numbers, adjust ErrorBound as explained in the Modification section.

Sample Usage

```
program SampleUsageOfMatInv;

const
   MatrixSize = 3;

type
   MatrixType = array[1..MatrixSize, 1..MatrixSize] of real;

var
   I, J              : integer;
   MatrixA, MatrixB : MatrixType;
   OK               : boolean;

{$I MatInv.PSL}
{$I MatShow.PSL}

BEGIN
   MatrixA[1,1] := 3;   MatrixA[1,2] := 5;   MatrixA[1,3] := -1;
   MatrixA[2,1] := 1;   MatrixA[2,2] := 4;   MatrixA[2,3] := -0.7;
   MatrixA[3,1] := 2;   MatrixA[3,2] := 5;   MatrixA[3,3] := -1;
   writeln(' Input Matrix =');   MatShow(MatrixA);
   MatInv(MatrixA, MatrixB, OK);
   if OK then
      begin
         writeln(' Inverted Matrix =');   MatShow(MatrixB)
      end
   else
      writeln('Matrix is singular' )
END.
```

Running this test program produces the following output:

```
Input Matrix =
        3.00       5.00       -1.00
        1.00       4.00       -0.70
        2.00       5.00       -1.00

Inverted Matrix =
        1.00       0.00       -1.00
        0.80       2.00       -2.20
        6.00      10.00      -14.00
```

Subprogram Listing of MatInv.PSL

```
procedure MatInv(MatrixA: MatrixType; var MatrixB: MatrixType;
                 var OK: boolean);

const
   ErrorBound = 1.0E-10;                                    {Mod. #1}

var
   I, J, K, M   : integer;
   Factor, Temp : real;

begin
   for I := 1 to MatrixSize do
      for J := 1 to MatrixSize do
         if I = J then
            MatrixB[I, J] := 1.0
         else
            MatrixB[I, J] := 0.0;
      for J := 1 to MatrixSize do
         begin
            I := J;
            while abs(MatrixA[I, J]) < ErrorBound do
               begin
                  if I = MatrixSize then
                     begin
                        OK := false;
                        exit
                     end;
                  I := I + 1
               end;
            for K := 1 to MatrixSize do
               begin
                  Temp         := MatrixA[I, K];
                  MatrixA[I, K] := MatrixA[J, K];
                  MatrixA[J, K] := Temp;
                  Temp         := MatrixB[I, K];
                  MatrixB[I, K] := MatrixB[J, K];
                  MatrixB[J, K] := Temp
               end;
```

```
         Factor := 1.0 / MatrixA[J, J];
         for K := 1 to MatrixSize do
            begin
                MatrixA[J, K] := Factor * MatrixA[J, K];
                MatrixB[J, K] := Factor * MatrixB[J, K]
            end;
         for M := 1 to MatrixSize do
            if M <> J then
               begin
                   Factor := - MatrixA[M, J];
                   for K := 1 to MatrixSize do
                      begin
                         MatrixA[M, K] := MatrixA[M, K] +
                                         Factor * MatrixA[J, K];
                         MatrixB[M, K] := MatrixB[M, K] +
                                         Factor * MatrixB[J, K]
                      end
               end
      end;
   OK := true
end;
```

Variables

ErrorBound	Maximum allowable deviation of a value from zero (needed because of round-off and truncation errors)
I, J, K, M	Subscripts in the two-dimensional arrays
Factor	Multiplicative factor applied to a row of MatrixA and a row of MatrixB
Temp	Temporary value of an array element

Discussion

The inverse of a matrix is, in effect, the "reciprocal" of that matrix. Matrix division can thus be accomplished. Instead of dividing one matrix by another, you multiply one matrix by the inverse of the other. It follows that multiplying a matrix by its own inverse will result in a unity matrix. A unity matrix has ones on its main diagonal and zeros everywhere else. Any square matrix multiplied by the unity matrix (of the same size) simply results in the original matrix.

A matrix is singular (and thus cannot be inverted) if one of its rows (or columns) consists of all zeros or if one of its rows (or columns) is an exact multiple of another. In these cases, MatInv will terminate and set the boolean flag OK to false. Be careful not to assume anything about the values in the MatrixB array in such cases. The values are indeterminate.

Modification

ErrorBound must be adjusted if your input array contains elements much different from order unity. This adjustment is discussed in the Limitations and Error Conditions section. You may set ErrorBound to any real number greater than zero. If you set ErrorBound to zero, you will likely cause the procedure to terminate unsuccessfully (OK = false) for most practical cases.

Determ

Name: *Determ*

Type: real *function*

Purpose: *To evaluate the determinant of a matrix*

Calling Sequence: Determ(MatrixA)

Description

Determ calculates the determinant of a two-dimensional square matrix. Matrix elements are of type real, and the result is also of type real.

Input

MatrixA   real   Array containing the matrix for which the determinant is to be evaluated

The following global const and type declarations must be specified in your main program:

```
const
   MatrixSize = 3;

type
   MatrixType = array[1..MatrixSize, 1..MatrixSize] of real;
```

The constant MatrixSize defines the size of the square array. (In other words, the value of MatrixSize is the number of elements on the main diagonal of MatrixA.) MatrixSize can be any positive integer. The value 3 is only an example.

Output

Determ   real   The function Determ returns the determinant of
                          MatrixA.

Limitations and Error Conditions

Determ contains an embedded recursive procedure named DoIt. As MatrixSize
increases, computational time and memory use rise dramatically because of the
recursion. For matrices with nonzero elements, table 12.1 shows typical computation times on a standard IBM PC.

Table 12.1
Execution Speed of Determ

MatrixSize	Approximate Time (in Seconds)
4 or less	Less than 1
5	1
6	4
7	24
8	190
9 or more	1100 or more

Overflow or underflow can occur if your matrix elements are several orders of
magnitude larger or smaller than 1, especially when MatrixSize is greater than 5.
Underflow can occur also when individual matrix elements differ greatly from each
other in order of magnitude. Determ does no internal checking for these possibilities.

Sample Usage

```
program SampleUsageOfDeterm;

const
   MatrixSize = 3;

type
   MatrixType = array[1..MatrixSize, 1..MatrixSize] of real;

var
   MatrixA : MatrixType;
   I, J    : integer;
   Value   : real;
```

```
{$I Determ. PSL}
{$I MatShow. PSL}

BEGIN
   for I := 1 to MatrixSize do
      for J := 1 to MatrixSize do
         MatrixA[I, J] := I + J;
   MatrixA[1, 2] := 1.8;
   writeln('MatrixA =');
   MatShow(MatrixA);
   Value := Determ(MatrixA);
   writeln ('Determinant of MatrixA =', Value:6:2)
END.
```

Running this test program produces the following output:

```
MatrixA =
        2.00    1.80    4.00
        3.00    4.00    5.00
        4.00    5.00    6.00

Determinant of MatrixA = -2.40
```

Subprogram Listing of Determ.PSL

```
function Determ(MatrixA: MatrixType): real;

var
   ValDeterm : real;
   J         : integer;
   Done      : array[1..MatrixSize] of boolean;

   procedure DoIt(Term: real; M, K: integer);

   var
      J, N, Sign: integer;

   begin {procedure DoIt}
      if K > MatrixSize then
         begin
```

```
            Sign := 1;
            if odd(M) then Sign := -1;
            ValDeterm := ValDeterm + Sign * Term
        end
    else
        if Term <> 0.0 then
            begin
                N := 0;
                for J := MatrixSize downto 1 do
                    if Done[J] then
                        N := N + 1
                    else
                        begin
                            Done[J] := true;
                            DoIt(Term * MatrixA[K, J], M + N, K + 1);
                            Done[J] := false
                        end
            end
    end; {procedure DoIt}

begin {function Determ}
    for J := 1 to MatrixSize do
        Done[J] := false;
    ValDeterm := 0.0;
    DoIt(1.0, 0, 1);
    Determ := ValDeterm
end; {function Determ}
```

Variables

Variables for the Function Determ

ValDeterm	Current (temporary) value of the determinant
J	Index variable
Done	boolean array indicating completion of evaluation at level J

Variables for the Embedded Recursive Procedure DoIt

Term	Next term in ValDeterm calculation
Sign	Sign (+ or -) for next Term in ValDeterm

N	Number of term being computed
M	Offset to N
K, J	Indices into MatrixA array

Discussion

Most algorithms to calculate determinants depend on triangulating the original matrix (reducing it to a form with all zeros on one side of the main diagonal). This process requires row and column manipulation as well as scaling. For best mathematical precision, the appropriate pivot element must be searched for at each step of the calculation before the critical divisions and multiplications are performed. All this activity typically requires quite lengthy program code.

Determ, however, calculates the determinant by implementing the combinatorial definition of a determinant. The resultant recursive code is more elegant but often takes longer to run than the code from a typical triangulation scheme.

Modifications

None

Integral

Name: *Integral*

Type: *Procedure*

Purpose: *To evaluate a definite integral of a given function*

Calling Sequence: Integral(LowX, HighX, Result, Code)

Description

Integral calculates a numerical approximation of a definite integral, using Simpson's rule. You provide the function to be integrated and the upper and lower bounds of the integration domain. You can also specify the accuracy of the solution.

Input

| LowX | real | Lower integration limit |
| HighX | real | Upper integration limit |

The integration domain is considered to range in X from X = LowX to X = HighX. But there is no restriction that HighX be greater than LowX. In fact, HighX can be greater than, smaller than, or equal to LowX.

You must provide the function to be integrated. It is called MyFunc and should be specified in your main program as

```
function MyFunc(X: real): real;
```

When called with a value for X, MyFunc must return the value of your function at that X. MyFunc can be as simple or as complicated as you require. It can be a one-line formula or a table (with a routine to interpolate between discretely specified values). What matters is that the function be continuous over the integration domain. For our purposes, this means that MyFunc returns a finite real value for any X in the integration domain.

The integral is the "area under the curve." This is the shaded area shown in figure 12.1.

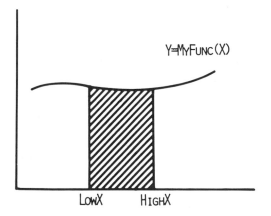

Fig. 12.1. *The integral of* MyFunc *from* LowX *to* HighX.

Output

Result	real	Value of the integral
Code	real	Accuracy of the solution. (See Limitations and Error Conditions.)

Limitations and Error Conditions

Integral works by dividing the integration domain into a number of subintervals, calculating the integral of each subinterval, and summing the results. The procedure then doubles the number of subintervals and recalculates the entire solution. This process continues until two successive iterations are sufficiently close to each other (convergence) or until the number of subintervals reaches a specified maximum (nonconvergence). The variables MaxError and MaxNumSegs control these convergence criteria. See the Modifications section for an explanation of how to adjust these variables.

The real variable Code provides information about the accuracy of the solution. If Code is greater than zero, the solution converged, and Code is the number of subintervals used in the final calculation. If Code is less than zero, the iteration did not converge, and the absolute value of Code is the relative error between the last two approximations. In this case, the procedure still returns its best solution in the variable Result. Although the value is often acceptable for the integral, be careful using Result when Code is less than zero.

Sample Usage

```
program SampleUsageOfIntegral;

var
   LowX, HighX, Result, Code: real;

function MyFunc(X: real): real;                        {Mod. #3}

begin
   MyFunc := 4.0 / (1.0 + X * X)                       {Mod. #3}
end;

{$I Integral.PSL}

BEGIN
   LowX  := 0.0;
   HighX := 1.0;
   Integral(LowX, HighX, Result, Code);
   if Code > 0.0 then
      writeln('Value of integral =', Result)
   else
      writeln('Integral calculation did not converge')
END.
```

Running this test program produces the following output:

```
Value of integral =  3.1415926530E+00
```

Subprogram Listing of Integral.PSL

```pascal
procedure Integral(LowX, HighX: real; var Result, Code: real);

const
  MaxNumSegs = 1000;                                      {Mod. #1}
  MaxError   = 1.0E-6;                                    {Mod. #2}

var
  J, M, NumSegs                              : integer;
  X, OldVal, Error, SegWidth, CurrentSum, Temp : real;

  function Simpson: real;

  begin {function Simpson}
    SegWidth   := (HighX - LowX) / NumSegs;
    CurrentSum := MyFunc(LowX) + MyFunc(HighX);          {Mod. #3}
    M          := NumSegs div 2;
    Temp       := 0.0;
    for J := 1 to M do
      begin
        X := LowX + SegWidth * (2.0 * J - 1);
        Temp := Temp + MyFunc(X)                         {Mod. #3}
      end;
    CurrentSum := CurrentSum + 4.0 * Temp;
    M          := M - 1;
    Temp       := 0.0;
    for J := 1 to M do
      begin
        X := LowX + SegWidth * 2.0 * J;
        Temp := Temp + MyFunc(X)                         {Mod. #3}
      end;
    CurrentSum := CurrentSum + 2.0 * Temp;
    Simpson    := SegWidth * CurrentSum / 3.0
  end; {function Simpson}
```

```
begin {procedure Integral}
   NumSegs := 10;                              {Mod. #4}
   Code    := 0.0;
   OldVal  := Simpson;
   repeat
      NumSegs := NumSegs * 2;
      Result  := Simpson;
      if Result = 0.0 then
         Error := 0.0
      else
         Error := abs((Result - OldVal) / Result);
      if NumSegs > MaxNumSegs then
         Code := - Error;
      if Error < MaxError then
         Code := NumSegs;
      OldVal := Result
   until Code <> 0.0
end; {procedure Integral}
```

Variables

MaxNumSegs	Constant that determines the maximum number of subintervals allowed
MaxError	Constant equal to the maximum percentage error allowed between successive iterations
J	Loop index
M	Number of terms in the summation loop
NumSegs	Number of subintervals in the current iteration
X	Current value of X (along the integration domain)
OldVal	Solution calculated by the last iteration
Error	Percentage error between the last two iterations
SegWidth	Width of one subinterval
CurrentSum	Working total of terms during an iteration
Temp	Temporary value of terms during an iteration

Discussion

If your function consists of experimental data at discrete values of X, you must enable MyFunc to calculate the function at intermediate values of X. We recommend one of two approaches. The first is to write the function to interpolate linearly (or in higher order) between the appropriate values of X. For this approach, you search your data table for the experimental X values that bound the value of X where the function is to be evaluated. The second method is to use the program PolyFit (see Chapter 18), which can produce an approximate polynomial expression to fit your experimental data. This expression can then be used in MyFunc.

Be sure that you specify MyFunc in your main program before the procedure Integral appears. MyFunc must be global to Integral.

Integral contains the embedded function Simpson, which calculates the value of the integral depending on the current value of NumSegs. After Simpson is invoked for each iteration, the percentage error between the last two iterates is computed. This is the absolute value of the difference between the two iterates divided by the last iterate. When this percentage error drops below MaxError, the procedure is considered to have converged to the desired solution.

Modifications

1. MaxNumSegs is the maximum number of subintervals allowed. The number of subintervals doubles with each iteration if convergence is not achieved. The algorithm terminates if MaxNumSegs is exceeded and convergence is still not achieved. You may change its value from 1000 to any positive integer.

2. MaxError is the required percentage error for successful convergence. The algorithm terminates when MaxError is satisfied. You may change its value from 1.0E-6 to any positive real number.

3. If you prefer to call your input function something other than MyFunc, change its name in all the indicated lines.

4. The number of subintervals used in the initial iteration is specified by NumSegs. You may want to raise its value from 10 if you know that your case will require many more subintervals for successful convergence. NumSegs must be a positive even integer greater than or equal to 4.

Root

> **Name:** *Root*
>
> **Type:** *Procedure*
>
> **Purpose:** *To calculate real roots of a given function*
>
> **Calling Sequence:** `Root(LowX, HighX, Result, OK)`

Description

`Root` attempts to find a value of X so that `MyFunc(X)` = 0, in which `MyFunc` is any function of X that you provide. You specify the range of X over which the search takes place. You can optionally specify the accuracy of the solution and the resolution of the search domain.

Input

`LowX`　　　　`real`　　　The lower end of the search domain

`HighX`　　　`real`　　　The upper end of the search domain

The search domain is considered to range in X from X = `LowX` to X = `HighX`. But there is no restriction that `HighX` be greater than `LowX`. The algorithm works correctly if `HighX` is greater than, equal to, or less than `LowX`.

You must provide the function `MyFunc`. Specify it in your main program as

```
function MyFunc(X: real): real;
```

When invoked with a value for X, `MyFunc` returns the value of the function at that X. `MyFunc` can be as simple or as complicated as you require. It can be a one-line formula or a table (with a routine to interpolate between discretely specified values). What matters is that the function be continuous over the search domain. For our purposes, this means that `MyFunc` returns a finite real value for any X in the search domain.

Output

Result   real   The value of X for which MyFunc(X) = 0

OK   boolean   The outcome of the procedure. If OK is true, a root
                        was found; if OK is false, no root was found.

If OK is false, the value of Result is meaningless.

Limitations and Error Conditions

Root works by trying to find a bounded interval in which a root occurs. The procedure first checks whether MyFunc(LowX) and MyFunc(HighX) have opposite signs.
If the signs are opposite, a root occurs at some X in this search domain. Otherwise,
Root continually divides the search interval into smaller and smaller subintervals,
looking for one bounding a root. This partitioning process continues until the number of segments (subintervals) becomes larger than the constant MaxNumSegs. If
MaxNumSegs is too small, the algorithm may terminate unsuccessfully even though
a root theoretically exists. See the Modifications section for an explanation of how
to adjust MaxNumSegs.

Once the search interval is bounded, Root iterates until the solution is found to a
tolerance of less than the constant MaxError. More specifically, X is a solution when
the absolute value of MyFunc(X) is less than MaxError. See the Modifications section
for information about adjusting MaxError.

The boolean flag OK reveals the outcome of the procedure. When OK is true, a
successful root is contained in the variable Result. When OK is false, no root was
found. Be sure to test OK after calling Root, because Result is meaningless if OK is
false.

Sometimes multiple roots exist. Root cannot detect this condition and terminates
successfully once any root is found. If you find a root but suspect that another one
exists, try the following technique. Invoke Root twice more. First, leave LowX unchanged but set HighX just below the found root. Second, set LowX just above the
found root but leave HighX at its original value. (For this technique, it is assumed
that the original LowX is less than the original HighX.)

Sample Usage

```
program SampleUsageOfRoot;

var LowX, HighX, Result : real;
    OK                  : boolean;

function MyFunc(X: real): real;                      {Mod. #3}

begin
  MyFunc := sin(X)                                   {Mod. #3}
end;

{$I Root.PSL}

BEGIN
  LowX  := 1.0;
  HighX := 5.0;
  Root(LowX, HighX, Result, OK);
  if OK then
     writeln('Root =', Result)
  else
     writeln('No root found')
END.
```

Running this test program produces the following output:

```
Root =  3.1415920258E+00
```

Subprogram Listing of Root.PSL

```
procedure Root(LowX, HighX: real; var Result: real;
               var OK: boolean);

const
  MaxNumSegs = 500;                                  {Mod. #1}
  MaxError   = 1.0E-6;                               {Mod. #2}

var
  X, XLo, XHi, FLo, FHi, Width, Test : real;
  J, NumSegs                         : integer;

  procedure Iterate;
```

```pascal
  begin {procedure Iterate}
    repeat
      X    := (XLo + XHi) / 2.0;                    {Mod. #4}
      Test := MyFunc(X);                            {Mod. #3}
      if abs(Test) < MaxError then
        begin
          Result := X;
          OK     := true
        end
      else
        if (Test * FLo) > 0.0 then
          begin
            XLo := X;
            FLo := Test
          end
        else
          begin
            XHi := X;
            FHi := Test
          end
    until OK
  end; {procedure Iterate}

begin {procedure Root}
  OK  := false;
  XLo := LowX;
  XHi := HighX;
  FLo := MyFunc(XLo);                               {Mod. #3}
  FHi := MyFunc(XHi);                               {Mod. #3}
  if abs(FLo) < MaxError then
    begin
      OK     := true;
      Result := XLo;
      exit
    end;
  if abs(FHi) < MaxError then
    begin
      OK     := true;
      Result := XHi;
      exit
    end;
```

```
  if (FLo * FHi) < 0.0 then
     begin
        Iterate;
        exit
     end;
   NumSegs := 2;
   repeat
     Width := (XHi - XLo) / NumSegs;
     for J := 1 to (NumSegs div 2) do
        begin
           X    := XLo + Width * (2 * J - 1);
           FHi := MyFunc(X);                               {Mod. #3}
           if (FHi * FLo) < 0.0 then
              begin
                 XHi := X;
                 Iterate;
                 exit
              end
        end;
     NumSegs := NumSegs * 2
   until NumSegs > MaxNumSegs
end; {procedure Root}
```

Variables

MaxNumSegs	Constant equal to the maximum number of subintervals allowed to bound a solution
MaxError	Constant equal to the error tolerance allowed in a solution
X	Current value of X in the search domain
XLo	Lower X boundary on the current subinterval
XHi	Higher X boundary on the current subinterval
FLo	Value of MyFunc(XLo)
FHi	Value of MyFunc(XHi)
Width	Length in X of a specific subinterval
Test	Value of MyFunc(X) for the current X
J	Loop index
NumSegs	Number of subintervals in the current partitioning

Discussion

If your function consists of data at discrete values of X, the comments in the Discussion section of the Integral subprogram pertain here also.

Be sure that you specify MyFunc in your main program before the procedure Root appears. MyFunc must be global to Root.

Root contains the embedded procedure Iterate. This procedure homes in on the correct solution once the search domain has been bounded. Iterate works by continually bisecting the search domain and retaining the half interval that still contains the root. The process is repeated until the root is obtained to the required accuracy. Although Iterate is a zero-order method, and thus relatively slow compared to higher-order techniques, it works for any continuous function. Higher-order methods converge faster for most practical cases but can be slow for certain pathological ones. One higher-order method is detailed in the Modifications section.

Modifications

1. MaxNumSegs is the maximum number of subintervals allowed in the search for a bounded solution domain. The width of each subinterval is continually halved until a solution domain is found. If you increase MaxNumSegs, the procedure will have increased resolution in its attempt to find a solution domain. If one cannot be found, the cost is additional computation time.

2. MaxError specifies the solution criterion by requiring that abs(MyFunc(X)) < MaxError for X is a satisfactory solution. You may change MaxError from 1.0E-6 to any positive real number.

3. If you prefer to call your input function something other than MyFunc, change its name in all the indicated lines.

4. A higher-order convergence formula can be used for X. Try the following replacement for the entire line:

   ```
   X := (FHi * XLo - FLo * XHi) / (FHi - FLo);
   ```

   This formula converges faster for most practical functions but can be slower in certain pathological cases.

Deriv

> **Name:** *Deriv*
>
> **Type:** *Procedure*
>
> **Purpose:** *To calculate the derivative of a given function*
>
> **Calling Sequence:** Deriv(XVal, Result, OK)

Description

Deriv calculates a numerical approximation of the derivative of MyFunc at XVal, which is a given value of the independent variable. MyFunc is a function of X that you provide. You can also specify the desired accuracy of the numerical solution.

Input

XVal   real   The value of X at which the derivative is to be calculated

You must provide the function MyFunc. Specify it in your main program as

```
function MyFunc(X: real): real;
```

When invoked with a value for X, MyFunc returns the value of your function at that X. MyFunc can be as simple or as complicated as you require. It can be a one-line formula or a bivariate table (with a routine to interpolate between discretely specified values). What matters is that the function be continuous near XVal. See the Limitations and Error Conditions section for more details.

Output

Result   real   The derivative of MyFunc at XVal

OK   boolean   Outcome of the procedure. If OK is true, a solution was found; if OK is false, no solution was found.

If OK is false, the value in Result may still be a reasonable approximation of the desired derivative. See the Limitations and Error Conditions section.

Limitations and Error Conditions

Deriv calculates the derivative by using a forward-differencing technique. MyFunc is evaluated for values of X in the range XVal <= X <= (XVal + 2Delta). Delta is set to 0.01 initially. This setting is reasonable if your function is to be evaluated with X approximately of order unity. If your typical X values are several orders of magnitude higher or lower than 1, you may want to change Delta appropriately as explained in the Modifications section.

If your function is not well behaved for X > XVal, you may want to use a backward-differencing technique to evaluate the derivative. For instance, you would use such a technique if MyFunc is not defined for X > XVal. Again, see the Modifications section.

Deriv iterates by continually halving Delta. This process continues until the percentage change in the derivative becomes less than MaxError. If the iteration does not converge in MaxNumTries, the procedure returns with OK set to false. But Result still contains the last iterate to the derivative. This last iterate may cautiously be used as an approximate solution. The control variables MaxError and MaxNumTries can be adjusted. See the Modifications section.

Sample Usage

```
program SampleUsageOfDeriv;

var XVal, Result : real;
    OK           : boolean;

function MyFunc(X: real): real;                    {Mod. #3}

begin
  MyFunc := sin(x)                                 {Mod. #3}
end;

{$I Deriv.PSL}

BEGIN
  XVal := 0.0;
  Deriv(XVal, Result, OK);
  if OK then
    writeln('Derivative =', Result, '  at  X =', XVal:6:2)
  else
    writeln('Error')
END.
```

Running this test program produces the following output:

```
Derivative =  1.0000001302E+00  at  X =  0.00
```

Subprogram Listing of Deriv.PSL

```
procedure Deriv(XVal: real; var Result: real; var OK: boolean);

const
   MaxNumTries  = 100;                                  {Mod. #1}
   MaxError     = 1.0E-6;                               {Mod. #2}
   InitialDelta = 0.01;                                 {Mod. #4}

var
   Delta, FPrime, OldFPrime, F1, F2, F3, Error : real;
   NumTries                                    : integer;

begin
   OK        := false;
   OldFPrime := 0.0;
   Delta     := InitialDelta;                           {Mod. #5}
   NumTries  := 0;
   repeat
      F1     := MyFunc(XVal);                           {Mod. #3}
      F2     := MyFunc(XVal + Delta);                   {Mod. #3}
      F3     := MyFunc(XVal + 2.0 * Delta);             {Mod. #3}
      FPrime := (-3.0 * F1 + 4.0 * F2 - F3) / 2.0 / Delta;
      if FPrime = 0.0 then
         Error := 0.0
      else
         Error := abs((FPrime - OldFPrime) / FPrime);
      NumTries := NumTries + 1;
      if NumTries > MaxNumTries then
         begin
            Result := FPrime;
            exit
         end;
```

```
      if Error < MaxError then
         begin
            OK      := true;
            Result := FPrime
         end;
      Delta      := Delta / 2.0;
      OldFPrime := FPrime
   until OK
end;
```

Variables

MaxNumTries	Constant equal to the maximum number of iterations allowed
MaxError	Constant equal to the maximum percentage error allowed for convergence
InitialDelta	Initial value of Delta
Delta	The current step size for X used in the difference equation
FPrime	The value of the derivative at the current iterate
OldFPrime	The value of the derivative at the last iterate
F1	MyFunc(XVal)
F2	MyFunc(XVal + Delta)
F3	MyFunc(XVal + 2Delta)
Error	Percentage error between the last two iterates
NumTries	Number of iterations already completed

Discussion

If your function consists of data at discrete values of X, the comments in the Discussion section of the Integral subprogram pertain here also.

Be sure that you specify MyFunc in your main program before the procedure Deriv appears. MyFunc must be global to Deriv.

To approximate the derivative, Deriv uses a second-order (quadratic) difference equation. MyFunc is evaluated at three points (XVal, XVal + Delta, and XVal + 2Delta) in each iteration. This method is quite accurate for a wide range of functions if Delta is picked appropriately. The algorithm adjusts Delta by continually halving it until convergence is achieved.

Modifications

1. If your case is not converging, allow the procedure more iterations by raising the value of MaxNumTries. Its value can be any positive integer.

2. MaxError specifies the maximum allowable percentage error between two iterates for successful convergence. You may change the value of MaxError from 1.0E-6 to any positive real number.

3. If you prefer to call your input function something other than MyFunc, change its name in all the indicated lines.

4. InitialDelta is the value of Delta in the first iteration. The variable's value of 0.01 assumes that the difference between MyFunc(Delta) and MyFunc(Delta + 0.01) is reasonable. Reasonable here means something large enough to be recognized within Turbo's real-number precision but smaller than several orders of magnitude. You may (rarely) need to make InitialDelta larger or smaller to achieve a reasonable difference. InitialDelta must be a positive real number.

5. You may want to try a backward-differencing technique if your function is not defined or not well behaved for $X > XVal$. Change the line indicated by {Mod. #5} to

```
Delta := - InitialDelta;
```

Even for well-behaved functions, this technique can be a worthwhile redundancy check on the calculated derivative. Your answer should not change significantly.

DiffEqn

Name: *DiffEqn*
Type: *Procedure*
Purpose: *To solve a specified differential equation*
Calling Sequence: DiffEqn(Xinitial, Yinitial, Xfinal, Yfinal, OK)

Description

You specify DYDX, the function of X and Y to be solved. DYDX must be a first-order, ordinary differential equation. X is the independent variable, and Y is the dependent variable. You must provide the initial values of X and Y and the final value of X.

The procedure calculates the final value of Y. You can specify also the desired accuracy of the numerical solution.

Input

Xinitial	real	The initial value of the independent variable
Yinitial	real	The initial value of the dependent variable
Xfinal	real	The final value of the independent variable

You must provide the differential equation through the function DYDX. Specify it in your main program as

```
function DYDX(X, Y: real): real;
```

DYDX returns the value of the differential equation when invoked with values for X and/or Y. DYDX should be continuous over the range of X and Y expected in the computation. For our purposes, this means that DYDX will return a finite real value for any X and Y occurring in the calculation.

Output

Yfinal	real	The value of Y at Xfinal
OK	boolean	Result of the procedure. If OK is true, a solution was found; if OK is false, no solution was found.

If OK is false, the value of Yfinal may still be a reasonable approximation of the desired answer. See the Limitations and Error Conditions section.

Limitations and Error Conditions

DiffEqn iterates by continually doubling NumSegs, the number of segments in the X domain. The value of Yfinal is progressively updated while each iteration improves the numerical accuracy (unless round-off errors dominate). This process continues until the percentage change in Yfinal is less than MaxError. If the iteration does not converge before NumSegs reaches MaxNumSegs, the procedure returns with OK set to false. However, Yfinal still contains the last (best) iterated value. This last iterate may cautiously be used as a good approximation of the desired solution. The control variables MaxError and MaxNumSegs can be adjusted. See the Modifications section.

Sample Usage

```
program SampleUsageOfDiffEqn;

var
   Xinitial, Yinitial, Xfinal, Yfinal' : real;
   OK                                  : boolean;

function DYDX(X, Y: real): real;                        {Mod. #3}

begin
   DYDX := Y * sin(X)                                   {Mod. #3}
end;

{$I DiffEqn.PSL}

BEGIN
   Xinitial := 0.0;
   Yinitial := 1.0;
   Xfinal   := 1.0;
   DiffEqn(Xinitial, Yinitial, Xfinal, Yfinal, OK);
   if OK then
      writeln('Yfinal =', Yfinal, '  at  Xfinal =', Xfinal)
   else
      writeln('Error')
END.
```

Running this test program produces the following output:

```
Yfinal = 1.5835951659E+00  at  Xfinal = 1.0000000000E+00
```

Subprogram Listing for DiffEqn.PSL

```
procedure DiffEqn(Xinitial, Yinitial, Xfinal: real;
                  var Yfinal: real; var OK: boolean);

const
   MaxNumSegs = 2000;                                   {Mod. #1}
   MaxError   = 1.0E-6;                                 {Mod. #2}
```

```
var
   XI, XF, YI, YF, Yprevious          : real;
   Width, HalfW, Error, KA, KB, KC, KD : real;
   J, NumSegs                         : integer;

begin
   OK      := false;
   NumSegs := 1;
   repeat
      Width  := (Xfinal - Xinitial) / NumSegs;
      HalfW  := Width / 2.0;
      for J := 1 to NumSegs do
         begin
            XI := Xinitial + (J - 1) * Width;
            XF := XI + Width;
            if J = 1 then
               YI := Yinitial
            else
               YI := YF;
            KA := DYDX(XI, YI);                        {Mod. #3}
            KB := DYDX(XI + HalfW, YI + KA * HalfW);    {Mod. #3}
            KC := DYDX(XI + HalfW, YI + KB * HalfW);    {Mod. #3}
            KD := DYDX(XI + Width, YI + KC * Width);    {Mod. #3}
            YF := YI + Width *
                  (KA + 2.0 * KB + 2.0 * KC + KD) / 6.0
         end;
      if NumSegs = 1 then
         Error := MaxError
      else
         if YF = 0.0 then
            Error := 0.0
         else
            Error := abs((YF - Yprevious) / YF);
      if NumSegs > MaxNumSegs then
         begin
            Yfinal := YF;
            exit
         end;
```

```
      if (Error < MaxError) or (Width = 0.0) then
        begin
            OK      := true;
            Yfinal := YF
        end;
      Yprevious := YF;
      NumSegs   := 2 * NumSegs
   until OK
end;
```

Variables

MaxNumSegs	Constant used to determine the maximum number of segments allowed in the X domain
MaxError	Constant equal to the maximum percentage error allowed for convergence
XI	Initial X in the current working segment
XF	Final X in the current working segment
YI	Initial Y in the current working segment
YF	Final Y in the current working segment
Yprevious	Final Y in the previous working segment
Width	Length (in X) of the current working segment
HalfW	Half of Width
Error	Percentage error between the last two iterates
KA, KB	Runge-Kutta coefficients
KC, KD	Runge-Kutta coefficients
J	Loop index
NumSegs	Number of segments in the current iteration

Discussion

Solving differential equations is often necessary in practical engineering problems. For many of these equations, a closed-form (or exact analytical expression) solution is obtainable. Frequently, however, such a solution is not possible. Then you must solve the equation numerically, using computer software like DiffEqn.

DiffEqn uses the fourth-order, Runge-Kutta method to solve your differential equation. The Runge-Kutta technique is explained in detail in many numerical analysis books.

You may want to produce a table of X and Y pairs instead of just the final values. Such a table is needed to draw a smooth graph of the solution curve while X varies from Xinitial to Xfinal. To create the table, place a loop in your main program where DiffEqn is invoked. Set the first value of Xfinal to be the first value you want in your table. Make the call to DiffEqn. Then reset Xinitial to your last Xfinal, and Yinitial to your last Yfinal. Reset Xfinal to be the next value you want in your table. Invoke DiffEqn again and continue the process until Xfinal reaches your true final value. This technique can produce a table of any resolution you want.

By the way, Xfinal does not have to be larger than Xinitial. This procedure works fine if X is decreasing. The procedure works fine also if Xfinal equals Xinitial, although Yfinal will simply equal Yinitial in this case.

Modifications

1. If your case is not converging, allow the procedure more iterations by raising the value of MaxNumSegs. It can be any positive integer greater than 1.

2. MaxError specifies the maximum allowable percentage error between two iterates for successful convergence. MaxError can be any positive real number.

3. If you prefer to call your input differential equation something other than DYDX, change its name in all the indicated lines.

13

Statistics and Probability

Although often maligned in the popular press ("There are three kinds of lies: lies, damned lies, and statistics"), the science of statistics provides valuable tools for data analysis. In this chapter are nine subprograms drawn from a variety of useful subjects in statistics and probability.

Stats provides elemental statistical analysis of a set of real numbers. The subprogram computes the mean, the standard deviation, and other basic statistical quantities.

Permutations and combinations of a collection of objects occur regularly in combinatorial probability. NumPerm and NumComb make these calculations. As a bonus, NumPerm provides a way to calculate factorials of integer numbers.

Probability distribution functions enable you to model a myriad of physical phenomena by quantitative analysis. BinomDis and NormDis calculate the two most important cases: binomial distributions in the discrete case, and normal distributions in the continuous case.

The subprogram RndNorm provides random numbers drawn from a specified normal distribution. This subprogram complements Turbo's random function, which provides random numbers drawn from a uniform distribution.

Paired X-Y data often results from experiments and from data collected in surveys. LinReg calculates correlation coefficients, which provide a measure of how well the data fits on a straight line.

The chi-square test has far-reaching applications in several areas. It provides a quantitative means of testing experimental hypotheses. GetChiSq computes the value of the chi-square statistic for a given experiment. ChiProb calculates the probability that a given range of chi-square will occur. Although few references provide a computational procedure for calculating the chi-square tables, ChiProb can do the calculation to any resolution you want.

367

Stats

Name:	*Stats*
Type:	*Procedure*
Purpose:	*To calculate statistics for a set of discrete values*
Calling Sequence:	Stats(NumArray, Count, Mean, Median, StanDev, MinValue, MaxValue)

Description

You provide the data in the one-dimensional array NumArray. Stats then computes the mean, median, standard deviation, minimum value, and maximum value of your data. The data is assumed to be real. See the Modification section for an explanation of how to use integer instead.

Input

NumArray	real	Array of the data values
Count	integer	Number of data elements in NumArray to use in computing statistics

The following global const and type declarations must be specified in your main program:

```
const
   ArraySize = 250;

type
   ArrayType = array[1..ArraySize] of real;
```

The number 250 for the array size is just an example. Your array size can be any positive integer.

Output

Mean	real	Mean of the values in NumArray
Median	real	Median of the values in NumArray
StanDev	real	Standard deviation of the values in NumArray
MinValue	real	Minimum value in NumArray
MaxValue	real	Maximum value in NumArray

Limitations and Error Conditions

If Count is less than 1, the procedure is bypassed. No error message is displayed, and the results returned for the statistics are meaningless. The same is true if Count is greater than ArraySize. In this case, irrelevant calculations are done, and the results are again meaningless. Your responsibility is to be sure that Count is set accurately.

If Count is 1, Stats returns a value of zero for the standard deviation. All of the other statistics have the value of NumArray[1]. If Count has a positive value less than ArraySize, statistics are computed for the first Count elements in NumArray.

Sample Usage

```
program SampleUsageOfStats;

const
   ArraySize = 250;

type
   ArrayType = array[1..ArraySize] of real;             {Mod. #1}

var
   NumArray                                : ArrayType;
   Count                                   : integer;
   Mean, Median, StanDev, MinValue, MaxValue : real;

{$I Stats.PSL}

BEGIN
   NumArray[1] := 4.2;  NumArray[2] := 1.9;  NumArray[3] := -3.3;
   NumArray[4] := 0.0;  NumArray[5] := 5.4;  NumArray[6] := 2.6;
   Count := 6;
   Stats(NumArray, Count, Mean, Median, StanDev,
                   MinValue, MaxValue);
   writeln('Number of Values =', Count:3);
   writeln('Minimum Value    =', MinValue:8:4);
   writeln('Maximum Value    =', MaxValue:8:4);
   writeln('Mean             =', Mean:8:4);
   writeln('Median           =', Median:8:4);
   writeln('Std. deviation   =', StanDev:8:4)
END.
```

Running this test program produces the following output:

```
Number of values =   6
Minimum value    = -3.3000
Maximum value    =  5.4000
Mean             =  1.8000
Median           =  2.2500
Std. deviation   =  3.1183
```

Subprogram Listing of Stats.PSL

```pascal
procedure Stats(NumArray: ArrayType; Count: integer; var Mean,
                Median, StanDev, MinValue, MaxValue: real);

var
  J, K, Mid            : integer;
  Temp                 : real;                              {Mod. #1}
  ValueSum, SquareSum  : real;

begin
  if Count < 1 then
     exit;
  for J := 2 to Count do
     begin
        Temp := NumArray[J];
        K    := J - 1;
        while (Temp < NumArray[K]) and (K > 0) do
           begin
              NumArray[K + 1] := NumArray[K];
              K := K - 1
           end;
        NumArray[K + 1] := Temp
     end;
  ValueSum  := 0.0;
  SquareSum := 0.0;
  for J := 1 to Count do
     begin
        ValueSum  := ValueSum + NumArray[J];
        SquareSum := SquareSum + sqr(NumArray[J])
     end;
```

```
    MinValue := NumArray[1];
    MaxValue := NumArray[Count];
    if odd(Count) then
       Median := NumArray[(Count + 1) div 2]
    else
       begin
          Mid    := Count div 2;
          Median := (NumArray[Mid] + NumArray[Mid + 1]) / 2.0
       end;
    Mean := ValueSum / Count;
    if Count = 1 then
       StanDev := 0.0
    else
       StanDev := sqrt((SquareSum - Count * Mean * Mean) /
                       (Count - 1))
end;
```

Variables

J	Looping index
K	Subscript in sorting algorithm
Mid	Half of Count when Count is even
Temp	Element of NumArray being sorted
ValueSum	Sum of the first Count elements of NumArray
SquareSum	Sum of the squares of the first Count elements of NumArray

Discussion

Stats computes statistical parameters that describe a group of data. In statistical terminology the values in NumArray make up a "population sample." They can be drawn from almost any sample group—for example, heights or weights of people, piston diameters from a manufacturing facility, or combustion times from a chemical experiment.

A primary measure of the data is its central tendency—one number that in some way represents the data or is typical of it. The most common of such measures is the mean, more correctly called the arithmetic mean and usually called the average. The mean is the sum of the data values divided by the number of values. Another description of central tendency is the median. It is the midpoint between the number of data values. That is, half of the data values are larger and half are smaller than the median. For an odd number of values, the median is the middle value when the data is sorted in numeric order. For an even number of values, the median is the number halfway between the two middle values.

Another measure of the data is its variation, or dispersion. This measure indicates how closely the data tends to be dispersed around the mean. The standard deviation is computed by first summing the squares of each data value subtracted from the mean. This sum is then divided by the number of data values - 1. The calculation produces the *variance* of the sample. The standard deviation is simply the square root of the variance. When the standard deviation is small, the data tends to be clustered close to the mean. When the standard deviation is large, the data tends to be spread farther from the mean.

Stats also returns the minimum and maximum values of the sample. So that these values can be found and the median computed, the data is first sorted with the algorithm presented in the subprogram SortSIR. In Stats, however, the subprogram does not change NumArray in the main program. The data in NumArray is in the same order before and after the call to Stats is made. Only the local copy of NumArray in Stats is modified.

Modification

To compute statistics on an integer array, change the word real to integer in the indicated lines. The data in NumArray is then assumed to be integer, of course. The statistical quantities computed by Stats remain of type real.

NumPerm

Name:	*NumPerm*
Type:	integer *function*
Purpose:	*To calculate the number of permutations*
Calling Sequence:	NumPerm(NumThings, NumTake)

Description

NumPerm calculates the number of permutations of a specified number of objects taken a specified number of times. The result is of type integer. The Modification section provides an explanation of how to change the result to type real.

Input

NumThings	integer	Number of objects available
NumTake	integer	Number to take

Output

NumPerm	integer	The function NumPerm returns the number of permutations of NumThings taken NumTake at a time.

Limitations and Error Conditions

NumPerm returns a value of zero if the input conditions are not sensible. A sensible case must have NumThings $>= 1$, NumTake $>= 1$, and NumThings $>=$ NumTake.

If NumThings is greater than 7, integer overflow is possible depending on the value of NumTake. See the Modification section.

Sample Usage

```
program SampleUsageOfNumPerm;

var
    NumThings, NumTake, J : integer;
    Answer                : integer;                    {Mod. #1}

{$I NumPerm.PSL}

BEGIN
    writeln('# Things':15, '# To Take':19, '# Permutations':24);
    NumThings := 6;
    for NumTake := 1 to NumThings do
        begin
            Answer := NumPerm(NumThings, NumTake);
            writeln(NumThings:10, NumTake:21, Answer:21)
        end
END.
```

Running this test program produces the following output:

```
  # Things        # To Take        # Permutations
     6                1                   6
     6                2                  30
     6                3                 120
     6                4                 360
     6                5                 720
     6                6                 720
```

Subprogram Listing of NumPerm.PSL

```pascal
function NumPerm(NumThings, NumTake: integer): integer;  {Mod. #1}

var
   Result   : integer;                                   {Mod. #1}
   J, Limit : integer;

begin
   if (NumThings < 1) or (NumTake < 1) or
                         (NumThings < NumTake) then
      Result := 0
   else
      begin
         Result := 1;
         Limit  := NumThings - NumTake + 1;
         for J := NumThings downto Limit do
            Result := Result * J;
      end;
   NumPerm := Result
end;
```

Variables

Result	Accumulating value of the number of permutations
J	Looping variable
Limit	Lower limit of loop

Discussion

The need for permutation calculations arises regularly in statistical analyses, particularly discrete probability computations. The number of permutations of a collection of objects is the number of different arrangements you can make of those objects. Consider three billiard balls labeled 1, 2, and 3. If you were to place them in a straight line, you could do so in six different ways: 123, 132, 213, 231, 312, and 321. Thus, there are six permutations of three objects.

More generally, you can ask how many permutations exist if you take only so many objects at a time from your collection. For example, from four billiard balls labeled 1 through 4, you can generate 12 permutations of the balls taken two at a time: 12, 13, 14, 21, 23, 24, 31, 32, 34, 41, 42, and 43.

NumPerm can be used to compute factorials. The number of permutations of n objects taken n at a time is simply n factorial. To calculate the factorial of a positive integer, therefore, you set both NumThings and NumTake equal to the desired factorial, and NumPerm returns the answer.

Modification

Integer overflow is threatened whenever NumThings is greater than 7. You can circumvent this overflow by having the function do real arithmetic and return a real result. Change the type declaration integer to real in the designated lines. In the function declaration, change only the last occurrence of integer. Afterward, the line should appear as

```
function NumPerm(NumThings, NumTake: integer): real;
```

NumComb

Name: *NumComb*

Type: integer *function*

Purpose: *To calculate the number of combinations*

Calling Sequence: NumComb(NumThings, NumTake)

Description

NumComb calculates the number of combinations of a specified number of objects taken a specified number of times. The result is of type integer. See the Modification section for information about changing the result to type real.

Input

NumThings	integer	Number of objects available
NumTake	integer	Number to take

Output

NumComb	integer	The function NumComb returns the number of combinations of NumThings taken NumTake at a time.

Limitations and Error Conditions

NumComb returns a value of zero if the input conditions are not sensible. A sensible case must have NumThings >= 1, NumTake >= 1, and NumThings >= NumTake.

If NumThings is greater than 10, integer overflow is possible depending on the value of NumTake. See the Modification section.

Sample Usage

```
program SampleUsageOfNumComb;

var
   NumThings, NumTake, J : integer;
   Answer                : integer;                        {Mod. #1}

{$I NumComb.PSL}

BEGIN
   writeln('# Things' :15, '# To Take' :19, '# Combinations' :24);
   NumThings := 6;
   for NumTake := 1 to NumThings do
      begin
         Answer := NumComb(NumThings, NumTake);
         writeln(NumThings:10, NumTake:21, Answer:21)
      end
END.
```

Running this test program produces the following output:

# Things	# To Take	# Combinations
6	1	6
6	2	15
6	3	20
6	4	15
6	5	6
6	6	1

Subprogram Listing of NumComb.PSL

```
function NumComb(NumThings, NumTake: integer): integer;  {Mod. #1}

var
   Result  : integer;                                    {Mod. #1}
   J, Limit : integer;

begin
   if (NumThings < 1) or (NumTake < 1) or
                      (NumThings < NumTake) then
      Result := 0
   else
      if NumThings = NumTake then
         Result := 1
      else
         if NumTake > (NumThings - NumTake) then
            Result := NumComb(NumThings, NumThings - NumTake)
         else
            begin
               Result := 1;
               Limit  := NumThings - NumTake + 1;
               for J := NumThings downto Limit do
                  Result := Result * J;
               for J := 2 to NumTake do
                  Result := Result div J               {Mod. #1a}
            end;
   NumComb := Result
end;
```

Variables

Result	Accumulating value of the number of combinations
J	Looping variable
Limit	Lower limit of loop

Discussion

Like permutation calculations, the calculation of combinations arises in discrete probability computations. A combination is a distinct subset of a group of objects without regard to order. A particular combination contains specific items, but there is no differentiation between the various ways these items can be arranged.

Consider the example used in the discussion of permutations. You had four billiard balls labeled 1 through 4. There were 12 permutations of them taken two at a time. But there are only 6 combinations of them taken two at a time: balls 1 and 2, (without respect to order), 1 and 3, 1 and 4, 2 and 3, 2 and 4, and 3 and 4. If you specify the total number of items and the particular number to take, the number of combinations is always less than or equal to the number of permutations.

We use a small trick in this subprogram to minimize the danger of integer overflow. If we have x number of objects and take them y at a time, the number of combinations is the same as taking them (x - y) at a time instead. Therefore, NumComb checks which calculation results in the least chance of integer overflow. If overflow is indicated with no adjustment to NumTake, NumComb makes a recursive call to itself with NumTake adjusted.

Modification

Integer overflow is possible whenever NumThings is greater than 10. You can circumvent this overflow by having the function do real arithmetic and return a real result. Change the type declaration integer to real in the lines designated by {Mod. #1}. Change only the last occurrence of integer in the function declaration. Afterward, that line should appear as

```
function NumComb(NumThings, NumTake: integer): real;
```

In addition, change the line designated as {Mod. #1a} to

```
Result := Result / J
```

BinomDis

> **Name:** *BinomDis*
>
> **Type:** `real` *function*
>
> **Purpose:** *To compute binomial distribution probabilities*
>
> **Calling Sequence:** `BinomDis(NumTrials, NumHits, ProbHit)`

Description

`BinomDis` calculates the probability of a given number of successes in a given number of independent trials according to the discrete binomial distribution. You must specify the chance of success in a single trial.

Input

NumTrials	integer	Number of trials
NumHits	integer	Number of successes in NumTrials
ProbHit	real	Probability of success in a single trial

Output

BinomDis	real	The function BinomDis returns the probability of exactly NumHits in NumTrials.

Limitations and Error Conditions

If the input is not sensible, `BinomDis` returns a negative probability of -1.0. All of the following conditions must be true for a case to be sensible: `NumTrials` must be at least 1, `NumHits` must be at least zero and no more than `NumTrials`, and `ProbHit` must be at least zero and no more than 1.

As `NumTrials` increases, large factorials are computed by `BinomDis`. Numeric overflow can occur even though the subprogram is coded to avoid such overflow whenever possible. The biggest danger occurs when `NumHits` is approximately half of `NumTrials`. If `NumTrials` is less than 50, there is no problem. For larger values, `NumHits` must be closer to zero (or to `NumTrials`) in order for `BinomDis` to avoid overflow. See the Discussion section.

`BinomDis` returns a probability of exactly zero whenever the true result is less than 1.0E-38. This zero probability occurs when Turbo's `exp` function is taxed by too large a negative number. `BinomDis` treats such a result as zero instead of allowing a (presumably meaningless) overflow. See the Modification section.

Sample Usage

```
program SampleUsageOfBinomDis;

var
   NumTrials, NumHits : integer;
   ProbHit, Result    : real;

{$I BinomDis.PSL}

BEGIN
   ProbHit   := 0.25;
   NumTrials := 5;
   writeln('Probability of a hit in one trial =', ProbHit:6:3);
   writeln;
   writeln('# Trials':10, '# Hits':13, 'Probability':18);
   for NumHits := 0 to NumTrials do
      begin
         Result := BinomDis(NumTrials, NumHits, ProbHit);
         writeln(NumTrials:5, NumHits:15, Result:18:4)
      end
END.
```

Suppose that you randomly draw one card from a full pack (no jokers) of playing cards. Your chance of drawing a spade is 1 in 4. Now suppose that you repeat the selection 5 times (replacing the drawn card after each trial). The test program just presented computes the probability of achieving 0 through 5 hits (spades) in your experiment. The program produces the following output:

```
Probability of a hit in one trial = 0.250

    # Trials        # Hits        Probability
       5              0             0.2373
       5              1             0.3955
       5              2             0.2637
       5              3             0.0879
       5              4             0.0146
       5              5             0.0010
```

Subprogram Listing of BinomDis.PSL

```
function BinomDis(NumTrials, NumHits: integer;
                  ProbHit: real): real;

var
   Factorials, Temp   : real;
   Smaller, Larger, J : integer;

begin
   if (NumTrials < 1) or (NumHits < 0) or (NumHits > NumTrials)
                      or (ProbHit < 0.0) or (ProbHit > 1.0) then
      begin
         BinomDis := -1.0;
         exit
      end;
   if ProbHit = 0.0 then
      begin
         if NumHits = 0 then
            BinomDis := 1.0
         else
            BinomDis := 0.0;
         exit
      end;
   if ProbHit = 1.0 then
       begin
          if NumHits = NumTrials then
             BinomDis := 1.0
          else
             BinomDis := 0.0;
          exit
       end;
   if (NumHits = 0) or (NumHits = NumTrials) then
      Factorials := 1.0
   else
      begin
         Larger  := NumHits;
         Smaller := NumTrials - NumHits;
         if (NumTrials - NumHits) > NumHits then
            begin
               Larger  := NumTrials - NumHits;
               Smaller := NumHits
            end;
```

```
        Factorials := 1.0;
        for J := NumTrials downto (Larger + 1) do
            Factorials := Factorials * J;
        for J := 2 to Smaller do
            Factorials := Factorials / J
    end;
  Temp := ln(Factorials) + NumHits * ln(ProbHit) +
            (NumTrials - NumHits) * ln(1.0 - ProbHit);
  if Temp < -88.0 then                              {Mod. #1}
      BinomDis := 0.0                               {Mod. #1}
  else                                              {Mod. #1}
      BinomDis := exp(Temp)
end;
```

Variables

Factorials	NumTrials! / NumHits! / (- NumHits)!
Temp	The natural log of the answer
Smaller	The smaller of NumHits and (NumTrials - NumHits)
Larger	The larger of NumHits and (NumTrials - NumHits)
J	Looping index

Discussion

Binomial distribution, which is a fundamental tool of discrete probability analysis, applies to any experiment in which each individual trial (or sample) has two distinct possible outcomes. These could be a hit or miss, a good item or a defective one, a head or tail, a success or failure, and so on. The binomial distribution gives the probability that a specific number of hits will be achieved with a certain number of trials. All trials must be independent of each other so that the result of one trial cannot affect the result of any other trial. The probability of success in one trial must be known and must remain constant throughout the experiment.

As indicated previously, BinomDis aborts with numeric overflow if NumTrials is too large and NumHits is not extreme. If you run cases in this range, you might consider using the Poisson distribution as an approximation of the binomial distribution. The bibliography contains references to some books that discuss using the Poisson distribution in this manner.

Modification

You can eliminate the check for extremely small answers (less than 1.0E-38) by removing the lines indicated by {Mod. #1}. You may want to remove these lines if you are working in a range in which extremely small probabilities are important. As discussed in the Limitations and Error Conditions section, overflow may occur if you make this change.

NormDis

Name:	*NormDis*
Type:	*Procedure*
Purpose:	*To evaluate frequencies and probabilities of a normal distribution function*
Calling Sequence:	NormDis(Mean, StanDev, X, Frequency, Probability)

Description

You specify a particular normal distribution curve by giving its mean and standard deviation. NormDis computes the probability density function (that is, the frequency, or ordinate) and the cumulative distribution function (probability) at a given value of X (the abscissa). These quantities are shown in figure 13.1.

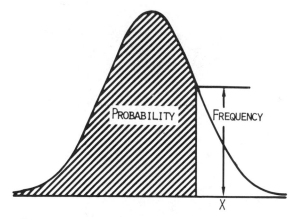

Fig. 13.1. *A normal distribution.*

Input

Mean	real	Mean of the normal distribution
StanDev	real	Standard deviation of the normal distribution
X	real	Abscissa value

Output

Frequency	real	The probability density function (the ordinate) of the normal distribution evaluated at X
Probability	real	The cumulative distribution function of the normal distribution function evaluated at X. This function specifies the probability that a random sample from the normal distribution has a value less than or equal to X.

Limitations and Error Conditions

StanDev must be positive for any meaningful case. If StanDev is not positive, NormDis returns the (impossible) value of -1.0 for both Frequency and Probability.

The accuracy of the solution is controlled by MaxError. By adjusting MaxError, you can control the number of (correct) significant digits in the result. Of course, as resolution of the solution increases, the computation time increases also. See the Modifications section.

Sample Usage

```
program SampleUsageOfNormDis;

var
  Mean, StanDev, X, Frequency, Probability : real;
  J                                        : integer;

{$I NormDis.PSL}

BEGIN
  Mean    := 160.0;
  StanDev := 20.0;
  writeln('Mean =', Mean:6:1, 'Standard Deviation =' :25,
                StanDev:5:1);
```

```
writeln;
writeln('X' :3, 'Frequency' :20, 'Probability' :19);
for J := 5 to 11 do
    begin
        X := 20.0 * J;
        NormDis(Mean, StanDev, X, Frequency, Probability);
        writeln (X:5:1, Frequency:18:7, Probability:18:7)
    end
END.
```

Running this test program produces the following output:

```
Mean = 160.0      Standard Deviation = 20.0

    X              Frequency            Probability
  100.0            0.0002216            0.0013499
  120.0            0.0026995            0.0227501
  140.0            0.0120985            0.1586552
  160.0            0.0199471            0.5000000
  180.0            0.0120985            0.8413448
  200.0            0.0026995            0.9772499
  220.0            0.0002216            0.9986501
```

Subprogram Listing of NormDis.PSL

```
procedure NormDis(Mean, StanDev, X: real;
                  var Frequency, Probability: real);

const
   MaxError = 1.0E-6;                                    {Mod. #1}

var
   Z, Area, OldVal, Error : real;
   NumSegs                : integer;

   function NormFunc(Z: real): real;

   begin {function NormFunc}
      NormFunc := exp(- Z * Z / 2.0);
   end;   {function NormFunc}

   function Simpson: real;
```

```pascal
var
    SegWidth, CurrentSum, Temp, LocalZ : real;
    NumTerms, J                        : integer;

begin {function Simpson}
    SegWidth   := Z / NumSegs;
    CurrentSum := NormFunc(Z) + 1.0;
    NumTerms   := NumSegs div 2;
    Temp       := 0.0;
    for J := 1 to NumTerms do
       begin
          LocalZ := SegWidth * (2.0 * J - 1.0);
          Temp   := Temp + NormFunc(LocalZ)
       end;
    CurrentSum := CurrentSum + 4.0 * Temp;
    NumTerms   := NumTerms - 1;
    Temp       := 0.0;
    for J := 1 to NumTerms do
       begin
          LocalZ := SegWidth * 2.0 * J;
          Temp   := Temp + NormFunc(LocalZ)
       end;
    CurrentSum := CurrentSum + 2.0 * Temp;
    Simpson    := SegWidth * CurrentSum / 3.0
  end; {function Simpson}

begin {procedure NormDis}
   if StanDev <= 0.0 then
      begin
         Frequency   := -1.0;
         Probability := -1.0
      end
   else
      begin
         Z := abs(X - Mean) / StanDev;
         if Z > 13.0 then                                {Mod. #2}
            begin
               Frequency := 0.0;
               Area      := 0.5
            end
```

```
        else
          begin
            Frequency := NormFunc(Z) / sqrt(2.0 * pi) /
                         StanDev;
            NumSegs    := 10;
            OldVal     := Simpson;
            repeat
               NumSegs := NumSegs * 2;
               Area    := Simpson;
               if Area = 0.0 then
                  Error := 0.0
               else
                  Error := abs((Area - OldVal) / Area);
               OldVal := Area
            until Error <= MaxError;
            Area := Area / sqrt(2.0 * pi);
            if X < Mean then
               Probability := 0.5 - Area
            else
               Probability := 0.5 + Area;
          end
      end
end; {procedure NormDis}
```

Variables

Variables for the Procedure NormDis

Z	X transformed to a standard normal distribution variable: $Z = (X - Mean) / StanDev$
MaxError	Constant equal to the maximum percentage error allowed between successive iterations
Area	Integral of the function NormFunc, from 0.5 to Z
OldVal	Area calculated by the previous iteration
Error	Percentage error between the last two iterations
NumSegs	Number of subintervals in the current iteration

Variables for the Embedded Function Simpson

SegWidth	Width of one subinterval
CurrentSum	Working total of terms during an iteration

Temp	Temporary value of terms during an iteration
LocalZ	Current value of the abscissa in Z coordinates
NumTerms	Number of subintervals in the current iteration
J	Loop index

Discussion

The normal distribution is the most important continuous probability distribution, occurring regularly in both theoretical and applied statistics. The familiar bell-shaped curves describe a myriad of practical distributions, ranging from the weights of people to collision frequencies in a physics lab experiment.

You can describe a particular normal distribution by giving its mean and standard deviation. With a simple change of variable, any normal distribution can be mapped into the standard normal distribution, having a mean of zero and a standard deviation of 1. NormDis uses this technique. (Refer to any statistics text for additional details. The bibliography contains some references.)

The probability calculation requires integrating this standardized curve. This is done by Simpson, an embedded iterative function that implements Simpson's rule. The embedded function NormFunc defines the active part of the necessary function to be integrated. See the Integral subprogram for a brief discussion of Simpson's rule.

For a given normal distribution, the frequency is simply defined as the value of the ordinate corresponding to a given value of X. The frequency is symmetric about the mean. (That is, the frequency at X is the same as that at -X.) The probability is defined as the integral from minus infinity to X. When X equals the mean, the probability is 0.5. (It's equally likely that a sample is greater than or less than the mean.) As X approaches plus infinity, the probability approaches 1.

Modifications

1. MaxError is the percentage error required for successful convergence of the integration. This variable controls the accuracy of the output. The number of correct significant digits in the result is approximately equal to the exponent in MaxError. Thus, when MaxError = 1.0E-6, there are approximately 6 correct digits. When MaxError = 1.0E-3, there are approximately 3 correct digits. You may change MaxError to any positive real number.

2. NormDis checks whether X is 13 or more standard deviations away from the mean. If so, NormDis sets the frequency to zero and the area to one-half. Potential overflow in NormFunc is therefore avoided. The adjustment should not cause any numeric inaccuracies because the normal

distribution is essentially zero and unchanging past 5 or 6 standard deviations (and the distribution is seldom needed in that range for any practical work). Still, you may want to change the 13 to something smaller (say, 6) to speed up slightly the calculation in the unlikely event that you invoke NormDis in this range.

RndNorm

> **Name:** *RndNorm*
>
> **Type:** real *function*
>
> **Purpose:** *To generate random numbers from a normal distribution*
>
> **Calling Sequence:** RndNorm(Mean, StanDev)

Description

RndNorm calculates a random normal deviate. This is a number randomly drawn from a normal distribution. You identify the specific normal distribution by giving the mean and the standard deviation.

Input

Mean	real	Mean of the normal distribution
StanDev	real	Standard deviation of the normal distribution

Output

RndNorm	real	The function RndNorm returns a random number drawn from the normal distribution described by Mean and StanDev.

Limitations and Error Conditions

RndNorm returns results even for nonsensical values of the standard deviation. If StanDev is negative, the function returns the same random number produced by the absolute value of StanDev. If StanDev is zero, RndNorm returns the value of Mean each time.

See modification 2 for the description of a rare potential error condition.

Sample Usage

```
program SampleUsageOfRndNorm;

var
  Mean, StanDev : real;
  J             : integer;

{$I RndNorm.PSL}

BEGIN
  Mean    := 0.0;
  StanDev := 1.0;
  randomize;                                    {Mod. #1}
  for J := 1 to 5 do
     writeln(RndNorm(Mean, StanDev):10:4);
  writeln;
  for J := 1 to 5 do
     writeln(RndNorm(100.0, 20.0):10:4)
END.
```

This test program produces different numbers each time it is run. Because Turbo's random-number generator is used, the output changes from run to run. (See modification 1 for further details.) The following output is typical:

```
    1.1064
   -1.2204
    0.3812
   -0.1491
   -0.5719

  106.4968
   87.1966
  108.6470
   78.4213
   60.8757
```

Subprogram Listing of RndNorm.PSL

```
function RndNorm(Mean, StanDev: real): real;

var
   RandomA, RandomB, Radius2, Deviate: real;

begin
   repeat
      RandomA := 2.0 * random - 1.0;
      RandomB := 2.0 * random - 1.0;
      Radius2 := sqr(RandomA) + sqr(RandomB)
   until
      Radius2 < 1.0;                                        {Mod. #2}
   Deviate := RandomA * sqrt((- 2.0 * ln(Radius2)) / Radius2);
   RndNorm := Mean + Deviate * StanDev
end;
```

Variables

RandomA   A random number between -1 and +1

RandomB   Another random number between -1 and +1

Radius2   The square of the distance between the point (RandomA, RandomB) and the origin (0, 0)

Deviate   Resultant random number. This number is drawn from the normal distribution with a mean of zero and a standard deviation of 1

Discussion

The need for random numbers drawn from a normal distribution arises frequently in computational statistics, especially in computer modeling and Monte Carlo simulation. (A Monte Carlo simulation is one that requires random numbers in a particular probability distribution for part of the algorithm used.) Consider an actuarial life expectancy represented by a normal distribution with a mean of 70 (years) and a standard deviation of 10. A life insurance company might base its premiums on the results of a simulation, using RndNorm to generate sample death statistics.

RndNorm uses random numbers drawn from the continuous uniform distribution. (The numbers are supplied by Turbo's built-in random function.) The algorithm depends on generating two such random numbers, each between -1 and +1. If you think of these numbers as X and Y coordinates, they define a point on a plane. The algorithm needs this point to be on the unit circle; therefore, a new random point must be generated if Radius2 is greater than 1. The probability that Radius2 is greater than 1 is $(4-\pi)/\pi$ (about 27 percent of the time, by the way). A random point on the standard normal distribution can be generated by using the formula beginning with Deviate := from the subprogram. This algorithm, called the "polar method for normal deviates," was developed by Box, Muller, and Marsaglia. (These applied mathematicians, especially Marsaglia, developed and refined many important numeric techniques to produce numbers from various distributions.) An excellent discussion of the algorithm and other methods of generating random deviates is contained in Section 3.4.1 in Knuth's book, *The Art of Computer Programming*, Volume 2. Refer to Knuth for a more complete explanation.

A second normal deviate can be generated from the same pass through the subprogram. If RandomA is replaced by RandomB in the Deviate := formula, a second deviate is generated. Even though the same Radius2 is used for both calculations, both random deviates are independent of each other and normally distributed. Thus, if your application requires generating many random deviates, consider turning RndNorm into a procedure and passing both random deviates back to your main program. This approach significantly saves computation time.

Modifications

1. You must be careful whenever you use Turbo Pascal's randomize procedure. During testing, you may want to remove this statement. Removing it causes RndNorm to generate the same sequence of random numbers each time the program is run, but only if you reboot Turbo between runs. For production runs, call randomize once, before any calls to random are made. Do not place randomize between successive rapid calls to random (such as inside RndNorm itself). If you do, Turbo generates similar "random" numbers and destroys the validity of your results.

2. Theoretically, it is possible for Radius2 to equal zero and thus cause a division by zero error. This possibility requires that random return two successive numbers exactly equal to 0.5 (to full computer accuracy). The odds against this are theoretically about 1 in 10 to the 22nd power, and probably zero, given Turbo's pseudo-random-number generator. If you are paranoid about this possibility, change the indicated line to

    (Radius2 < 1.0) and (Radius2 > 0.0);

This formula causes a small increase in computation time.

LinReg

> **Name:** *LinReg*
>
> **Type:** *Procedure*
>
> **Purpose:** *To perform linear regression on a set of data pairs*
>
> **Calling Sequence:** LinReg(Num2Array, NumDataPairs, Intercept, Slope, CorrCoeff)

Description

Given a table of X-Y data pairs, LinReg finds the equation of the straight line that best represents the data. The method of least squares is used to calculate the slope and Y intercept of the line. The correlation coefficient is also computed.

Input

Num2Array   real   A two-dimensional array representing the data. The first subscript identifies the ordinal number of the data pair. The second subscript is 1 when the array element is an X value (independent variable), or 2 when the array element is a Y value (dependent variable).

NumDataPairs integer   Number of data pairs in Num2Array.

In addition, the following const and type global declarations must be specified in your main program:

```
const
   RowSize = 250;
   ColSize = 2;

type
   Array2Type = array[1..RowSize, 1..ColSize] of real;
```

The constant RowSize identifies the maximum number of data pairs you allow Num2Array to contain. The number 250 is just an example; you can make RowSize any positive integer greater than 1. (The active number of data pairs is controlled by NumDataPairs, which must be less than or equal to RowSize.) The constant ColSize is fixed at 2.

Output

Intercept	real	The Y intercept of the best straight line. Intercept is the value of Y when X equals 0.
Slope	real	The slope of the best straight line. Slope is the rate of change of Y with respect to X.
CorrCoeff	real	The correlation coefficient. This is a number between 0 and 1. The higher its value, the better the fit. A perfect fit (with the data all on a straight line) has CorrCoeff = 1. The poorer the fit, the closer CorrCoeff is to 0.

Limitations and Error Conditions

You must pass at least two data pairs to LinReg. Otherwise, it cannot calculate any meaningful straight line. If NumDataPairs is less than 2, the procedure returns a value of zero for both Intercept and Slope. In addition, the (otherwise impossible) value of -5.0 is returned for CorrCoeff as an arbitrary code to indicate this error.

Another meaningless case occurs when all of your data pairs have identical X values. If this happens, LinReg again returns zero for both Intercept and Slope. Here, however, the (otherwise impossible) value of -10.0 is returned for CorrCoeff.

If all the Y values are identical (and all the X values are not equal), Slope is set to zero, and Intercept is set to the value of Y. In addition, CorrCoeff is set to 1.0 to indicate a perfect fit.

Sample Usage

```
program SampleUsageOfLinReg;

const
   RowSize = 250;
   ColSize = 2;

type
   Array2Type = array[1..RowSize, 1..ColSize] of real;

var
   Num2Array                        : Array2Type;
   NumDataPairs                     : integer;
   Intercept, Slope, CorrCoeff : real;

{$I LinReg.PSL}
```

```
BEGIN
   Num2Array[1, 1] := 14. 0;   Num2Array[1, 2] := 62. 1;
   Num2Array[2, 1] := 17. 0;   Num2Array[2, 2] := 69. 5;
   Num2Array[3, 1] := 18. 0;   Num2Array[3, 2] := 73. 6;
   Num2Array[4, 1] :=  5. 0;   Num2Array[4, 2] := 37. 2;
   Num2Array[5, 1] := -3. 0;   Num2Array[5, 2] := 31. 1;
   Num2Array[6, 1] := 25. 0;   Num2Array[6, 2] := 88. 0;
   NumDataPairs := 6;
   LinReg(Num2Array, NumDataPairs, Intercept, Slope, CorrCoeff);
   writeln('Intercept = ', Intercept:9:6);
   writeln('Slope      = ', Slope:9:6);
   writeln('Correlation Coefficient = ', CorrCoeff:8:6)
END.
```

Running this test program produces the following output:

```
Intercept = 32. 943140
Slope      =  2. 155805
Correlation Coefficient = 0. 985471
```

Subprogram Listing of LinReg.PSL

```
procedure LinReg(Num2Array: Array2Type; NumDataPairs: integer;
                 var Intercept, Slope, CorrCoeff: real);

var
   J: integer;
   SumX, SumY, SumXY, SumXSq, SumYSq, XVal, YVal, Denom: real;

begin
   if NumDataPairs < 2 then
      begin
         Slope     := 0. 0;
         Intercept := 0. 0;
         CorrCoeff := -5. 0;
         exit
      end;
```

```
   SumX    := 0.0;
   SumY    := 0.0;
   SumXY   := 0.0;
   SumXSq  := 0.0;
   SumYSq  := 0.0;
   for J := 1 to NumDataPairs do
      begin
         XVal     := Num2Array[J,1];
         YVal     := Num2Array[J,2];
         SumX     := SumX + XVal;
         SumY     := SumY + YVal;
         SumXY    := SumXY + XVal * YVal;
         SumXSq   := SumXSq + XVal * XVal;
         SumYSq   := SumYSq + YVal * YVal
      end;
   Denom := SumXSq - SumX * SumX / NumDataPairs;
   if Denom = 0.0 then
      begin
         Slope     := 0.0;
         Intercept := 0.0;
         CorrCoeff := -10.0;
         exit
      end
   else
      Slope := (SumXY - SumX * SumY / NumDataPairs) / Denom;
   Intercept := (SumY - Slope * SumX) / NumDataPairs;
   Denom     := SumYSq - SumY * SumY / NumDataPairs;
   if Denom = 0.0 then
      CorrCoeff := 1.0
   else
      CorrCoeff := sqrt(Slope * (SumXY - SumX * SumY /
                     NumDataPairs) / Denom);
end;
```

Variables

J	Loop index ranging from 1 to NumDataPairs
SumX	The sum of all the X values in your data. SumX is the sum of Num2Array[J,1] for J ranging from 1 to NumDataPairs.
SumY	The sum of all the Y values in your data. SumY is the sum of Num2Array[J,2] for J ranging from 1 to NumDataPairs.

SumXY	The sum of (X * Y) for all data pairs
SumXSq	The sum of (X * X) for all data pairs
SumYSq	The sum of (Y * Y) for all data pairs
XVal	The current value of X
YVal	The current value of Y
Denom	The value of a denominator in the expression currently being calculated

Discussion

Linear regression provides a computational procedure to approximate a set of X-Y data by a straight line. The method of least squares is used. It calculates the line that minimizes the sum of the squares of the calculated Y values subtracted from the actual Y values. Once the straight line is defined, you can get a calculated value of Y for a given X. If you subtract this calculated Y from the actual Y at that X, square the difference, and add the squares together, you get a measure of the error in the straight line. The least-squares method provides the straight line that minimizes this error.

LinReg defines the straight line by providing its Y intercept and its slope. Intercept is the value of Y when X equals 0. Slope is the relative change of Y with respect to X. The straight line is thus given by the following formula:

```
Y = Intercept + (Slope * X)
```

The correlation coefficient provides information about how good the fit to the straight line actually is. Often this information is valuable by itself. You might do an experiment in which you expect a linear dependent relationship to exist. For example, assume that the height of (adult) sons can be linearly expressed as a function of the height of their fathers. After sampling sufficient data, you can run LinReg and find out whether the relationship exists by checking CorrCoeff.

For each data pair, consider (calculated Y - actual Y) divided by (actual Y - mean Y). Suppose that you square these ratios, sum them for all the data pairs, and then subtract the answer from 1. CorrCoeff is the square root of this result. CorrCoeff has the value 1 when the linear relationship is exact. Smaller values indicate less linear correlation. A value of 0 means no correlation—Y values are unpredictable from a knowledge of the X values.

Modifications

None

GetChiSq

Name:	*GetChiSq*
Type:	*Procedure*
Purpose:	*To calculate the chi-square statistic*
Calling Sequence:	GetChiSq(ProbPerTrial, NumObserved, NumCells, ChiSq)

Description

For GetChiSq, it is assumed that an experiment is conducted (or statistical data is available) consisting of a finite number of individual trials. Each trial results in one of several predetermined outcomes or "cells." Furthermore, the probability of achieving each outcome on an individual trial is known (or hypothesized). When used with ChiProb, GetChiSq provides a statistical test of hypotheses your experiment may be trying to resolve.

Input

ProbPerTrial   real   Array of the probabilities of achieving each particular cell in one trial. Each array element is a number between zero and 1. The sum of the elements over all the cells must equal 1.

NumObserved   real   Array of the actual totals achieved for each cell

NumCells   integer   Number of cells. The first NumCells elements of ProbPerTrial and NumObserved contain the relevant data.

In addition, you must provide the following global const and type declarations in your main program. The number 250 is an example; your array size may differ.

```
const
   ArraySize = 250;

type
   ArrayType = array[1..ArraySize] of real;
```

Output

ChiSq   real   Value of chi-square. If ChiSq is negative, an error has occurred. (See Limitations and Error Conditions.)

Limitations and Error Conditions

GetChiSq sets ChiSq to special negative values if GetChiSq detects an error in your input data. (Correct values of chi-square are always nonnegative.) Table 13.1 shows the four possible error conditions and the corresponding values of chi-square.

Table 13.1
Input Errors Detected by GetChiSq

ChiSq	*Error*
-1.0	NumCells is less than 2.
-2.0	An element of ProbPerTrial is nonpositive.
-3.0	An element of NumObserved is negative.
-4.0	The sum of the first NumCells elements of ProbPerTrial does not equal 1.

A certain tolerance is allowed in the summation of the elements of ProbPerTrial before ChiSq is set to 4.0. (See the Modification section.)

Be sure that NumCells is not larger than the constant ArraySize set in the const block of your main program.

Sample Usage

```
program SampleUsageOfGetChiSq;

const
   ArraySize = 250;

type
   ArrayType = array[1..ArraySize] of real;

var
   ProbPerTrial, NumObserved : ArrayType;
   NumCells, J               : integer;
   Val, ChiSq                : real;

{$I GetChiSq.PSL}
```

```
BEGIN
   NumCells        := 3;
   ProbPerTrial[1] := 0.25;
   ProbPerTrial[2] := 0.25;
   ProbPerTrial[3] := 0.5;
   NumObserved[1]  := 21;
   NumObserved[2]  := 27;
   NumObserved[3]  := 64;
   GetChiSq(ProbPerTrial, NumObserved, NumCells, ChiSq);
   writeln('Chi-square =', ChiSq)
END.
```

Running this test program produces the following output:

```
Chi-square =   2.9285714285E+00
```

Subprogram Listing of GetChiSq.PSL

```
procedure GetChiSq(ProbPerTrial, NumObserved: ArrayType;
                   NumCells: integer; var ChiSq: real);

var
   NumTrials, ErrorValue, Sum : real;
   J                          : integer;

begin
   ErrorValue := 0.0;
   if NumCells < 2 then
      ErrorValue := -1.0
   else
      begin
         Sum       := 0.0;
         NumTrials := 0.0;
         for J := 1 to NumCells do
            begin
               if ProbPerTrial[J] <= 0.0 then
                  ErrorValue := -2.0;
               if NumObserved[J] < 0.0 then
                  ErrorValue := -3.0;
               Sum       := Sum + ProbPerTrial[J];
               NumTrials := NumTrials + NumObserved[J]
            end;
```

```
      if ErrorValue = 0.0 then
          if (Sum < 0.999) or (Sum > 1.001) then        {Mod. #1}
             ErrorValue := -4.0
   end;
 if ErrorValue < 0.0 then
    ChiSq := ErrorValue
 else
    begin
       Sum   := 0.0;
       for J := 1 to NumCells do
          Sum := Sum + sqr(NumObserved[J]) / ProbPerTrial[J];
       ChiSq := Sum / NumTrials - NumTrials
    end
end;
```

Variables

NumTrials	The total number of trials performed in the experiment. NumTrials is the sum of the first NumCells elements of NumObserved.
ErrorValue	A negative value for chi-square, indicating an error in the input data
Sum	The sum of the elements in an array
J	Looping variable

Description

The chi-square test is a valuable statistical tool for evaluating whether the results of an experiment validate a particular hypothesis. When you use GetChiSq with ChiProb, a numerical probability can be assigned to the chance of achieving your particular experimental result. If this probability is extremely high or extremely low, you have cause to doubt your experimental assumptions.

Chi-square can be used in a wide variety of practical applications. A gambler might consider cells to be the various types of poker hands and then test whether a particular dealer seems to cheating. A programmer might write a random-number generator and test whether it produces good random numbers. Or an emergency room staff might test whether admissions are statistically biased toward particular days of the week.

As chi-square is used here, certain assumptions are made about your experiment. The probability of achieving each outcome (or "cell" in our terminology) must be known beforehand. Often, however, this hypothesis is the one being tested, and the chi-square test can be repeated for different probability distributions. Each individual trial must be independent. The test is not valid if the result of one trial might influence the result of another trial. In addition, the total number of trials (NumTrials) must be large enough to produce a statistically significant result. The rule of thumb is that, for each cell, the value of NumTrials times the ProbPerTrial for that cell should be at least 5. If the value is less, the results achieved with the ChiProb subprogram lose some validity.

The calculation of chi-square is straightforward. For each cell, the difference between the expected number (NumTrials times ProbPerTrial for that cell) and the actual number (NumObserved for that cell) is calculated. This difference is squared and then divided by the expected number, thus giving the chi-square contribution for each cell. The final value is the sum across all the cells of these individual contributions.

Modification

The sum of ProbPerTrial across all cells must equal 1. You need to allow a certain tolerance away from exactly 1 because you (and the computer) cannot represent all decimal fractions exactly. (One-fourth is exactly 0.25, but one-third has no such finite decimal representation. You may be nonchalant and enter a ProbPerTrial value of one-third as 0.33.) In any case, we allow the sum of ProbPerTrial to lie between 0.999 and 1.001. You may change this tolerance if you want.

ChiProb .

Name:	*ChiProb*
Type:	real *function*
Purpose:	*To calculate the probability of achieving particular values of chi-square*
Calling Sequence:	ChiProb(ChiSq, DegFreedom)

Description

For this function, it is assumed that you have experimental results (or statistical data) characterized by known values for the chi-square statistic and the number of degrees of freedom. ChiProb calculates the probability that your experiment will result in a larger value for chi-square.

Input

ChiSq   real   The value of chi-square. ChiSq must be nonnegative.

DegFreedom   integer   The number of degrees of freedom. DegFreedom must be at least 1.

Output

ChiProb   real   Given DegFreedom, the function ChiProb returns the probability that an empirical chi-square statistic has a value larger than ChiSq. ChiProb is expressed as a number between 0 and 1.

Limitations and Error Conditions

The computational algorithm depends on series summations that can cause real-number overflow if the number of degrees of freedom becomes large. Thus, the constant MaxDegFreedom defines the largest acceptable value of DegFreedom. See the Modifications section for more details. The program DoChiSq presented in Chapter 18 provides a complete chi-square capability that overcomes this limitation.

A fatal run-time error (overflow) may occur if the value of ChiSq is exceedingly large (larger than possible in any realistic, practical case). In this instance, the desired value of ChiProb is extremely small (probably less than 0.00001).

ChiProb returns special negative values if it detects an error in your input data. (Correct values of ChiProb are always nonnegative.) Table 13.2 shows the three detectable error conditions and the corresponding values of ChiProb.

Table 13.2
Input Errors Detected by ChiProb

ChiProb	*Error*
-1.0	DegFreedom is less than 1.
-2.0	DegFreedom is greater than MaxDegFreedom.
-3.0	ChiSq is negative.

Sample Usage

```
program SampleUsageOfChiProb;

var
   ChiSq       : real;
   DegFreedom  : integer;

{$I ChiProb.PSL}

BEGIN
   DegFreedom := 5;
   ChiSq      := 8.36;
   writeln('Degrees of freedom = ', DegFreedom);
   writeln('Chi-square =', ChiSq:5:2);
   writeln;
   writeln('Probability of a larger chi-square =',
           ChiProb(ChiSq, DegFreedom):7:4)
END.
```

Running this test program produces the following output:

```
Degrees of freedom = 5
Chi-square = 8.36

Probability of a larger chi-square = 0.1375
```

Subprogram Listing of ChiProb.PSL

```
function ChiProb(ChiSq: real; DegFreedom: integer): real;

const
   MaxDegFreedom = 30;                              {Mod. #1}

var
   Term                                 : integer;
   Denom, Z, ZPartial, Value, Numerator : real;
```

```
begin
   if DegFreedom < 1 then
      begin
         ChiProb := -1.0;
         exit
      end;
   if DegFreedom > MaxDegFreedom then
      begin
         ChiProb := -2.0;
         exit
      end;
   if ChiSq < 0.0 then
      begin
         ChiProb := -3.0;
         exit
      end;
   if ChiSq = 0.0 then
      begin
         ChiProb := 1.0;
         exit
      end;
   Z        := 1.0;
   ZPartial := 1.0;
   Term     := DegFreedom;
   repeat
      Term     := Term + 2;
      ZPartial := ZPartial * ChiSq / Term;
      Z        := Z + ZPartial
   until
      ZPartial < 1.0E-8;                              {Mod. #2}
   if odd(DegFreedom) then
      Term := 1
   else
      Term := 2;
   Denom := Term;
   while Term < DegFreedom do
      begin
         Term  := Term + 2;
         Denom := Denom * Term
      end;
```

```
    if odd(DegFreedom) then
        begin
            Value        := ((DegFreedom + 1) / 2) * ln(ChiSq) -
                            ChiSq / 2.0;
            Numerator := exp(Value) * sqrt(2.0 / ChiSq / pi)
        end
    else
        begin
            Value        := DegFreedom / 2 * ln(ChiSq) - ChiSq / 2.0;
            Numerator := exp(Value)
        end;
    ChiProb := 1.0 - Numerator * Z / Denom
end;
```

Variables

Term	Current value of terms used in series summations
Denom	Denominator in the final division for ChiProb
Z	Approximate value of an infinite series involving ChiSq and DegFreedom
ZPartial	Intermediate value in the calculation of Z
Value	The natural log of Numerator
Numerator	Numerator in the final division for ChiProb

Discussion

The following discussion expands the ideas presented with the GetChiSq subprogram. Some of the terminology used here is developed and explained in the Discussion section of GetChiSq.

The number of degrees of freedom (DegFreedom) is one less than the number of distinct outcomes (cells) possible in one trial of the experiment. Thus, if ChiProb and GetChiSq are used together, DegFreedom is always one less than the variable NumCells used in GetChiSq.

A remarkable thing about ChiProb is that the function does not depend on the total number of trials in the experiment nor on the probabilities of achieving each possible outcome. Once chi-square is known, only the value of DegFreedom determines the probability that ChiProb calculates.

The chi-square distribution is a continuous, finite-valued (positive) curve defined for positive values of chi-square. The chi-square distribution is actually a family of curves (one for each value of DegFreedom) in much the same way that the normal distribution is a family of curves (one for each value of the mean and the standard deviation). As chi-square goes toward infinity, the distribution curve approaches zero asymptotically. The total area under the curve (that is, the integral) equals 1. The probability calculated by ChiProb is the integral of the distribution curve for chi-square, ranging from ChiSq to infinity. As chi-square increases, the value of ChiProb decreases.

If your value of ChiProb is extremely low (maybe less than 0.05 or even less than 0.01), you have cause to doubt your experimental hypothesis. In the poker example mentioned previously, a ChiProb of 0.01 means that the gambler has only a one percent chance of being dealt poker hands according to their true probabilities. (He should look for a different game.) A very high value of ChiProb (say, greater than 0.95) is also suspicious. A value this high means that, cell by cell, the experimental results match the expected probabilities almost exactly. Such a case typically indicates insufficient randomness. Whenever a suspicious value of ChiProb occurs, repeating the experiment is recommended, if possible.

Modifications

1. You may raise the value of MaxDegFreedom to calculate ChiProb for larger degrees of freedom. However, fatal run-time errors may occur even if ChiSq contains "reasonable" values. (See Limitations and Error Conditions.) The computational method still gives correct values if no error occurs.

2. The calculation of Z involves an infinite (converging) sum. We stop the series when terms become less than 1.0E-8. (The leading term of the series is 1. Thus, this convergence criterion guarantees at least 7 correct decimal digits.) You may adjust the convergence criterion if you like. A smaller value improves accuracy (slightly); a larger value saves (a small amount of) computation time.

14

Business and Finance

The microcomputer has found an ever-growing niche in productivity applications. This chapter presents 15 subprograms that perform fundamental business and financial calculations. Most of the subprograms apply to home financial management as well as to conventional business.

Forecasting is a continual concern of most businesses. FutGrow uses a technique to make projections based on a growth rate. If you have past-performance data, GrowRate can determine the correct growth rate to use. FutGrow has many applications, including sales, employment, and production.

Most of this chapter deals with money management calculations. The subprograms cover four types of time-dependent monetary transactions: (1) investments (InvestFV, InvestP, InvestIR, and InvestNM); (2) loans (LoanPay, LoanPrin, and LoanTNP); (3) annuities (AnnuFV, AnnuDep, and AnnuTND); and (4) investments with withdrawals (WDrawP, WDrawWD, and WDrawTNW). Each transaction type is characterized by a principal, an interest rate, a term, a compounding frequency, and a final value. Some transaction types have a periodic payment or withdrawal. Each subprogram calculates an unknown quantity, given the known quantities.

Unfortunately, many banking institutions don't follow conventional computational formulas exactly. For instance, the regular payment on a loan is often rounded up, sometimes to a full dollar, and sometimes even more. For the subprograms in this chapter, no results are rounded. Computations in dollars result in full-precision real numbers. Figures are rounded to the nearest cent if you display them with two decimal digits, using Turbo's real-number formatting. For example, the following statement displays the principal to the nearest cent:

```
write(Principal:10:2)
```

You may find discrepancies between values computed with these subprograms and values quoted by banks. Many banks are quite "imaginative" in their interpretations of the correct computational formulas.

A word of warning to those using the BCD version of Turbo is necessary. Several of the subprograms in this chapter do not work with that compiler. See the Limitations and Error Conditions section of each subprogram you are considering using.

FutGrow

> **Name:** *FutGrow*
>
> **Type:** real *function*
>
> **Purpose:** *To project future values based on a growth rate*
>
> **Calling Sequence:** FutGrow(Rate, Base, NewTime)

Description

This function projects a future value at a specified time, based on an initial value and an average growth rate. The business applications are numerous, including sales, salaries, employee count, and computer use. (Many applications are possible outside of business also.) If you have actual past-performance data, GrowRate can compute the growth rate and initial value needed for FutGrow.

Input

Rate   real   The average growth rate, expressed as a percentage, for a specific period of time (yearly, monthly, daily, etc.). If Rate is negative, growth is declining. If Rate is positive, growth is increasing.

Base   real   The initial value of the item to be projected. Base should be positive for any meaningful case.

NewTime   integer   The time for which the projection is to be made, in units of the basic time period. That is, if Rate represents daily growth, than each unit of NewTime represents one day.

Output

FutGrow   real   The function FutGrow calculates a future value at NewTime, given an initial value (Base) and a growth rate (Rate).

Limitations and Error Conditions

If NewTime is less than 2, FutGrow returns the value Base as NewTime's projection.

Sample Usage

```
program SampleUsageOfFutGrow;

var
   Rate, Base, Prediction : real;
   NewTime                : integer;

{$I FutGrow.PSL}

BEGIN
   Rate := 7.723;
   Base := 48.281;
   NewTime := 12;
   Prediction := FutGrow(Rate, Base, NewTime);
   writeln('Expected Customers in 12th Month =', Prediction:6:1);
   writeln;
   writeln('Dollar Value after 8 years at 10.9 % =',
           FutGrow(10.8, 1.0, 8):6:3)
END.
```

Running this test program produces the following output. The first line represents a projection based on the Sample Usage program from GrowRate.

```
Expected Customers in 12th Month = 109.4

Dollar Value after 8 years at 10.9 % = 2.050
```

Subprogram Listing of FutGrow.PSL

```
function FutGrow(Rate, Base: real; NewTime: integer): real;

var
   Term, Product : real;
   J             : integer;

begin
   Product := 1.0;
   Term    := Rate / 100.0 + 1.0;
   for J := 1 to NewTime - 1 do
      Product := Product * Term;
   FutGrow := Base * Product
end;
```

Variables

Term	The periodic growth factor
Product	Term to the NewTime power
J	Loop index

Discussion

You need to understand clearly the concept of time as used in FutGrow. NewTime expresses the future time in integral values of some time unit. This time unit can be days, years, microseconds—whatever you have. However, Rate must express the percentage growth rate per one unit of that interval. Thus, if NewTime is expressed in weeks, be sure that Rate is the percentage growth rate per week (not per year, per month, or per anything else).

If you use GrowRate to get Rate and Base, time is automatically in the same unit represented by successive values in PastDataArray. NewTime, therefore, should be in these units also. For example, if GrowRate used monthly sales figures for the last 6 months (Count was 6), then units of NewTime should be months also. To get a projection of monthly sales one month after the PastDataArray data ended, set NewTime to 7. To project the monthly sales one year after the PastDataArray ended, set NewTime to 18.

Modifications

None

GrowRate

> **Name:** *GrowRate*
>
> **Type:** *Procedure*
>
> **Purpose:** *To calculate the average growth rate of time-series data*
>
> **Calling Sequence:** `GrowRate(PastDataArray, Count, Rate, Base, OK)`

Description

`GrowRate` calculates the average percentage growth rate (and adjusted initial value) of time-series data. This kind of data is used regularly in most business environments. Examples are sales revenues, positive profits, customer service calls, and manufacturing production. (Many applications outside the business arena are possible also.) The past-performance data must be available at equally spaced intervals (years, months, days, etc.). `GrowRate` then provides the average percentage growth rate per this interval. Once the growth rate is determined, you can use `FutGrow` to predict future performance.

Input

PastDataArray	real	Array containing the past data. The first element contains the oldest data. Successive array elements represent data at equally spaced intervals. All data must be positive.
Count	integer	Number of elements of `PastDataArray` to use. `Count` must be at least 2.

In addition, you must specify the following global `type` declaration in your main program, preferably using the global `const` declaration shown. The number 250 is an example; the size of your array may differ.

```
const
   ArraySize = 250;

type
   ArrayType = array[1..ArraySize] of real;
```

Output

Rate	real	The average percentage growth rate per interval. Rate may be positive, zero, or negative.
Base	real	The adjusted initial value of your data
OK	boolean	Data validation flag. If OK is true, your input data is fine. If OK is false, an error is in your data—either Count is less than 2, or an element of PastDataArray is not positive.

Limitations and Error Conditions

If an error is detected in your data (Count < 2, or an element in PastDataArray is nonpositive), OK is set to false, and the procedure returns to the calling program. In this case, the values of Rate and Base are meaningless. If Count is less than ArraySize, only the first Count elements in PastDataArray are used.

This procedure will not work with the BCD version of Turbo because that compiler does not support the ln function on which GrowRate depends.

Sample Usage

```
program SampleUsageOfGrowRate;

const
   ArraySize = 250;

type
   ArrayType = array[1..ArraySize] of real;

var
   PastDataArray : ArrayType;
   Rate, Base    : real;
   Count, J      : integer;
   OK            : boolean;

{$I GrowRate.PSL}
```

```
BEGIN
   Count := 5;
   PastDataArray[1] := 49;
   PastDataArray[2] := 54;
   PastDataArray[3] := 52;
   PastDataArray[4] := 59;
   PastDataArray[5] := 68;
   GrowRate(PastDataArray, Count, Rate, Base, OK);
   if OK then
      begin
         write('Customer Growth Rate for Last');
         writeln(Count:2, ' Months');
         writeln;
         writeln('Growth Rate % =', Rate:7:3);
         writeln('Base Value     =', Base:7:3)
      end
   else
      writeln('Bad input data.')
END.
```

Running this test program produces the following output:

```
Customer Growth Rate for Last 5 Months

      Growth Rate % =  7.723
      Base Value    = 48.281
```

Subprogram Listing of GrowRate.PSL

```
procedure GrowRate(PastDataArray: ArrayType; Count: integer;
                   var Rate, Base: real; var OK: boolean);

var
   SumOfLogs, WeightedSum, Value, LogValue, Temp : real;
   J                                             : integer;

begin
   if Count < 2 then
      begin
         OK := false;
         exit
      end;
```

```
   SumOfLogs    := 0.0;
   WeightedSum := 0.0;
   for J := 1 to Count do
      begin
         Value := PastDataArray[J];
         if Value <= 0.0 then
            begin
               OK := false;
               exit
            end;
         LogValue     := ln(Value);
         SumOfLogs    := SumOfLogs + LogValue;
         WeightedSum := WeightedSum + (J - 1) * LogValue
      end;
   OK    := true;
   Temp := 6.0 * (2.0 * WeightedSum / (Count - 1) -
                  SumOfLogs) / Count / (Count + 1);
   Rate := 100.0 * (exp(Temp) - 1.0);
   Base := exp(SumOfLogs / Count - Temp * (Count - 1) / 2.0)
end;
```

Variables

SumOfLogs	The sum of the natural logs of the first Count elements in PastDataArray
WeightedSum	The sum of the logs weighted toward the most recent data
Value	A value from PastDataArray
LogValue	The natural log of Value
Temp	Temporary quantity
J	Loop index

Discussion

Coupled with FutGrow, GrowRate provides a powerful tool for describing past performance and forecasting future results. GrowRate is best used when your data tends to show some semblance of an overall growth trend (whether up or down) instead of a scattered, random pattern.

If Rate is negative, your data shows an overall decreasing growth rate. Positive values represent increasing growth.

GrowRate fits a weighted exponential curve to your data. The procedure requires that you have data at regular intervals. If your data is irregularly spaced (or you have some missing data), try the PolyFit and TryCurvs programs in Chapter 18.

Modifications

None

InvestFV

> **Name:** *InvestFV*
>
> **Type:** real *function*
>
> **Purpose:** *To calculate the final value of an investment*
>
> **Calling Sequence:** InvestFV(Principal, InterestRate, CompoundYear, NumberMonths)

Description

InvestFV computes the final value of an investment. You must provide the principal (initial investment), interest rate, compounding frequency, and term of the investment.

Input

Principal	real	The initial amount invested
InterestRate	real	The annual interest rate expressed as a percentage
CompoundYear	integer	The compounding frequency expressed as the number of compounding periods per year
NumberMonths	integer	The term (length) of the investment, in months. For example, NumberMonths is 36 for a 3-year investment.

Output

InvestFV	real	The function InvestFV returns the final value of the investment.

Limitations and Error Conditions

This function does no range checking on your input parameters. If they have non-sensical values, a fatal error is possible. Principal should be positive. A negative value results in a negative answer; a value of zero results in an answer of zero. InterestRate should be positive (or zero); a large negative value can cause a fatal error. CompoundYear should be positive, or a fatal error is possible. Finally, NumberMonths should be positive, but a negative value does not cause a fatal error.

InvestFV will not work with the BCD version of Turbo because that compiler does not support the ln function on which InvestFV depends.

Sample Usage

Suppose that you have $15,000 to invest. Two different banks offer 3-year investments at 14.5 percent annual interest rate. One bank compounds yearly (simple interest), but the other bank advertises monthly compounding. The following Sample Usage program compares the results of the investment in each case.

```
program SampleUsageOfInvestFV;

var
   Principal, FinalValue, InterestRate : real;
   CompoundYear, NumberMonths          : integer;

{$I InvestFV.PSL}

BEGIN
   Principal    := 15000;
   InterestRate := 14.5;
   CompoundYear := 12;
   NumberMonths := 36;
   FinalValue   := InvestFV(Principal, InterestRate,
                            CompoundYear, NumberMonths);
   writeln('Final value (compound monthly) = $', FinalValue:8:2);
   FinalValue := InvestFV(Principal, InterestRate,
                          1, NumberMonths);
   writeln('Final value (compound yearly)  = $', FinalValue:8:2)
END.
```

Running this test program produces the following output:

```
Final value (compound monthly) = $23114.11
Final value (compound yearly)  = $22516.85
```

Subprogram Listing of InvestFV.PSL

```
function InvestFV(Principal, InterestRate: real;
                  CompoundYear, NumberMonths: integer): real;

var
   Growth: real;

begin
   Growth := exp(NumberMonths / 12.0 * CompoundYear *
                 ln(1.0 + InterestRate / 100.0 / CompoundYear));
   InvestFV := Principal * Growth
end;
```

Variables

Growth
Multiplicative factor expressing the growth ratio of the investment between its initial value and its final value

Discussion

Be sure that you express the length of the investment correctly with the input parameter NumberMonths. It is the number of months of your investment. Don't mistakenly set this parameter to the number of years. The results will be quite different!

CompoundYear specifies the compounding rate as the number of compounding periods per year. Thus, yearly, quarterly, monthly, and daily compounding are expressed with 1, 4, 12, and 365, respectively. Some banks consider daily compounding to be 360 times a year. Occasionally someone offers continuous or infinite compounding. To simulate this kind of compounding, set CompoundYear to a large value, say, 10000. The answer will be accurate to (at least) 6 significant digits.

You can use InvestFV to calculate the annual yield of an investment, given the interest rate and compounding frequency. For the calculation, set InterestRate and CompoundYear as you normally would. Then, if you have declared a real variable named AnnualYield, the following statement calculates the annual yield as a percentage:

```
AnnualYield := InvestFV(100.0, InterestRate, CompoundYear,
                        12) - 100.0;
```

Interestingly, the annual yield does not get infinitely large as CompoundYear increases. Instead, the annual yield asymptotes (converges) to a finite value.

Modifications

None

InvestP

Name:	*InvestP*
Type:	real *function*
Purpose:	*To calculate the principal of an investment*
Calling Sequence:	InvestP(FinalValue, InterestRate, CompoundYear, NumberMonths)

Description

InvestP calculates the principal (initial investment) necessary to reach a certain final value, given the investment specifications. You must provide the final value, interest rate, compounding frequency, and term of the investment.

Input

FinalValue	real	The final value of the investment
InterestRate	real	The annual interest rate expressed as a percentage
CompoundYear	integer	The compounding frequency expressed as the number of compounding periods per year
NumberMonths	integer	The term (length) of the investment, in months. For example, NumberMonths is 36 for a 3-year investment.

Output

InvestP	real	The function InvestP returns the initial amount invested (principal).

Limitations and Error Conditions

This function does no range checking of your input parameters. If they have nonsensical values, a fatal error is possible. FinalValue should be positive. A negative value results in a negative answer; a value of zero results in an answer of zero. InterestRate should be positive (or zero); a large negative value can cause a fatal error. CompoundYear should be positive, or a fatal error is likely. Finally, NumberMonths should be positive, but a negative value does not cause a fatal error.

InvestP will not work with the BCD version of Turbo because that compiler does not support the ln function on which InvestP depends.

Sample Usage

Suppose that you want to invest a lump sum in a college fund for your child. You need the investment to mature in 10 years at a value of $20,000. Two different banks offer 10-year time deposits at 11.2 percent annual interest rate. One bank compounds yearly (simple interest), but the other bank advertises daily compounding. The following Sample Usage program shows the initial investment needed to reach your goal in each case.

```
program SampleUsageOfInvestP;

var
   Principal, FinalValue, InterestRate : real;
   CompoundYear, NumberMonths          : integer;

{$I InvestP.PSL}

BEGIN
   FinalValue   := 20000.00;
   InterestRate := 11.2;
   CompoundYear := 1;
   NumberMonths := 120;
   Principal    := InvestP(FinalValue, InterestRate,
                           CompoundYear, NumberMonths);
   writeln('Principal (compound yearly) = $', Principal:7:2);
   Principal := InvestP(FinalValue, InterestRate,
                        365, NumberMonths);
   writeln('Principal (compound daily)  = $', Principal:7:2)
END.
```

Running this test program produces the following output:

```
Principal (compound yearly) = $6918. 02
Principal (compound daily)  = $6526. 72
```

Subprogram Listing of InvestP.PSL

```
function InvestP(FinalValue, InterestRate: real;
                 CompoundYear, NumberMonths: integer): real;

var
  Growth: real;

begin
  Growth := exp(NumberMonths / 12. 0 * CompoundYear *
                ln(1. 0 + InterestRate / 100. 0 / CompoundYear));
  InvestP := FinalValue / Growth
end;
```

Variables

Growth   Multiplicative factor expressing the growth ratio of the
                        investment between its initial value and its final value

Discussion

In the Discussion section of InvestFV, the comments regarding the correct specification of NumberMonths and CompoundYear are relevant here. See InvestFV.

Modifications

None

InvestIR

> **Name:** *InvestIR*
>
> **Type:** real *function*
>
> **Purpose:** *To calculate the interest rate of an investment*
>
> **Calling Sequence:**   InvestIR(Principal, FinalValue, CompoundYear,
>   NumberMonths)

Description

InvestIR calculates the annual interest rate required for an investment to produce a specified return. You must provide the principal, final value, compounding frequency, and term of the investment.

Input

Principal	real	The initial amount invested
FinalValue	real	The final value of the investment
CompoundYear	integer	The compounding frequency expressed as the number of compounding periods per year
NumberMonths	integer	The term (length) of the investment, in months. For example, NumberMonths is 36 for a 3-year investment.

Output

InvestIR	real	The function InvestIR returns the nominal (annual) interest rate expressed as a percentage.

Limitations and Error Conditions

This function does no range checking of your input parameters. If they have non-sensical values, a fatal error is possible. Principal and FinalValue must be positive. A fatal error results if either of these parameters is negative or zero. CompoundYear and NumberMonths should be positive, but a negative value for either one does not cause a fatal error.

InvestIR will not work with the BCD version of Turbo because that compiler does not support the ln function on which InvestIR depends.

Sample Usage

Suppose that you have $10,000 to invest, and you want to triple the amount. You need the investment to mature in 7 or 8 years. The following Sample Usage program shows the nominal (annual) interest required to achieve your goal for each of the two maturity terms if your bank compounds interest monthly.

```pascal
program SampleUsageOfInvestIR;

var
   Principal, FinalValue, InterestRate : real;
   CompoundYear, NumberMonths          : integer;

{$I InvestIR.PSL}

BEGIN
   Principal    := 10000.00;
   FinalValue   := 30000.00;
   CompoundYear := 12;
   NumberMonths := 84;
   InterestRate := InvestIR(Principal, FinalValue,
                            CompoundYear, NumberMonths);
   writeln(' Interest Rate (7-year term) = ', InterestRate:6:3);
   InterestRate := InvestIR(Principal, FinalValue,
                            CompoundYear, 96);
   writeln(' Interest Rate (8-year term) = ', InterestRate:6:3)
END.
```

Running this test program produces the following output:

```
Interest Rate (7-year term) = 15.798
Interest Rate (8-year term) = 13.812
```

Subprogram Listing of InvestIR.PSL

```pascal
function InvestIR(Principal, FinalValue: real;
                  CompoundYear, NumberMonths: integer): real;

begin
   InvestIR := CompoundYear * (exp(ln(FinalValue / Principal) /
               CompoundYear / NumberMonths * 12.0) - 1.0) * 100.0
end;
```

Variables

None

Discussion

The interest rate computed by InvestIR is the nominal (annual) rate. This is the rate before any compounding takes effect. It is consistent with the variable InterestRate in the other investment subprograms.

In the Discussion section of InvestFV, the comments regarding the correct specification of NumberMonths and CompoundYear are relevant here. See InvestFV.

Modifications

None

InvestNM

> **Name:** *InvestNM*
>
> **Type:** integer *function*
>
> **Purpose:** *To calculate the term of an investment*
>
> **Calling Sequence:** InvestNM(Principal, FinalValue, InterestRate, CompoundYear)

Description

InvestNM calculates the term (length of time) required for an investment to mature, given the investment specifications. The term is expressed in months, with any partial month rounded to the next higher integer value. You must provide the principal (initial investment), final value, interest rate, and compounding frequency of the investment.

Input

Principal	real	The initial amount invested
FinalValue	real	The final value of the investment
InterestRate	real	The annual interest rate expressed as a percentage
CompoundYear	integer	The compounding frequency expressed as the number of compounding periods per year

Output

InvestNM   integer   The function InvestNM returns the term (length) of
                      the investment, in months.

Limitations and Error Conditions

This function does no range checking of your input parameters. If they have non-
sensical values, a fatal error is possible. Principal and FinalValue should be positive. Otherwise, a fatal error results (unless both parameters are negative).
InterestRate and CompoundYear make sense only if they are both positive. A fatal
error is likely if either parameter has a large negative value.

InvestNM will not work with the BCD version of Turbo because that compiler does
not support the ln function on which InvestNM depends.

See the Discussion section for a general limitation of this function.

Sample Usage

Suppose that you have $10,000 to put in a time-deposit investment, and your bank
offers 10.6 percent interest compounded monthly. This Sample Usage program determines how long it will take to double your money.

```
program SampleUsageOfInvestNM;

var                                          ı
   Principal, FinalValue, InterestRate : real;
   CompoundYear, NumberMonths          : integer;

{$I InvestNM.PSL}

BEGIN
   Principal    := 10000.00;
   FinalValue   := 20000.00;
   InterestRate := 10.6;
   CompoundYear := 12;
   NumberMonths := InvestNM(Principal, FinalValue,
                            InterestRate, CompoundYear);
   writeln('Term (months) =', NumberMonths:3)
END.
```

Running this test program produces the following output:

```
Term (months) = 79
```

Subprogram Listing of InvestNM.PSL

```
function InvestNM(Principal, FinalValue, InterestRate: real;
                  CompoundYear: integer): integer;      {Mod. #1a}

var
   RealNM: real;

begin
   RealNM := ln(FinalValue / Principal) / ln(InterestRate /
             100.0 / CompoundYear + 1.0) / CompoundYear * 12.0;
   if frac(RealNM) = 0.0 then                    {Mod. #1b}
      InvestNM := trunc(RealNM)                   {Mod. #1b}
   else                                           {Mod. #1b}
      InvestNM := trunc(RealNM) + 1               {Mod. #1b}
end;
```

Variables

RealNM — The term of the investment in months, expressed as a real number. This number is rounded up to produce the output of InvestNM.

Discussion

For consistency with the other subprograms in the investment family, the term of the investment is an integer value, in months. If the real value of the term contains a fraction of a month, the value is rounded to the next full month.

An inaccuracy in the results of InvestNM is possible if the compounding frequency (CompoundYear) is not at least 12, that is, if compounding is not at least monthly. This inaccuracy arises because the subprogram may calculate the end of the term in the middle of a compounding period. The results are exact only if the end of each month coincides with the end of a compounding period.

Modification

You can have the function return a real value instead of an integer value. A real value shows a fraction of a month if the term is not an integral number of months. Change the last `integer` to `real` in the line denoted by {Mod. #1a}. Then replace all four lines indicated by {Mod. #1b} with the following single statement:

```
InvestNM := RealNM
```

LoanPay

Name:	*LoanPay*
Type:	`real` *function*
Purpose:	*To calculate the regular payment for a loan*
Calling Sequence:	LoanPay(Principal, InterestRate, TotalNumPay, NumPayPerYr)

Description

LoanPay computes the amount of each payment required to pay back a loan. For most loans, these payments are made monthly, but LoanPay accommodates other payment schedules as well. All payments (except possibly the last) are assumed to be equal. You must provide the amount of the loan, the annual interest rate, the term of the loan, and the number of payments made per year.

Input

Principal	real	The principal of the loan (amount borrowed)
InterestRate	real	The annual interest rate expressed as a percentage
TotalNumPay	integer	The term of the loan, expressed as the total number of payments to be made
NumPayPerYr	integer	The number of payments made per year. For most loans, this number is 12 (monthly repayment). The term of the loan in years is TotalNumPay / NumPayPerYr.

Output

LoanPay   real   The function LoanPay returns the amount of each
                           payment required to pay back the loan.

Limitations and Error Conditions

This function does no range checking of your input parameters. If they have non-sensical values, a fatal error is possible. Principal should be positive, but a non-positive value does not cause a fatal error. InterestRate, TotalNumPay, and NumPayPerYr should also be positive. A value of zero or a large negative value for any of these parameters can cause a fatal error.

LoanPay will not work with the BCD version of Turbo because that compiler does not support the ln function on which LoanPay depends.

Sample Usage

Suppose that you want to finance a house for $82,000. Your lending company offers 20- or 30-year loans at 11.5 percent. The following Sample Usage program shows the monthly payment required to pay back either a 20-year loan or a 30-year loan.

```
program SampleUsageOfLoanPay;

var
   Principal, Payment, InterestRate : real;
   TotalNumPay, NumPayPerYr         : integer;

{$I LoanPay.PSL}

BEGIN
   Principal    := 82000.00;
   InterestRate := 11.5;
   TotalNumPay  := 240;
   NumPayPerYr  := 12;
   Payment      := LoanPay(Principal, InterestRate, TotalNumPay,
                           NumPayPerYr);
   writeln('Payment (20-year term) = $', Payment:6:2);
   writeln('Payment (30-year term) = $', LoanPay(Principal,
           InterestRate, 360, NumPayPerYr):6:2)
END.
```

Running this test program produces the following output:

```
Payment (20-year term) = $874.47
Payment (30-year term) = $812.04
```

Subprogram Listing of LoanPay.PSL

```pascal
function LoanPay(Principal, InterestRate: real; TotalNumPay,
                 NumPayPerYr: integer): real;

var
   Temp: real;

begin
   Temp     := exp(-TotalNumPay * ln(1.0 + InterestRate /
                  100.0 / NumPayPerYr));
   LoanPay := Principal * InterestRate / 100.0 / NumPayPerYr /
                  (1.0 - Temp)
end;
```

Variables

Temp   Temporary quantity

Discussion

Most loans are paid back monthly. In such a case, NumPayPerYr is 12, and
TotalNumPay is 12 times the length of the loan in years. However, LoanPay can
handle other payment schedules as well. For example, a loan paid back quarterly
over 15 years has NumPayPerYr equal to 4 and TotalNumPay equal to 60.

This subprogram computes the regular (constant) payment made each payment
period. Typically, the last payment is not equal to the regular payment because the
remaining loan balance in the last payment period is often less than the regular
payment. Use the Mortgage program in Chapter 18 to calculate the amount of the
last payment.

Modifications

None

LoanPrin

> **Name:** *LoanPrin*
>
> **Type:** real *function*
>
> **Purpose:** *To calculate the principal for a loan*
>
> **Calling Sequence:** LoanPrin(Payment, InterestRate, TotalNumPay,
> NumPayPerYr)

Description

LoanPrin computes the principal (initial amount borrowed) for a loan. You must provide the amount of each payment, the annual interest rate, the term of the loan, and the number of payments made per year. For most loans, payment is made monthly, but LoanPrin accommodates other payment schedules as well.

Input

Payment	real	The amount of each payment
InterestRate	real	The annual interest rate expressed as a percentage
TotalNumPay	integer	The term of the loan, expressed as the total number of payments to be made
NumPayPerYr	integer	The number of payments made per year. For most loans, this number is 12 (monthly repayment). The term of the loan in years is TotalNumPay / NumPayPerYr.

Output

LoanPrin	real	The function LoanPrin returns the principal of the loan (the initial amount borrowed).

Limitations and Error Conditions

This function does no range checking of your input parameters. If they have non-sensical values, a fatal error is possible. Payment should be positive, but a nonpositive value does not cause a fatal error. InterestRate, TotalNumPay, and NumPayPerYr should also be positive. A value of zero or a large negative value for any of these parameters can cause a fatal error.

LoanPrin will not work with the BCD version of Turbo because that compiler does not support the ln function on which LoanPrin depends.

Sample Usage

Suppose that you want to finance the purchase of a new car. You can afford a monthly payment of up to $300. Your lending company offers car loans for 4 or 5 years at 16 percent. The following Sample Usage program shows how much you can borrow for each of these loan terms.

```pascal
program SampleUsageOfLoanPrin;

var
   Principal, Payment, InterestRate : real;
   TotalNumPay, NumPayPerYr          : integer;

{$I LoanPrin.PSL}

BEGIN
   Payment      := 300.00;
   InterestRate := 16.0;
   TotalNumPay  := 48;
   NumPayPerYr  := 12;
   Principal    := LoanPrin(Payment, InterestRate, TotalNumPay,
                           NumPayPerYr);
   writeln('Principal (4-year term) = $', Principal:8:2);
   writeln('Principal (5-year term) = $', LoanPrin(Payment,
           InterestRate, 60, 12):8:2)
END.
```

Running this test program produces the following output:

```
Principal (4-year term) = $10585.64
Principal (5-year term) = $12336.51
```

Subprogram Listing of LoanPrin.PSL

```
function LoanPrin(Payment, InterestRate: real; TotalNumPay,
                  NumPayPerYr: integer): real;

var
   Temp: real;

begin
   Temp      := exp(-TotalNumPay * ln(1.0 + InterestRate /
                   100.0 / NumPayPerYr));
   LoanPrin := Payment * NumPayPerYr * 100.0 / InterestRate *
                      (1.0 - Temp)
end;
```

Variables

Temp   Temporary quantity

Discussion

In the Discussion section of LoanPay, the comments regarding the specification of the loan payment schedules are relevant here. See LoanPay.

Modifications

None

LoanTNP

Name: *LoanTNP*

Type: integer *function*

Purpose: *To calculate the total number of payments required to pay back a loan*

Calling Sequence: LoanTNP(Principal, Payment, InterestRate,
NumPayPerYr)

Description

LoanTNP calculates the term (length of time) required to pay back a loan. This term is expressed as the total number of payments required. You must provide the principal (amount borrowed), amount of each payment, annual interest rate, and number of payments made per year. The payback in years can be found by dividing the total number of payments by the number of payments made per year.

Input

Principal	real	The amount borrowed
Payment	real	The amount of each payment
InterestRate	real	The annual interest rate expressed as a percentage
NumPayPerYr	integer	The number of payments made per year. For most loans, this number is 12 (monthly repayment).

Output

LoanTNP	integer	The function LoanTNP returns the total number of payments required to pay back the loan.

Limitations and Error Conditions

LoanTNP checks that the quantity (Principal * InterestRate / Payment / NumPayPerYr) does not exceed 100. If it does, your loan payments are too small to achieve amortization, and the number of payments required is infinite. LoanTNP returns a value of 0 (zero) as an error warning if this condition occurs.

No other range checking of your input parameters is done. All input values should be positive. A fatal error is possible if a value is negative or zero.

LoanTNP will not work with the BCD version of Turbo because that compiler does not support the ln function on which LoanTNP depends.

Sample Usage

Imagine that a friend is willing to loan you $15,000 at 15.5 percent interest on the condition that you pay him back in monthly payments of $325. The following Sample Usage program shows how many payments you must make to repay this loan.

```
program SampleUsageOfLoanTNP;

var
   Principal, Payment, InterestRate : real;
   TotalNumPay, NumPayPerYr         : integer;

{$I LoanTNP.PSL}

BEGIN
   Principal   := 15000.00;
   Payment     := 325.00;
   InterestRate := 15.5;
   NumPayPerYr := 12;
   TotalNumPay  := LoanTNP(Principal, Payment, InterestRate,
                           NumPayPerYr);
   writeln('Total number of payments =', TotalNumPay:3)
END.
```

Running this test program produces the following output:

```
Total number of payments = 71
```

Subprogram Listing of LoanTNP.PSL

```
function LoanTNP(Principal, Payment, InterestRate: real;
                 NumPayPerYr: integer): integer;        {Mod. #1a}

var
   Temp, RealTNP: real;

begin
   Temp := Principal * InterestRate / 100.0 /
                       Payment / NumPayPerYr;
   if Temp >= 1 then
      RealTNP := 0.0
   else
      RealTNP := -ln(1.0 - Temp) / ln(1.0 + InterestRate /
                    100.0 / NumPayPerYr);
   if frac(RealTNP) = 0.0 then                          {Mod. #1b}
      LoanTNP := trunc(RealTNP)                          {Mod. #1b}
   else                                                  {Mod. #1b}
      LoanTNP := trunc(RealTNP) + 1                      {Mod. #1b}
end;
```

Variables

Temp   Temporary quantity. It must be less than 1.

RealTNP   The total number of payments, expressed as a real
                        number. This number is rounded up to produce the
                        output of LoanTNP.

Discussion

For consistency with the other subprograms in the loan family, the term of the
loan is an integer value equal to the total number of payments to be made. If the
real value of this term contains a fractional part, the value is rounded up to produce
the integer output required.

Modification

You can have the function return a real value for the total number of payments
instead of returning an integer value. A real value shows whether a fraction of
a payment is required. Change the last integer to real in the line indicated by
{Mod. #1a}. Then replace all four lines designated by {Mod. #1b} with the following
single statement:

```
LoanTNP := RealTNP
```

AnnuFV

> **Name:** *AnnuFV*
>
> **Type:** real *function*
>
> **Purpose:** *To calculate the final value of an annuity*
>
> **Calling Sequence:** AnnuFV(Deposit, InterestRate, TotalNumDep,
>   NumDepPerYr)

Description

AnnuFV computes the final value of an investment in which equal deposits are made
at regular intervals. Interest is assumed to compound with each deposit. You must
provide the amount of each deposit, the nominal (annual) interest rate, the term
of the annuity, and the number of deposits made yearly.

Input

Deposit	real	The amount of each deposit
InterestRate	real	The annual interest rate expressed as a percentage
TotalNumDep	integer	The term of the annuity, expressed as the total number of deposits to be made
NumDepPerYr	integer	The number of deposits made each year. The term of the annuity in years is TotalNumDep / NumDepPerYr.

Output

AnnuFV	real	The function AnnuFV returns the final value of the annuity.

Limitations and Error Conditions

All of your input parameters should be positive. AnnuFV does not do any range checking. If an input parameter is negative, a nonsensical answer results. A fatal error occurs if InterestRate or NumDepPerYr is zero. AnnuFV returns a value of 0 (zero) if Deposit is zero or TotalNumDep is not positive.

Sample Usage

Suppose that you deposit $75 into a savings account at the end of every two weeks. Your bank offers 8.5 percent interest, which is compounded with each deposit. The following Sample Usage program shows the value of this account after 1 year and after 2 years.

```
program SampleUsageOfAnnuFV;

var
   Deposit, FinalValue, InterestRate : real;
   TotalNumDep, NumDepPerYr          : integer;

{$I AnnuFV.PSL}
```

```
BEGIN
   Deposit        := 75.00;
   InterestRate  := 8.5;
   TotalNumDep   := 26;
   NumDepPerYr   := 26;
   FinalValue     := AnnuFV(Deposit, InterestRate,
                        TotalNumDep, NumDepPerYr);
   writeln('Final Value (1 year) = $', FinalValue:7:2);
   FinalValue := AnnuFV(Deposit, InterestRate, 52, NumDepPerYr);
   writeln('Final Value (2 years) = $', FinalValue:7:2)
END.
```

Running this test program produces the following output:

```
Final value (1 year)  = $2031.81
Final value (2 years) = $4243.57
```

Subprogram Listing of AnnuFV.PSL

```
function AnnuFV(Deposit, InterestRate: real;
              TotalNumDep, NumDepPerYr: integer): real;

var
   Product : real;
   J       : integer;

begin
   Product := 1.0;
   for J := 1 to TotalNumDep do
      Product := Product * (1.0 + InterestRate / 100.0 /
                            NumDepPerYr);
   AnnuFV := Deposit * (Product - 1.0) * NumDepPerYr * 100.0 /
                       InterestRate
end;
```

Variables

Product	Temporary multiplicative product
J	Loop index

Discussion

Annuities come in many forms. For our purposes, they refer to any fixed-amount deposits made at regular intervals into savings. The interest is assumed to compound at each deposit.

Be sure that you express the term of the annuity correctly. NumDepPerYr is the number of deposits made per year. For annual deposits to an annuity, NumDepPerYr is simply 1. For monthly deposits into a "Christmas Club" account, NumDepPerYr is 12. TotalNumDep is the total number of deposits made over the life of the annuity. This number does not need to be an even multiple of NumDepPerYr. (That is, the term of the annuity does not have to be an integral number of years.) For example, if you start a Christmas Club in April, TotalNumDep is 9, whereas NumDepPerYr is 12.

Modifications

None

AnnuDep

> **Name:** *AnnuDep*
>
> **Type:** real *function*
>
> **Purpose:** *To calculate the regular deposit for an annuity*
>
> **Calling Sequence:** AnnuDep(FinalValue, InterestRate, TotalNumDep, NumDepPerYr)

Description

AnnuDep computes the amount of each deposit required for an annuity to reach a specified final value in a given amount of time. All deposits are equal and made at regular intervals. Interest is assumed to compound with each deposit. You must provide the final value of the annuity, nominal (annual) interest rate, term of the annuity, and number of deposits made yearly.

Input

FinalValue	real	The final value of the annuity
InterestRate	real	The annual interest rate expressed as a percentage

| TotalNumDep | integer | The term of the annuity, expressed as the total number of deposits to be made |
| NumDepPerYr | integer | The number of deposits made each year. The term of the annuity in years is TotalNumDep / NumDepPerYr. |

Output

| AnnuDep | real | The function AnnuDep returns the amount of each deposit. |

Limitations and Error Conditions

All of your input parameters should be positive. AnnuDep does not do any range checking. If an input parameter is negative, a nonsensical answer results. A fatal error occurs if InterestRate is zero, NumDepPerYr is zero, or TotalNumDep is not positive. AnnuFV returns a value of 0 (zero) if FinalValue is zero.

Sample Usage

Suppose that you want to start an annuity that matures at $15,000 in 10 years. Your bank offers 9 percent interest. You can make deposits yearly or quarterly. The following Sample Usage program compares the size of your required regular deposits for each depositing alternative. Interest is assumed to compound with each deposit.

```
program SampleUsageOfAnnuDep;

var
   Deposit, FinalValue, InterestRate : real;
   TotalNumDep, NumDepPerYr          : integer;

{$I AnnuDep.PSL}

BEGIN
   FinalValue   := 15000.00;
   InterestRate := 9.0;
   TotalNumDep  := 10;
   NumDepPerYr  := 1;
   Deposit      := AnnuDep(FinalValue, InterestRate,
                           TotalNumDep, NumDepPerYr);
   writeln('Deposit (yearly)    = $', Deposit:6:2);
   Deposit := AnnuDep(FinalValue, InterestRate, 40, 4);
   writeln('Deposit (quarterly) = $', Deposit:6:2)
END.
```

Running this test program produces the following output:

```
Deposit (yearly)    = $987.30
Deposit (quarterly) = $235.16
```

Subprogram Listing of AnnuDep.PSL

```
function AnnuDep(FinalValue, InterestRate: real;
                TotalNumDep, NumDepPerYr: integer): real;

var
   Product : real;
   J       : integer;

begin
   Product := 1.0;
   for J := 1 to TotalNumDep do
      Product := Product * (1.0 + InterestRate / 100.0 /
                            NumDepPerYr);
   AnnuDep := FinalValue * InterestRate / 100.0 / NumDepPerYr /
                            (Product - 1.0);
end;
```

Variables

Product   Temporary multiplicative product

J   Loop index

Discussion

In the Discussion section of AnnuFV, the comments regarding the correct specifications of TotalNumDep and NumDepPerYr are relevant here. See AnnuFV.

Modifications

None

AnnuTND

> **Name:** *AnnuTND*
>
> **Type:** integer *function*
>
> **Purpose:** *To calculate the total number of deposits for an annuity*
>
> **Calling Sequence:** AnnuDep(Deposit, FinalValue, InterestRate,
>   NumDepPerYr)

Description

AnnuTND computes the term (length of time) required for an annuity to mature. This term is expressed as the total number of deposits required. You must specify the amount of each deposit, the final (maturity) value, the annual interest rate, and the number of deposits made per year. All deposits are equal and made at regular intervals. Interest is assumed to compound with each deposit.

Input

Deposit	real	The amount of each deposit
FinalValue	real	The final value of the annuity
InterestRate	real	The annual interest rate expressed as a percentage
NumDepPerYr	integer	The number of deposits made each year

Output

AnnuTND	integer	The function AnnuTND returns the total number of deposits required for the annuity to mature.

Limitations and Error Conditions

Each input parameter should be positive. AnnuTND does not do any range checking. If any input parameter is zero or sufficiently negative, a fatal error occurs.

This function will not work with the BCD version of Turbo because that compiler does not support the ln function on which AnnuTND depends.

Sample Usage

Suppose that you want to start an annuity that matures at $7,500. You can make monthly payments of $100, and your bank offers 7.75 percent annual interest for such an account. The interest compounds with each deposit. The following Sample Usage program shows how many deposits you must make to achieve your goal.

```
program SampleUsageOfAnnuTND;

var
   Deposit, FinalValue, InterestRate : real;
   TotalNumDep, NumDepPerYr          : integer;

{$I AnnuTND.PSL}

BEGIN
   Deposit      := 100.00;
   FinalValue   := 7500.00;
   InterestRate := 7.75;
   NumDepPerYr  := 12;
   TotalNumDep  := AnnuTND(Deposit, FinalValue, InterestRate,
                           NumDepPerYr);
   writeln('Total number of deposits =', TotalNumDep:3)
END.
```

Running this test program produces the following output:

```
Total number of deposits = 62
```

Subprogram Listing of AnnuTND.PSL

```
function AnnuTND(Deposit, FinalValue, InterestRate: real;
               NumDepPerYr: integer): integer;        {Mod. #1a}

var
   Temp, RealTND: real;
```

```
begin
  Temp    := InterestRate / 100.0 / NumDepPerYr;
  RealTND := ln(1.0 + FinalValue * Temp / Deposit) /
             ln(1.0 + Temp);
  if frac(RealTND) = 0.0 then                          {Mod. #1b}
    AnnuTND := trunc(RealTND)                           {Mod. #1b}
  else                                                  {Mod. #1b}
    AnnuTND := trunc(RealTND) + 1                       {Mod. #1b}
end;
```

Variables

Temp	Temporary value
RealTND	The total number of payments, expressed as a real number. This number is rounded up to produce the output of AnnuTND.

Discussion

For consistency with the other subprograms in the annuity family, the term of the annuity is an integer value equal to the total number of deposits to be made. If the term's real value contains a fractional part, the value is rounded up to produce the integer output required.

Modification

You can have the function return a real value for the total number of deposits instead of returning an integer value. A real value shows whether a fraction of a deposit is required. Change the last integer to real in the line indicated by {Mod. #1a}. Then replace all four lines designated by {Mod. #1b} with the following single statement:

```
AnnuTND := RealTND
```

WDrawP

Name:	*WDrawP*
Type:	real *function*
Purpose:	*To calculate the principal for an investment with withdrawals*
Calling Sequence:	WDrawP(Withdrawal, InterestRate, TotalNumW, NumWPerYr)

Description

WDrawP computes the principal (initial investment) required to sustain an investment with regular withdrawals for a given length of time. The amount of each withdrawal is the same. Withdrawals are made at fixed intervals, and interest is assumed to compound with each withdrawal. The balance of the investment is zero at maturity. You must specify the amount of each withdrawal, the nominal (annual) interest rate, the term of the investment, and the number of withdrawals made per year.

Input

Withdrawal	real	The amount of each withdrawal
InterestRate	real	The annual interest rate expressed as a percentage
TotalNumW	integer	The term of the investment, expressed as the total number of withdrawals to be made
NumWPerYr	integer	The number of withdrawals made each year. The term of the loan in years is TotalNumW / NumWPerYr.

Output

WDrawP	real	The function WDrawP returns the principal (initial investment) required.

Limitations and Error Conditions

Each input parameter should be positive. The function does not do any range checking. A fatal error can occur if InterestRate or NumWPerYr is zero or negative. WDrawP returns a value of 0 (zero) if Withdrawal is zero or TotalNumW is not positive.

Sample Usage

Suppose that you want to make monthly withdrawals of $150 from a savings account over a period of 3 or 4 years. (The balance of the account is zero at maturity.) Your bank offers 10.5 percent annual interest compounded with each withdrawal. The following Sample Usage program compares the initial investment required for each of these two terms.

```
program SampleUsageOfWDrawP;

var
   Principal, Withdrawal, InterestRate : real;
   TotalNumW, NumWPerYr                : integer;

{$I WDrawP.PSL}

BEGIN
   Withdrawal   := 150.00;
   InterestRate := 10.5;
   TotalNumW    := 36;
   NumWPerYr    := 12;
   Principal    := WDrawP(Withdrawal, InterestRate, TotalNumW,
                          NumWPerYr);
   writeln('Principal (3-year term) = $', Principal:7:2);
   writeln('Principal (4-year term) = $', WDrawP(Withdrawal,
                   InterestRate, 48, NumWPerYr):7:2)
END.
```

Running this test program produces the following output:

```
Principal (3-year term) = $4615.04
Principal (4-year term) = $5858.60
```

Subprogram Listing of WDrawP.PSL

```
function WDrawP(Withdrawal, InterestRate: real;
               TotalNumW, NumWPerYr: integer): real;

var
   Product : real;
   J       : integer;
```

```
begin
   Product := 1.0;
   for J := 1 to TotalNumW do
      Product := Product * (1.0 + InterestRate / 100.0 /
                           NumWPerYr);
   WDrawP := Withdrawal * NumWPerYr .* (1.0 - 1.0 / Product) *
                        100.0 / InterestRate
end;
```

Variables

Product   Temporary multiplicative product

J   Loop index

Discussion

Be sure that you express the term of the investment correctly. NumWPerYr is the number of withdrawals per year. The number is 12 for monthly withdrawals and 1 for yearly withdrawals. The entire term of the investment is reflected in TotalNumW, which is the total number of withdrawals over the life of the investment. TotalNumW does not have to be an integral multiple of NumWPerYr. In other words, the maturity term does not have to be an integral number of years (unless NumWPerYr is 1). For example, if withdrawals are quarterly for 3 1/2 years, NumWPerYr is 4, and TotalNumW is 14.

Modifications

None

WDrawWD

Name:	*WDrawWD*
Type:	real *function*
Purpose:	*To calculate the maximum periodic withdrawal from an investment*
Calling Sequence:	WDrawWD(Principal, InterestRate, TotalNumW, NumWPerYr)

Description

WDrawWD computes the maximum regular withdrawal amount that enables an investment to sustain itself for a given length of time. The amount of each withdrawal is the same. Withdrawals are made at fixed intervals, and interest is assumed to compound with each withdrawal. The balance of the investment is zero at maturity. You must specify the principal (amount of the initial investment), nominal (annual) interest rate, term of the investment, and number of withdrawals made per year.

Input

Principal	real	The principal (initial investment)
InterestRate	real	The annual interest rate expressed as a percentage
TotalNumW	integer	The term of the investment, expressed as the total number of withdrawals to be made
NumWPerYr	integer	The number of withdrawals made each year. The term of the loan in years is TotalNumW / NumWPerYr.

Output

WDrawWD	real	The function WDrawWD returns the amount of each withdrawal.

Limitations and Error Conditions

Each input parameter should be positive. The function does not do any range checking. A fatal error can occur if InterestRate, TotalNumW, or NumWPerYr is zero or negative. WDrawWD returns a value of 0 (zero) if Principal is zero.

Sample Usage

Suppose that you have $12,500 to invest in an income-producing time deposit. Your bank offers 11 percent annual interest if withdrawals (and compounding) are once a year. You do not want the account balance to reach 0 (zero) until 10 or 12 years. The following Sample Usage program compares the maximum withdrawal you can make for each of these two terms.

```
program SampleUsageOfWDrawWD;

var
   Principal, Withdrawal, InterestRate : real;
   TotalNumW, NumWPerYr                : integer;

{$I WDrawWD.PSL}

BEGIN
   Principal    := 12500.00;
   InterestRate := 11.0;
   TotalNumW    := 10;
   NumWPerYr    := 1;
   Withdrawal   := WDrawWD(Principal, InterestRate, TotalNumW,
                          NumWPerYr);
   writeln('Withdrawal (10-year term) = $', Withdrawal:7:2);
   writeln('Withdrawal (12-year term) = $', WDrawWD(Principal,
                     InterestRate, 12, NumWPerYr):7:2)
END.
```

Running this test program produces the following output:

```
Withdrawal (10-year term) = $2122.52
Withdrawal (12-year term) = $1925.34
```

Subprogram Listing of WDrawWD.PSL

```
function WDrawWD(Principal, InterestRate: real;
                TotalNumW, NumWPerYr: integer): real;

var
   Product : real;
   J       : integer;

begin
   Product := 1.0;
   for J := 1 to TotalNumW do
      Product := Product * (1.0 + InterestRate / 100.0 /
                           NumWPerYr);
   WDrawWD := Principal * InterestRate / 100.0 / NumWPerYr *
                     (1.0 + 1.0 / (Product - 1.0))
end;
```

Variables

Product	Temporary multiplicative product
J	Loop index

Discussion

In the Discussion section of WDrawP, the comments regarding the specification of the length of the investment are relevant here. See WDrawP.

Modifications

None

WDrawTNW

Name:	*WDrawTNW*
Type:	integer *function*
Purpose:	*To calculate the total number of withdrawals until an investment is depleted*
Calling Sequence:	WDrawTNW(Principal, Withdrawal, InterestRate, NumWPerYr)

Description

WDrawTNW computes the term (length of time) an investment can sustain itself if periodic withdrawals are made. This term is expressed as the total number of withdrawals before the investment is depleted to zero value. The amount of each withdrawal is the same, and the withdrawals occur at regular intervals. Interest is compounded with each withdrawal. You must specify the principal (initial investment), amount of each withdrawal, nominal (annual) interest rate, and number of withdrawals made per year.

Input

Principal	real	The principal (initial investment)
Withdrawal	real	The amount of each withdrawal

InterestRate	real	The annual interest rate expressed as a percentage
NumWPerYr	integer	The number of withdrawals made each year

Output

WDrawTNW	integer	The function WDrawTNW returns the total number of withdrawals until the investment depletes to zero value.

Limitations and Error Conditions

WDrawTNW checks that the quantity (Principal * InterestRate / NumWPerYr / Withdrawal) does not exceed 100. If it does, your withdrawals are not large enough to deplete the investment, and the number of withdrawals required is infinite. WDrawTNW returns a value of 0 (zero) as an error warning if this condition occurs.

No other range checking of your input parameters is done. All values should be positive. A fatal error is possible if a value is negative or zero.

This function will not work with the BCD version of Turbo because that compiler does not support the ln function on which WDrawTNW depends.

Sample Usage

Suppose that you have $10,000 to invest in an income-producing time deposit. Your bank offers 11.5 percent annual interest if withdrawals (and compounding) are either monthly or every other month. You want to withdraw $400 each time. The following Sample Usage program compares the total number of withdrawals possible in each case before the balance reaches zero.

```
program SampleUsageOfWDrawTNW;

var
    Principal, Withdrawal, InterestRate : real;
    TotalNumW, NumWPerYr                : integer;

{$I WDrawTNW.PSL}

BEGIN
    Principal    := 10000.00;
    Withdrawal   := 400.00;
    InterestRate := 11.5;
    NumWPerYr    := 6;
```

```
  TotalNumW   := WDrawTNW(Principal, Withdrawal, InterestRate,
                           NumWPerYr);
  writeln('Total number of withdrawals (bimonthly) =',
        TotalNumW:3);
  TotalNumW := WDrawTNW(Principal, Withdrawal,
                        InterestRate, 12);
  writeln('Total number of withdrawals (monthly)   =',
        TotalNumW:3)
END.
```

Running this test program produces the following output:

```
Total number of withdrawals (bimonthly) = 35
Total number of withdrawals (monthly)   = 29
```

Subprogram Listing of WDrawTNW.PSL

```
function WDrawTNW(Principal, Withdrawal, InterestRate: real;
                 NumWPerYr: integer): integer;          {Mod. #1a}

var
   Temp, RealTNW: real;

begin
   Temp := 1.0 - Principal * InterestRate / 100.0 /
             NumWPerYr / Withdrawal;
   if Temp <= 0.0 then
     RealTNW := 0
   else
     RealTNW := -ln(Temp) / ln(1.0 + InterestRate / 100.0 /
                          NumWPerYr);
   if frac(RealTNW) = 0.0 then                          {Mod. #1b}
     WDrawTNW := trunc(RealTNW)                          {Mod. #1b}
   else                                                 {Mod. #1b}
     WDrawTNW := trunc(RealTNW) + 1                      {Mod. #1b}
end;
```

Variables

Temp   Temporary quantity. It must be greater than zero, or the error condition occurs.

RealTNW   The total number of withdrawals, expressed as a real number. This number is rounded up to produce the output of WDrawTNW.

Discussion

For consistency with the other subprograms in the investment withdrawal family, the term of the investment is an integer value equal to the total number of withdrawals allowed. If the real value of this term contains a fractional part, the value is rounded up to produce the integer output required.

Modification

You can have the function return a real value for the total number of withdrawals instead of returning an integer value. The real value shows whether a fraction of a withdrawal occurs. Change the last integer to real in the line denoted by (Mod. #1a). Then replace all four lines designated as (Mod. #1b) with the following single statement:

```
WDrawTNW := RealTNW
```

15

Examining and Altering
the Computer Environment

This chapter presents three subprograms that examine the computer environment and one subprogram that changes the environment. GetSysID determines which type of IBM PC the program is running on, GetEquip determines what equipment is attached to the computer, and VidMode determines what video mode the program is currently using. The fourth subprogram, VideoChg, changes the currently active screen if the computer has both the Monochrome Adapter and the Color/Graphics Adapter.

GetSysID

> **Name:** *GetSysID*
>
> **Type:** char *function*
>
> **Purpose:** *To determine which type of IBM PC is in use*
>
> **Calling Sequence:** GetSysID

Description

GetSysID examines a location in the IBM PC's ROM (read-only memory) to determine which computer model is being used. Because the different models have different characteristics and capabilities, you may want to use this subprogram if your main program is being distributed to other people. The technique used in GetSysID distinguishes among the original IBM PC, the IBM PC XT, the IBM PC*jr*™, and the IBM Personal Computer AT.

Input

None

Output

GetSysID   char   The function GetSysID returns a char value with the
following meanings:

P   IBM PC

X   IBM PC XT or Portable PC

J   IBM PC*jr*

A   IBM Personal Computer AT

U   Unknown

Limitations and Error Conditions

IBM is not perfectly consistent in the way it implements the system identification
byte in ROM, but the results of this subprogram are generally accurate. Some original
PCs and XTs may be branded with the same ID, but the PC*jr* and the Personal
Computer AT always should be indicated correctly. Fortunately, these discrepancies
are not a practical problem. The PC and the XT are extremely similar, but the PC*jr*
and the AT have many differences. Confusing the PC and the XT (or Portable) is
seldom a problem, and the other IDs are reliable. Some "compatible" computers,
however, are inconsistent in the implementation of the system identification feature.
Some computers use the same indicators IBM uses, but other computers use other
values.

Sample Usage

```
program SampleUsageOfGetSysID;

{$I GetSysID.PSL}

BEGIN
  writeln('This computer has a system ID of ', GetSysID)
END.
```

This sample program produces the following output when the program is run on
an original IBM PC:

```
This computer has a system ID of P
```

Subprogram Listing of GetSysID.PSL

```
function GetSysID: char;

var
   SysID: byte;

begin
   SysID := mem[$F000:$FFFE];
   case SysID of
      $FF: GetSysID := 'P';
      $FE: GetSysID := 'X';
      $FD: GetSysID := 'J';
      $FC: GetSysID := 'A'                            {Mod. #1}
      else
         GetSysID := 'U'
   end;
end;
```

Variables

SysID   The contents of the system identification memory location

Discussion

None

Modifications

You can update the list of computer models as new computers are announced.
Add a semicolon to the end of the line indicated by {Mod. #1} and insert more
lines after it. For example, if a new model called the QT becomes available and it
has a system ID of hex FA (decimal 250), you add the following line (the semicolon
on the last line before else should be omitted):

```
   $FA: GetSysID := 'Q'
```

GetEquip

> **Name:** *GetEquip*
>
> **Type:** *Procedure*
>
> **Purpose:** *To determine the computer's equipment configuration*
>
> **Calling Sequence:** `GetEquip(EquipList, MemSize)`

Description

The `GetEquip` subprogram uses two ROM BIOS services to retrieve information about the equipment configuration of the computer. Of most interest are the number of printers installed, the number of RS-232 serial ports installed, the number of floppy disk drives, and the amount of memory installed. This information is helpful for programs that deal with peripheral devices. For example, if the computer has no printer interface installed, a program should not attempt to send data to a printer. This subprogram provides a means of checking.

Input

None

Output

`EquipList`	integer	Two bytes of bit settings that indicate the current equipment configuration. See table 15.1 in the Discussion section for details.
`MemSize`	integer	The amount of RAM, in kilobytes (K), the computer has, based on the system board switch settings. In other words, 256 means 256K of RAM (256 times 1,024, or 262,144 bytes).

Limitations and Error Conditions

The information provided by this subprogram is limited by the accuracy of the ROM BIOS services used. In particular, the `EquipList` bit settings were devised when the original IBM PC was designed, and the settings have not been updated to include all subsequent peripherals. Even with these limitations, however, the available information can be useful in many programming cases.

Sample Usage

```
program SampleUsageOfGetEquip;

type
   String4 = string[4];

var
   EquipList, MemSize : integer;
   Temp               : byte;

{$I GetEquip.PSL}
{$I IntToHex.PSL}

BEGIN
   GetEquip(EquipList, MemSize);
   writeln('EquipList = ', IntToHex(EquipList), ' (hex)' );
   writeln(MemSize, 'K of RAM installed' );
   Temp := hi(EquipList) shr 6;
   writeln(Temp, ' printer(s) installed' );
   Temp := hi(EquipList) and $0F shr 1;
   writeln(Temp, ' RS-232 serial port(s)' );
   if (lo(EquipList) and $01) = 1 then
      begin
         Temp := lo(EquipList) shr 6 + 1;
         writeln(Temp, ' floppy disk drive(s)' )
      end
   else
      writeln('No floppy disk drives' )
END.
```

This sample program displays the EquipList data in hexadecimal notation (using the IntToHex subprogram, which you must make available), and the memory size in decimal notation. The program then demonstrates how to select some peripheral information from the bits in EquipList, displaying on the screen the peripherals found.

```
EquipList = 427D (hex)
512K of RAM installed
1 printer(s) installed
1 RS-232 serial port(s)
2 floppy disk drive(s)
```

Subprogram Listing of GetEquip.PSL

```
procedure GetEquip(var EquipList, MemSize: integer);

type
   RegList = record
      AX, BX, CX, DX, BP, SI, DI, DS, ES, Flags: integer
   end;

var
   Reg: RegList;

begin
   intr($11, Reg);
   EquipList := Reg.AX;
   intr($12, Reg);
   MemSize := Reg.AX
end;
```

Variables

Reg   The standard internal registers used in passing data to and
                          from Turbo's msdos procedure

Discussion

Table 15.1 explains the bit settings in EquipList. A few more details are available
in IBM's *Personal Computer Technical Reference* and in *The Peter Norton Programmer's Guide to the IBM® PC* (Microsoft Press, 1985).

The standard bit-numbering scheme for the IBM PC (Intel 808x microprocessor
chip family) is used. In other words, bit 15 is the high-order bit of the high-order
byte [byte hi(EquipList) in Turbo]. Bit 7 is the high-order bit of the low-order
byte [lo(EquipList)]. CGA refers to the IBM Color/Graphics Adapter. The Sample
Usage program demonstrates how to test bits and retrieve numbers from EquipList.

Modifications

None

Table 15.1
Bit Settings in EquipList

Bits Set	Interpretation
15, 14	Number of printers attached
13	On if serial printer attached to PC*jr*
12	On if game I/O attached
11–9	Number of RS-232 serial ports
8	Off if DMA chip installed
7, 6	Number of floppy disk drives minus 1
5, 4	Initial video mode (01 = 40x25 CGA, 10 = 80x25 CGA, and 11 = monochrome)
3, 2	System board RAM (11 = 64K or full)
1	Not used (0)
0	On if there are floppy disks. Bit must be on for bits 6 and 7 to be valid.

VidMode

> **Name:** *VidMode*
>
> **Type:** *Procedure*
>
> **Purpose:** *To determine information about the current video mode*
>
> **Calling Sequence:** VidMode(Mode, TextWidth, Page)

Description

The VidMode subprogram uses a ROM BIOS video service to retrieve information about the video mode currently in effect. With this information, you can adapt your programs to take appropriate action depending on whether you are running them on a color/graphics or monochrome video screen, in graphics mode or text mode, in black-and-white or color, using page 0 or not, or with a text-line length of 40 or 80 characters.

Input

None

Output

Mode	byte	A number from 0 through 15 that indicates the current video display mode. Modes 0 through 6 are for the Color/Graphics Adapter (CGA), 7 is for the Monochrome Adapter, 8 through 10 are for the PC*jr*, and 13 through 15 are for the Enhanced Color/ Graphics Adapter (EGA). See table 15.2 in the Discussion section for details.
TextWidth	byte	The text-line width of the current video display mode (20, 40, or 80)
Page	byte	The current active page number in use (0 through 3 for 80-column text widths, or 0 through 7 for color/ graphics in 40-column width). Turbo Pascal normally uses page 0 at all times.

Limitations and Error Conditions

Turbo Pascal does not provide commands for setting the video mode to all the possible settings indicated here. Table 15.2 shows the Turbo commands for setting standard video modes with the Monochrome and Color/Graphics Adapters. Activating the modes that have no Turbo command indicated may require some fancy footwork (assembler language interface, direct memory access, etc.). As new video interfaces are created, other Mode values may be added.

Sample Usage

```
program SampleUsageOfVidMode;

var
   Mode, TextWidth, Page: byte;

{$I VidMode.PSL}
```

```
BEGIN
   VidMode(Mode, TextWidth, Page);
   writeln('Mode=', Mode, ' Width=', TextWidth, ' Page=', Page);
   delay(5000);
   graphmode;
   VidMode(Mode, TextWidth, Page);
   writeln('Mode=', Mode, ' Width=', TextWidth, ' Page=', Page);
   delay(5000);
   textmode
END.
```

When you run this sample program with an 80-column, black-and-white monitor attached to the Color/Graphics Adapter, the program displays the first line shown in the following sample output and then waits five seconds, clears the screen, and displays the second line in large (40-column) characters. (The graphmode command causes the screen to be cleared and enables the subsequent generation of the large characters.) If the program is run with the Monochrome Adapter, the three output values are instead 7, 80, and 0 both times.

```
Mode=2 Width=80 Page=0
Mode=5 Width=40 Page=0
```

Subprogram Listing of VidMode.PSL

```
procedure VidMode(var Mode, TextWidth, Page: byte);

type
   RegList = record
      AX, BX, CX, DX, BP, SI, DI, DS, ES, Flags: integer
   end;

var
   Reg: RegList;

begin
   Reg.AX := $0F00;
   intr($10, Reg);
   TextWidth := hi(Reg.AX);
   Mode      := lo(Reg.AX);
   Page      := hi(Reg.BX)
end;
```

Variables

Reg   The standard internal registers used in passing data to and
                       from Turbo's msdos procedure

Discussion

Table 15.2 shows the Mode values returned as a result of Turbo's various graphics
and text mode commands for activating the standard modes.

Table 15.2
Interpretation of the Mode Value

Mode	Turbo Command	Display Type	Adapter Type	Length and Height
0	textmode(bw40)	bw text	CGA	40, 25
1	textmode(c40)	color text	CGA	40, 25
2	textmode(bw80)	bw text	CGA	80, 25
3	textmode(c80)	color text	CGA	80, 25
4	graphcolormode	color graphics	CGA	320, 200
5	graphmode	bw graphics	CGA	320, 200
6	hires	bw graphics	CGA	640, 200
7	textmode	bw text	mono	80, 25
8		color graphics	PCjr	160, 200
9		color graphics	PCjr	320, 200
10		color graphics	PCjr, EGA	640, 200
13		color graphics	EGA	320, 200
14		color graphics	EGA	640, 200
15		color graphics	EGA	640, 350

Although Page is always zero when you use standard Turbo Pascal commands, you
can use other pages through other languages (assembler subroutines, for example).
We have experimented in trying to cause Turbo to use other video pages (by
changing the active page through another ROM BIOS service), but Turbo insists
on using page zero all the time for its standard graphics and text output. Apparently

you must manipulate memory locations in order to make effective use of other pages in Turbo. Despite this limitation, we include Page in this subprogram because of the parameter's potential usefulness with subroutines in other languages.

Modifications

None

VideoChg

Name:	*VideoChg*
Type:	*Procedure*
Purpose:	*To change between monochrome and color/graphics video screens or determine which screen is in use*
Calling Sequence:	VideoChg(WhichVideo)

Description

Turbo Pascal has plenty of extensions for the IBM PC so that you can switch between text and graphics modes, but Turbo provides no way to switch between the two physical video monitors you can have on your computer. (The graphics commands are based on the assumption that you are currently using the Color/Graphics Adapter.) If you have an IBM PC with both the Monochrome Adapter and the Color/ Graphics Adapter, this subprogram enables you to switch from one to the other while your Turbo Pascal program is running. You do not need to stop your program, use the PC DOS or MS-DOS MODE command to switch to the other monitor, and then restart your program. VideoChg also has an option to determine which of the two screens is currently being used. Before issuing any graphics commands, you should find out whether the computer has the capability of performing graphics. If the Monochrome Adapter is currently in use, you cannot perform graphics.

Input

WhichVideo   char   A single character that indicates the action you want VideoChg to perform. If the character is M or m, you want to switch to the Monochrome Adapter. If the character is C or c, you want to switch to the Color/ Graphics Adapter. If WhichVideo is any other character, you want to find out which video adapter is currently in use.

Output

WhichVideo   char   If the character you pass to VideoChg is something
                            other than M, m, C, or c, then WhichVideo is changed
                            to M or C, depending on whether the current video
                            adapter is Monochrome or Color/Graphics,
                            respectively. Otherwise, WhichVideo is changed to E
                            (error) if you try to switch to a video display you
                            don't have installed, or unchanged if the switch is
                            successfully made.

In addition, if you specify M, m, C, or c, and you have the appropriate video adapter
installed, that video adapter becomes the active one. The previous video screen is
not cleared (blanked) unless you clear it yourself with Turbo's clrscr procedure
before you use VideoChg. However, the new video screen (that you are switching
to) is cleared by VideoChg.

Limitations and Error Conditions

The subprogram sets your Color/Graphics Adapter to 80-column mode in black
and white. This is the same mode that results from the DOS command MODE BW80.
You can switch to 40-column mode and/or color mode with Turbo's textmode
procedure after you use VideoChg.

There is a complication in using this subprogram during program development.
Turbo Pascal apparently checks to see which video adapter is in use only when
Turbo starts up. If you use VideoChg to switch to the other adapter, Turbo does
not recheck which video screen to use after you compile and run your program.
Turbo continues to write to the old screen, even though some system information
is changed by VideoChg, making such output impossible. The result is that neither
screen is properly used by Turbo from then on.

You can deal with this complication in two ways. One approach is to press the Q
key to quit Turbo at that point and then restart Turbo, using the new screen. Be
sure that you remember to use option S to save your source program before running
it. (This advice is always sound.) The other approach is to design your test program
so that it switches back to the original screen before ending. In this case, you can
continue using Turbo with no problems.

This subprogram was tested on a standard IBM PC with both standard video adapters. Whether VideoChg works on other "compatible" computers and adapters depends on just how compatible they are. Be aware that some hardware technicians
recommend against having both video displays in use at the same time. Check with
your computer manufacturer or dealer to be sure.

Sample Usage

```
program SampleUsageOfVideoChg;

var
   WhichVideo: char;

{$I VideoChg.PSL}

BEGIN
   WhichVideo := 'X';
   VideoChg(WhichVideo);
   write('Current video is ');
   case WhichVideo of
      'M': writeln('monochrome');
      'C': writeln('color/graphics')
      else
         begin
            writeln('** error - recheck your typing **');
            exit
         end
      end;
   writeln('Switching to your second video after 5 seconds');
   delay(5000);
   clrscr;
   if WhichVideo = 'M' then
      WhichVideo := 'C'
   else
      WhichVideo := 'M';
   VideoChg(WhichVideo);
   if WhichVideo = 'E' then
      begin
         writeln('** Error - video adapter not available **');
         halt
      end;
```

```
   writeln('Now using your second video');
   writeln('Switching back to your first video after 5 seconds');
   if WhichVideo = 'M' then
      WhichVideo := 'C'
   else
      WhichVideo := 'M';
   delay(5000);
   clrscr;
   VideoChg(WhichVideo);
   writeln('Now back on your first video')
END.
```

This sample program indicates the type of video display currently in use, waits five seconds, and attempts to switch to the other video display. If the other video display is not installed, the program displays an error message and stops. If the switch is successful, the program displays a message on the second display, waits five seconds, and switches back to the original display. In each case, the program clears the video display screen just before leaving it. (VideoChg automatically clears the new screen it switches to.)

Subprogram Listing of VideoChg.PSL

```
procedure VideoChg(var WhichVideo: char);

const
   ColorSeg = $B800;
   ColorOfs = $FFF;
   MonoSeg  = $B000;
   MonoOfs  = $3FFF;
   TestA    = $55;
   TestB    = $AA;

type
   RegList = record
      AX, BX, CX, DX, BP, SI, DI, DS, ES, Flags: integer
   end;

var
   Reg     : RegList;
   VideoOK : boolean;
```

```
    begin
      case WhichVideo of
        'C', 'c' :
          begin
            VideoOK := true;
            mem[ColorSeg:ColorOfs] := TestA;
            if mem[ColorSeg:ColorOfs] <> TestA then
                VideoOK := false;
            mem[ColorSeg:ColorOfs] := TestB;
            if mem[ColorSeg:ColorOfs] <> TestB then
                VideoOK := false;
            if VideoOK then
                begin                                      {Mod. #1}
                  mem[0:$410] := (mem[0:$410] and $CF) or $20;
                  Reg.AX := $0002;
                  intr($10, Reg)
                end
            else
                WhichVideo := 'E'
          end;
        'M', 'm' :
          begin
            VideoOK := true;
            mem[MonoSeg:MonoOfs] := TestA;
            if mem[MonoSeg:MonoOfs] <> TestA then
                VideoOK := false;
            mem[MonoSeg:MonoOfs] := TestB;
            if mem[MonoSeg:MonoOfs] <> TestB then
                VideoOK := false;
            if VideoOK then
                begin                                      {Mod. #1}
                  mem[0:$410] := mem[0:$410] or $30;
                  Reg.AX := $0007;
                  intr($10, Reg)
                end
            else
                WhichVideo := 'E'
          end
```

```
      else
         begin
            if mem[0:$449] = 7 then
               WhichVideo := 'M'
            else
               WhichVideo := 'C'
         end
      end
end;
```

Variables

Reg	A record of integer variables representing the microprocessor's registers and flags. Reg is used to pass values to Turbo's intr procedure.
VideoOK	boolean variable that is set to true if the video screen to be switched to exists, but false if it does not exist
ColorSeg	Segment address of the color/graphics screen area
ColorOfs	Offset address of the byte tested in the color screen area
MonoSeg	Segment address of the monochrome screen area
MonoOfs	Offset address of the byte tested in the monochrome screen area
TestA	The first test value that is placed in the screen area in order to test whether the screen is installed
TestB	The second test value

Discussion

We tried to use a method that would make this subprogram not only easy to understand but also less likely to become obsolete because of hardware and software developments from IBM and other vendors. Time will tell whether we guessed right. The subprogram tests whether the new screen (you want to switch to) is installed by putting a value into the screen's memory area and then checking whether the value actually stays there (thus verifying that the screen's memory area exists). If the value doesn't stay, you don't have the adapter installed for that screen, and WhichVideo is set to E to indicate an error. The screen-memory test is done twice, with different values, to ensure that the first value is not coincidentally the value obtained when the subprogram tries to access nonexistent memory.

If the other screen exists on your system, the subprogram modifies a location (hex 410) in the data area that is used by the PC's ROM-resident BIOS (Basic Input/Output System) in order to indicate the equipment attached to your computer. The subprogram changes the necessary bits (in location hex 410) to reflect the video mode you want and then invokes the ROM BIOS video service interrupt (hex 10), using service 0 to set the video mode. The BIOS routine does the work to switch to the monitor you select, and the change is reflected in another BIOS data location (hex 449). We use this location to check which video adapter is currently in use.

Modification

You can revise the subprogram so that it clears the old video screen just before you switch to the new one. This change eliminates the need for your main program to clear the screen just before calling VideoChg each time (assuming that clearing the screen is what you want to do). Add a new line following each of the two lines indicated by {Mod. #1} in the subprogram. Each new line should be simply

```
clrscr;
```

16

Handling Errors

Turbo Pascal has limited facilities for handling error conditions while a program is running, but this chapter has two subprograms that deal with errors. IOError simplifies the task of checking for errors after I/O operations. RunError intercepts run-time errors and displays informative messages instead of mysterious error code numbers.

IOError

> **Name:** *IOError*
>
> **Type:** byte *function*
>
> **Purpose:** *To perform error checking after an I/O operation*
>
> **Calling Sequence:** IOError

Description

If the default {$I+} (I/O error handling) compiler directive is in effect, Turbo Pascal aborts a program if any I/O error condition occurs. Such drastic action is often unwanted, for instance, when a program is trying to open a disk file that is not found. A better programming approach is to inactivate the I/O error-handling compiler directive with {$I-} and have the program check whether the file open is successful. If the open is not successful, the program can display an error message and ask for a new file name. This subprogram does some of the work in checking for error conditions by displaying a brief error message for any known I/O error. The main program must then determine the action to take.

Input

IOError has no input variables, but the I/O error-handling compiler directive must be inactive ({$I-}) in order for Turbo's ioresult to be set after an I/O operation.

Output

Error   byte   The function IOError returns the numeric error code
                     obtained from ioresult. If Error is zero, no error
                     occurred. The error codes are explained in Appendix
                     G of the Turbo manual.

In addition, the subprogram beeps and displays a general I/O error message at the
current cursor position, then a message with the error code in decimal, and then
a message for the particular type of I/O error that occurred.

Limitations and Error Conditions

If ioresult does not contain either zero or any of the error numbers listed in
Appendix G of the Turbo manual, the error type is displayed as "unknown I/O
error type" on the screen. Note that ioresult must be examined after every I/O
operation, either by IOError or by your main program, so that error conditions
can be handled.

Sample Usage

```
program SampleUsageOfIOError;

var
   Code     : byte;
   FileA    : text;
   TextLine : string[255];

{$I IOError.PSL}

BEGIN
   {$I-}
   assign(FileA, 'NONEXIST.ENT');
   Code := IOError;
   if Code <> 0 then
      begin
         writeln('Error in assign statement');
         halt
      end;
```

```
      reset(FileA);
      Code := IOError;
      if Code <> 0 then
         begin
            writeln('Error in reset statement');
            halt
         end;
      readln(FileA, TextLine);
      Code := IOError;
      if Code <> 0 then
         begin
            writeln('Error in readln statement');
            halt
         end;
      close(FileA);
      Code := IOError;
      if Code <> 0 then
         begin
            writeln('Error in close statement');
            halt
         end
END.
```

This sample program demonstrates how to use IOError after disk I/O operations. The program tries to open a file that doesn't exist on disk. Note that the assign statement doesn't cause the error, but the subsequent reset does.

```
** I/O error encountered. **
** error code = 1 (decimal)
** no such filename in directory
Error in reset statement
```

Subprogram Listing of IOError.PSL

```
function IOError: byte;

var
   Code : byte;
   Msg  : string[40];
```

```
begin
   Code := ioresult;
   if Code = 0 then
      begin
         IOError := Code;
         exit;
      end;
   case Code of
      $01: Msg := 'no such filename in directory';
      $02: Msg := 'file not prepared to be read from';
      $03: Msg := 'file not prepared to be written to';
      $04: Msg := 'file not prepared with reset or rewrite';
      $10: Msg := 'illegal numeric format in data';
      $20: Msg := 'illegal operation for a logical device';
      $21: Msg := 'illegal operation in direct mode';
      $22: Msg := 'illegal to assign to standard file';
      $90: Msg := 'unmatched record lengths';
      $91: Msg := 'attempted seek after end of file';
      $99: Msg := 'physical end of file not expected';
      $F0: Msg := 'disk data area full';
      $F1: Msg := 'disk directory full';
      $F2: Msg := 'file exceeds 65535 records';
      $F3: Msg := 'too many files open';
      $FF: Msg := 'filename no longer in directory'
   else    Msg := 'unknown I/O error type'
   end;
   writeln(#7, '** I/O error encountered. **' );
   writeln('** error code = ', Code, ' (decimal)' );
   writeln('** ', Msg);
   IOError := Code                              {Mod. #1}
end;
```

Variables

Code	I/O error code retrieved from Turbo's ioresult
Msg	Error message for the error code

Discussion

If you choose not to do your own I/O error checking (either with this subprogram or with your own ioresult checking), then I/O errors are handled like any other run-time error. As a result, I/O errors may be either detected by the RunError subprogram or left undetected to cause normal run-time errors. If you are the only one using your programs, error handling may not be especially important. If, however, you write programs for others to use, error handling should occupy a large part of your programming efforts. Displaying cryptic error messages and aborting a program abruptly are two signs of unprofessional programming.

Modification

Replace the indicated line with a halt statement to make the subprogram end for any I/O error condition. This change is not recommended for polished programs, but it is a handy way to expedite program development by postponing the need to add error-handling logic to your main program until you have the program working.

RunError

> **Name:** *RunError*
>
> **Type:** *Procedure*
>
> **Purpose:** *To intercept run-time errors and display informative messages before aborting*
>
> **Calling Sequence:** errorptr := ofs(RunError)

Description

RunError can be activated to take control in the event of a run-time error (such as division by zero or an illegal string length). Unfortunately, Turbo Pascal provides no means of recovering from the error and continuing with the program. Instead, you can only display informative messages and let Turbo either continue with its regular abort actions (as this subprogram does) or come to a more graceful, "normal" end. (See the Modification section.) Even with these limitations, a program for distribution to others (and one that is prone to certain types of run-time errors) can be made more understandable and usable if you incorporate this subprogram or something like it.

Input

RunError requires no input variables (the two parameters shown on the procedure statement are passed by Turbo, not your program), but the subprogram must be activated by the following statement:

```
errorptr := ofs(RunError);
```

(For 8-bit versions of Turbo, replace ofs with addr.) This statement puts the address of the error-handling subprogram into the reserved location called errorptr.

Output

No output variables are changed. The subprogram displays two error messages. The first message indicates the type of error that occurred (user-interrupt error, I/O error, run-time error, or unknown error). The second message is displayed only if the error is a run-time error. This message specifies the type of error that took place. After one or both messages are displayed, the subprogram attempts to return control to the main program through an exit statement. Because Turbo does not allow the main program to continue, the result is that Turbo takes control and performs its regular run-time error handling. If you are running the program in memory mode, Turbo displays its normal error messages and searches through your source code for the statement that caused the error.

Limitations and Error Conditions

The error messages are displayed beginning at the current cursor location. If the error code does not match one of the codes in Appendix F of the Turbo manual, the second message calls the error an "unknown run-time error type."

Sample Usage

```
program SampleUsageOfRunError;

type
   Caps = 'A'..'Z';

var
   X    : real;
   J    : integer;
   Str  : string[255];
   Alph : Caps;

{$I RunError.PSL}
```

```
BEGIN
   {$R+}
   errorptr := ofs(RunError);
{The following statements all cause run-time errors.}
   X := 10E35;   for J := 1 to 10 do X := X * X;
   X := 5.0 / 0.0;
   X := sqrt(-2);
   X := ln(0);
   Str[0] := #200;   Str := Str + Str;
   Str := copy(str,0,1);
   J := 260;   Str[J] := #0;
   Alph := 'a';
   J := trunc(33000.0);
END.
```

This sample program has a series of lines that can cause various run-time errors. The first line of this series causes a fatal error, as shown in the sample output that follows. To see the effect of the next error, either delete the line that causes the first error or surround that line with braces, thus turning it into a comment. Then rerun the program to get the next error. Note that the {R+} statement at the beginning of the sample program is not needed by RunError. The statement is there only to force a run-time error later in the program. Running this sample program produces the following output:

```
** Error — Run-time error caused by
** floating point overflow
```

At this point, Turbo takes over to abort the program.

Subprogram Listing of RunError.PSL

```
procedure RunError(ErrorType, ErrorAddr: integer);

var
   ErrorCat, ErrorNum: byte;
   Msg: string[40];

begin
   ErrorCat := hi(ErrorType);
   ErrorNum := lo(ErrorType);
   case ErrorCat of
```

```
        0: Msg := 'User break/interruption';
        1: Msg := 'I/O error';
        2: Msg := 'Run-time error caused by';
        else Msg := 'Unknown type of error'
        end;
    writeln('** Error — ', Msg);
    if ErrorCat <> 2 then exit;                                {Mod. #1}
    case ErrorNum of
        $01: Msg := 'floating point overflow';
        $02: Msg := 'division by zero';
        $03: Msg := 'negative sqrt argument';
        $04: Msg := 'zero or negative ln argument';
        $10: Msg := 'illegal string length';
        $11: Msg := 'string index not within 1..255';
        $90: Msg := 'index not within range for an array';
        $91: Msg := 'scalar or subrange out of range';
        $92: Msg := 'real value out of integer range';
        $F0: Msg := 'overlay file not found';
        $FF: Msg := 'heap and stack collision';
    else    Msg := 'unknown run-time error type'
    end;
    writeln('** ', Msg);
    exit                                                       {Mod. #1}
end;
```

Variables

ErrorCat	The error category (0 = user interrupt, 1 = I/O error, 2 = run-time error, other = unknown)
ErrorNum	The run-time error number, as listed in Appendix F of the Turbo manual
Msg	An error message that corresponds to the error number

Discussion

If you encounter an I/O error in a program that has activated RunError, the error causes RunError to get control only if {$I+} is in effect. (See IOError.) If {$I-} is in effect, your program is doing its own error handling instead (either by checking ioresult itself or by using a subprogram like IOError). RunError is not designed to give details about an I/O error (IOError does that), but does display a message indicating that an I/O error has occurred.

Modification

Replace exit with halt in the two indicated lines, causing the program to come to a normal end instead of forcing Turbo to invoke its abort actions. See the Output section for details.

17

Manipulating Times and Dates

Turbo Pascal has a built-in delay procedure that causes a program to pause for a specified amount of time. Nothing else relating to times and dates is available, however. Because many programs must work with times and dates, this chapter contains 10 subprograms for that purpose. Internal clocks and calendars vary among different computers; therefore, most of these subprograms are based on the capabilities of PC DOS (or MS-DOS) and the IBM PC, and most of the subprograms make use of Turbo's msdos facility.

Four subprograms deal with the computer's time of day. GetTime retrieves the current time of day from the computer's internal clock. ShowTime displays the current time of day in a standardized form. SetTime sets the current time to the time you specify. Finally, TimeDiff calculates in seconds the elapsed time between two times.

Three subprograms are date-oriented counterparts of the first three time subprograms. GetDate retrieves the current date, ShowDate displays the current date, and SetDate sets the current date. The remaining three subprograms also deal with dates but are independent of PC DOS and the IBM PC. Julian converts a date into the corresponding Julian day number, which is useful for computing differences between dates. JulToYMD converts a Julian day number to year-month-day form. Finally, DayWeek determines the day of the week (Sunday through Saturday) on which a date falls.

GetTime

> **Name:** *GetTime*
>
> **Type:** *Procedure*
>
> **Purpose:** *To retrieve the current time of day in numeric form*
>
> **Calling Sequence:** GetTime(Hr, Min, Sec, Hun)

Description

GetTime uses DOS function call hex 2C to retrieve the current time of day in numeric form. After retrieving the time, your calling program can display it (or use ShowTime), calculate elapsed times (see TimeDiff), time-stamp events that are recorded in a disk file, and even act as an alarm clock.

Input

None

Output

Hr	byte	The hours portion of the time of day (0–23)
Min	byte	The minutes portion (0–59)
Sec	byte	The seconds portion (0–59)
Hun	byte	The hundredths-of-a-second portion (0–99)

Limitations and Error Conditions

The IBM PC's internal clock is updated about 18.2 times per second (actually 18.206482), or about once every .055 seconds (actually .0549255). Even though you can invoke GetTime many times in .055 seconds, the time of day remains the same until the next tick of the clock adds another .055 seconds. In practice, the time increases by either .05 or .06 seconds (depending on rounding) even though the clock appears to have .01-seconds resolution. Thus, for accuracy, rounding times to the nearest one-tenth of a second is recommended.

Sample Usage

```
program SampleUsageOfGetTime;

var
   Hr, Min, Sec, Hun: byte;

{$I GetTime.PSL}

BEGIN
   GetTime(Hr, Min, Sec, Hun);
   writeln('The time is ', Hr, ':', Min, ':', Sec, '.', Hun:2)
END.
```

The sample program displays the current time of day in a simple form, without leading zeros for each portion. The hundredths portion, if less than 10, has a leading space. Note that the 24-hour form is used. To convert to p.m., you subtract 12 from the hours portion when that portion is greater than 12. The time shown is 2.51 seconds after 6:57 p.m.:

```
The time is 18:57:2. 51
```

Subprogram Listing of GetTime.PSL

```
procedure GetTime(var Hr, Min, Sec, Hun: byte);

type
   RegList = record
      AX, BX, CX, DX, BP, SI, DI, DS, ES, Flags: integer
   end;

var
   Reg: RegList;

begin
   Reg.AX := $2C00;
   msdos(Reg);
   Hr  := hi(Reg.CX);
   Min := lo(Reg.CX);
   Sec := hi(Reg.DX);
   Hun := lo(Reg.DX)
end;
```

Variables

Reg   The standard internal registers used in passing data to and from Turbo's msdos procedure

Discussion

None

Modifications

None

ShowTime

Name:	*ShowTime*
Type:	*Procedure*
Purpose:	*To display the current time of day on the screen*
Calling Sequence:	ShowTime

Description

ShowTime retrieves the current internal time and uses a writeln statement to display the time on the screen. All components are displayed with two digits. (That is, a zero precedes each component that would otherwise be a single digit.) Colons separate hours, minutes, and seconds. A decimal point separates seconds and hundredths of a second.

Input

None

Output

The current time of day is displayed as an 11-byte string at the existing cursor location. The cursor moves to the beginning of the next line after the time is displayed.

Limitations and Error Conditions

See the clock-resolution limitations explained in GetTime.

Sample Usage

```
program SampleUsageOfShowTime;

{$I ShowTime.PSL}

BEGIN
   write('The time is ');
   ShowTime
END.
```

The sample program displays the current time of day:

The time is 18:57:06.08

Subprogram Listing of ShowTime.PSL

```
procedure ShowTime;

type
  RegList = record
    AX, BX, CX, DX, BP, SI, DI, DS, ES, Flags: integer
  end;

var
  Hr, Min, Sec, Hun : string[2];
  Reg               : RegList;

begin
  Reg.AX := $2C00;
  msdos(Reg);
  str(hi(Reg.CX):2, Hr);
  str(lo(Reg.CX):2, Min);
  str(hi(Reg.DX):2, Sec);
  str(lo(Reg.DX):2, Hun);
  if Hr[1]  = ' ' then Hr[1]  := '0';          {Mod. #1}
  if Min[1] = ' ' then Min[1] := '0';
  if Sec[1] = ' ' then Sec[1] := '0';
  if Hun[1] = ' ' then Hun[1] := '0';
  writeln(Hr, ':', Min, ':', Sec, '.', Hun)    {Mod. #2}
end;
```

Variables

Hr	Two-byte string of current hour, permitting a leading zero to be added, if necessary
Min	Two-byte string of current minute
Sec	Two-byte string of current second
Hun	Two-byte string of current hundredths of a second
Reg	The standard internal registers used in passing data to and from Turbo's msdos procedure

Discussion

None

Modifications

1. To eliminate the leading zero before the time's hour component, delete the line indicated by {Mod. #1}. This change causes a leading space to be displayed when the hour is 0 (zero) through 9.

2. To change the form in which the time is displayed, alter the indicated writeln statement. For example, if you want only the hour and the minute to be displayed, change the statement to

   writeln(Hr, ' :', Min)

   You may want to change writeln to write. This prevents ShowTime from moving the cursor to the beginning of the next line after displaying the time.

SetTime

Name:	*SetTime*
Type:	*Procedure*
Purpose:	*To set the computer's internal clock to a specified time*
Calling Sequence:	SetTime(Hr, Min, Sec, Hun)

Description

SetTime uses DOS function call hex 2D to set the internal clock to the time you specify. Some programs require an accurate clock setting; this subprogram provides a means of forcing the user to enter the correct time. (Users sometimes get lazy and skip the time-entry procedure during the boot process.)

Input

Hr	byte	The hours portion of the time of day (0–23)
Min	byte	The minutes portion (0–59)
Sec	byte	The seconds portion (0–59)
Hun	byte	The hundredths-of-a-second portion (0–99)

Output

The time-of-day clock in the computer is set to the specified time. If illegal values are specified, Hr is set to 25.

Limitations and Error Conditions

The four specified values (Hr, Min, Sec, and Hun) must be set to legal values, as shown in the Input section. If any value is not legal, Hr is set to 25 to indicate an error.

Sample Usage

```
program SampleUsageOfSetTime;

var
   Hr, Min, Sec, Hun: byte;

{$I SetTime.PSL}
{$I ShowTime.PSL}

BEGIN
   Hr  := 14;
   Min := 35;
   Sec := 0;
   Hun := 0;
   SetTime(Hr, Min, Sec, Hun);
   if Hr > 24 then
      writeln(' ** Error - illegal time **' )
   else
      begin
         write('The new time is ' );
         ShowTime
      end
END.
```

The sample program sets the internal clock to 14:35 (2:35 p.m.) and then immediately displays the new time. Note that such time settings are not always precise. Running the program produces the following output:

```
The new time is 14:34:59.98
```

Subprogram Listing of SetTime.PSL

```
procedure SetTime(var Hr, Min, Sec, Hun: byte);

type
   RegList = record
      AX, BX, CX, DX, BP, SI, DI, DS, ES, Flags: integer
   end;

var
   Reg: RegList;

begin
   Reg.CX := 256 * Hr + Min;
   Reg.DX := 256 * Sec + Hun;
   Reg.AX := $2D00;
   msdos(Reg);
   if lo(Reg.AX) <> 0 then
      Hr := 25
end;
```

Variables

Reg   The standard internal registers used in passing data to and
                       from Turbo's msdos procedure

Discussion

None

Modifications

None

TimeDiff

Name:	*TimeDiff*
Type:	real *function*
Purpose:	*To calculate the number of seconds between two times*
Calling Sequence:	TimeDiff(Hr, Min, Sec, Hun, Hr2, Min2, Sec2, Hun2)

Description

This subprogram calculates the number of seconds between two times of day, which are in the same form used in other subprograms in this chapter. The times can be obtained from the GetTime subprogram, in which case TimeDiff calculates the elapsed time between two real-time events. Or the times can come from any other source, as long as they are converted to the form shown here.

Input

Hr	byte	The first time's hours
Min	byte	The first time's minutes
Sec	byte	The first time's seconds
Hun	byte	The first time's hundredths of seconds
Hr2	byte	The second time's hours
Min2	byte	The second time's minutes
Sec2	byte	The second time's seconds
Hun2	byte	The second time's hundredths of seconds

Output

TimeDiff	real	The function TimeDiff returns a real value that is the number of seconds between the two times (with two decimal places). If TimeDiff is negative, the second time is earlier (smaller) than the first. For details, see the next section.

Limitations and Error Conditions

As discussed in GetTime, the resolution of the IBM PC clock is about .055 seconds. If the PC's timer is the source of the two times, TimeDiff can be no more accurate than the timer, even though two decimal places are carried in the result. The arithmetic is accurate to two decimal places.

If the calculated time difference is negative, the second time is earlier (smaller) than the first because of one of two reasons. Either you did not know which time would be earlier (or you accidentally reversed them), or midnight took place between the two times. In the first case, if you know that both times are from the same day, you can simply take the absolute value of TimeDiff (using Turbo's abs function) to get the correct answer. In the second case, you can add 86400.0 (the number of seconds in 24 hours) to TimeDiff. The Sample Usage program contains an example of two times, with midnight between them. The values passed to TimeDiff are not required to fall within the normal ranges. (For instance, Min does not need to be in the 0–59 range.) Sixty-five minutes is treated as 1 hour and 5 minutes. Because all values are defined as byte, however, each value must be from 0 to 255.

Sample Usage

```
program SampleUsageOfTimeDiff;

var
   Hr, Min, Sec, Hun, Hr2, Min2, Sec2, Hun2: byte;
   Seconds: real;

{$I TimeDiff.PSL}
{$I GetTime.PSL}

BEGIN
   GetTime(Hr, Min, Sec, Hun);
   delay(1000);
   GetTime(Hr2, Min2, Sec2, Hun2);
   Seconds := TimeDiff(Hr, Min, Sec, Hun, Hr2, Min2, Sec2, Hun2);
   writeln('End time   = ', Hr2:2, Min2:3, Sec2:3, Hun2:3);
   writeln('Start time = ', Hr:2,  Min:3,  Sec:3,  Hun:3);
   writeln('Time difference =', Seconds:7:2, ' seconds');
   Hr := 23;  Min  := 59;  Sec  := 54;  Hun  := 0;
   Hr2 := 0;  Min2 := 0;   Sec2 := 7;   Hun2 := 0;
   Seconds := TimeDiff(Hr, Min, Sec, Hun, Hr2, Min2, Sec2, Hun2);
   if Seconds < 0.0 then
      Seconds := Seconds + 86400.0;
   writeln('Second time difference = ', Seconds:6:2, ' seconds')
END.
```

This sample program produces two results that illustrate two different points. The first result tests the accuracy of Turbo's delay procedure using the PC's internal clock. The Turbo manual warns that the exact delay may vary in different operating environments. Our experience is that delay pauses about 6 or 7 percent less than the delay indicated by the PC clock. You can experiment on your system by changing the number in the delay statement. The first time difference should be 1.00 seconds for a 1,000 millisecond delay. Try 10,000 milliseconds (10 seconds) also. The coding for the second time difference shows how to handle a case in which you know that the second time should be later than the first, but midnight may intervene.

Note that the sample program makes use of GetTime to get the current time of day. Thus, GetTime.PSL is required on your default disk drive for this sample program. Running the program produces the following output:

```
End time    = 14 23 19 38
Start time  = 14 23 18 45
Time difference =    0.93 seconds
Second time difference =   13.00 seconds
```

Subprogram Listing of TimeDiff.PSL

```
function TimeDiff(Hr, Min, Sec, Hun, Hr2, Min2, Sec2, Hun2:
                  byte): real;

begin
   TimeDiff := 3600.0 * Hr2 + 60.0 * Min2 + Sec2 + 0.01 * Hun2 -
              (3600.0 * Hr  + 60.0 * Min  + Sec  + 0.01 * Hun)
end;
```

Variables

None

Discussion

You can use many tricky ways to subtract one time from another. This subprogram uses a straightforward method: simply convert each time into the number of seconds that have elapsed since midnight, and then subtract one time from the other.

Modifications

None

GetDate

Name: *GetDate*

Type: *Procedure*

Purpose: *To retrieve the current date in numeric form*

Calling Sequence: GetDate(Yr, Mon, Day)

Description

GetDate uses DOS function call hex 2A to retrieve the current date in numeric form. After retrieving the date, the calling program can display it (or use ShowDate), calculate date differences (see Julian), date-stamp events that are recorded in a disk file, and so on.

Input

None

Output

Yr	byte	The year portion of the date (0–99)
Mon	byte	The month portion (1–12)
Day	byte	The day portion (1–31)

Limitations and Error Conditions

The year (Yr) is returned as a 2-digit number. The years 1980 through 1999 are returned as 80 through 99. The years 2000 through 2079 are returned as 0 through 79. The years 2080 through 2099 are returned also as 80 through 99.

Sample Usage

```
program SampleUsageOfGetDate;

var
   Yr, Mon, Day: byte;

{$I GetDate.PSL}

BEGIN
  GetDate(Yr, Mon, Day);
  writeln('The date is ', Yr, '-', Mon, '-', Day)
END.
```

The sample program displays the current date in a simple form (year-month-day) without leading zeros for each portion:

The date is 86-2-27

Subprogram Listing of GetDate.PSL

```
procedure GetDate(var Yr, Mon, Day: byte);

type
   RegList = record
      AX, BX, CX, DX, BP, SI, DI, DS, ES, Flags: integer
   end;

var
   Reg: RegList;

begin
   Reg.AX := $2A00;
   msdos(Reg);
   Yr  := Reg.CX - 1900;
   if Yr > 99 then
      Yr := Yr - 100;
   Mon := hi(Reg.DX);
   Day := lo(Reg.DX)
end;
```

Variables

Reg   The standard internal registers used in passing data to and from Turbo's msdos procedure

Discussion

None

Modifications

None

ShowDate

Name:	*ShowDate*
Type:	*Procedure*
Purpose:	*To display the current date on the screen*
Calling Sequence:	ShowDate

Description

ShowDate retrieves the current internal date and uses a writeln statement to display the date on the screen. The date is displayed in year-month-day form. A leading zero precedes each single-digit component, and the components are separated by hyphens. You can easily change the form with a modification that is provided.

Input

None

Output

The current date is displayed as an eight-byte string at the existing cursor location. The cursor moves to the beginning of the next line after the date is displayed.

Limitations and Error Conditions

The year is converted to a two-digit number, as explained in GetDate.

Sample Usage

```
program SampleUsageOfShowDate;

{$I ShowDate.PSL}

BEGIN
   write('The date is ');
   ShowDate
END.
```

The sample program displays the current date in year-month-day form:

```
The date is 86-06-13
```

Subprogram Listing of ShowDate.PSL

```
procedure ShowDate;

type
  RegList = record
    AX, BX, CX, DX, BP, SI, DI, DS, ES, Flags: integer
  end;

var
  Yr, Mon, Day : string[2];
  Reg          : RegList;

begin
  Reg.AX := $2A00;
  msdos(Reg);
  Reg.CX := Reg.CX - 1900;
  if Reg.CX > 99 then
    Reg.CX := Reg.CX - 100;
  str(Reg.CX:2, Yr);
  str(hi(Reg.DX):2, Mon);
  str(lo(Reg.DX):2, Day);
  if Yr[1]  = ' ' then Yr[1]  := '0';
  if Mon[1] = ' ' then Mon[1] := '0';
  if Day[1] = ' ' then Day[1] := '0';
  writeln(Yr, '-', Mon, '-', Day)                              {Mod. #1}
end;
```

Variables

Yr	The year in two-byte string form, permitting addition of a leading zero, if necessary
Mon	Two-byte string of the month
Day	Two-byte string of the day
Reg	The standard internal registers used in passing data to and from Turbo's msdos procedure

Discussion

None

Modification

To change the form in which the date is displayed, alter the line indicated by {Mod. #1}. Change the year-month-day form into month/day/year form by using the statement

```
writeln(Mon, '/', Day, '/', Yr)
```

SetDate

Name:	*SetDate*
Type:	*Procedure*
Purpose:	*To set the computer's internal date*
Calling Sequence:	SetDate(Yr, Mon, Day)

Description

SetDate uses DOS function call hex 2B to set the internal date to the date you specify. Some programs require an accurate date setting; this subprogram provides a means of forcing the user to enter the current date. (Users sometimes get lazy and skip the date-entry procedure during the boot process.)

Input

Yr	byte	The year portion of the date (0–199)
Mon	byte	The month portion (1–12)
Day	byte	The day portion (1–31)

Output

The internal date in the computer is set to the date specified. If illegal values are specified, Yr, Mon, and Day are all set to zero.

Limitations and Error Conditions

The three specified values (Yr, Mon, and Day) must be set to legal values, as shown in the Input section. If the values are not legal, all three values are set to zero to indicate an error. The Yr values of 80 through 99 are interpreted as 1980 through 1999. For 0 through 79 (or 100 through 179), the interpretation is 2000 through

2079. For 180 through 199, the year is set to 2080 through 2099. DOS does not allow the current year to be earlier than 1980.

Sample Usage

```
program SampleUsageOfSetDate;

var
   Yr, Mon, Day: byte;

{$I SetDate.PSL}
{$I ShowDate.PSL}

BEGIN
   Yr  := 87;
   Mon := 12;
   Day := 31;
   SetDate(Yr, Mon, Day);
   if Mon = 0 then
      writeln('** Error — illegal date **')
   else
      begin
         write('The new date is ');
         ShowDate
      end
END.
```

The sample program sets the internal date to December 31, 1987, and displays the new date immediately afterward:

```
The new date is 87-12-31
```

Subprogram Listing of SetDate.PSL

```
procedure SetDate(var Yr, Mon, Day: byte);

type
   RegList = record
      AX, BX, CX, DX, BP, SI, DI, DS, ES, Flags: integer
   end;

var
   Reg: RegList;
```

```
begin
   if Yr < 80 then
      Yr := Yr + 100;
   Reg.CX := 1900 + Yr;
   Reg.DX := 256 * Mon + Day;
   Reg.AX := $2B00;
   msdos(Reg);
   if lo(Reg.AX) <> 0 then
      begin
         Yr  := 0;
         Mon := 0;
         Day := 0
      end
end;
```

Variables

Reg   The standard internal registers used in passing data to and
                                 from Turbo's msdos procedure

Discussion

None

Modifications

None

Julian

> **Name:** *Julian*
>
> **Type:** real *function*
>
> **Purpose:** *To calculate the Julian day number for a given year,*
> *month, and day*
>
> **Calling Sequence:** Julian(Year, Mon, Day)

Description

This subprogram calculates the day number within the Julian period for the specified year, month, and day. The Julian day number is commonly used by astronomers to indicate the dates of astronomical events. The number is also useful to computer programmers in determining the number of days between two dates. The start of the Julian period was January 1, 4713 B.C., as determined by the Julian calendar. The starting point for the current Gregorian calendar is a date that is a few weeks away from that. See the Limitations and Error Conditions section and the Discussion section for details.

Input

Year	integer	The year portion of the date. (See Limitations and Error Conditions.)
Mon	byte	The month portion (1–12)
Day	byte	The day portion (1–31)

Output

Julian	real	The function Julian returns the day number within the Julian period for the date provided.

Limitations and Error Conditions

If Mon or Day is out of the range shown in the Input section, or if Year is negative, Julian is set to -1.0 to indicate an error. When Year is from 0 (zero) to 99, it is assumed to mean 1900 through 1999. Note that Year in this subprogram is defined as an integer variable, whereas Yr is defined as a byte variable in the previous date subprograms. As used by astronomers, the Julian day begins at noon. Thus, each night's astronomical observations occur on one day, without the date changing at midnight. The day number calculated by this subprogram is the day beginning at noon on the date specified.

The algorithm used for this subprogram provides a valid result for any Gregorian calendar date that produces a Julian day number greater than zero. Julian day number 1 corresponds to the Gregorian date November 25, 4714 B.C., or November 25 of year -4713. The difference occurs because the Gregorian calendar has no year 0 (zero) between 1 B.C. and A.D. 1, but the Julian period requires a zero year between years -1 and 1. Even though ancient dates are technically valid, be aware that the English-speaking world converted to the Gregorian calendar on September 14, 1752. Earlier dates produce correct results only if you provide the dates in Gregorian terms.

Sample Usage

```
program SampleUsageOfJulian;

var
   Year       : integer;
   Mon, Day   : byte;
   NumDays    : real;

{$I Julian.PSL}

BEGIN
   repeat
      writeln('Enter date');
      write('Year: ');      read(Year);
      write('  Month: ');   read(Mon);
      write('  Day: ');     read(Day);
      writeln;
      NumDays := Julian(Year, Mon, Day);
      if NumDays < 0.0 then
         writeln('** Illegal date **')
      else
         writeln('Julian day = ', NumDays:8:0)
   until NumDays < 0.0
END.
```

The sample output that follows shows the Julian day for several dates. The sample
program continues until you enter an illegal date.

```
Enter date
Year: 1985 Month: 12 Day: 31
Julian day = 2446431
Enter date
Year: 86 Month: 1 Day: 1
Julian day = 2446432
Enter date
Year: 1776 Month: 7 Day: 4
Julian day = 2369916
Enter date
Year: 2000 Month: 2 Day: 29
Julian day = 2451604
Enter date
Year: 0 Month: 0 Day: 0
** Illegal date **
```

Subprogram Listing of Julian.PSL

```
function Julian(Year: integer; Mon, Day: byte): real;

var
   Temp: real;

begin
   if (Year < 0) or (Mon < 1) or (Mon > 12)                {Mod. #1}
                  or (Day < 1) or (Day > 31) then
      begin
         Julian := -1.0;
         exit
      end;
   if Year < 100 then Year := Year + 1900;                 {Mod. #1}
   Temp    := int((Mon - 14.0) / 12.0);
   Julian := Day - 32075.0 +
             int(1461.0 * (Year + 4800.0 + Temp) / 4.0) +
             int(367.0 * (Mon - 2.0 - Temp * 12.0) / 12.0) -
             int(3.0 * int((Year + 4900.0 + Temp) / 100.0) / 4.0)
end;
```

Variables

Temp   A partial result, used in calculating the Julian day number

Discussion

The most frequent application of this subprogram is finding differences between
two dates. Every modern Julian day number is a large positive integer; therefore,
determining how many days elapse between two dates is a matter of simple sub-
traction, even if the two dates are hundreds of years apart. If you have defined a
real variable DaysApart, you can use the following approach. Of course, you can
remove the abs (absolute value) function to find out which date is earlier, if
necessary.

```
DaysApart := abs(Julian(Y1, M1, D1) - Julian(Y2, M2, D2))
```

Another use of this subprogram is to find the date that is n days in the future (or
past) from a given date. Use Julian to get the Julian day of the given date, add or
subtract n (as appropriate), and then use the JulToYMD subprogram to convert back
to year-month-day form.

For details about calendar differences and the Julian period, see *The World Almanac and Book of Facts* (Newspaper Enterprise Association, 1985). Beware of the 1985 edition, however, which contains an error in the sample Julian day for December 31, 1984. The correct Julian day is 2,446,066. (The 1986 edition has a similar error.) For a discussion of the origins of the Julian period, see Chapter 6 of *Counting the Eons*, by Isaac Asimov (Doubleday, 1983).

Modification

To eliminate the conversion of year numbers from 0 (zero) through 99 into 1900 through 1999, delete entirely the second statement indicated by {Mod. #1}. In the first indicated statement, delete only the portion that reads (Year < 0) or. These changes open the valid Year range to -4713 (4714 B.C.) through A.D. 99, in addition to later dates. See the Limitations and Error Conditions section for a warning about dates before 1752.

JulToYMD

> **Name:** *JulToYMD*
>
> **Type:** *Procedure*
>
> **Purpose:** *To convert a Julian day number into year-month-day form*
>
> **Calling Sequence:** JulToYMD(JulianDay, Year, Mon, Day)

Description

JulToYMD converts a Julian day number into year-month-day form of the Gregorian calendar. This subprogram is the inverse of Julian, which has details about calendars and the Julian period.

Input

JulianDay	real	The Julian day number to be converted into year-month-day form

Output

Year	integer	The year portion of the date
Mon	byte	The month portion (1–12)
Day	byte	The day portion (1–31)

Limitations and Error Conditions

JulianDay must be a positive integer value, but no error checking is done. The output values correspond to the Gregorian calendar, even for a date before the Gregorian calendar's use. See Julian for more information.

Sample Usage

```
program SampleUsageOfJulToYMD;

var
   JulianDay : real;
   Year      : integer;
   Mon, Day  : byte;

{$I JulToYMD.PSL}

BEGIN
   repeat
      write('Enter Julian Day: ');
      readln(JulianDay);
      JulToYMD(JulianDay, Year, Mon, Day);
      if JulianDay > 0.0 then
         writeln('Date is ', Year, '/', Mon, '/', Day)
   until JulianDay <= 0.0
END.
```

The sample output that follows converts Julian days into year-month-day form. Many of the same dates are used that were in the Julian sample run. The program ends when you enter a negative or zero Julian day.

```
Enter Julian day: 2446431
Date is 1985/12/31
Enter Julian day: 2446432
Date is 1986/1/1
Enter Julian day: 2369916
Date is 1776/7/4
Enter Julian day: 2451605
Date is 2000/3/1
Enter Julian day: 1
Date is -4713/11/25
Enter Julian day: 0
```

Subprogram Listing of JulToYMD.PSL

```
procedure JulToYMD(JulianDay: real; var Year: integer;
                   var Mon, Day: byte);

var
  TempA, TempB: real;

begin
  TempA := JulianDay + 68569.0;
  TempB := int(4.0 * TempA / 146097.0);
  TempA := TempA - int((146097.0 * TempB + 3.0) / 4.0);
  Year  := trunc(4000.0 * (TempA + 1.0) / 1461001.0);
  TempA := TempA - int(1461.0 * Year / 4.0) + 31.0;
  Mon   := trunc(80.0 * TempA / 2447.0);
  Day   := trunc(TempA - int(2447.0 * Mon / 80.0));
  TempA := int(Mon / 11.0);
  Mon   := trunc(Mon + 2.0 - 12.0 * TempA);
  Year  := trunc(100.0 * (TempB - 49.0) + Year + TempA)
end;
```

Variables

TempA, TempB   Two work variables used during the calculations

Discussion

See the Discussion section of Julian.

Modifications

None

DayWeek

Name:	*DayWeek*
Type:	*Procedure*
Purpose:	*To determine the day of the week for a given date*
Calling Sequence:	DayWeek(Year, Mon, Day, DayNum, DayName)

Description

The DayWeek subprogram uses a method called Zeller's congruence to determine the day of the week for any date. The day is provided in both numeric form (zero through six for Sunday through Saturday) and string form (a three-character abbreviation for each day).

Input

Year	integer	The year portion of the date. (See Limitations and Error Conditions.)
Mon	byte	The month portion (1–12)
Day	byte	The day portion (1–31)

In addition, you must specify in your main program the following global type declaration:

```
type
   String3 = string[3];
```

Output

DayNum	byte	The numeric day of the week (0 = Sunday, 1 = Monday, etc.). DayNum is set to 9 if an illegal date is specified.
DayName	string	The text day of the week, containing three characters, of which the first is capitalized (Sun, Mon, Tue, etc.). DayName is set to ERR if an illegal date is specified.

Limitations and Error Conditions

Mon and Day must be set to legal values, as shown in the Input section. Year must be positive. If any of these parameters is not within bounds, DayNum is set to 9, and DayName is set to ERR. If Year is 0 through 99, the year is interpreted as 1900 through 1999. Note that English-speaking countries converted to the Gregorian calendar (our present calendar) in 1752. (Other countries converted at other times over a period of several hundred years.) An earlier date yields a day of the week that does not correspond to the calendar in use at the time.

Sample Usage

```
program SampleUsageOfDayWeek;

type
   String3 = string[3];

var
   Year            : integer;
   Mon, Day, DayNum : byte;
   DayName         : String3;

{$I DayWeek.PSL}

BEGIN
   Year := 1986;
   Mon  := 2;
   Day  := 27;
   DayWeek(Year, Mon, Day, DayNum, DayName);
   writeln('Feb 27, 1986 = DayNum ', DayNum, ' or ', DayName);
   DayWeek(1941, 12, 7, DayNum, DayName);
   writeln('Dec 7, 1941, was ', DayName)
END.
```

The sample program displays the day of the week for two dates:

```
Feb 27, 1986 = DayNum 4 or Thu
Dec 7, 1941, was Sun
```

Subprogram Listing of DayWeek.PSL

```
procedure DayWeek(Year: integer; Mon, Day: byte;
                  var DayNum: byte; var DayName: string3);

const
   DayText = 'SunMonTueWedThuFriSat';

var
   Cent, Yr : byte;
   Temp     : integer;
```

```
begin
   if (Year < 0) or (Mon < 1) or (Mon > 12)
                or (Day < 1) or (Day > 31) then
      begin
         DayNum  := 9;
         DayName := 'ERR';
         exit
      end;
   if Year < 100 then Year := Year + 1900;
   Mon    := Mon - 2;
   if (Mon < 1) or (Mon > 10) then
      begin
         Mon  := Mon + 12;
         Year := Year - 1
      end;
   Cent := Year div 100;
   Yr   := Year mod 100;
   Temp := (trunc(int(2.6 * Mon - 0.2)) + Day + Yr + (Yr div 4)
            + (Cent div 4) - Cent - Cent) mod 7;
   if Temp < 0 then Temp := Temp + 7;
   DayNum  := Temp;
   DayName := copy(DayText, DayNum + DayNum + DayNum + 1, 3)
end;
```

Variables

DayText	A string constant that contains the text values for the seven days
Cent	The century number of the year specified
Yr	The year within the century (0–99)
Temp	An intermediate numeric variable that holds the modulus remainder for conversion to a positive byte value

Discussion

Zeller's congruence is discussed in several sources, including *Problems for Computer Solution* by Fred Gruenberger and George Jaffray (Wiley & Sons, 1965). Once you calculate the numeric day of the week, it is a simple matter to look up the text equivalent in the DayText string table. Or you can look up a different text name in your main program by using DayNum. In different programming cases, you may need the full name of the day (such as Sunday), or you may need only the first one or two letters of the name (to label a crowded graph axis, for example).

Modifications

None

18

Full Programs Constructed from Subprograms

Here is where the concept of the Turbo Pascal Program Library really shines! A primary goal of this book is to show how easily you can incorporate our integrated subprograms into your main programs. Now is our chance.

This chapter presents 10 complete Turbo programs that demonstrate the method in action. Each program uses several subprograms from the book. On disk, each subprogram is saved with the three-letter file extension .PSL (for Pascal Subprogram Library, the subprogram portion of this program library). A main program invokes one of the subprograms by using Turbo's {$I} *include* compiler directive. Early in the source listing of each full program is a series of these directives for reading the necessary subprograms from disk. A typical part of this section of code looks like the following:

```
{$I GetReply.PSL}
{$I Key2Arr.PSL}
{$I MatMult.PSL}
{$I WaitKey.PSL}
```

Syntax is critical to ensure that Turbo treats these as compiler directives and not ordinary comments. The {$I part must appear with no intervening spaces. Then comes a space followed by the name of the subprogram to be read in from disk. Don't forget the PSL extension. (Capitalization is irrelevant in the subprogram name.) Finally, a right brace (}) terminates the compiler directive. See Appendix A for details about storing the subprogram library on disk.

An Overview of the Programs

The complete programs represent a potpourri of applications. Each program uses at least five different subprograms. In all, about one-third of the subprograms in the book are used.

The program NewsWire displays moving "ticker tape" type messages on the screen. You enter the desired text, and your message continually scrolls right to left in a framed message box. This program is great for announcements, advertisements, or special messages.

Two math programs analyze paired X-Y data for correlation. TryCurvs calculates particular nonlinear curve fits, and PolyFit calculates polynomial fits of arbitrary degree. Your data can be typed from the keyboard, saved on disk, and retrieved later.

SortDir provides a display of a disk directory in alphabetical order. This program also displays file attributes, the time and date of a file, and hidden files. SortText sorts text data from a disk file and creates a new disk file from the result of the sort. The program is handy for many word-processing applications.

SimulEqn solves systems of simultaneous linear equations.

Mortgage calculates loan repayment schedules that include balloon payments and monthly payment overrides.

DoChiSq generates chi-square tables for validation of experiments. For any number of degrees of freedom, you can specify either chi-square or the probability.

Finally, two programs create graphs of your data quickly and conveniently on the screen. XYGraph plots functional curves, and BarChart draws bar charts and histograms. Complete axis annotation is included with both programs.

Documenting the Programs

The documentation of each full program in this chapter differs somewhat from that of the individual subprograms. Each explanation begins with a statement of the purpose and consists of the following sections.

Usage

This section provides an explanation of when and how to use the program. Included is a step-by-step description of input required and output produced.

Sample Output

A sample case is presented to illustrate the program in action. Figures are included to depict the representative session.

Program Listing

This section contains a complete listing of the Turbo Pascal source code for the program, printed on a shaded background for easy reference. When you save one of these full programs on disk, use the extension . PGM (for example, SortText. PGM) or choose some other extension that differentiates a full program from a subprogram. (See Appendix A.)

Variables

Each variable in the program is listed with an explanation of its use.

Discussion

This section contains information to help you make effective use of the program. The discussion may include cross-references to the included subprograms; applications of the program that may not be obvious; theoretical foundations; details of the programming techniques involved; and information about speed, memory use, or other resource requirements.

Modifications

In this section are offered specific changes you can make in the source code so that the program will work slightly differently. Thus, you can tailor the program to your exact needs.

NewsWire

Purpose: *To display moving messages on the screen*

Usage

NewsWire turns your computer into a moving "ticker tape" message center. With this program, you can enter any message up to 8,000 characters long and then have it repeatedly scroll from right to left inside a framed message box. This technique creates an attention-getting display for announcements, advertising promotion, or just plain fun.

To use NewsWire, you must first type the message you want displayed. The program stores the message in a string array. Each array element can be up to 80 characters long; a maximum of 100 elements is allowed in the array. Thus, your message can contain up to 8,000 characters. If this is insufficient, see the Modifications section.

The program prompts you for the text to place in each element of the array. For the purposes of NewsWire, these elements are concatenated into one long message. Therefore, you place a blank space (if appropriate) at the end of each entry line so that the message is readable after concatenation. As the message is displayed, it is continually repeated. Because of this, you may want to put several blank spaces at the end of the message. When you are finished entering the entire message, type **END** (all uppercase) to signal the end of data entry. For an illustration of this entry process, here is how you might enter one of Woody Allen's pearls[1]:

```
1: "More than any other time in history, mankind faces a
2: crossroads. One path leads to despair and utter
3: hopelessness. The other, to total extinction. Let
4: us pray we have the wisdom to choose correctly."
5:         — Woody Allen. . . .
6: END
```

One blank space is included at the end of each of the first four lines, and several blank spaces appear at both the beginning and end of line 5.

If you try to make an input line longer than 80 characters, that line is truncated to 80 characters. Data entry terminates automatically if you input 100 lines.

Once the data entry is complete, the program prompts you to press a key to begin the display. Your message scrolls from right to left inside a framed display box. The message repeats until you press a key to terminate the program.

Sample Output

It's hard to show a moving video display in a static book, but we can give you some of the flavor of NewsWire. Figure 18.1 shows the data entry for a short, promotional message from a couple of objective authors. Figure 18.2 is a "snapshot" look at (part of) the moving message in progress.

---

[1]From Woody Allen, *Side Effects* (New York: Ballantine Books, 1981).

```
NewsWire - Create moving messages.

** Enter text data.  Array size = 100 lines **
** Enter END to end data entry. **
  1: Look for more books by Rugg & Feldman!!
  2: from Que -- the leading microcomputer book
  3: publisher......
  4: END
** Data entry complete **

Press a key to start the news wire.
Once it begins, you can press any key to stop it.

** PRESS ANY KEY TO CONTINUE **
```

Fig. 18.1. *The data entry for* NewsWire *is complete.*

```
Look for more books by Rugg & Feldman!
```

Fig. 18.2. *A snapshot look at the moving message.*

Program Listing of NewsWire.PGM

```
program NewsWire;   {Display moving messages}

const
   TextSize = 100;                                      {Mod. #1}

type
   LineSize      = string[80];
   TextArrayType = array[1..TextSize] of LineSize;

var
   TextArray                                  : TextArrayType;
   J, K, LineCount, LeftX, RightX, Y, DelayTime : integer;
   Reply, Reply2                              : char;

{$I CursorOn.PSL}
{$I KeyHit.PSL}
{$I KeyTxt.PSL}
{$I Scroll.PSL}
{$I TextBox.PSL}
{$I WaitKey.PSL}
```

```
BEGIN
    textmode(bw80);
    clrscr;
    writeln('NewsWire - Create moving messages.');
    writeln;
    LeftX      := 2;                                          {Mod. #2}
    RightX     := 39;                                         {Mod. #2}
    Y          := 12;                                         {Mod. #2}
    DelayTime := 150;                                         {Mod. #3}
    LineCount := 0;
    KeyTxt(TextArray, LineCount);
    writeln;
    writeln('Press a key to start the news wire.');
    writeln('Once it begins, you can press any key to stop it.');
    waitkey;
    textmode(bw40);                                          {Mod. #4}
    textbox(LeftX - 1, Y - 1, RightX + 1, Y + 1);
    repeat
        for J := 1 to LineCount do
            for K := 1 to length(TextArray[J]) do
                begin
                    CursorOn(false);
                    gotoxy(RightX, Y);
                    write(TextArray[J][K]);
                    delay(DelayTime);
                    scroll(LeftX, Y, RightX, Y, 0);
                    if KeyHit(Reply, Reply2) then
                        begin
                            textmode(bw80);
                            CursorOn(true);
                            halt
                        end
                end
    until false
END.
```

Variables

TextSize	The maximum number of input lines that define your message. Each line can be up to 80 characters long.
TextArray	The string array that holds your message. It has TextSize number of elements, with each element containing up to 80 characters.
J, K	Loop indices
LineCount	The number of lines of text entered into TextArray
LeftX	The leftmost X (horizontal) position (in text-character units) of the scrolling window
RightX	The rightmost X (horizontal) position (in text-character units) of the scrolling window
Y	The Y (vertical) position (in text-character units) of the scrolling window
DelayTime	The wait time, in milliseconds, between each (one character) scroll of the message. DelayTime defines the speed of the scrolling.
Reply, Reply2	Keyboard characters detected by KeyHit

Discussion

If you have a business with customer foot traffic, consider using NewsWire to attract attention. You can use the program in a display window or inside the store to announce sale prices and upcoming events, or just to wax poetic. People are always attracted to movement.

Modifications

1. TextSize is the maximum number of elements allowed in TextArray. The number is currently set to 100. If you need more space for your message, make TextSize a larger integer by changing the line denoted by {Mod. #1}.

2. The size and location of the scrolling window (and box frame) are controlled by the variables LeftX, RightX, and Y in the three lines denoted by {Mod. #2}. Make the window smaller by bringing the values of LeftX and RightX closer together. Move the window up or down by changing the value of Y.

3. The speed of the scrolling is set by DelayTime. Raise its value to slow the scrolling speed, or lower its value to increase the speed.

4. You can try other text modes by changing the line denoted by {Mod. #4}. Try textmode(c40) to use color. Add a textcolor and/or textbackground statement to set any color(s) you choose. In addition, you can try textmode(bw80) with {Mod. #2} in order to create a larger (in terms of number of characters) scrolling window. And you can place a constant message or title on your screen to accompany the moving message. For example, you might add the following code right after the textcolor statement:

```
gotoxy(10, 3);
writeln('MY MESSAGE FOR THE DAY');
```

TryCurvs

> **Purpose:** *To calculate four nonlinear curve fits of X-Y data*

Usage

TryCurvs analyzes X-Y data to see whether the curve fit of a nonlinear function fits the data better than the best linear fit. The program begins by prompting you for the data entry. Each "row number" is a pair of points, one for X and one for the corresponding Y. The X point is Entry [R, 1], and the Y point is Entry [R, 2], in which R is the row number. Type **END** (all uppercase) to indicate that the data entry is complete. You must enter at least two data pairs, and all values must be positive.

Next, you can save the data to a disk file. Before saving, however, you are asked if you would like to see the directories on either disk drive (assuming that you have a system with two floppy disks). A menu displays the various options. If you do elect to save the data, you must type the filespec you want. If you don't include a drive specification, the default drive is used.

Last, the curve fits are displayed. Four nonlinear forms are compared to the linear (straight line) curve fit. A correlation value for each curve fit enables you to see which one works best.

Sample Output

Suppose that a technician runs a series of lab experiments. Each one results in rapidly rising X-Y data. She uses TryCurvs to find the best functional fit because she wants to approximate the data with a mathematical formula. Previously, she has run three experiments and saved the data in a file named EXPTn.DTA, in which n is one of the three experiment numbers. Figures 18.3 through 18.5 show how she applies TryCurvs to her fourth experiment.

```
TryCurvs - Fit nonlinear functions to X-Y data

Type END (all caps) when all data is input.
The data must now be input.
--Row number 1--
    Entry [1,1]: 1.3
    Entry [1,2]: 0.26
--Row number 2--
    Entry [2,1]: 1.9
    Entry [2,2]: 0.45
--Row number 3--
    Entry [3,1]: 2.3
    Entry [3,2]: 0.81
--Row number 4--
    Entry [4,1]: 2.8
    Entry [4,2]: 1.51
--Row number 5--
    Entry [5,1]: 3.6
    Entry [5,2]: 3.92
--Row number 6--
    Entry [6,1]: 4.1
    Entry [6,2]: 8.03
--Row number 7--
    Entry [7,1]: END
```

Fig. 18.3. *The data entry is complete.*

```
--Row number 6--
    Entry [6,1]: 4.1
    Entry [6,2]: 8.03
--Row number 7--
    Entry [7,1]: END
** 6 rows entered. **
** Data entry complete **

You can save the data on disk.  Choose an option.

  1 - I don't want to save the data on disk.
  2 - Show me the directory (A:*.*) first.
  3 - Show me the directory (B:*.*) first.
  4 - I do want to save the data on disk but don't
      need to see a directory.

Enter reply from 1 to 4.
3

** Directory listing for B:*.*
EXPT1.DTA          EXPT2.DTA          EXPT3.DTA
** End of directory listing. **
** Enter filespec for output file, or **
** press [Enter] key to cancel.        **
expt4.dta
```

Fig. 18.4. *A file name is chosen for the data storage.*

```
expt4.dta
** 6 sets of 2 element(s) written to file expt4.dta **

Linear          Y = a + (b X)          Correlation = 0.9042670
a = -4.4297590361E+00
b =  2.5974096385E+00

Logarithmic     Y = a (X ** b)         Correlation = 0.9412909
a =  8.3676543959E-02
b =  3.0025391560E+00

Semilog         Y = (a) exp(b X)       Correlation = 0.9973810
a =  4.7426052954E-02
b =  1.2372865514E+00

Hyperbolic      Y = X / (a + b X)      Correlation is negative
a =  7.3332741787E+00
b = -1.7981330154E+00

Reciprocal      Y = 1 / (a + b X)      Correlation is negative
a =  4.7199116637E+00
b = -1.2484149572E+00
```

Fig. 18.5. *The curve fits are calculated and displayed.*

As you can see, the semilog fit is best because it has the highest correlation number. The semilog fit is a substantial improvement over the simple linear fit.

Program Listing of TryCurvs.PGM

```pascal
program TryCurvs;   {Nonlinear curve fits to X-Y data}

const
   MaxNumPairs = 250;                              {Mod. #1}
   RowSize     = MaxNumPairs;
   ArraySize   = MaxNumPairs;
   ColSize     = 2;

type
   Array2Type = array[1..RowSize, 1..ColSize] of real;
   ArrayType  = array[1..ArraySize] of real;
   String80   = string[80];
```

```pascal
var
   DataArray, ConvertedArray      : Array2Type;
   XArray, YArray, YfromX         : ArrayType;
   NumDataPairs, Code, J          : integer;
   A, B, Variance, Temp, YStanDev : real;
   MinX, MinY, Unused             : real;
   Reply                          : char;

{$I GetReply.PSL}
{$I Key2Arr.PSL}
{$I LinReg.PSL}
{$I Power.PSL}
{$I Save2Arr.PSL}
{$I ShowDir.PSL}
{$I Stats.PSL}

procedure ShowResults;

var
   J   : integer;
   Sum : real;

begin
   Sum := 0.0;
   for J := 1 to NumDataPairs do
      Sum := Sum + sqr(YArray[J] - YfromX[J]);
   if YStanDev = 0.0 then
      Variance := 1.0
   else
      Variance := 1.0 - Sum / (NumDataPairs - 1) / sqr(YStanDev);
   if Variance < 0.0 then
      writeln('Correlation is negative' )
   else
      writeln('Correlation =', sqrt(Variance):10:7);
   writeln('a =', A);
   writeln('b =', B);
   writeln
end;
```

```
BEGIN
  clrscr;
  writeln('TryCurvs - Fit nonlinear functions to X-Y data');
  writeln;
  writeln('Type END (all caps) when all data is input.');
  writeln('The data must now be input.');
  NumDataPairs := 0;
  Key2Arr(DataArray, NumDataPairs);
  writeln;
  if NumDataPairs < 2 then
    begin
      writeln(chr(7));
      writeln('At least 2 data pairs are required.');
      exit
    end;
  writeln('You can save the data on disk.  Choose an option.');
  writeln;
  writeln(' 1 - I don''t want to save the data on disk.');
  writeln(' 2 - Show me the directory (A:*.*) first.');
  writeln(' 3 - Show me the directory (B:*.*) first.');
  writeln(' 4 - I do want to save the data on disk but don''t');
  writeln('       need to see a directory.');
  writeln;
  GetReply('1', '4', Reply);
  writeln(Reply);
  writeln;
  case Reply of
    '2' : ShowDir('A:*.*', $10);
    '3' : ShowDir('B:*.*', $10)
  end;
  if Reply <> '1' then
    Save2Arr(DataArray, NumDataPairs, Code);
  if Code > 0 then
    writeln('Unsuccessful file save');
  for J := 1 to NumDataPairs do
    begin
      XArray[J] := DataArray[J,1];
      YArray[J] := DataArray[J,2]
    end;
```

```
Stats(XArray, NumDataPairs, Unused, Unused,
                            Unused, MinX, Unused);
Stats(YArray, NumDataPairs, Unused, Unused,
                            YStanDev, MinY, Unused);
writeln;
if (MinX <= 0.0) or (MinY <= 0.0) then
   begin
      writeln(chr(7));
      writeln('Cannot fit your data because it contains');
      writeln(' some value(s) less than or equal to zero.');
      exit
   end;
write('Linear          Y = a + (b X)         ');
for J := 1 to NumDataPairs do
   begin
      ConvertedArray[J, 1] := XArray[J];
      ConvertedArray[J, 2] := YArray[J]
   end;
LinReg(ConvertedArray, NumDataPairs, A, B, Unused);
for J := 1 to NumDataPairs do
   YfromX[J] := A + B * XArray[J];
ShowResults;
write('Logarithmic    Y = a (X ** b)        ');
for J := 1 to NumDataPairs do
   begin
      ConvertedArray[J, 1] := ln(XArray[J]);
      ConvertedArray[J, 2] := ln(YArray[J])
   end;
LinReg(ConvertedArray, NumDataPairs, Temp, B, Unused);
A := exp(Temp);
for J := 1 to NumDataPairs do
   YfromX[J] := A * Power(XArray[J], B);
ShowResults;
write('Semilog         Y = (a) exp(b X)     ');
for J := 1 to NumDataPairs do
   begin
      ConvertedArray[J, 1] := XArray[J];
      ConvertedArray[J, 2] := ln(YArray[J])
   end;
```

```
       LinReg(ConvertedArray, NumDataPairs, Temp, B, Unused);
       A := exp(Temp);
       for J := 1 to NumDataPairs do
           YfromX[J] := A * exp(B * XArray[J]);
       ShowResults;
       write('Hyperbolic      Y = X / (a + b X)    ');
       for J := 1 to NumDataPairs do
           begin
               ConvertedArray[J, 1] := 1.0 / XArray[J];
               ConvertedArray[J, 2] := 1.0 / YArray[J]
           end;
       LinReg(ConvertedArray, NumDataPairs, B, A, Unused);
       for J := 1 to NumDataPairs do
           YfromX[J] := XArray[J] / (A + B * XArray[J]);
       ShowResults;
       write('Reciprocal      Y = 1 / (a + b X)    ');
       for J := 1 to NumDataPairs do
           begin
               ConvertedArray[J, 1] := XArray[J];
               ConvertedArray[J, 2] := 1.0 / YArray[J]
           end;
       LinReg(ConvertedArray, NumDataPairs, A, B, Unused);
       for J := 1 to NumDataPairs do
           YfromX[J] := 1.0 / (A + B * XArray[J]);
       ShowResults
END.
```

Variables

DataArray	Two-dimensional array of the input data. The first subscript references the data-pair number. The second subscript references an X value when the subscript is 1, or a Y value when it is 2.
ConvertedArray	Array with the same specifications as DataArray. Here either the X data or the Y data (or both) has been transformed, depending on the functional form being fit.
XArray	One-dimensional array of the X values
YArray	One-dimensional array of the Y values
YfromX	One-dimensional array of Y values calculated from X values, using one of the functional fits

NumDataPairs	Number of data pairs input
Code	Parameter from Save2Arr, indicating whether a file save was successful
J	Looping index
A, B	Solutions to the various curve fits
Variance	Variance of the errors in each data point
Temp	Temporary variable
YStanDev	Standard deviation of the input Y values
MinX	Minimum X value input (must be greater than 0)
MinY	Minimum Y value input (must be greater than 0)
Unused	Placeholder for an unneeded procedure parameter
Reply	Continuation option selected from a menu

Discussion

TryCurvs compares four different nonlinear curve fits to the best linear fit. The four nonlinear curve types are logarithmic, semilog, hyperbolic, and reciprocal. All these types have two parameters (A and B) and thus require at least two points in order to produce a curve fit. If your data has an exponential type rise or an asymptotic decay, one of these four curve fits will probably be a substantial improvement over the linear fit.

The program uses a least-squares technique to fit the data. A functional transformation (logarithmic, exponential, inverse, etc.) is made to the X data or the Y data (or both) as appropriate. (Look for the ConvertedArray assignments in the code.) Then LinReg is called for the functional fits. A reverse transformation provides A and B, the two output constants for each fit.

For each fit, the embedded function ShowResults computes the correlation. This provides a quantitative measure of the quality of the fit. ShowResults compares the differences between the actual Y values and the Y values that the particular curve fit produces for the corresponding X values. A perfect fit has a correlation of 1. The smaller the correlation, the worse the fit. A negative value means that the correlation is poor although the values of A and B are still displayed for these cases. It is not unusual to get negative correlations for the hyperbolic and reciprocal fits if the Y data increases with increasing X data.

For simplicity, because of possible division by zero, all input data must be positive. This applies to both X data and Y data. In addition, at least two data pairs must be provided.

Modification

The maximum allowable number of data pairs is currently set to 250 in the constant MaxNumPairs. Raise this number if you have more data.

PolyFit

Purpose: *To calculate polynomial curve fits of X-Y data*

Usage

The degree of the polynomial curve fit is under your control. PolyFit can be used as a powerful forecasting tool. (See the Discussion section.)

The input data (X-Y values) is read from a disk file you must have available. You can create this file with the TryCurvs program. PolyFit requires that all values of X be positive. If some are not, the results are meaningless.

The program begins by requesting the filespec of your data file. After the file is read, you select the degree of the polynomial that is used to fit your data. This degree is an integer from 0 to 1 less than the number of data pairs you have. PolyFit prompts you by showing the allowable range. At this point, you can type **Q** (uppercase) to quit the program.

The polynomial coefficients are now calculated and displayed. In addition, the correlation coefficient is given, which provides a quantitative measure of the accuracy of the fit.

Now you can request that values of Y be calculated for any positive X, using the functional fit just found. This step allows interpolation and extrapolation of your data. To leave this mode, simply type **E** (uppercase) instead of an X value. Finally, you can request a different degree fit to your data.

Sample Output

For TryCurvs, you considered a technician who ran lab experiments. She created a disk file of X-Y data named EXPT4.DTA. TryCurvs found that the best nonlinear curve fit for her data was a semilog fit. This fit had a correlation of 0.99738+ compared to the linear fit with a correlation of 0.90426+.

The technician now uses PolyFit to find a better polynomial fit. In addition, she wants to calculate what values Y would have for X values of 3.0 and 4.5. Figures 18.6 and 18.7 show the results.

```
PolyFit - Polynomial curve fitter

The input data must now be read from a disk file.
** Enter filespec of input file, or **
** press [Enter] key to cancel.      **
EXPT4.DTA
** 6 sets of 2 element(s) now in array. **


Degree to fit (0-5) or Q to Quit the program
Entry? 2

X Power            Coefficient
   0             4.8037107970E+00
   1            -5.1249181340E+00
   2             1.4140337212E+00

Correlation =  9.8846296380E-01

X value to evaluate or E to End evaluations
Entry? E

Degree to fit (0-5) or Q to Quit the program
Entry? 3
```

Fig. 18.6. *A second degree fit is calculated.*

```
Entry? 3

X Power            Coefficient
   0            -5.5114531475E+00
   1             8.6479143756E+00
   2            -4.1832187075E+00
   .3            7.0117687070E-01

Correlation =  9.9860794848E-01

X value to evaluate or E to End evaluations
Entry? 3.0
Y =  1.7150971208E+00

X value to evaluate or E to End evaluations
Entry? 4.5
Y =  1.2588725058E+01

X value to evaluate or E to End evaluations
Entry? E

Degree to fit (0-5) or Q to Quit the program
Entry? Q

>
```

Fig. 18.7. *A third degree fit is calculated and evaluated.*

The third degree fit has a correlation of 0.99860+, and that fit is therefore the lowest degree polynomial that improves on the semilog fit found by *TryCurvs*.

Program Listing of PolyFit.PGM

```
program PolyFit;   {Polynomial Curve Fitter}

const
  RowSize   = 250;                                    {Mod. #1}
  ColSize   = 2;
  MaxDegree = 7;                                      {Mod. #2}

type
  Array2Type    = array[1..RowSize, 1..ColSize] of real;
  ArrayType     = array[1..RowSize] of real;
  CoeffArrayType = array[0..30] of real;

var
  DataArray                 : Array2Type;
  XArray, YArray            : ArrayType;
  PowerArray, RHS, Coeffs   : CoeffArrayType;
  Factors                   : array[1..15, 1..15] of real;
  NumDataPairs, Degree, TwoDegree, NumEqns, Code : integer;
  J, K, L, M, Last                               : integer;
  CharFlag                                       : char;
  TimeToQuit, NoMoreToDo                         : boolean;
  Work, Numer, Denom, Correlation, MeanY, X, Y   : real;

{$I GetNumI.PSL}
{$I GetNumR.PSL}
{$I Load2Arr.PSL}
{$I Power.PSL}
{$I Stats.PSL}


procedure Interpolate;
```

```
begin
   NoMoreToDo := false;
   repeat;
      writeln;
      writeln('X value to evaluate or E to End evaluations');
      GetNumR(X, CharFlag, Code);
      case Code of
         -1: if CharFlag = 'E' then
                NoMoreToDo := true;
          0: begin
                Y := 0.0;
                for K := 1 to NumEqns do
                   Y := Y + Coeffs[K] * Power(X, K - 1);
                writeln('Y =', Y)
             end
      end
   until
      NoMoreToDo
end;

procedure SolveEqns;

begin
   TwoDegree := Degree * 2;
   NumEqns   := Degree + 1;
   for J := 0 to TwoDegree do
      begin
         PowerArray[J] := 0.0;
         for K := 1 to NumDataPairs do
            PowerArray[J] := PowerArray[J] + Power(XArray[K], J)
      end;
   for J := 1 to NumEqns do
      begin
         RHS[J] := 0.0;
         for K := 1 to NumDataPairs do
            RHS[J] := RHS[J] + YArray[K] *
                                 Power(XArray[K], J - 1)
      end;
   for J := 1 to NumEqns do
      for K := 1 to NumEqns do
         Factors[J,K] := PowerArray[J + K - 2];
   for K := 1 to Degree do
```

```
    begin
       M := K + 1;
       L := K;
       repeat
          if abs(Factors[M, K]) > abs(Factors[L, K]) then
             L := M;
          M := M + 1
       until
          M > NumEqns;
       for J := K to NumEqns do
          begin
             Work          := Factors[K, J];
             Factors[K, J] := Factors[L, J];
             Factors[L, J] := Work;
          end;
       Work := RHS[K];   RHS[K] := RHS[L];   RHS[L] := Work;
       M := K + 1;
       repeat
          Work          := Factors[M, K] / Factors[K, K];
          Factors[M, K] := 0.0;
          for J := K + 1 to NumEqns do
             Factors[M, J] := Factors[M, J] -
                             Work * Factors[K, J];
          RHS[M] := RHS[M] - Work * RHS[K];
          M       := M + 1
       until
          M > NumEqns
    end;
Coeffs[NumEqns] := RHS[NumEqns] / Factors[NumEqns, NumEqns];
for M := Degree downto 1 do
    begin
       Work := 0.0;
       for J := M + 1 to NumEqns do
          begin
             Work       := Work + Factors[M, J] * Coeffs[J];
             Coeffs[M] := (RHS[M] - Work) / Factors[M, M]
          end
    end;
```

```
    writeln;
    writeln('X Power', 'Coefficient':22);
    for J := 1 to NumEqns do
        writeln(J - 1:3, Coeffs[J]:28);
    Numer := 0.0;
    Denom := 0.0;
    for J := 1 to NumDataPairs do
        begin
            Work := 0.0;
            for K := 1 to NumEqns do
                Work := Work + Coeffs[K] * Power(XArray[J], K - 1);
            Numer := Numer + sqr(YArray[J] - Work);
            Denom := Denom + sqr(YArray[J] - MeanY)
        end;
    if Denom = 0.0 then
        Correlation := 1.0
    else
        Correlation := sqrt(1.0 - Numer / Denom);
    writeln;
    writeln('Correlation =', Correlation)
end;

BEGIN
    clrscr;
    writeln('PolyFit - Polynomial curve fitter');
    writeln;
    writeln('The input data must now be read from a disk file.');
    NumDataPairs := 0;
    Load2Arr(DataArray, NumDataPairs, Code);
    writeln;
    if Code <> 0 then
        begin
            writeln('File was not read successfully.');
            exit
        end;
    for J := 1 to NumDataPairs do
        begin
            XArray[J] := DataArray[J, 1];
            YArray[J] := DataArray[J, 2]
        end;
```

```
    Stats(YArray, NumDataPairs, MeanY, Work, Work, Work, Work);
    Last := NumDataPairs - 1;
    if Last > MaxDegree then
       Last := MaxDegree;
    TimeToQuit := false;
    repeat
       writeln;
       writeln('Degree to fit (0-', Last,
                      ') or Q to Quit the program');
       GetNumI(Degree, CharFlag, Code);
       case Code of
          -1: if CharFlag = 'Q' then
                 TimeToQuit := true;
           0: if (Degree >= 0) and (Degree <= Last) then
                 begin
                    SolveEqns;
                    Interpolate
                 end
       end
    until
       TimeToQuit
END.
```

Variables

DataArray	Two-dimensional array of the input data. The first subscript references the data-pair number. The second subscript references an X value when the subscript is 1, or a Y value when it is 2.
XArray	Array of the X data from DataArray
YArray	Array of the Y data from DataArray
PowerArray	Array of various powers of X
RHS	Array of the right-hand sides of the equations
Coeffs	Array of the solutions to the equations. These solutions are the coefficients of the various X powers.
Factors	Two-dimensional array of the factors needed to solve the equations for Coeffs
NumDataPairs	Number of data pairs

Degree	Degree of the polynomial to be fitted
TwoDegree	Twice Degree
NumEqns	Number of equations to solve (Degree + 1)
Code	Parameter from Load2Arr, indicating whether a file was read successfully
J, K, L, M	Looping variables and array subscripts
Last	Highest degree that can be fit
CharFlag	Character read in from keyboard
TimeToQuit	boolean flag set to true when program is finished
NoMoreToDo	boolean flag set to true when no more X values are to be evaluated for the current polynomial
Work	Dummy variable and placeholder in call to Stats
Numer	Numerator used in calculation of correlation
Denom	Denominator used in calculation of correlation
Correlation	Coefficient indicating the goodness of fit
MeanY	Mean value of the Y data
X	Value of X for which to evaluate the current polynomial
Y	Value of Y for a given X

Discussion

Both TryCurvs and PolyFit provide analytic functions to fit a set of X-Y data. In TryCurvs, various nonlinear functions are tried; here polynomials of arbitrary degree are computed. PolyFit fits a curve of the following form to your data:

$$Y = C_0 + C_1 X^1 + C_2 X^2 + \ldots + C_D X^D$$

The maximum value allowed for D is seven (or one less than NumDataPairs if you have fewer than eight data pairs). The values of C are the constant coefficients calculated by PolyFit. A correlation value is also displayed. This correlation is analogous to the correlations calculated by TryCurvs. Thus, the correlations from the two programs can be directly compared for the goodness of fit.

There are many reasons why you might want an analytic function to represent your X-Y data. Such a function can smooth out the fluctuations in Y found in most physical experiments. Using an analytic function also is a convenient way to represent your data in a computer program. Most important, an analytic function provides a way to compute functional values of Y for values of X not explicitly in your data. These can be values of X between known points (interpolation), or values outside known points (extrapolation). If used cautiously, such a function can become a forecasting tool. By extrapolating your known data, you can make predictions of future results.

The least-squares technique is used for the curve fitting. This technique minimizes the sum of the squares of the errors at each data point. Because the Power function does not allow negative bases, all values of X in PolyFit should be positive. This applies to your input data and to values of X you want evaluated after the fit is found. Negative X values result in meaningless answers.

TryCurvs and PolyFit work nicely together. Your data file can be created with TryCurvs and later used by PolyFit. Be careful if your file contains duplicate data pairs. The degree of fit must be at least one less than the number of unique data pairs. Otherwise, division by zero is possible.

Modifications

1. The maximum allowable number of data pairs is controlled by the constant RowSize, which is currently set to 250. Raise the number if you have more data in your data file.

2. The constant MaxDegree determines the largest degree fit that PolyFit allows you to choose. You can make the degree larger than the current value of 7 if you want. However, unless your data is well behaved (X and Y values are near 1), computational accuracy degrades quickly for fits higher than the seventh degree. PolyFit is dimensioned adequately to accept MaxDegree up to 14, but a practical limit for MaxDegree is 7.

SortDir

> **Purpose:** *To display a sorted listing of a disk directory*

Usage

This program displays in alphabetical order the file names in a root directory or subdirectory. When prompted, you simply provide the disk drive and path you want. The output format of SortDir is similar to the output format of the DOS DIR command, but this program displays a bit more. In addition to the file name, size, and date and time of the last update, SortDir displays the file attributes and the day of the week of the last update. In addition, the time of the last update is shown to the second, not just to the minute. Unlike DIR, this program shows hidden files also.

Sample Output

Figure 18.8 shows the output produced by SortDir if a test disk is in drive B. Note that all the files, except the subdirectory, have the archive attribute set (A at the far right). Note also that the two DOS files with names starting with IBM (these files are from DOS V2.0, by the way) are marked as hidden, read-only, and system files.

```
Enter drive and path for sorted directory listing
B:
8 files found.   Sorted listing:
CHKDSK.COM          6400   83- 3- 8   Tue   12: 0: 0    A
COMMAND.COM        17664   83- 3- 8   Tue   12: 0: 0    A
DAYWEEK.PSL          887   86- 2-11   Tue   14:19:52    A
FILEINFO.PSL        1603   86- 2- 2   Sun   19:57:42    A
IBMBIO.COM          4608   83- 3- 8   Tue   12: 0: 0    A HRS
IBMDOS.COM         17152   83- 3- 8   Tue   12: 0: 0    A HRS
SORTDIR.PGM         1966   86- 2-14   Fri    4:23:12    A
[D]MONTHLY.DAT         0   86- 2-15   Sat   18:12:32    D

>
```

Fig. 18.8. *A sample session with* SortDir.

Program Listing of SortDir.PGM

```
program SortDir;    {Sorted disk directory listing}

const
   TextSize = 200;                                    {Mod. #1}

type
   String80 = string[80];
   String15 = string[15];
   String5  = string[5];
   String3  = string[3];
   LineSize = string[15];
   TextArrayType = array[1..TextSize] of LineSize;
```

```pascal
var
   FileSpec  : String80;
   Path      : String80;
   Name      : String15;
   AttrList  : String5;
   DayName   : String3;
   TextArray : TextArrayType;
   FileBytes : real;
   Code, J, K, Year                         : integer;
   Attr, Yr, Mon, Day, Hr, Min, Sec, DayNum : byte;

{$I DayWeek.PSL}
{$I FileInfo.PSL}
{$I NextFile.PSL}
{$I SortHT.PSL}
{$I Tab.PSL}

BEGIN
   Path := '';
   Attr := $16;
   Code := 0;
   J    := 0;
   writeln('Enter drive and path for sorted directory listing');
   readln(Path);
   FileSpec := Path + '*.*';
   repeat
      NextFile(FileSpec, Attr, Code, Name);
      if Code = 1 then
         begin
            J := J + 1;
            TextArray[J] := Name
         end
   until
      Code <> 1;
   write(J, ' files found.');
   if J > 0 then write('  Sorted listing:');
   writeln;
   SortHT(TextArray, J, 1, 15);
   for K := 1 to J do
```

```
    begin
       FileSpec := TextArray[K];
       if FileSpec[1] = '[' then
          FileSpec := copy(FileSpec, 4, 12);
       FileSpec := Path + FileSpec;
       FileInfo(FileSpec, FileBytes, Yr, Mon, Day, Hr, Min,
                Sec, AttrList);
       Year := Yr;
       DayWeek(Year, Mon, Day, DayNum, DayName);
       write(TextArray[K], Tab(16), FileBytes:8:0, Tab(26));
       if FileBytes < 0.0 then
          writeln('** File not found **')
       else
          begin
             write(Yr, '-', Mon:2, '-', Day:2, Tab(36));
             write(DayName, Tab(41), Hr:2, ':', Min:2, ':');
             writeln(Sec:2, Tab(52), AttrList)
          end
    end
END.
```

Variables

FileSpec	The file specification, used for retrieving the file names at the beginning of the program, and the FileInfo data at the end
Path	The drive and path entered from the keyboard
Name	The file name found by NextFile
AttrList	The list of attributes found by FileInfo
DayName	The weekday name found by DayWeek
TextArray	Array of file names, sorted by SortHT
FileBytes	The size of a file in bytes
Code	Condition code returned from NextFile
J	Subscript of file names as found; counter of number of files found
K	Subscript of sorted file names as displayed
Year	Year of a file's last update (integer form)

Attr	Attribute byte NextFile uses when searching the directory
Yr	Year of a file's last update (byte form)
Mon	Month of a file's last update
Day	Day of a file's last update
Hr	Hour of a file's last update
Min	Minute of a file's last update
Sec	Second of a file's last update
DayNum	Day number of the weekday that a file was last updated

Discussion

This program uses NextFile to retrieve all the file names in the specified directory, then SortHT to sort the names into alphabetical order, and finally FileInfo and DayWeek to retrieve information about each file name. SortDir does not pause after the screen fills with file names, although you could easily modify the program for pausing. Instead, you can simply press Ctrl-S to make the displaying pause and then continue.

Modification

To allow for more file names, change 200 in the line indicated by {Mod. #1}. For the root directory of a floppy disk, 200 is plenty. For subdirectories (especially for fixed disks), you may need to allow for more file names.

SortText

> **Purpose:** *To sort text data from a disk file, creating a new disk file*

Usage

Many word-processing programs have no sorting capability, yet you may occasionally need to alphabetize text data. This program enables you to sort a text file. The sort key can be located anywhere within the text line, as long as the key is in the same location (column) in each line. For example, suppose that you have a list of names and addresses for which each entry (name and address combination) occupies one line. The last name starts in the first position of each line and occupies the first 14 characters. Following the last name is the first name, which is no more than 12 characters. In this case, the sort key you want begins in position 1 and is 26 characters long.

SortText asks you for the location and length of the sort key (that is, the portion of each text line which is the basis for alphabetizing the data). The program then displays the disk directory that is currently active and asks you to enter a filespec (disk drive, path, and filename; only filename is required) to indicate the file you want sorted. The program reads the input file into memory, sorts the file, and asks you for a filespec for the output file. After writing the output file to disk, the program displays a message showing that the file is successfully saved. Then the program ends.

Sample Output

Figures 18.9 and 18.10 show a typical run of SortText in which a small test file is sorted.

```
**** SortText Program ****

Maximum text lines that can be sorted = 500
Maximum length of each text line = 80

For the sort key:

Enter the position number it starts in.
Entry? 1

Enter the sort key length.
Entry? 26


Files in current active directory are
** Directory listing for *.*
COMMAND.COM      INDEX.DAT         SORTTEXT.PGM
** End of directory listing. **

** Enter filespec of input text file, or **
** press [Enter] key to cancel.          **
```

Fig. 18.9. *The filespec must now be input.*

```
Enter the sort key length.
Entry? 26


Files in current active directory are
** Directory listing for *.*
COMMAND.COM       INDEX.DAT        SORTTEXT.PGM
** End of directory listing. **

** Enter filespec of input text file, or **
** press [Enter] key to cancel.          **
INDEX.DAT
** 5 lines now in text array. **

5 lines of text sorted

** Enter filespec for text output file, or **
** press [Enter] key to cancel.           **
INDEX.SRT
5 text lines written to file INDEX.SRT

Sorted file successfully saved


>
```

Fig. 18.10. SortText *creates the sorted text file.*

Program Listing of SortText.PGM

```pascal
program SortText;  {Load text file, sort, save on disk.}

const
   TextSize   = 500;                              {Mod. #1}
   LineLength = 80;                               {Mod. #1}

type
   LineSize = string[LineLength];
   String80 = string[80];
   TextArrayType = array[1..TextSize] of LineSize;

var
   TextArray                        : TextArrayType;
   LineCount, Code, Position, Width : integer;
   CharEntry                        : char;
   FileSpec                         : String80;
```

```
{$I GetNumI.PSL}
{$I LoadTxt.PSL}
{$I SaveTxt.PSL}
{$I ShowDir.PSL}
{$I SortHT.PSL}

BEGIN
  clrscr;
  writeln('**** SortText Program ****');
  writeln;
  writeln('Maximum text lines that can be sorted = ', TextSize);
  writeln('Maximum length of each text line = ', LineLength);
  writeln;
  writeln('For the sort key:');
  writeln;
  repeat
     writeln('Enter the position number it starts in.');
     GetNumI(Position, CharEntry, Code);
     if (Position < 1) or (Position > 255) then
        Code := -3;
     if Code <> 0 then writeln(#7, '** Illegal entry **')
  until Code = 0;
  writeln;
  repeat
     writeln('Enter the sort key length.');
     GetNumI(Width, CharEntry, Code);
     if (Width < 1) or (Width > 255) then
        Code := -4;
     if Code <> 0 then writeln(#7, '** Illegal entry **')
  until Code = 0;
  writeln;
  writeln;
  FileSpec := '*.*';                                      {Mod. #2}
  writeln('Files in current active directory are');       {Mod. #2}
  ShowDir(FileSpec, 0);
  writeln;
  LineCount := 0;
  LoadTxt(TextArray, LineCount, Code);
  if Code <> 0 then
     begin
        writeln('** Program aborted **');
        halt
     end;
```

```
    SortHT(TextArray, LineCount, Position, Width);
    writeln;
    writeln(LineCount, ' lines of text sorted');
    writeln;
    SaveTxt(TextArray, LineCount, Code);
    writeln;
    if Code <> 0 then
       writeln('Unsuccessful file save.')
    else
       writeln('Sorted file successfully saved');
    writeln
END.
```

Variables

TextArray	string array that holds the data read from the input file and in which the data is sorted
LineCount	Number of text lines read from the input file
Code	Error code used by several subprograms
Position	Starting position of the sort key
Width	Size of the sort key
CharEntry	Possible single-character entry returned from GetNumI subprogram. CharEntry is not used.
FileSpec	The file specification ShowDir uses to display the directory contents

Discussion

The logic of SortText is straightforward. The program's "backbone" consists of LoadTxt, which loads the file into an array; SortHT, which sorts the array; and SaveTxt, which saves the sorted array back to disk. Other parts of the program exist only for communicating through the screen to obtain necessary information (the sort-key specifications) and to display status messages (number of lines sorted, error messages, etc.).

Modifications

1. Change the two numbers in the lines indicated by {Mod. #1} to fit the text data you are working with. TextSize is the maximum number of text lines, and LineLength is the maximum length of each line. Because

Turbo limits the size of your data area to no more than 64K, you cannot make these numbers excessively large. As shown here, the text array takes up 500 times 81, or 40,500 bytes.

2. As written, this program displays the active directory before asking for an input file name. You can change this directory by altering the two indicated lines. For example, to display the root directory of disk drive B, change the first line to

```
FileSpec := 'B:*.*';
```

Another possibility is to replace both indicated lines with a brief dialogue, asking at run-time which directory should be displayed.

SimulEqn

> **Purpose:** *To solve a set of simultaneous linear equations*

Usage

The need to solve simultaneous equations arises regularly in scientific and numerical work. Algebra students encounter such equations regularly. Many "word" problems can be solved by constructing the correct set of simultaneous equations.

The program is set to solve three equations in three unknowns. You can easily change this number (3) by redefining the values of two constants in the const block. (See the Modification section.)

First, the program prompts you for the data entry. For each equation, you must provide the coefficients of each unknown and the right-hand side. When you complete the data entry, a prompting message tells you to press a key to continue. The screen then clears, and the program reformats the data and displays it for your review.

You now have three continuation options: (1) proceed (the data is OK), (2) reenter the data (the data is entered incorrectly), and (3) abort (an error in problem formulation exists). If you proceed, SimulEqn calculates and displays the solution.

Sample Output

Consider the following set of three equations with the unknowns X, Y, and Z:

```
1.5 X -  2.0 Y -  6.2 Z =  3.7
0.5 X +  2.5 Y          = -2.4
2.1 X +  1.4 Y -  1.5 Z =  4.8
```

Figures 18.11 through 18.13 show SimulEqn being used to solve this problem for X, Y, and Z.

```
SIMULEQN - A simultaneous linear equation solver

The program is currently set to do 3 equations in 3 unknowns.

The data must now be input.  You will be prompted
for the coefficients and right-hand side of each
equation (or row) one at a time.   The notation
Entry [A,B] means coefficient B of equation A.
When B = 4, provide the right-hand side.

--Row number 1--
   Entry [1,1]:
```

Fig. 18.11. *The data entry is ready to begin.*

```
When B = 4, provide the right-hand side.

--Row number 1--
   Entry [1,1]:  1.5
   Entry [1,2]:  -2
   Entry [1,3]:  -6.2
   Entry [1,4]:  3.7
--Row number 2--
   Entry [2,1]:  0.5
   Entry [2,2]:  2.5
   Entry [2,3]:  0
   Entry [2,4]:  -2.4
--Row number 3--
** Last row **
   Entry [3,1]:  2.1
   Entry [3,2]:  1.4
   Entry [3,3]:  -1.5
   Entry [3,4]:  4.8
** 3 rows entered. **
** Data entry complete **

You now have a chance to review the data.

** PRESS ANY KEY TO CONTINUE **
```

Fig. 18.12. *The data entry is complete.*

```
[1,1]  1.5000      [1,2] -2.0000     [1,3] -6.2000     [1,4]  3.7000
[2,1]  0.5000      [2,2]  2.5000     [2,3]  0.0000     [2,4] -2.4000
[3,1]  2.1000      [3,2]  1.4000     [3,3] -1.5000     [3,4]  4.8000
** Press a key to continue **

This is the data you entered.  Is it correct?

  1 - Yes it is; please continue.
  2 - No it's not; let me reenter it.
  3 - No it's not; please abort the program.

Enter reply from 1 to 3.
1

The solution is

Unknown 1 =   4.2000000000E+00
Unknown 2 = -1.8000000000E+00
Unknown 3 =  1.0000000000E+00

>
```

Fig. 18.13. *The solution is calculated and displayed.*

Thus, the answer to the sample problem is the following:

$$X = 4.2$$
$$Y = -1.8$$
$$Z = 1.0$$

Program Listing of SimulEqn.PGM

```
program SimulEqn;   {Simultaneous Linear Equation Solver}

const
  NumEqn      = 3;                                    {Mod. #1}
  NumEqnPlus1 = 4;                                    {Mod. #1}

  { The above constants must be set correctly by you.
      NumEqn      = The number of equations to be solved.
      NumEqnPlus1 = NumEqn + 1.   }

  ColSize    = NumEqnPlus1;
  RowSize    = NumEqn;
  MatrixSize = NumEqn;
```

```
type
    Array2Type = array[1..RowSize, 1..ColSize] of real;
    MatrixType = array[1..MatrixSize, 1..MatrixSize] of real;

var
    EqnArray                                : Array2Type;
    EqnCount, J, K                          : integer;
    OK                                      : boolean;
    Reply                                   : char;
    CoeffMatrix, RHSMatrix, InvertedMatrix  : MatrixType;
    AnswerMatrix                            : MatrixType;

{$I GetReply.PSL}
{$I Key2Arr.PSL}
{$I MatInv.PSL}
{$I MatMult.PSL}
{$I Show2Arr.PSL}
{$I WaitKey.PSL}

BEGIN
    clrscr;
    writeln('SIMULEQN - A simultaneous linear equation solver');
    writeln;
    if (NumEqnPlus1 <> NumEqn + 1) or (NumEqn < 1) then
        begin
            writeln(chr(7));
            writeln('** Bad settings in the const block **');
            exit
        end;
    writeln('The program is currently set to do', NumEqn:2,
            ' equations in', NumEqn:2, ' unknowns.');
    writeln;
    writeln('The data must now be input.  You will be prompted');
    writeln('for the coefficients and right-hand side of each');
    writeln('equation (or row) one at a time.  The notation');
    writeln('Entry [A,B] means coefficient B of equation A.');
    writeln('When B =', NumEqnPlus1:2,
            ', provide the right-hand side.');
    Reply := '0';
    repeat
```

```
      writeln;
      EqnCount := 0;
      Key2Arr(EqnArray, EqnCount);
      writeln;
      writeln('You now have a chance to review the data.');
      WaitKey;
      Show2Arr(EqnArray, EqnCount, 8, 4, 4);
      writeln;
      writeln('This is the data you entered.  Is it correct?');
      writeln;
      writeln('  1 - Yes it is; please continue.');
      writeln('  2 - No it''s not; let me reenter it.');
      writeln('  3 - No it''s not; please abort the program.');
      writeln;
      GetReply('1', '3', Reply);
      writeln(Reply)
   until
      Reply <> '2';
   if Reply = '3' then
      exit;
   writeln;
   for J := 1 to NumEqn do
      for K := 1 to NumEqn do
         CoeffMatrix[J,K] := EqnArray[J,K];
   for J := 1 to NumEqn do
      RHSMatrix[J,1] := EqnArray[J,NumEqnPlus1];
   for J := 1 to NumEqn do
      for K := 2 to NumEqn do
         RHSMatrix[J,K] := 0.0;
   MatInv(CoeffMatrix, InvertedMatrix, OK);
   if not OK then
      begin
         writeln(chr(7));
         writeln('Bad input, no solution is possible.');
         exit
      end;
   MatMult(InvertedMatrix, RHSMatrix, AnswerMatrix);
   writeln('The solution is');
   writeln;
   for J := 1 to NumEqn do
      writeln('Unknown', J:2, ' =', AnswerMatrix[J,1])
END.
```

Variables

EqnArray	Array of the input data. The array is two-dimensional of size [NumEqn, NumEqn + 1], in which NumEqn is the number of equations. The first subscript references the equation number; the second subscript references the unknown. When the second subscript equals NumEqn + 1, the reference is to the right-hand side of the current equation.
EqnCount	The number of equations for which data was entered
J, K	Loop indices
OK	boolean flag indicating whether the solution is possible. If OK is true, a solution was found. If OK is false, no solution is possible.
Reply	Keystroke made in response to a program prompt
CoeffMatrix	Array containing the input coefficients for each equation and each unknown
RHSMatrix	Array containing the values for the right-hand side of each equation
InvertedMatrix	The inverse array of CoeffMatrix
AnswerMatrix	Array containing the solution for each unknown

Discussion

Because Turbo does not allow you to pass variable-sized arrays to procedures and functions, the size of the arrays (that is, the number of equations being solved) must be "hardwired" into the program as a global declaration. The constant NumEqn is thus set to the number of equations to be solved. For compatibility with the included subprograms Key2Arr (Chapter 2) and Show2Arr (Chapter 4), a second constant, NumEqnPlus1, is set also. It has a value of NumEqn + 1. These two constants are defined at the beginning of the const block. Make sure that they are set appropriately for your particular case.

Data input is under the control of Key2Arr. This subprogram prompts you for data for a two-dimensional array. Key2Arr displays Row number on the screen, prompting (in the general case) for array input one row at a time. For the purposes of SimulEqn, a *row* is simply an equation, and the terms *row number* and *equation number* are synonymous.

If your data is ill-conditioned, the program cannot calculate a solution. When this happens, the program beeps, and a message is displayed to indicate this error condition. The two most likely causes of this error are that all the coefficients of one equation are zero, or that one equation is an exact multiple of another.

SimulEqn solves the matrix equation (A)(X)=(B). Here, A is the square coefficient matrix. X is the column matrix of the unknowns, and B is the column matrix of the right-hand sides. The solution is given by (X)=(A inverse)(B). Thus, the solution technique is to invert CoeffMatrix and multiply it by RHSMatrix.

MatMult, which is the subprogram that does the multiplication, operates only on square matrices. Therefore, the matrix RHSMatrix is expanded from its natural column form into a full square matrix and filled with zeros in the extraneous elements. The resultant matrix, from its multiplication with (the naturally square) CoeffMatrix, is AnswerMatrix. It contains the solution for all the unknowns in its first column.

Modification

Reset NumEqn and NumEqnPlus1 when the number of equations to be solved changes. Set NumEqn to the number of equations (and thus the number of unknowns also). Set NumEqnPlus1 to one more than NumEqn.

Mortgage

> **Purpose:** *To calculate and display loan repayment schedules*

Usage

This program can help take the frustration and mystery out of many loan decisions. When you are faced with financing a house, a car, or any major purchase, many questions arise. How is your monthly payment affected by the size of your down payment? How does a 25-year loan compare with a 30-year loan? How much of your payments this year go toward tax-deductible interest? How large is your "balloon" payment if you take that second mortgage? This program shows you the answers.

First, the program prompts you for the fundamental loan specifications. These are the principal, annual interest rate (as a percentage), and length of the loan in months.

A conventional mortgage is assumed. This means that a payment is made every month, all payments (except perhaps the last) are equal, and interest is compounded with each payment. Some of these assumptions can be adjusted. See the Modifications section.

After you supply the input, the regular monthly payment is shown. You now have the option of overriding this payment and, instead, specifying a different monthly payment. Using this option results in a balloon payment (if you reduce the normal payment) or an early amortization of the loan (if you increase the normal payment). See the Discussion section.

Next, an analysis of each year of the loan is presented. For each month, you are shown the current loan balance, the contribution paid toward interest, and the contribution paid toward principal. The cumulative totals are shown also.

After a year's worth of information is displayed, you can either see the next year of information or go immediately to the final totals. A prompt asks you to press the Enter key for the next year of information, or the T (or t) key to see the totals.

The final totals include the amount of the last payment, the sum total of all payments, the total number of payments, and the ratio of the total of the payments made to the principal of the loan.

Sample Output

Suppose that you need a short-term second mortgage for $5,000. Your bank offers an 18-month loan at 14.5 percent interest. You initially can afford to pay only $250 a month in repayment. Because the normal payment is over $300 a month, the bank agrees to a balloon payment at the end. Figures 18.14 through 18.16 show the analysis of this loan.

```
Mortgage - Analysis of a loan repayment

Please enter the principal.
Entry? 5000

Please enter the annual interest rate.
Entry? 14.5

Please enter the length of the loan in months.
Entry? 18

Regular payment is      310.75
Do you want to override this (Y or N)? Y

Please enter the desired payment.
Entry? 250
```

Fig. 18.14. *The loan data is entered.*

```
Mortgage - Analysis of a loan repayment

Principal        =     5000.00
Interest rate    =       14.50
Regular payment  =      250.00
Term in months   =          18

          Remaining    ---Interest Paid---    -Amount Amortized-
Paymt.    Balance    This time    To date    This time    To date
   1      4810.42      60.42        60.42      189.58      189.58
   2      4618.55      58.13       118.55      191.87      381.45
   3      4424.36      55.81       174.36      194.19      575.64
   4      4227.82      53.46       227.82      196.54      772.18
   5      4028.91      51.09       278.91      198.91      971.09
   6      3827.59      48.68       327.59      201.32     1172.41
   7      3623.84      46.25       373.84      203.75     1376.16
   8      3417.63      43.79       417.63      206.21     1582.37
   9      3208.93      41.30       458.93      208.70     1791.07
  10      2997.70      38.77       497.70      211.23     2002.30
  11      2783.92      36.22       533.92      213.78     2216.08
  12      2567.56      33.64       567.56      216.36     2432.44

Press T for Totals or [Enter] for next screen.
```

Fig. 18.15. *The first year of the loan is analyzed.*

```
Mortgage - Analysis of a loan repayment

Principal        =     5000.00
Interest rate    =       14.50
Regular payment  =      250.00
Term in months   =          18

          Remaining    ---Interest Paid---    -Amount Amortized-
Paymt.    Balance    This time    To date    This time    To date
  13      2348.58      31.02       598.58      218.98     2651.42
  14      2126.96      28.38       626.96      221.62     2873.04
  15      1902.66      25.70       652.66      224.30     3097.34
  16      1675.65      22.99       675.65      227.01     3324.35
  17      1445.90      20.25       695.90      229.75     3554.10
  18         0.00      17.47       713.37     1445.90     5000.00

Last payment      =    1463.37
Total payments =       5713.37
Total number of payments =      18
Ratio of total payments to principal =   1.1427

>
```

Fig. 18.16. *The last six months are analyzed, and the final totals are shown.*

Program Listing of Mortgage.PGM

```
program Mortgage;   {Mortgage Analyzer}

const
   TermString  = 'months';                        {Mod. #1}
   NumPayPerYr = 12;                              {Mod. #2}

type
   KeyListType = string[4];

var
   Principal, Payment, FirstPayment, InterestRate    : real;
   Interest, Balance, IntFactor, Amortized           : real;
   TotalPayments, TotalInterest, TotalAmort          : real;
   TotalNumPay, Code, LineCount, PayNum, LinesToShow : integer;
   CharFlag, Reply, Reply2                           : char;
   WantToSeeIt                                       : boolean;

{$I GetKey.PSL}
{$I GetNumI.PSL}
{$I GetNumR.PSL}
{$I LoanPay.PSL}
{$I Tab.PSL}

procedure Header;

begin
   clrscr;
   writeln('Mortgage - Analysis of a loan repayment');
   writeln;
   writeln('Principal', Tab(17), '=', Principal:11:2);
   writeln('Interest rate', Tab(17), '=', InterestRate:11:2);
   writeln('Regular payment =', FirstPayment:11:2);
   writeln('Term in ', TermString, '  =', TotalNumPay:8);
   writeln;
   write(Tab(8), 'Remaining', Tab(20), '--Interest Paid--');
   writeln(Tab(43), '-Amount Amortized-');
   writeln('Paymt.', Tab(9), 'Balance', Tab(20), 'This time',
           Tab(32), 'To date', Tab(43), 'This time',
           Tab(54), 'To date')
end;
```

```
BEGIN
  clrscr;
  writeln('Mortgage - Analysis of a loan repayment');
  repeat
     writeln;
     writeln('Please enter the principal.');
     GetNumR(Principal, CharFlag, Code)
  until
     (Principal > 0.0) and (Code = 0);
  repeat
     writeln;
     writeln('Please enter the annual interest rate.');
     GetNumR(InterestRate, CharFlag, Code)
  until
     (Code = 0) and (InterestRate > 0.0) and
                    (InterestRate < 100.0);
  repeat
     writeln;
     write('Please enter the length of the loan in');
     writeln(Tab(40), TermString, '.');
     GetNumI(TotalNumPay, CharFlag, Code)
  until
     (Code = 0) and (TotalNumPay > 0) and (TotalNumPay < 2000);
  Payment := LoanPay(Principal, InterestRate,
                     TotalNumPay, NumPayPerYr);
  writeln;
  writeln('Regular payment is', Payment:11:2);
  write('Do you want to override this (Y or N)?', Tab(40));
  GetKey('YyNn', Reply, Reply2);
  writeln(Reply);
  if (Reply = 'Y') or (Reply = 'y') then
     begin
        repeat
           writeln;
           writeln('Please enter the desired payment.');
           GetNumR(Payment, CharFlag, Code)
        until
           (Code = 0) and (Payment > 0.0)
     end;
```

```
Payment        := int(Payment * 100.0 + 0.5) / 100.0;
FirstPayment := Payment;
Header;
Balance        := int(Principal * 100.0 + 0.5) / 100.0;
IntFactor      := InterestRate / NumPayPerYr;
TotalPayments := 0.0;
TotalInterest := 0.0;
TotalAmort     := 0.0;
WantToSeeIt    := true;
LinesToShow    := 12;                              {Mod. #3}
LineCount      := 0;
PayNum         := 0;
repeat
   PayNum    := PayNum + 1;
   Interest := int(Balance * IntFactor + 0.5) / 100.0;
   if PayNum = TotalNumPay then
      Payment := Balance + Interest;
   Amortized := Payment - Interest;
   Balance   := Balance - Amortized;
   if Balance < 0.0 then
      begin
         Payment   := Payment + Balance;
         Amortized := Amortized + Balance;
         Balance   := 0.0
      end;
   TotalPayments := TotalPayments + Payment;
   TotalInterest := TotalInterest + Interest;
   TotalAmort    := TotalAmort + Amortized;
   if WantToSeeIt then
      begin
         write(PayNum:4, Tab(7), Balance:10:2, Tab(18));
         write(Interest:10:2, Tab(29), TotalInterest:10:2);
         write(Tab(40), Amortized:10:2);
         writeln(Tab(51), TotalAmort:10:2);
         LineCount := LineCount + 1;
         if LineCount = LinesToShow then
```

```
            begin
                writeln;
                write('Press T for Totals', Tab(20));
                writeln(' or [Enter] for next screen.');
                GetKey('Tt' + chr(13), Reply, Reply2);
                if Reply in ['T', 't'] then
                    WantToSeeIt := false;
                Header;
                LineCount := 0
            end
        end
until
    (PayNum = TotalNumPay) or (Balance = 0.0);
writeln;
writeln('Last payment   =', Payment:11:2);
writeln('Total payments =', TotalPayments:11:2);
writeln('Total number of payments =', PayNum:5);
writeln('Ratio of total payments to principal =',
        TotalPayments / Principal:8:4)
END.
```

Variables

Principal	Principal of the loan
Payment	Current monthly payment
FirstPayment	Payment for the first month
InterestRate	Annual interest rate as a percentage
Interest	Interest paid in the current month
Balance	Current loan balance
IntFactor	Monthly interest rate
Amortized	Amount paid to principal in the current month
TotalPayments	Cumulative sum of the payments to date
TotalInterest	Total paid to interest to date
TotalAmort	Total paid to principal to date
TotalNumPay	Total number of payments to be made
Code	Return flag from GetNumR or GetNumI

LineCount	Number of months of information displayed to date
PayNum	Payment number
LinesToShow	Number of months of information to display on one screen
CharFlag	Character returned by GetNumR or GetNumI
Reply, Reply2	Characters returned by GetKey
WantToSeeIt	boolean flag indicating whether more output is wanted

Discussion

Unfortunately, many lending institutions differ in how they compute amortization tables, especially in calculating the monthly payment. Many institutions round the true value up, often to the next whole dollar, and sometimes even more. In Mortgage, all dollar figures are rounded (up or down) to the nearest cent.

The interest rate you provide should be the annual percentage interest, such as 12.0 or 8.75. Mortgage assumes that repayment is monthly, that all payments are equal (except the last), and that interest is compounded with each monthly payment.

Don't overlook the flexibility allowed by the option of overriding the standard monthly payment. This option accommodates the common practice of second mortgage loans to allow smaller monthly payments with a large balloon payment at the end. You can try various monthly payments to see how they affect that last big payment. And you can try making larger than normal payments to see how fast the principal is paid off.

The following restrictions apply to your input. Principal must be a positive real number. InterestRate must be a real number greater than 0 (zero) and less than 100. TotalNumPay must be a positive integer less than 2000. Payment (if you override it) must be a positive real number. Principal and Payment are rounded to the nearest penny, if necessary.

Mortgage includes the subprograms GetKey, GetNumI, and GetNumR (all in Chapter 2) for data input; Tab (Chapter 4) for output formatting, and LoanPay (Chapter 14) for calculating the standard loan payment.

Modifications

1. The string constant TermString identifies the time period between payments. The constant is set to months (TermString = 'months'), which is appropriate for most loans. Thus, the word months is displayed in the annotations. However, you can change TermString to something

else for consistency with the next modification. Change TermString by altering the constant in the line denoted by {Mod. #1}.

2. The constant NumPayPerYr identifies the number of payments to be made per year. This number is set to 12 for the usual monthly repayment. You may want to set the constant to 1 (annual payments), 4 (quarterly payments), or something else. Adjust NumPayPerYr in the line denoted by {Mod. #2}.

3. The number of payment lines to display on one screen is set in the variable LinesToShow. The number is nominally 12 to show one year's worth of data at a time. Make the variable bigger or smaller by changing its value in the line denoted by {Mod. #3}.

DoChiSq

> **Purpose:** *To generate chi-square tables*

Usage

This program provides the seldom-found capability of calculating your own tables of the chi-square distribution. Most references simply provide a (frequently sparse) table. Sometimes you need more accuracy or values not found explicitly in your reference. See the GetChiSq and ChiProb subprograms in Chapter 13 for a general explanation of the chi-square test and the terminology used here.

First, the program prompts you for the number of degrees of freedom in your problem. This number can be any positive integer. Next, you can either specify the value of chi-square and have the probability calculated, or specify the probability and have chi-square calculated. The program asks which you prefer. Type **C** to specify chi-square, or **P** to specify the probability. You can use either uppercase or lowercase.

Finally, you must give your input value for either chi-square or the probability. Chi-square values are positive real numbers. Probabilities are real numbers between 0 and 1. (See the Modifications section.) The answer is then computed and displayed.

Sample Output

Two sample runs are shown in figures 18.17 and 18.18. A value of chi-square is specified in the first, and a probability is specified in the second.

```
DoChiSq - Generate chi-square tables

Degrees of freedom?
Entry? 8

Which would you like to specify, C or P ?
    C - Chi-square
    P - Probability
Which one? C

Value for Chi-square?
Entry? 11.4
Probability =   1.8004807437E-01

>
```

Fig. 18.17. *The probability is calculated from chi-square.*

```
DoChiSq - Generate chi-square tables

Degrees of freedom?
Entry? 50

Which would you like to specify, C or P ?
    C - Chi-square
    P - Probability
Which one? P

Value for Probability?
Entry? 0.95
Chi-square =   3.4763431549E+01

>
```

Fig. 18.18. *Chi-square is calculated from the probability.*

Program Listing of DoChiSq.PGM

```
program DoChiSq;   {Calculate chi-square tables}

const
   LoProb = 0.005;                          {Mod. #1}
   HiProb = 0.995;                          {Mod. #1}
   OneThird = 0.33333333333;

type
   KeyListType = string[4];
```

```
var
    ChiSq, Probability, Unused, CumDis   : real;
    LoChiSq, HiChiSq, Numer, Term, NormX : real;
    DegFreedom, Code                     : integer;
    OK                                   : boolean;
    CharFlag, Reply, Reply2              : char;

function MyFunc(X: real): real; forward;

{$I ChiProb.PSL}
{$I GetKey.PSL}
{$I GetNumI.PSL}
{$I GetNumR.PSL}
{$I NormDis.PSL}
{$I Power.PSL}
{$I Root.PSL}

function GetProb(X: real): real;

begin
    if DegFreedom < 30 then
        GetProb := ChiProb(X, DegFreedom)
    else
        begin
            Term  := 2.0 / 9.0 / DegFreedom;
            Numer := Power(X / DegFreedom, OneThird) - 1.0 + Term;
            NormX := Numer / sqrt(Term);
            NormDis(0.0, 1.0, NormX, Unused, CumDis);
            GetProb := 1.0 - CumDis
        end
end;

function MyFunc;

begin
    MyFunc := GetProb(X) - Probability
end;
```

```
BEGIN
  clrscr;
  writeln('DoChiSq - Generate chi-square tables');
  writeln;
  repeat
     writeln('Degrees of freedom?');
     GetNumI(DegFreedom, CharFlag, Code)
  until
     (Code = 0) and (DegFreedom > 0);
  writeln;
  writeln('Which would you like to specify, C or P ?');
  writeln('   C - Chi-square');
  writeln('   P - Probability');
  write('Which one? ');
  GetKey('CcPp', Reply, Reply2);
  writeln(Reply);
  writeln;
  if (Reply = 'C') or (Reply = 'c') then
     begin
        repeat
           writeln('Value for Chi-square?');
           GetNumR(ChiSq, CharFlag, Code);
        until
           (Code = 0) and (ChiSq > 0.0);
        writeln('Probability =', GetProb(ChiSq))
     end
  else
     begin
        repeat
           writeln('Value for Probability?');
           GetNumR(Probability, CharFlag, Code);
        until
           (Code = 0) and (Probability >= LoProb) and
                          (Probability <= HiProb);
        if DegFreedom < 40 then
           if DegFreedom < 9 then
              LoChiSq := 1.0E-6                       {Mod. #2}
           else
              LoChiSq := 0.05 * Power(DegFreedom, 1.6) {Mod. #2}
```

```
      else
         LoChiSg := DegFreedom / 2.0;                  {Mod. #2}
         HiChiSg := 2.0 * DegFreedom + 7.0;            {Mod. #2}
         Root(LoChiSg, HiChiSg, ChiSg, OK);
         if OK then
            writeln('Chi-square =', ChiSg)
         else
            writeln('Can''t converge on your answer.')
      end
END.
```

Variables

LoProb	Lowest probability you are allowed to input
HiProb	Highest probability you are allowed to input
ChiSg	Value of chi-square (input or calculated)
Probability	Probability that an experiment characterized by DegFreedom will result in a chi-square higher than ChiSg. Probability must be between 0 and 1.
Unused	Placeholder for an unused parameter in the call to NormDis
CumDis	The normal cumulative distribution function as returned by NormDis
LoChiSg	A lower bound on chi-square (see Modifications)
HiChiSg	An upper bound on chi-square (see Modifications)
Numer	The numerator in the calculation of NormX
Term	Temporary term
NormX	Abscissa value of X for the call to NormDis
DegFreedom	Degrees of freedom. DegFreedom must be a positive integer.
Code	Return code from GetNumI or GetNumR
OK	Convergence indicator. If OK is true, Root successfully converged to an answer.

CharFlag	Character returned by GetNumI or GetNumR
Reply	Character returned by GetKey
Reply2	Character returned by GetKey

Discussion

The subprogram ChiProb provides the capability of calculating probabilities, given chi-square for degrees of freedom less than 30. DoChiSq extends that capability to larger degrees of freedom. In addition, you can do the reverse problem—finding chi-square given the probability.

The technique for solving the problem is interesting. (We'll have to gloss over the mathematics because of space limitations.) The embedded function GetProb calculates the probability given DegFreedom and ChiSq. This calculation is simple when DegFreedom is less than 30, because the subprogram ChiProb does the calculation directly. For a larger DegFreedom, the desired probability can be excellently approximated with a normal distribution. A transformation along the abscissa (X) of this distribution is required. This transformed X, called NormX, is a function of DegFreedom and ChiSq. (In ChiProb the variable X is chi-square and equals the value ChiSq has outside ChiProb.) When NormX has been computed, the subprogram NormDis is called to get the probability.

The inverse problem uses Root (Chapter 12) to solve for chi-square given the probability. The function MyFunc is simply GetProb minus the desired probability. Root adjusts ChiSq until MyFunc becomes zero.

For ease of reference, the included files are grouped together near the top of the listing. The Root subprogram, however, needs MyFunc defined within Root's block. Therefore, MyFunc is declared with a forward reference before the included files. The body of MyFunc comes later.

Modifications

1. LoProb and HiProb control, respectively, the lowest and highest values you are allowed to use for Probability. The current ranges should be adequate for any practical problems, but you may adjust the ranges if you want. Of course, LoProb must be greater than 0, and HiProb must be less than 1.

2. LoChiSq and HiChiSq provide bounds on the range of chi-square when Root is called. (Root is used when you specify Probability and want to calculate ChiSq.) Overflow can occur if this range in chi-square is much wider than the chi-square values that LoProb and HiProb would compute for a given DegFreedom. The lines indicated by {Mod. #2} provide

functional approximations for LoChiSq and HiChiSq. You may need to change these lines if you use modification 1. If an overflow (or "can't converge" message) occurs, adjusting these lines appropriately should cure the problem.

XYGraph

Purpose: *To draw a graph of X-Y data on the screen*

Usage

Nothing conveys bivariate numerical data more effectively than a well-posed graph. Trends, minima, and maxima are easily discerned. This program provides a full-featured graphics presentation tool.

You have control over the size of the graph, the axis labeling, and the scaling. (See the Modifications section for several ways to adjust the final appearance of your graph.) The data to be plotted must be in a disk file containing the X and Y points as paired data entries. You can use the subprogram Save2Arr (Chapter 6) to create this file.

The program begins by prompting you for the filespec of the disk file containing the X-Y data. The data is then read from disk into an array for use by XYGraph. The data pairs are sorted to ensure that the X values are in ascending order.

Now you must provide the specifications for the graph (scaling, axis labeling, etc.). First, the x-axis is considered. This is the abscissa, or horizontal axis, of the graph. The program requests the X values to use at the left and right ends of the axis. To aid you in deciding, the program displays the lowest and highest values of X occurring in your input data file. Typically, you want round numbers at the axis extrema in order to create easily readable graphs, but any real numbers are acceptable (as long as they aren't equal).

Next, you provide the number of primary tick marks to use along the axis. This number must be an integer greater than or equal to zero. One tick mark is placed at each end of the axis. The remaining tick marks, if any, are equally spaced along the axis. If you request less than two tick marks, none is displayed. Secondary tick marks are provided automatically between the primary tick marks. Last, you provide the label for the whole axis. This label should be limited to about 60 characters. If you prefer, you can simply press Enter to eliminate the label completely.

A similar dialogue then transpires for the y-axis specifications. The y-axis is the ordinate, or vertical axis, of your graph.

When prompted, you simply press any key to produce the graph on the screen. The graph is drawn in high-resolution graphics with white lines on a black background. Axis labeling and centering are done automatically. After viewing the graph, you press any key to clear the screen, return to text mode, and end the program.

Sample Output

XYGraph can be readily used to plot mathematical functions. This application is demonstrated here with a plot of the SIN function. Before this run of XYGraph, the Save2Arr subprogram was used to create a disk file called SINDEMO.DTA. This file contains pairs of X-Y data points for one full period of the SIN function. X runs from 0 to 6.28 in steps of 0.04. Y is the corresponding value of SIN(X). In figures 18.19 and 18.20, the graph specifications are provided. Figure 18.21 shows the resultant graph. (This figure was created on an EPSON printer by using Shift-PrtSc with GRAPHICS.COM to get an image of the screen.)

```
XYGraph - High-resolution graph of X-Y data

The input data must be on a data file.
** Enter filespec of input file, or **
** press [Enter] key to cancel.     **
SINDEMO.DTA
** 158 sets of 2 element(s) now in array. **
Sorting the data ...

  -- X-Axis Specifications --

Smallest X value in data file = 0.000000E+00
Largest X value in data file  = 6.280000E+00

X value at the left end of the axis?
Entry? 0.0
X value at the right end of the axis?
Entry? 7.0

Number of primary tick marks on axis?
Entry? 8

Label for x-axis?
? X (Radians)
```

Fig. 18.19. *Reading the data file and specifying the x-axis.*

```
   -- Y-Axis Specifications --

Smallest Y value in data file = -9.99971E-01
Largest Y value in data file  = 9.999417E-01

Y value at the bottom of the axis?
Entry? -1.0
Y value at the top of the axis?
Entry? 1.0

Number of primary tick marks on axis?
Entry? 5

Label for y-axis?
? SIN

Press a key to see the graph.  When finished,
press a key to clear the screen.
```

Fig. 18.20. *Specifying the y-axis.*

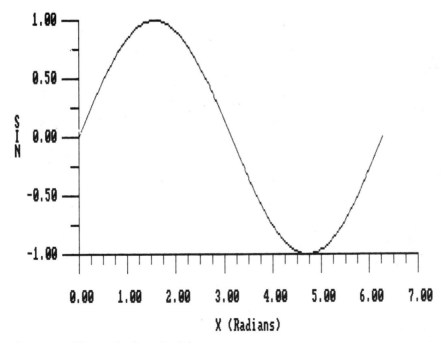

Fig. 18.21. *The graph of Y = SIN(X).*

Program Listing of XYGraph.PGM

```
program XYGraph;   {Draw graphs of X-Y data}

const
   ColSize = 2;
   RowSize = 300;                                    {Mod. #1}
   MaxNumAxisAnn = 50;                               {Mod. #2}

type
   AxisAnnSize  = string[80];
   ArrayType    = array[1..RowSize] of real;
   Array2Type   = array[1..RowSize, 1..ColSize] of real;
   AnnArrayType = array[0..MaxNumAxisAnn] of AxisAnnSize;

var
   TestArray            : ArrayType;
   XYDataArray          : Array2Type;
   XTextArr, YTextArr   : AnnArrayType;
   RowCount, Code, Code2, J, NumTicks, OldX, OldY        : integer;
   NewX, NewY, XOrigin, YOrigin, XAxisL, YAxisL, Color   : integer;
   NumSegsX, NumSegsY, SubTicksX, SubTicksY              : integer;
   LowestX, HighestX, LowestY, HighestY, Unused          : real;
   LoXAxis, HiXAxis, LoYAxis, HiYAxis, ScaleX, ScaleY    : real;
   CharFlag, Reply, Reply2                               : char;
   RealFormatX, RealFormatY, Mid                         : boolean;


{$I AnnXAxis.PSL}
{$I AnnYAxis.PSL}
{$I AxisText.PSL}
{$I DoXAxis.PSL}
{$I DoYAxis.PSL}
{$I GetNumI.PSL}
{$I GetNumR.PSL}
{$I KeyHit.PSL}
{$I Load2Arr.PSL}
{$I SortH2R.PSL}
{$I Stats.PSL}
```

```
BEGIN
   clrscr;
   writeln('XYGraph - High-resolution graph of X-Y data');
   XOrigin     := 100;                                      {Mod. #3}
   YOrigin     := 148;                                      {Mod. #3}
   XAxisL      := 448;                                      {Mod. #4}
   YAxisL      := 128;                                      {Mod. #4}
   Color       := white;                                 {Mod. #5, 10}
   RealFormatX := true;                                     {Mod. #6}
   RealFormatY := true;                                     {Mod. #6}
   Mid         := false;
   SubTicksX   := 3;                                        {Mod. #7}
   SubTicksY   := 1;                                        {Mod. #7}
   RowCount    := 0;
   writeln;
   writeln('The input data must be on a data file.');
   Load2Arr(XYDataArray, RowCount, Code);
   if (Code <> 0) or (RowCount < 2) then
      begin
         writeln('Error in reading input - program aborted.');
         halt
      end;
   writeln('Sorting the data ...');                         {Mod. #8}
   SortH2R(XYDataArray, RowCount, 1);                       {Mod. #8}
   LowestX   := XYDataArray[1, 1];
   HighestX  := XYDataArray[RowCount, 1];
   for J := 1 to RowCount do
      TestArray[J] := XYDataArray[J, 2];
   Stats(TestArray, RowCount, Unused, Unused, Unused,
                              LowestY, HighestY);
   writeln;
   {— Beginning of input dialogue —}                       {Mod. #9}
   writeln('  — X-Axis Specifications —');
   writeln;
   writeln('Smallest X value in data file = ', LowestX:12);
   writeln('Largest X value in data file  = ', HighestX:12);
   repeat
      writeln;
      writeln('X value at the left end of the axis?');
      GetNumR(LoXAxis, CharFlag, Code);
      writeln('X value at the right end of the axis?');
      GetNumR(HiXAxis, CharFlag, Code2)
```

```
until
   (Code = Ø) and (Code2 = Ø) and (LoXAxis <> HiXAxis);
repeat
   writeln;
   writeln('Number of primary tick marks on axis?');
   GetNumI(NumTicks, CharFlag, Code)
until
   (Code = Ø) and (NumTicks >= Ø);
if NumTicks < 2 then
   NumSegsX := Ø
else
   NumSegsX := NumTicks - 1;
AxisText(XTextArr, NumSegsX, LoXAxis, HiXAxis, RealFormatX);
writeln;
writeln('Label for x-axis?');
write('? ');
readln(XTextArr[Ø]);
writeln;
writeln(' — Y-Axis Specifications —');
writeln;
writeln('Smallest Y value in data file = ', LowestY:12);
writeln('Largest Y value in data file  = ', HighestY:12);
repeat
   writeln;
   writeln('Y value at the bottom of the axis?');
   GetNumR(LoYAxis, CharFlag, Code);
   writeln('Y value at the top of the axis?');
   GetNumR(HiYAxis, CharFlag, Code2)
until
   (Code = Ø) and (Code2 = Ø) and (LoYAxis <> HiYAxis);
repeat
   writeln;
   writeln('Number of primary tick marks on axis?');
   GetNumI(NumTicks, CharFlag, Code)
until
   (Code = Ø) and (NumTicks >= Ø);
if NumTicks < 2 then
   NumSegsY := Ø
```

```
   else
      NumSegsY := NumTicks - 1;
   AxisText(YTextArr, NumSegsY, LoYAxis, HiYAxis, RealFormatY);
   writeln;
   writeln('Label for y-axis?' );
   write('? ' );
   readln(YTextArr[0]);
   {— End of input dialogue —}                          {Mod. #9}
   writeln;
   writeln('Press a key to see the graph.  When finished,' );
   writeln('press a key to clear the screen.' );
   repeat until keypressed;
   hires;                                               {Mod. #10}
   hirescolor(color);                                   {Mod. #10}
   ScaleX := XAxisL / (HiXAxis - LoXAxis);
   ScaleY := YAxisL / (HiYAxis - LoYAxis);
   NewX   := round(XOrigin + (XYDataArray[1, 1] -
                              LoXAxis) * ScaleX);
   NewY   := round(YOrigin - (XYDataArray[1, 2] -
                              LoYAxis) * ScaleY);
   DoXAxis(XOrigin, YOrigin, XAxisL, NumSegsX, SubTicksX, Color);
   DoYAxis(XOrigin, YOrigin, YAxisL, NumSegsY, SubTicksY, Color);
   AnnXAxis(XOrigin, YOrigin, XAxisL, NumSegsX, XTextArr, Mid);
   AnnYAxis(XOrigin, YOrigin, YAxisL, NumSegsY, YTextArr, Mid);
   for J := 2 to RowCount do
      begin
         OldX := NewX;
         OldY := NewY;
         NewX := round(XOrigin + (XYDataArray[J, 1] -
                                  LoXAxis) * ScaleX);
         NewY := round(YOrigin - (XYDataArray[J, 2] -
                                  LoYAxis) * ScaleY);
         draw(OldX, OldY, NewX, NewY, Color)
      end;
   repeat until KeyHit(Reply, Reply2);
   textmode(bw80)
END.
```

Variables

XYDataArray	The two-dimensional array containing the X-Y data read from the input disk file
TestArray	One-dimensional array of either the X data or the Y data
XTextArray	string array of the annotations for the x-axis. The zero element contains the label for the whole axis. The elements from 1 upward contain the labels for the primary tick marks.
YTextArray	string array of the annotations for the y-axis
RowCount	Number of data pairs in XYDataArray
Code, Code2	Return codes from GetNumI and GetNumR
J	Loop index
NumTicks	Number of tick marks to put on an axis
OldX, OldY	Last value of X and Y in graphing coordinates
NewX, NewY	Current value of X and Y in graphing coordinates
XOrigin	X location of the origin in graphing coordinates
YOrigin	Y location of the origin in graphing coordinates
XAxisL	Length of the x-axis in graphing coordinates
YAxisL	Length of the y-axis in graphing coordinates
Color	Graphing color (usually white)
NumSegsX	Number of segments on the x-axis. This number is one less than the number of primary ticks marks; if there are no tick marks, NumSegsX is zero.
NumSegsY	Number of segments on the y-axis
SubTicksX	Number of secondary tick marks between each pair of primary tick marks on the x-axis
SubTicksY	Number of secondary tick marks on the y-axis
LowestX	Smallest value of X in the data file
HighestX	Largest value of X in the data file
LowestY	Smallest value of Y in the data file
HighestY	Largest value of Y in the data file

Unused	Placeholder for unneeded arguments in Stats
LoXAxis	Value for the left end of the x-axis
HiXAxis	Value for the right end of the x-axis
LoYAxis	Value for the bottom of the y-axis
HiYAxis	Value for the top of the y-axis
ScaleX	Scaling factor used to compute X in graphing units
ScaleY	Scaling factor used to compute Y in graphing units
CharFlag	Character value returned by GetNumR and GetNumI
Reply, Reply2	Character values returned by KeyHit
RealFormatX	boolean flag indicating whether the x-axis should be labeled with real numbers
RealFormatY	boolean flag indicating whether the y-axis should be labeled with real numbers
Mid	boolean flag indicating whether the annotations should be centered on the tick marks or between them

Discussion

You may have to adjust the input parameters a few times so that you can create the best-looking graph. Usually the tick mark annotations are too crowded (or too sparse) the first time you try a new graph. Although XYGraph centers all annotations the best it can, you may want to extend or shrink the length of one or both axes to cause the annotations to line up perfectly.

The creation of a pleasing graph is often an iterative process. You try one set of specifications and then adjust them to improve readability and aesthetics. XYGraph uses several variables to control the appearance of the graph. A dialogue with the user is a natural way to set these variables. However, the process can get tedious, especially if you want to rerun the program with one or two changes in order to fine-tune your graph. A compromise, therefore, was adopted. Most variables are set explicitly to default values, and the dialogue is restricted to the more essential variables.

You may want to remove the input dialogue completely, and simply set values for the necessary parameters explicitly. (Modification 9 explains how to do this.) Then you can adjust any stubborn variables before recompiling and rerunning the program. You might use two versions of this program: the regular version the first time you try a graph, and the modified version to hone it.

Producing a graph of an analytic function is a simple task. Use the Save2Arr sub-program in Chapter 6 to create a disk file of the X and Y data produced by your function. XYGraph can then plot the graph.

Modifications

1. RowSize controls the maximum number of data pairs allowed in your disk file. Increase RowSize if necessary.

2. MaxNumAxisAnn is the maximum number of tick mark annotations allowed on one axis. A practical limit for this number is 20. You may want to lower the default value to save memory.

3. XOrigin and YOrigin control the location of the graph origin on your screen. Adjust these variables if you want to move the whole graph orthogonally.

4. XAxisL and YAxisL control the length of each axis. Adjust them to change the size of the graph.

5. Color determines the color used to plot the high-resolution graphics. Color must be an integer from 0 to 15, or you can use Turbo's predefined color constants. (See the Turbo manual.)

6. If you want integer numbers (no decimal points) to be used for either axis annotation, change RealFormatX or RealFormatY to false as appropriate.

7. SubTicksX controls the number of secondary tick marks to be placed between each pair of primary tick marks on the x-axis. (If no primary tick marks are used, SubTicksX is irrelevant.) Similarly, SubTicksY controls the number of secondary tick marks on the y-axis. Adjust these variables as needed.

8. If your data is already sorted on X, you can remove the two statements indicated by {Mod. #8} to save computation time. You may also want to remove them if you want unsorted data to stay that way.

9. To remove the input dialogue (see the Discussion section), you can delete (or comment out) all the statements between the two lines denoted by {Mod. #9}. However, you must replace these lines with statements that explicitly set values for LoXAxis, HiXAxis, NumSegsX, XTextArr, LoYAxis, HiYAxis, NumSegsY, and YTextArr.

10. If you want to create a medium-resolution graph, change the hires statement to graphmode or graphcolormode. If you make this change, you need to set color, palette, and graphbackground compatibly.

BarChart

> **Purpose:** *To draw a bar chart on the screen*

Usage

A bar chart is an effective presentation tool for many kinds of business data. Such a chart is especially good for showing time-varying quantities—for example, sales, number of employees, or production capacities—per time period. BarChart provides this charting capability.

The data must be stored in a disk file. The file contains the Y value for each bar in the chart. (This Y value determines the height of the bar.) You can use the subprogram SaveArr (Chapter 6) to create this file. See the Discussion section.

First, BarChart prompts you for the filespec of the disk file containing the Y data. The program assumes that the bottom of each bar is at Y = 0. (That is, the horizontal axis of the chart is along the line Y = 0.) Values in the data file should not be negative. The bars are graphed vertically upward and represent positive values of Y.

You are then shown the largest value of Y read from the disk file. This value enables you to make a sensible choice for Y at the top of the vertical axis. Make sure that you select a value at least as large as the actual maximum Y. Your input value must be an integer. (It is therefore limited to 32767. See the Modifications section.)

Next, you must provide the number of primary tick marks to be placed on the y-axis. This number must be an integer greater than or equal to zero. If you supply 0 or 1, no tick marks are drawn. Otherwise, one tick mark is placed at each end of the axis, and the other tick marks, if any, are equally spaced in between. Secondary tick marks are provided automatically between the primary tick marks. Last, you must provide the label for the whole axis. If you prefer, you can press the Enter key to eliminate the label completely.

Now the annotation for the x-axis is required. Tick marks for this axis are automatically generated by the program because the number of bars is already determined. If you want the spaces between these tick marks to be annotated, you must create a disk file containing these annotations. Use SaveTxt (Chapter 6) to create this file. (See the Discussion section.) BarChart asks you for the name of the file. If you do not have this file (and thus do not want such annotations), simply press the Enter key. Finally, you must provide the label for the whole axis. Again, you can press Enter to nullify the label.

You have six choices for the shading style to be used in the bars. Try each one to determine the most pleasing choice for your graph.

When prompted, simply press any key to produce the chart on the screen. The chart is drawn in high-resolution graphics with white lines on a black background. Axis labeling and centering are done automatically. After viewing the graph, press any key to clear the screen, return to text mode, and end the program.

Sample Output

Consider a sporting goods company that manufactures self-contained home gymnasiums. The company wants to analyze its month-by-month sales. A disk file named UNITS.DTA contains the number of units sold during each month of 1986. This file was created with SaveArr. A string data file called MONTHS.TXT contains the abbreviations for each of the 12 months; the abbreviations are used as annotations on the x-axis. Figures 18.22 and 18.23 show the data entry phase of BarChart for this run. The resultant bar chart is shown in figure 18.24. (This figure was created on an EPSON printer by using Shift-PrtSc with GRAPHICS.COM to get an image of the screen.)

```
BarChart - Create bar charts

The input data must be on a disk file.
** Enter filespec of input file, or **
** press [Enter] key to cancel.    **
UNITS86.DTA
** 12 elements now in array. **

Y value at bottom of axis is set to 0

Largest value in data file = 4.352000E+03

Y value at top of axis?  (integer please)
Entry? 5000

Number of primary tick marks on y-axis?
Entry? 6

Label for y-axis?
? Units Sold
```

Fig. 18.22. *Reading the data file and specifying the y-axis.*

```
? Units Sold

If you want annotations for the x-axis tick marks,
the annotations must be retrieved from a disk
file.  Provide the filespec of that file now, or
press [Enter] to skip labeling of the tick marks.

** Enter filespec of input text file, or **
** press [Enter] key to cancel.            **
MONTHS.TXT
** 12 lines now in text array. **

Label for x-axis?
? 1986

Shading style options
  0 - No shading       3 - Vertical
  1 - Filled in        4 - Diagonal
  2 - Horizontal       5 - Herringbone
Enter reply from 0 to 5.
5

Press a key to see the bar chart.  When finished,
press a key to clear the screen.
```

Fig. 18.23. *Completing the input specifications.*

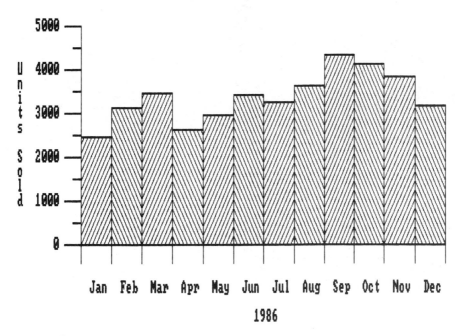

Fig. 18.24. *The resulting bar chart.*

Program Listing of BarChart.PGM

```
program BarChart;   {Draw bar charts}

const
   ArraySize      = 50;                                    {Mod. #1}
   TextSize       = ArraySize;
   MaxNumAxisAnn = ArraySize;

type
   LineSize       = string[80];
   ArrayType      = array[1..ArraySize] of real;
   TextArrayType = array[1..TextSize] of LineSize;
   AnnArrayType  = array[0..ArraySize] of LineSize;

var
   NumArray                                    : ArrayType;
   TempTextArr                                 : TextArrayType;
   XTextArr, YTextArr                          : AnnArrayType;
   XOrigin, YOrigin, XAxisL, YAxisL, Color     : integer;
   SubTicksX, SubTicksY, Count, Code, TextCount : integer;
   LoYAxis, HiYAxis, NumSegsX, NumSegsY        : integer;
   UpLeftX, UpLeftY, LoRightX, LoRightY        : integer;
   ShadingType, Density, FlipFlop, J, NumTicks : integer;
   Unused, LowestY, HighestY, WidthX, ScaleY   : real;
   CharFlag, Reply, Reply2                     : char;
   RealFormatY, MidX, MidY                     : boolean;


{$I AnnXAxis.PSL}
{$I AnnYAxis.PSL}
{$I AxisText.PSL}
{$I DoXAxis.PSL}
{$I DoYAxis.PSL}
{$I GetNumI.PSL}
{$I GetReply.PSL}
{$I GraphBox.PSL}
{$I KeyHit.PSL}
{$I LoadArr.PSL}
{$I LoadTxt.PSL}
{$I Stats.PSL}
```

```
BEGIN
  clrscr;
  writeln('BarChart - Create bar charts');
  XOrigin     := 100;                               {Mod.  #2}
  YOrigin     := 148;                               {Mod.  #2}
  XAxisL      := 480;                               {Mod.  #3}
  YAxisL      := 120;                               {Mod.  #3}
  Color       := white;                             {Mod.  #4, 10}
  RealFormatY := false;                             {Mod.  #5}
  MidX        := true;
  MidY        := false;
  SubTicksX   := 0;                                 {Mod.  #6}
  SubTicksY   := 1;                                 {Mod.  #6}
  LoYAxis     := 0;                                 {Mod.  #7}
  Density     := 5;                                 {Mod.  #8}
  Count       := 0;
  writeln;
  writeln('The input data must be on a disk file.');
  LoadArr(NumArray, Count, Code);
  if (Code <> 0) or (Count < 1) then
    begin
       writeln('Error in reading data - program aborted.');
       halt
    end;
  NumSegsX := Count;
  Stats(NumArray, Count, Unused, Unused, Unused,
                  LowestY, HighestY);
  writeln;
  writeln('Y value at bottom of axis is set to ', LoYAxis:1);
  if LowestY < LoYAxis then
    writeln('Warning - some data is less than ', LoYAxis:1);
  writeln;
  writeln('Largest value in data file = ', HighestY:12);
  repeat
    writeln;
    writeln('Y value at top of axis?  (integer please)');
    GetNumI(HiYAxis, CharFlag, Code)                {Mod. #5}
  until
    (Code = 0) and (HiYAxis > LoYAxis) and
               (HiYAxis >= HighestY);
```

```
repeat
   writeln;
   writeln('Number of primary tick marks on y-axis?');
   GetNumI(NumTicks, CharFlag, Code)
until
   (Code = 0) and (NumTicks >= 0);
if NumTicks < 2 then
   NumSegsY := 0
else
   NumSegsY := NumTicks - 1;
AxisText(YTextArr, NumSegsY, LoYAxis, HiYAxis, RealFormatY);
writeln;
writeln('Label for y-axis?');
write('? ');
readln(YTextArr[0]);
writeln;
writeln('If you want annotations for the x-axis tick marks,');
writeln('the annotations must be retrieved from a disk');
writeln('file.  Provide the filespec of that file now, or');
writeln('press [Enter] to skip labeling of the tick marks.');
writeln;
TextCount := 0;
LoadTxt(TempTextArr, TextCount, Code);
for J := 1 to Count do
   XTextArr[J] := '';
for J := 1 to TextCount do
   XTextArr[J] := TempTextArr[J];
writeln;
writeln('Label for x-axis?');
write('? ');
readln(XTextArr[0]);
writeln;
writeln('Shading style options');
writeln(' 0 - No shading      3 - Vertical');
writeln(' 1 - Filled in       4 - Diagonal');
writeln(' 2 - Horizontal      5 - Herringbone');
GetReply('0', '5', Reply);
writeln(Reply);
ShadingType := ord(Reply) - 48;
FlipFlop := 0;                              {Mod. #9}
if ShadingType = 5 then                     {Mod. #9}
   FlipFlop := 1;                           {Mod. #9}
```

```
writeln;
writeln('Press a key to see the bar chart.  When finished,');
writeln('press a key to clear the screen.');
repeat until keypressed;
hires;                                                    {Mod. #10}
hirescolor(color);                                        {Mod. #10}
DoXAxis(XOrigin, YOrigin, XAxisL, NumSegsX, SubTicksX, Color);
DoYAxis(XOrigin, YOrigin, YAxisL, NumSegsY, SubTicksY, Color);
AnnXAxis(XOrigin, YOrigin, XAxisL, NumSegsX, XTextArr, MidX);
AnnYAxis(XOrigin, YOrigin, YAxisL, NumSegsY, YTextArr, MidY);
ScaleY   := YAxisL / (HiYAxis - LoYAxis);
WidthX   := XAxisL / Count;
LoRightY := YOrigin;
for J := 1 to Count do
   begin
      UpLeftX := XOrigin + trunc(WidthX * (J - 1));
      UpLeftY := round(YOrigin - (NumArray[J] - LoYAxis) *
                                 ScaleY);
      LoRightX   := XOrigin + trunc(WidthX * J);
      FlipFlop   := - FlipFlop;
      ShadingType := ShadingType + FlipFlop;
      GraphBox(UpLeftX, UpLeftY, LoRightX, LoRightY, Color,
                               ShadingType, Density)
   end;
repeat until KeyHit(Reply, Reply2);
textmode(bw80)
END.
```

Variables

ArraySize	Maximum number of data values (bars) allowed
NumArray	Array containing the input data read from disk
TempTextArr	Array containing the string data for the X tick mark labeling. This data is read from disk.
XTextArr	string array of the annotations for the x-axis. The zero element contains the label for the whole axis. The elements from 1 upward contain the labels for the spaces between the primary tick marks. These (positive valued) elements are identical to those in TempTextArr.

YTextArr	string array of the annotations for the y-axis
XOrigin	X location of the origin in graphing coordinates
YOrigin	Y location of the origin in graphing coordinates
XAxisL	Length of the x-axis in graphing coordinates
YAxisL	Length of the y-axis in graphing coordinates
Color	Graphing color (usually white)
SubTicksX	Number of secondary tick marks (usually 0) between each pair of primary tick marks on the x-axis
SubTicksY	Number of secondary tick marks on the y-axis
Count	Number of data values in NumArray
Code	Return code from LoadArr and GetNumI
TextCount	Number of data values in TempTextArr
LoYAxis	Value (usually 0) for the bottom of the y-axis
HiYAxis	Value for the top of the y-axis
NumSegsX	Number of segments on the x-axis. This number is the same as the number of bars in the chart.
NumSegsY	Number of segments on the y-axis. This number is one less than the number of primary tick marks; if there are no tick marks, NumSegsY is zero.
UpLeftX	X graph coordinate of upper left corner of a bar
UpLeftY	Y graph coordinate of upper left corner of a bar
LoRightX	X graph coordinate of lower right corner of a bar
LoRightY	Y graph coordinate of lower right corner of a bar
ShadingType	Type of shading to use in each bar (0 = none, 1 = filled, 2 = horizontal, 3 = vertical, 4 = diagonal, 5 = herringbone)
Density	Amount of space between shading lines
FlipFlop	Shading indicator—alternating shading if positive, constant shading if 0
J	Looping index
NumTicks	Number of tick marks on axis
Unused	Placeholder for unneeded arguments in Stats

LowestY	Smallest Y value in data file
HighestY	Largest Y value in data file
WidthX	Width of a bar in graph coordinates
ScaleY	Scaling factor used to compute Y in graphing units
CharFlag	Character value returned by GetNumI
Reply, Reply2	Character values returned by KeyHit
RealFormatY	boolean flag indicating whether the y-axis should be annotated with real (or integer) numbers
MidX, MidY	boolean flags indicating whether the x-axis and y-axis annotations should be centered on the tick marks or between them

Discussion

As with XYGraph, the creation of a bar chart is frequently an iterative process. You need to try different shadings and labeling to find the most pleasing and effective chart.

Typically, the data for each bar chart is created externally in another program. The SaveArr subprogram is ideal for creating the disk file once the data is saved in an array. This array should have the Y value for the first bar in element 1, the Y value for the second bar in element 2, and so on. SaveArr can then put the data sequentially on disk in exactly the form needed by BarChart.

If you prefer, you can specify the data explicitly in BarChart. You must replace the LoadArr statement with code that stores the data into NumArray directly. Then set Count equal to the number of data values present.

Similarly, the string data for the bar labeling on the x-axis is expected to be in a disk file. You can use SaveTxt to create this file. The text strings in this file should directly correspond with the data values in NumArray. Again, you can set these strings explicitly in BarChart by filling TempTextArr through direct assignment statements. Remove the LoadTxt statement if you take this action.

Modifications

1. ArraySize controls the maximum number of data values allowed in your disk file. Increase the value of this variable if necessary.

2. XOrigin and YOrigin control the location of the chart origin on your screen. Adjust these variables to move the whole chart orthogonally.

3. XAxisL and YAxisL control the length of each axis. Adjust them to change the size of the chart.

4. Color determines the color used for the high-resolution graphics. Color must be an integer from 0 to 15, or you can use Turbo's predefined color constants. (See the Turbo manual.)

5. The program is now restricted to integer constants for the tick mark labeling on the y-axis. If you want to use real numbers (to accommodate values larger than 32767), change RealFormatY to true. In addition, the GetNumI call (at the line denoted by {Mod. #5}) must be replaced by GetNumR. You must also add GetNumR to the list of included subprograms.

6. SubTicksX controls the number of secondary tick marks to be placed between each pair of primary tick marks on the x-axis. This number is typically 0, indicating no secondary tick marks. But you can have them if you want. Similarly, SubTicksY is the number of secondary tick marks on the y-axis. You may want to adjust these variables.

7. LoYAxis is the value of Y to use as the base of each bar. This value is usually 0, but you may adjust the value.

8. Density controls the density of the shading. Adjust this variable to alter the number of shading lines in each bar.

9. To enhance the graphics effect, you can alternate the shading used in consecutive bars. First, determine the two integer values of ShadingType for the two kinds of shading you want to alternate. Second, replace the three lines denoted by {Mod. #10} with two statements like the following:

```
ShadingType := 4;
FlipFlop    := 2;
```

The value assigned to ShadingType is the higher of the two integer values specifying the shading types. The value assigned to FlipFlop is the positive difference between the two integer values.

10. If you want to create a medium-resolution graph, change the hires statement to graphmode or graphcolormode. If you make this change, you need to set color, palette, and graphbackground compatibly.

A

How To Create and Use
a Subprogram Library

To use a subprogram from this book, you need to type accurately the subprogram into your computer, save the subprogram on disk, and compile the subprogram as part of a larger main program. (The main program may be one of the Sample Usage programs accompanying each subprogram, a full program from Chapter 18, or an original program of your own.) You can organize your subprogram and program disk files in many ways. This appendix presents an approach for entering, saving, and testing these subprograms, thus creating an easy-to-use subprogram library on disk.

We assume that you have an IBM PC (or compatible) with two floppy disk drives (or one floppy disk and one fixed disk), and that you are running PC DOS (or MS-DOS) Version 2.0 or higher with Turbo Pascal Version 3.01A. Changes may be necessary for other configurations. We assume also that you are typing the subprograms yourself. A much better idea (though more expensive) is to use the associated disk with all the subprograms and programs from this book. This disk is available for purchase separately. If you have the disk, refer instead to the instructions accompanying it.

In addition, we assume that you are sufficiently familiar with Turbo Pascal to start it up, use the Turbo editor to enter and change a program, and compile and run the program. For the discussion that follows, we assume that you have a copy of the Turbo compiler disk in floppy disk drive A and a data disk in drive B. We'll discuss fixed disk systems, but you may need to make adjustments depending on how you installed Turbo and what subdirectories you use.

Starting Turbo Pascal

Start Turbo Pascal, respond with Y to include error messages or N if you don't want such messages (we recommend Y), and use the L command to make B the logged (default) disk drive. For a fixed disk system, you probably need to make C the logged disk drive and then use the A command to set the active directory; let's assume that TURBO is the subdirectory you use for all Turbo Pascal files. For floppy disk systems, let's assume for now that you do not use subdirectories.

Entering a Subprogram

Select a subprogram from this book. We'll use ShowTime as an example. Enter the W command and respond with the work file name ShowTime. PSL. All subprograms in this book require the file name extension . PSL for consistency with the associated Sample Usage programs, and for the remainder of this discussion to be accurate. Note that capitalization is irrelevant in file names. We use capitalization for readability only.

Enter the E (edit) command to edit the subprogram. The Turbo editor responds by displaying a blank screen with the file name at the top. Type the source code for the ShowTime subprogram extremely carefully. Although spacing is largely optional in Pascal programs, we strongly recommend that you duplicate our subprograms exactly as they are shown in the book. This includes spacing, comments, blank lines, and capitalization. Deviations make it much harder to check for typing errors later.

When typing, be especially careful that you get all the punctuation characters right (semicolons, commas, colons, equal signs, and periods). A missing or added semicolon in the wrong place may not cause a compilation error but can change the entire meaning of a Pascal program. In addition, be extremely careful not to confuse similar alphabetic and numeric characters when you type. In particular, look out for lowercase l (the letter "el") instead of the number 1 (one), or uppercase O (the letter "oh") instead of the number 0 (zero). Another common typing mistake is to use incorrect spacing between apostrophes. Pascal uses apostrophes to define character strings. In some subprograms and programs, you must type the number of spaces between apostrophes in an exact way in order for the program to work correctly. Often the number of spaces is zero; don't put a space between the apostrophes unless you see a space in the book.

After typing the complete subprogram, enter the Ctrl-K-D sequence (press the K key while holding down the Ctrl key and then press the D key) to end editing. Then enter the S command to save the subprogram on disk.

Typing a Sample Usage Program

Now you are ready to type the Sample Usage program that accompanies the subprogram. This short program demonstrates how the subprogram works, and provides a way to verify that you typed the subprogram correctly. Once again, use the W command to select a work file name. This time use the name ShowTime. SU for the file. The SU stands for Sample Usage and is our way of keeping the sample program distinguished from the subprogram yet still relating the two.

Enter the E command and then type the Sample Usage program from the book. Again, be extremely careful to type the program exactly as it is shown. When you have finished typing the program, enter the Ctrl-K-D sequence to end the edit, and then enter the S command to save the program on disk.

Testing the Subprogram with the Sample Program

The moment of truth is at hand. Enter the C command to compile the subprogram. This causes the Sample Usage program (still designated as the work file) to be compiled. During the compilation the subprogram is drawn into memory from disk by the {$I ShowTime.PSL} statement in the Sample Usage program. The program and the subprogram compile together. If there is an error in either the Sample Usage program or the subprogram, the compiler displays an error number and message (unless you responded with N when starting Turbo) and tells you to press the Esc key to continue. After you press the Esc key, Turbo indicates the place in the subprogram or program where an error is detected.

Usually the cause is a typing error in that line or the one immediately before it. If so, correct the error, end edit with Ctrl-K-D, save the revised file with the S command, and recompile with the C command. You may need to use the W command first to make the Sample Usage program the work file again. If the error is in the subprogram, Turbo automatically makes the subprogram the work file (so that you can make corrections).

Be aware that Turbo may report an error in one line when the actual typing error is in a previous line. If you get a compiler error and can't find the typing error that caused it, refer to Appendix B. A typing error in the subprogram may even cause Turbo to tell you that the error is in the Sample Usage program. If all else fails, you may need to search through every line, character by character, of both the subprogram and the Sample Usage program, looking for typing errors.

Eventually, all your typing errors will be fixed. (For all you infallible typists who always get "clean" compiles the first time, we applaud you. You are a small minority.) The result of an error-free compilation is three lines on the screen showing how much memory is required by the program. Enter the R command to run the program. You should see on the screen a duplication of the sample output shown or described in the book. For some subprograms, such as ShowTime, your output will be slightly different. ShowTime shows the current time of day, and the time of day when you run your test is unlikely to match exactly the time shown in the book. Other sample programs require that you enter data. If so, enter the same data shown in the sample to see whether you get the same results.

If your sample program output matches the output shown in the book, you can be fairly confident that you typed the subprogram (and Sample Usage program) correctly. You can't be *completely* confident because a short test program can't test all possible subprogram conditions. Modify the Sample Usage program to check other conditions if appropriate.

If you see unexplained differences between your output and the sample output in the book, reread the subprogram explanation to be sure that you understand what the subprogram is supposed to do. If you still can't explain the discrepancies, check once more for typing errors. If that fails, refer to Appendix B.

Building Up a Subprogram Library

Once you have one subprogram working, go back and begin the process again with another subprogram. Continue entering and testing the subprograms until you have built up the complete library or the subset appropriate for your needs. Two problems arise as you build up a substantial subprogram library if you have a system with two floppy disks. Neither problem affects the fixed disk system owner.

First, the root directory of a 360K floppy disk has room for only 112 file names, but you will create over 200 files if you enter all the code in this book (subprograms, Sample Usage programs, and full programs). The simplest solution is to create a subdirectory on your data disk and store all your files in the subdirectory instead of the root directory. Subdirectories do not have a limit of 112 file names. To create the subdirectory, use the DOS command MKDIR. If you are not familiar with subdirectories, see your DOS manual. Suppose that you decide to use the subdirectory name TPPL for the Turbo Pascal Program Library. Once you create the subdirectory, simply use the A command whenever you start Turbo to indicate that the active directory you want is \TPPL. That way, the 112-file limit will not be a problem.

The second problem on a system with two floppy disks is lack of disk space. All the subprograms, Sample Usage programs, and full programs fit on one 360K disk with little room to spare. This lack of space can be a problem if you want to do more program development with the subprogram library. The solution is to create a new data disk, create a subdirectory on the disk as just discussed, and copy all the subprogram files (named with extension .PSL) from the full disk to the new one. If you use the subdirectory name TPPL on both disks, you can easily copy all the subprogram files with a single DOS command because of our recommended file names. Use the following command:

```
COPY   A:\TPPL\*.PSL   B:\TPPL
```

Of course, your data disk containing all the subprograms must be in drive A, and your new data disk must be in drive B when you enter this command. After the copying is complete, you will have a data disk with all the necessary subprograms available on a disk, with room for more program development. The subprograms themselves occupy less than half the space of a 360K disk. Depending on your needs, you may want to copy only some of the subprograms, giving you even more room to work.

Entering and Running the Full Programs

Chapter 18 contains several full programs. These complete programs demonstrate the methodology of including numerous subprograms in a main program. Enter a full program the same way you enter a Sample Usage program, except give the work file name an extension of . PGM, identifying the file as a full program from Chapter 18. Each full program requires several subprograms, as explained in the chapter. Be sure that you have entered (and saved on disk) all the necessary subprograms before you try to run a full program.

B

What To Do If You Have Problems

We can't possibly anticipate every kind of problem you may encounter, but here are some steps to take when things go wrong.

1. Read Appendix A.

Appendix A explains the general procedures for entering, saving, and testing the subprograms. If you don't understand the procedures, or if you don't understand their intent, you may need to do some more studying before continuing with this book. If you have trouble entering, editing, compiling, and running programs, read the *Turbo Pascal Reference Manual* or an introductory Turbo Pascal book. If you don't understand subdirectories or DOS commands, read the documentation that came with DOS or a tutorial book about DOS.

2. Read about the subprogram or full program.

Your problem may be that you don't understand how the subprogram or full program is supposed to work. Reread the explanation of the subprogram or program that is causing the problem. Read the *entire* explanation. Many tips are contained in the Limitations and Error Conditions section, the Discussion section, and the chapter introduction. Don't make assumptions about how you think the subprogram *should* work. Be sure that you define all the input and output variables correctly.

3. Check your typing.

We can't emphasize this point enough. If you know the fundamentals of dealing with Turbo Pascal and DOS (as explained in step 1), and if you have read and understood the subprogram explanation, your problem is almost certainly a typing error. Yes, we admit the possibility that the error may be in our programming. (Refer to the Reader Feedback section near the end of the book.) But we *have* tested these subprograms, and you should *not* be getting certain types of errors unless some sort of production error occurred in printing this book. Almost certainly, *your* typing error will cause a compiler error message or a run-time error when you try to duplicate the output from the Sample Usage program.

Review the typing tips in Appendix A. Look for punctuation errors—that missing or extra semicolon, the parentheses instead of square brackets or braces, or the missing apostrophe. Check that all of those 1's aren't lowercase l's, and that you haven't confused capital O's with zeros. Look for that line you may have omitted entirely. *Carefully recheck every character on every line.* Often it is helpful to print out what you have typed and then compare the printed listing with what is in the book. Don't limit your search to the line that Turbo says has an error. A typing error in one line can often cause an error message in another. These "remote" errors may occur if you omit a `begin` or `end` statement, a right brace (thus turning a whole chunk of a program into a comment), or an apostrophe. If you can't find an error in your typing, ask a "nitpicking" friend to look for you.

Remember, if a subprogram doesn't work, assume that you have made a typing error until you prove otherwise.

4. Document the problem.

What if there really is a bug in a subprogram? Well, we want to fix it. If you are absolutely sure that you have not made any typing errors (please check one more time), then put together all the information you can about the problem and let us know. We'll be very appreciative. Our address is in the Reader Feedback section near the back of the book. Mentioned also in that section are specific things we want from you in explaining the problem. If you *really* did find a problem, we'll refund the dollar you send us. And if you are the first to find the problem, we'll probably even send you an extra dollar (one we received from a bad typist who thought he/she found an error).

C

Programming Style and Conventions

As Long As It Works,
Who Cares What It Looks Like?

Nothing seems to engender as much passionate partisanship among Pascal programmers as questions of programming style. For some reason, two seemingly intelligent, sane Pascallers [*sic*] can argue for hours about semicolons and where to put an else.

Perhaps the problem arises because of the freedom Pascal allows in program style. Pascal embraces a strange contradiction because the language is quite rigid in some ways yet extremely flexible in others. Pascal compilers insist that each variable be predeclared and assigned a specific type. Semantic meaning is rigorous. However, names are free-form, block structure is open, and many ways to do the same thing are available. Pascal is something like a piano. There are only a certain number of keys to play, but the ways you can play them and the music you can create are boundless.

Surprisingly, there is little agreement about what a Pascal program should actually look like. Most authorities agree that programs should consist of clean, modular units and should be organized in a top-down structure. But what about more mundane issues? Have you ever considered where to put the begin and end statements in a small coding block? Consider this code fragment:

```
if BigDeal then
   begin
      writeln('This is our style');
      Author1 := 'Rugg';
      Author2 := 'Feldman
   end
```

TURBO PASCAL PROGRAM LIBRARY

In the literature, respected authorities write this type of construct in several ways. The begin might be flush with the if or on the same line with then. The end could be in any of several places: indented parallel to the if, parallel to Author2, or on the same line with Feldman.

Coding Conventions

Programs in many popular Pascal textbooks use various coding conventions. Often there is little consistency within the same book—not that there is only one way to do things or that uniformity is always a virtue. We must remain masters of our tools, not slaves to them. Unabashedly, we have developed our own set of coding conventions. When there is good reason to override them, we do so—but sparingly.

For increased legibility, all Turbo Pascal reserved words, subprograms, full programs, and subprogram and program excerpts appear in Digital font.

Capitalization

Turbo reserved words (see Appendix E) are in lowercase. These are Turbo's key-words—the predefined identifier names such as program, true, for, writeln, pi, integer, and so on.

Identifier names we create (subprogram names, variables, type names, etc.) always begin with a capital letter. Furthermore, capital letters are used freely within the name to increase readability. Examples of names we create are GetReply, ArrayType, and Code.

The sole exceptions to these capitalization rules (why are there always exceptions?) are the single BEGIN and the single END. that delimit the executable part of a main program (not a subprogram). Those two words appear in uppercase. Any other begin and end appear in lowercase, as expected. (These exceptions help set off the main block of a program from the subordinate blocks.)

Names for Subprograms and Programs

Each subprogram has a name limited to eight characters. This limit ensures that the subprogram can be saved with that same name on an IBM PC disk. When a subprogram name is saved on disk, the file suffix .PSL is used.

Names of full programs in Chapter 18 are also limited to eight characters for the same reason. Here, however, the extension .PGM is added when a full program is saved on disk.

Variable Names

Many of our subprograms are designed for compatibility with one another. Variable names are identical across subprograms whenever possible. In addition, variables in the main part of Sample Usage programs are usually given the same names as those of their counterparts in the subprograms. (That is, the actual parameter list in a statement invoking a subprogram is usually the same as the formal parameter list in the subprogram header.) This convention is used for ease of reference.

Semicolons

In Pascal the semicolon is a statement separator, not a terminator. Consider the following:

```
for J := 1 to 5 do
   begin
      Count := Count + NumArray[J];
      writeln(J, NumArray[J]);
   end
```

The last semicolon (in the line with writeln) is unnecessary. (Putting the semi-colon there creates a blank statement between the semicolon and end.) We have avoided these superfluous semicolons. The same goes for the last line before until and other similar Pascal constructs. Note that keywords like end, else, and until are statement delimiters, not statements themselves. Thus, a semicolon is never required just before end or another delimiter.

Indentation and Rightward Creep

Indentation sets off block structure and makes a Pascal program much easier to read and understand. We use indentation liberally. Unfortunately, because of nested blocking, some programs seem to drift doggedly toward the right. (This problem is especially acute to us since we can't put any code past the 65th column position, as explained shortly.) Here is what we tried to do (occasionally we had to compromise):

- Indent new subblocks three characters from the previous block

- Place begin and end on distinct lines indented from the previous block

- Keep paired begin and end at the same indentation level

If..Then..Else

Our preferred form is as follows:

```
if Done then
   writeln('All data processed')
else
   begin
      Count := Count + 1;
      writeln('Still more to do')
   end;
writeln('This is the next statement');
```

The object phrases of then and else are indented. The else, if it appears, is on a separate line at the same indentation level as that of the corresponding if.

A similar form is used for repeat..until and other delimited statements.

Alignment and Split Lines

Writing a book puts pressure on a coding style. For purposes of reproduction in the book, line lengths are limited horizontally. The maximum number of characters on any program line is 65. Therefore, program statements must be broken in half much more often than normal.

When a single, logical line has to be broken in half (because it extends past position 65), we try to split it at a convenient identifier name and indent the continuation part several characters (at least 5) from the initial part. This convention maximizes readability.

When several consecutive lines contain assignment statements, we try to align the := operator at the same tab position if at all reasonable. This convention is also true for equal signs in consecutive type declarations, colon separators in var blocks, and other similar constructs.

Spacing

One space is put on either side of each operator symbol. Examples of operators are +, -, :=, >, and or.

If the colons are aligned in a var block, a space is put on either side of the colon. If the colons are not aligned, however, a space still appears after the colon, but no space appears before the colon.

One space is used after each comma, colon, and semicolon. The exceptions are these: no space after a comma in a multiple subscript reference, and two spaces after a semicolon if multiple statements appear on the same line. Rarely does more than one statement appear on the same line.

Ordering of the Program Parts

Unlike other Pascals, Turbo allows considerable flexibility in the declaration of the main program parts. Here, we are speaking of the `label`, `const`, `type`, and `var` sections. Turbo allows these sections to appear in any order, and the language even allows more than one section of a given kind. We have stayed with the nominal Pascal standard: one declaration of each part, if any, and always in the order just shown. In a full program, procedures and functions follow these declarations, and the executable part of the main program comes last.

Comments

Although all programs and subprograms are well documented in the book, comments in the source code have been kept to a minimum to discourage distribution of the programs to those without this book.

D

The Environment for
Turbo Pascal Timings

In this book, we refer to the amount of time required to run a Turbo Pascal program. Many factors can affect program timings. This appendix describes the methodology and equipment we used.

All timings were done on a standard IBM Personal Computer running PC DOS V2.0. There were no unusual peripherals, hardware modifications, or software modifications that would have any effect on the speed of the runs.

The version of Turbo Pascal we used was 3.01A. All the default compiler directives were in effect. You should be aware that some of the compiler directives, such as {$R+} and {$U+} can greatly change the speed at which programs run.

We used the PC's internal clock to make the timings, accessing the clock with the ShowTime or GetTime subprograms. In some cases (such as the searching subprograms), we had to repeat a subprogram many times (100 or 1,000) and divide by the number of repetitions in order to determine the time required to execute a fast subprogram once. We have rounded the timings to match the approximate precision of the clock. See GetTime (Chapter 17) for details about the clock's precision.

E

Reserved Words in Turbo Pascal

The following is a list of reserved words in Turbo Pascal Version 3.01A for the IBM PC. The lists in the Turbo manual are incomplete. Avoid using any of the following words as a variable or subprogram name. Words from extended graphics and turtlegraphics are excluded.

abs	case	dispose	freemem	intr
absolute	cbreak	div	function	ioresult
addr	chain	do	getdir	kbd
and	char	downto	getmem	keypressed
append	chdir	draw	goto	label
arctan	chr	dseg	gotoxy	length
array	close	else	graphbackground	lightblue
assign	clreol	end	graphcolormode	lightcyan
aux	clrscr	eof	graphmode	lightgray
auxinptr	con	eoln	graphwindow	lightgreen
auxoutptr	concat	erase	green	lightmagenta
begin	coninptr	errorptr	halt	lightred
black	conoutptr	execute	heapptr	ln
blink	const	exit	hi	lo
blockread	constptr	exp	highvideo	longfilepos
blockwrite	copy	external	hires	longfilesize
blue	cos	false	hirescolor	longseek
boolean	crtexit	file	if	lowvideo
brown	crtinit	filepos	in	lst
buflen	cseg	filesize	inline	lstoutptr
bw40	cyan	fillchar	input	magenta
bw80	darkgray	flush	insert	mark
byte	delay	for	insline	maxavail
c40	delete	forward	int	maxint
c80	delline	frac	integer	mem

599

memavail	palette	repeat	swap	while
memw	paramcount	reset	text	white
mkdir	paramstr	rewrite	textbackground	window
mod	pi	rmdir	textcolor	with
move	plot	round	textmode	write
msdos	port	seek	then	writeln
new	portw	seekeof	to	xor
nil	pos	seekeoln	trm	yellow
normvideo	pred	seg	true	
nosound	procedure	set	trunc	
not	program	shl	truncate	
odd	ptr	shr	type	
of	random	sin	until	
ofs	randomize	sizeof	upcase	
or	read	sound	usr	
ord	readln	sqr	usrinptr	
output	real	sqrt	usroutptr	
overlay	record	sseg	val	
ovrpath	red	str	var	
packed	release	string	wherex	
	rename	succ	wherey	

Reader Feedback

We welcome your feedback about this book. In particular, we welcome comments about (and improvements to) the subprograms themselves. We hope that interest will be high enough to call for a second volume. It could contain many more useful subprograms.

If you have developed a handy subprogram, or if you have suggestions about what kind of subprograms you would like to see in Volume 2, please let us know. If you send us a subprogram listing, by doing so you are agreeing to let us publish it if we choose to, and you are certifying that the subprogram is your original work. No plagiarism, please. We may use the subprogram as is, modify it, or ignore it. We'll also feel free to acknowledge you by name unless you plead for anonymity. In all cases, we'll be grateful. Please be aware that we are most interested in short, clearly written subprograms that are potentially interesting to a wide variety of people.

As for the book you now hold, we recognize that some errors may exist. We have carefully tested the subprograms, Sample Usage programs, and full programs, but some errors may have slipped through nevertheless. We take no responsibility for any damage you may suffer because of programming errors. You must bear the responsibility of testing all programming thoroughly in your own environment before making assumptions about accuracy.

If, however, we find errors in programming or ambiguities in explanations, we want you to have the opportunity to find out about corrections. We will accumulate an errata list that you can send for. As mentioned previously, we also welcome your corrections if you find errors. Our past experience with software books has taught us that many readers write to us with scrawled letters much like this:

I typed inn you're ShowTim porgram and it does'nt work.
Please send me the correctoins.

This is worse than most letters—but not all of them. Please be aware of a few facts before you write to us:

1. If a program in this book won't work for you, the overwhelming probability is that you have made typing errors. We are continually amazed at how many readers swear that they have rechecked their typing 5 (or 8 or 13) times and are *positive* that they have no errors.

Yet when we ask them to send us a printed listing of what they have typed, we immediately find numerous typing errors. The lesson is this: If you are not good at proofreading what you have typed (and many intelligent people are not), find a good proofreading friend to check your typing for you. If you send us a letter with numerous typing errors in it, your credibility as an accurate typist will not be high.

2. Once you are sure that your typing is accurate, read both Appendix A and Appendix B to be certain that you have done everything possible to find and fix the error. And reread the explanation of the subprogram (or full program) to make sure that you understand what the program is actually supposed to do. Don't complain to us because ShowTime doesn't gong 12 times at midnight.

3. Finally, if you write to claim that a program doesn't work, be sure to document exactly what you mean. We can't help you if we can't understand the problem. Be sure to send all of the following:

   a. A self-addressed, stamped envelope.

   b. A printed listing of the subprogram and/or program as you typed it so that we can verify your typing accuracy.

   c. A detailed explanation of exactly what went wrong. Is the error at compile time or run time? Is there an error message? If so, exactly what is it? Where in the program does Turbo indicate the error is? If there is no error message, exactly what goes wrong and when? What input did you provide, if any? For example, did the first four lines of output match the sample output in the book, but then the fifth line was wrong? What was different? Be specific! Include printed output that shows the error if possible.

   d. Information about your computer configuration if it is anything other than what is listed in Appendix D. What computer model and what version of DOS are you using? What version of Turbo? Are you using only the default compiler directives? Which video interface do you have? Anything else unusual?

   e. One dollar. Cash is preferred, but send a check if you're paranoid about sending cash through the mail.

As you may have concluded by now, our past experience with reader correspondence has made us cautious. But we still want you to have a chance for help if you need it. That's why the dollar is required along with everything else. We want you to demonstrate a little sincerity about your efforts to find the error before you write to us. Believe us, we don't make as much money per hour answering these letters as we would handing out Big Macs.

And if you don't want to complain about an error but just want to find out whether we have discovered any errors for our errata list, write to us and ask for the "TPPL Errata" at the following address:

Rugg and Feldman
TPPL Errata
P.O. Box 24815
Los Angeles, CA 90024

Be sure to include a self-addressed, stamped envelope (or a self-addressed, *un*-stamped envelope if you are writing from another country). We'd also appreciate a dollar (or even a quarter) to help cover copying and handling costs, but that's up to you.

Bibliography

Allen, Woody. *Side Effects*. New York: Ballantine Books, 1981.

Asimov, Isaac. *Counting the Eons*. New York: Doubleday & Co., 1983.

Borland International, Inc. *Turbo Pascal Version 3.0 Reference Manual*. 2nd ed. 1985.

Collected Algorithms. Communications of the ACM.

Croxton, Frederick, and others. *Applied General Statistics*. 3rd ed. Englewood Cliffs, New Jersey: Prentice-Hall, Inc., 1967.

Garrison, Paul. *Turbo Pascal for BASIC Programmers*. Indianapolis, Indiana: Que Corporation, 1985.

Gruenberger, Fred, and George Jaffray. *Problems for Computer Solution*. New York: John Wiley & Sons, 1965.

Jensen, Kathleen, and Niklaus Wirth. *Pascal User Manual and Report*. 3rd ed. New York: Springer-Verlag, 1985.

Kernighan, Brian, and P. J. Plaugher. *Software Tools in Pascal*. Reading, Massachusetts: Addison-Wesley, 1981.

Knuth, Donald E. *The Art of Computer Programming*. 3 vols. Reading, Massachusetts: Addison-Wesley, 1968, 1969, 1973.

"A Machine Algorithm for Processing Calendar Dates." *Communications of the ACM*. 11, No. 10 (1968).

Norton, Peter. *The Peter Norton Programmer's Guide to the IBM® PC*. Bellevue, Washington: Microsoft Press, 1985.

Personal Computer BASIC. Boca Raton, Florida: International Business Machines Corporation, 1981.

Personal Computer Disk Operating System (2.00), Boca Raton, Florida: International Business Machines Corporation, 1983.

Personal Computer Technical Reference, Boca Raton, Florida: International Business Machines Corporation, 1981.

Poole, Lon, and Mary Borchers. *Some Common BASIC Programs*. 2nd ed. Berkeley, California: Adam Osborne & Associates, 1978.

Rubinstein, Moshe. *Patterns of Problem Solving*. Englewood Cliffs, New Jersey: Prentice-Hall, Inc., 1975.

Rugg, Tom, and Phil Feldman. *More Than 32 BASIC Programs for the IBM Personal Computer*. Portland, Oregon: dilithium Press, 1983.

Sterling, Theodor, and Seymour Pollack. *Introduction to Statistical Data Processing*. Englewood Cliffs, New Jersey: Prentice-Hall, Inc., 1968.

White, Harvey E. *Modern College Physics*. New York: Van Nostrand Co., 1962.

The World Almanac and Book of Facts. New York: Newspaper Enterprise Association, 1985.

Index

More Computer Knowledge from Que

Que Order Line: **1-800-428-5331**

All prices subject to change without notice.

FOLD HERE

_____

_____

_____

_____

Que Corporation
P. O. Box 50507
Indianapolis, IN 46250